Perspectives on Minnesota Government and Politics

Fourth Edition

Steve Hoffman
Donald Ostrom
Homer Williamson
Kay Wolsborn

University of St. Thomas
St. Paul, Minnesota

Burgess Publishing

A Division of Burgess International Group, Inc.

Address orders to:

BURGESS INTERNATIONAL GROUP, Inc.
7110 Ohms Lane
Edina, Minnesota 55439-2143
Telephone 612-831-1344
Fax 612/831-3167

Burgess Publishing
A Division of BURGESS INTERNATIONAL GROUP, Inc.

CONTENTS

INTRODUCTION TO VOLUME

In his Editors Introduction to the first edition of *Minnesota Government and Politics*, Millard Gieske proffered that the book was "an experiment" designed to correct the fact that "too little has been written and regularly published about the whys and ways" of Minnesota's political processes (Gieske and Brandt, 1977). While the experiment appears to have been successful, at least if one accepts three successive editions as a measure of success, the problem raised by Gieske remains.

It is not hard to imagine why the study of state politics receives relatively little attention within the discipline of political science. Consider the characteristics of our world. The Internet is rapidly becoming the communications vehicle of choice for many, and in particular, for the students that will be using this text. Indeed it is oftentimes easier to connect with a distant member of the "global village" than with your next-door neighbor. Virtual communities, borne out of affiliations of interest, seem to be of greater concern than those communities forged out of the need to share and inhabit the space around us. And legislatures, not to mention city councils and local school boards, increasingly must adapt to the realities generated by decisions made in board rooms located in "global cities" far removed from statehouses and capitol rotundas.

Given such conditions, it is not hard to understand Gieske's concern. For a number of reasons, however, the rush to treat state and local politics as an afterthought, or simply in terms of their relevance to a global order, is shortsighted.

At its core, the study of American politics as a *federal* system of governance demands that it be grounded in the study of subnational

1

units of government. DeTocqueville long ago pointed out that the states are the laboratories of change and experimentation.   As demonstrated by several chapters in this volume, this is as true today as it was over two hundred years ago.

Moreover, the imperatives of globalization have not diminished the importance of the local. In fact, global integration might well be providing the basis for the long term *dis*-integration of stable civil societies at the subnational level. As W. Phillips Shively points out (1997: 36-37):

> Ethnic and regional conflicts have not diminished over recent decades. [Instead] they have flourished as states become more modern. Perhaps . . . in our increasingly mobile world, where we move from place to place and from relationship to relationship, people feel a lack of identity and seek out something to provide them with a stable core.

Certainly none of the authors who contributed to this volume would suggest that the political character of American states can be compared to situations in Quebec, Northern Ireland, or even Scotland. Minnesota is, however, subject to those forces which have marginalized the idea of place and which consistently undermine respect for the importance of the local. In this respect, the study of state politics and an understanding of what makes any place unique and valuable is critical as we enter a new century, the "stable core" of which has yet to be identified.

One final note. Readers of this book will note that the volume's previous editions are liberally referenced by many of the contributors. Surely, this is also the mark of a successful experiment.

Steven M. Hoffman
University of St. Thomas
January, 1998

REFERENCES

Gieske, Millard and Edward R. Brandt. 1977. *Perspectives on Minnesota Government and Politics.* Dubuque, IA: Kendall/Hunt Publishing Company.

Shively, W. Phillips. 1997. *Comparative Governance.* New York, NY: McGraw-Hill Companies.

SECTION I

THE STRUCTURE OF MINNESOTA POLITICS

Homer E. Williamson
St. Cloud State University

Kay Wolsborn
College of St. Benedict

Minnesota's political system, as is the case for any political system, exists not in a vacuum but in context. The social, demographic, and economic characteristics of a society create particular sets of interests, problems, and needs. These interests and needs become translated into demands on the political decision makers. The mix of people with differing ethnic, religious, racial, and economic backgrounds shapes both the level and nature of conflict in a community. The economic base for a state conditions problems facing the state. Does the state rely heavily on old, heavy manufacturing and so face job loss as demand for the products of that old industry decline? Will the state take action to attract newer, service oriented industries that promise a future growth?

Similarly, formal structures shape the manner in which political needs can be articulated and met. These structures probably don't absolutely determine the nature of political combat, but they channel it. Since this is so, political actors try to change the formal structure to provide advantage to themselves or their policy interests. And sometimes changing social and economic forces place strong pressure on those structures or either adapt or become irrelevant, encouraging political actors to evade the outdated form.

Despite these pressures, constitutions and institutions of governance change rarely and then only stubbornly and slowly over time. At least, this is the often frustrating assumption that many people make. The authors in this section ask the reader to set aside that assumption and to take a fresh look at the fundamental law of the State of Minnesota, its Constitution, and at the institutional structures responsible for the stewardship and implementation of the state's public policy. In all of the following chapters, the evidence is clear that Minnesota's institutions have adapted to the changing demands and needs of the state's population by means of technological innovation and by responding to increasingly broad participation from citizen groups.

In addition to change and adaptability, several other themes reverberate throughout each chapter in this section. Like many other states in recent decades, Minnesota has demonstrated increasing levels of professionalism in public service, a growing emphasis on public accountability, and a continuing expansion of roles and responsibilities of state government vis-a-vis the national government.   In each analysis, however, the author cautions the reader that change and adaptation do not happen without challenges that must also be addressed.

The increasing professionalism of elected officials and staff, for instance, brings greater expertise to the tasks of governance, yet the jargon of expertise can widen the communications gap between public servant and the populations to be served. A growing emphasis on public accountability allows for the vigilance essential in a well functioning democracy, yet the proliferation of venues for public participation can drag the progress of needed public policies to a standstill. Finally, in response to financial constraints on the federal budget, the expanding role of state governments has evolved at the same time that states like Minnesota have resources and policy ideas ready to exploit greater independence. Yet absent the stability of federal support and the tools of fiscal policymaking, states may soon find themselves buffeted by unpredictable shifts in the economy and in the needs of various population groups. In each of the following chapters, the author provides a framework for helping the reader to consider what circumstances might help the state to meet these challenges successfully.

The opening chapter by Homer Williamson relates the state Constitution to both political consequences arising from that basic document and the political and social forces that shape it. For example, an alteration in the requirements for popular ratification of constitutional amendments decreased, for a long period of time, the success rate in changing the basic document. The constitution also creates strong controls over local governments by the state legislature. However, because increasing socio-economic complexities put greater demands on them, both cities and counties in metropolitan areas have adopted various types of professional administrators through local action.

In his chapter on the Office of Governor, Williamson calls attention to the roles that governors have played in the state's recent political history and the legacies that Minnesota governors have passed along to their successors. The analysis differentiates among the legal, institutional, political, and personal resources available to the state's chief executive. Although Minnesota governors at the end of the twentieth century have considerably more power resources available to them than did their predecessors, Williamson reminds the reader that individual style remains an important factor in an assessment of gubernatorial success.

Donald Ostrom summarizes the professional evolution that has characterized many state legislatures, including the Minnesota Legislature, in recent decades. Incumbency, partisan dominance, and political culture also continue to be important factors in understanding the dynamics of the state's legislative representation.   Yet in the context of a virtually unified media market in a state where folks pay considerable attention to the decisions and behaviors of their public officials, voter preferences could shift very quickly. Consequently, Ostrom questions whether Minnesota's moralistic political culture will continue to produce traditional progressive policy outcomes.

Philip Kronebusch opens his analysis of the Minnesota courts with an example of judicial policymaking — an impact not often recognized in judicial decisions in specific cases. Although the court system may appear to be the most stable of government institutions, Kronebusch's description reminds the reader that this branch of government has been subject to dramatic organizational changes in the past three decades, and not without some loss of public accountability at the local level. Confronted with a variety of conflicting values and goals, Minnesota's courts are asked to provide a legal system that is responsive to calls for increased efficiency, more public accountability, and greater accessibility for the poor.

Kay Wolsborn's chapter provides an overview of Minnesota's administrative bureaucracy — the growing number and variety of agencies and personnel that do the work of the state in response to executive, statutory and judicial policymaking.   The state's bureaucracy includes political appointees, career civil servants, and expert professionals. Bureaucracies are by far the largest and most complex of the state's venues for policy formation and probably the least understood by the public. They make rules that carry the force of statutory law as well as quasi-judicial decisions in the context of missions, programs, and budgets defined by state institutions and authority.   Because state agencies must nevertheless conform to regulatory federalism and accommodate public input, Wolsborn emphasizes the particularly complex issues of accountability that accompany public service in this area.

Chapter 1

MINNESOTA'S CONSTITUTION AND INTERGOVERNMENTAL RELATIONS

Homer E. Williamson
St. Cloud State University

INTRODUCTION

Although formal structures may not determine political processes and policies, they certainly channel them. Further, political participants perceive that formal structures may provide them with advantages, or, conversely, impose disadvantages to either their political beliefs or their political power. For example, many commentators on state constitutions attribute their often excessive length to the power of interest groups anxious to embed items such as tax advantages or earmarked funds for favored programs into the fundamental law. Minnesota itself presents the unique feature of operating under two constitutional documents resulting from early fundamental political divisions (Minnesota Legislative Manual, 1997-98: 31-2). In the 1857 constitutional convention elections the then fledgling Republican party bitterly contested with the established Democratic party for majority control of the convention. The feelings generated on both sides were so intense that delegates from the two sides refused to meet in the same room and refused to sign the same document at the conclusion of the proceeding. However, more than petty partisan politics lay behind the conflict. The slavery question impelled the United States towards the most serious internal conflict in its history. In Minnesota the Republicans finally relented by withdrawing a Negro suffrage clause from the state constitution in return for an easy amendment process (Kane, 1984: 37).

In the United States government must function within the context of relationships with other governments. The fact of a federal system again conditions, although does not completely, control the political process and political power. The state constitution provides a "barebones" outline for local governments in the state. Essentially the document leaves the determination of most local government features to the state legislature. Minnesota State government owes its existence to the U.S. Constitution. The U.S. Congress had to approve the Minnesota constitution. The desirable relationship between the national government and Minnesota governments remains a matter for on going political controversy.

This chapter outlines fundamental features of the Minnesota constitution, highlighting political consequences emanating from the formal provisions. Secondly, the chapter examines major features of Minnesota local government showing where state legislative action fleshes out the minimal constitutional framework. Finally, we show how the Minnesota constitution may be revised.

MINNESOTA CONSTITUTIONAL FUNDAMENTALS

The state constitution serves as the state's fundamental law. As such it takes precedence over ordinary statutory law. The latter must be consistent with the former if challenged in the courts (Harrigan, 1993: 28). The constitution covers a long list of topics including bill of rights, legislature, judiciary, executive, voting qualifications, taxes, finance, highways and miscellaneous substantive policy, amendment procedure, and local government.

Bill of Rights

The original constitution directly incorporated the Minnesota bill of rights with pride of place as the first article. The article itself covers most of the basics found in the U.S. Constitution. These include free press, freedom of religion, and criminal due process. The state version does embody some unusual provisions not found at the national level. For instance Minnesota prohibits feudal tenure (Minnesota Constitution, Article I, Section 15). Why duplicate rights already found in the national version? State courts may interpret the state constitution differently than the U.S. Supreme Court views similar provisions in the U.S. Constitution. Interests who find the national level not congenial to their viewpoint may try again at the state level. The Amish challenged a state law requiring orange warning signs on slow moving vehicles (in this case horse drawn buggy) as a violation of freedom of religious conscience. The court rejected the challenge on the basis of the U.S. Constitution. On rehearing at the state level the plaintiffs raised the question of state constitution. The Minnesota Supreme Court took a more expansive view of the state constitution and upheld the challenge (Vogel, 1991: 35).

Decision Making Institutions

The Minnesota Constitution leaves no doubt as to its devotion to separation of powers. Article III states this principle directly. The legislative article outlines provisions governing selection of legislators, legislative structure, and basic procedures. Some procedural requirements go beyond basic provisions. For example passage of any general banking law requires the extraordinary majority of a two thirds vote in each house of the legislature for passage (Minnesota Constitution, Article IV, Section 26). Unlike its national counterpart, the Minnesota Constitution creates a plural executive. The voters directly choose six different executive officers. This, potentially at least, weakens the governor as the executive's leader. The attorney general's office plays a significant role independent of the governor. All of the executive officers might, and several have, become important rivals for the incumbent governor's position. Article V, Section 3 succinctly outlines most gubernatorial powers. The appointment power, in particular the authority to fill vacancies, stands out among these. The state constitution initially lays out a simple, "barebones" outline for the state court system (Article VI, Section 1). However, many subsequent additions circumscribe legislative freedom on details. The document requires at least two judges, residents of the district, per judicial district. It awards each county its own clerk of district court .

Elective Franchise

Article VII establishes basic voting requirements as well as the outlines for conducting elections. Voting requirements include basic personal characteristics for voting eligibility (persons convicted of a felony cannot vote until restored to civil rights and residence). Sections also cover timing of elections, procedures for processing election returns, and campaign spending limits. A blanket eligibility for office clause reveals a quirk in the constitution. In conformity with the U.S. Constitution, Minnesota establishes the age of 18 as the minimum for voting eligibility. However, every person who is otherwise eligible to vote, must be at least 21 to be eligible to hold any elective office in the state (Article VII, Sections 1 and 6).

Unlike the case in many so called "moralistic" states, the Minnesota Constitution makes no provision for initiative and referendum. Minnesota citizens, therefore, vote directly on state wide issues only through constitutional amendments. A 1980 amendment to establish initiative and referendum carried 54 percent of those voting in the election, but only 47 percent of those voting in the election, and so failed. Governor Al Quie supported the measure, but a number of interest groups, most notably the Minnesota Education Association campaigned vigorously against it.

However, Minnesotans now possess the right of recall. That is, they can vote to remove a state elective official or judge before the officers established term ends (Article VIII, Section 6). Throughout most of the state's history only the state legislature could impeach and remove these officers. (It could remove state legislators through judging the qualifications of its own members.) Voters added the recall provision in the 1996 elections by a lopsided 80 percent plus approval of a constitutional amendment. Perceived misbehavior by several state legislators over a period of years contributed to the one sided vote. However, skeptics argued that the grounds for recall are so narrow, especially for judges, and the procedures so difficult, petition by 25 percent of the voters in the district, that the provision will seldom be used.

Policy and Finance Provisions

Reformers conventionally criticize state constitutions for being too long, too detailed, and imposing unreasonable restrictions on the state legislature (Harrigan, 1993: 31). One Minnesota scholar concluded that this state's constitution was not too long, but in several instances it did impose excessive detail and restrictions (Harrigan, 1993: 31-34).

A 1974 constitutional amendment streamlined and modernized the wording for the constitutional document in popular use (Minnesota Legislative Manual, 1997-1998: 33). This accounts for the Minnesota Constitution's relative brevity compared to other states. However, for legal purposes, the original document remains the final authority. This remains more lengthy and detailed. For example, a trunk highway article adopted in 1920 runs to five and one-half pages of double column small print. Most of this details the starting city, cities along the route, and ending city for seventy highway routes in Minnesota.

Most state constitutional detail and restrictions appear in articles dealing with finances and specific public policy areas. The state constitution seemingly grants the legislature generally taxing authority.   Specific provisions on forests, iron ore, motor fuel, aircraft, and taconite create special conditions for taxing those items (Minnesota Constitution, Article 10). Some sections, such as that on taconite taxation, expired several years ago. Likewise the constitution sets aside, or "earmarks", revenues from certain sources to be spent only for specified purposes. These include part of iron ore taxes for schools, permanent school fund (some land sales), permanent university fund, environment and natural resources trust fund (lottery revenues), and highway user tax distribution fund (motor vehicle and motor fuel taxes). Finally, the constitution grants the state a general power to contract debt for public purposes. Then it provides a long laundry list of specific purposes, including the repelling of invasions and suppressing insurrections (Minnesota Constitution, Article 11, Section 5).

Articles on miscellaneous subjects and the state highway system contain the bulk, but not all, of special policy provisions. These range from the antiquarian (no license required to peddle the products of one's own farm or garden) to current political flashpoints (what exactly is a "uniform system of public schools"). The highway article covers the state road system previously discussed, various highway funds from taxation, and restrictions on highway bonding procedures (Minnesota Constitution, Article 14).

MINNESOTA LOCAL GOVERNMENT

The Minnesota Constitution authorizes the Minnesota Legislature to provide for the creation, organization, consolidation, and dissolution of local governments (Minnesota Constitution, Article 12, Section 3). Under the same provisions the legislature also establishes what local governments do, their boundaries, and their elective and appointive officials.   Traditional court interpretations grant the legislature broad discretion in controlling local governments through this constitutional authority.   As

creatures of the state, all U.S. Constitutional restrictions applying
to the states also control local governments.

The state constitution provides some limited protections for
local units. When authorized by law any local unit may adopt and
amend a home rule charter through a local vote under procedures
established by the constitution and the legislature (Minnesota
Constitution, Article 12, Section 4). To date the legislature
provides a home rule option only for cities. Special acts by the
state legislature that apply only to a single local government unit
must be approved by the voters or governing body of that unit
(Minnesota Constitution, Article 12, Sections 1 and 2). The
legislature may not change a county boundary line or move a
county seat without a majority of voters in each county affected
approving the change.

The state legislature, then, regulates most aspects of local
government by statute. The term "local government" in Minnesota
applies to townships, counties, special districts, and cities. We will
briefly discuss each of these in turn with the most extended
discussion reserved for cities.

Township Government

The Minnesota legislature created townships to exercise
governmental jurisdiction over unincorporated places characterized
by open countryside, agricultural uses, and rural residential
purposes. The 1,800 townships govern most of the land outside
cities, but often under restrictions imposed by county policy. Most
rural townships focus on the construction of road and bridge
maintenance, conducting elections, providing fire protection,
zoning, and tax levies. The legislature also created the possibility
for forming urban townships in unincorporated areas that have
platted portions and a population of 1,000 or more people (League
of Minnesota Cities, 1997: 8). These possess most powers granted
to cities except annexation and operating municipal liquor stores.

A three or five member (usually three) board of supervisors govern the township. Supervisors serve three year, staggered terms of office. Options allow for elected or appointed clerk and treasurer and an appointed town administrator (Minnesota Legislative Manual, 1997: 300). Townships provide the only approximation to direct democracy in Minnesota local governments. Citizens assemble once a year to elect officials, debate issues, and vote on proposed budget expenditures. Regular board of supervisor meetings provide an opportunity for direct dialogue between citizens and officials since rural townships over cover relatively small areas and populations. Academic observers often condemn township government for low participation rates and ineffective administration. Many rural residents positively support township government because of its accessibility and personal contacts (Tesdell and Obrecht, 1984: 283, 285).

County Government

Minnesota's 87 counties range in population from 4,000 to 1,000,000 (Minnesota Legislative Manual, 1997: 256). The state created most of the present counties in the mid nineteenth century to act as administrative units for specific services mandated by the state. (Tesdell and Obrecht, 1984: 273). These traditional functions included tax collection, record keeping, law enforcement, and court administration. Originally established to serve a rural society, the state gradually expanded county functions over time to serve an urbanizing society. The state never granted counties home rule but provides for differences between highly urban and rural counties through widespread use of special laws. Counties do not provide municipal services. Most county spending now focuses on three functional areas, highways, land use and human services, with a particular emphasis upon the latter two functional areas over the last twenty years.

Most Minnesota counties follow a uniform governing structure. A five member county board of commissioners, elected from districts, serves as the governing legislative body. Traditionally the voters directly elect five department heads: auditor, treasurer, recorder, sheriff, county attorney. Only about a dozen still elect a coroner. Thirty-seven counties appoint a coroner or medical examiner. Only about five retain a surveyor, all appointed (Minnesota Legislative Manual, 1997: 256-85). County government does not utilize an executive such as a mayor at the city level. The Optional Forms for County Government Act, passed in 1973, allows five alternatives to create some executive leadership. No county uses these alternatives. Some counties choose to use other options under the law. Six larger counties function under a seven member county board. Increasingly (thirty-two at present) counties combine the office of auditor and treasurer. A majority of counties have chosen to adopt some sort of appointed administrator either under the options act or by local resolution. Most commonly the local law designates these administrators as coordinators, but a substantial number use the term administrator.

Special Districts

State law authorizes local units to perform specific duties or provide specific services in a limited situation. Unlike general purpose governments these units usually provide a single service rather than multiple services. The Minnesota legislature resisted the move to special districts more than has been the case in many states, but these are still the most numerous unit of government. School districts, although diminished in numbers over the years, remain the most identifiable type of special district. The 355 independent school districts cover every area of the state (Minnesota Legislative Manual, 1997: 300). In addition there are 10 special school districts of various descriptions and 19 charter schools. The largest number of charter schools operate in metropolitan areas. Most county areas contain multiple school districts although a few have only one. At one time each school district was associated with one city. With the move toward consolidation more than twenty-five percent of school district titles now cover two or more communities. Separately elected six member boards govern school districts. These turn the day to day administration over to an appointed administrator called a superintendent.

Other significant special purpose districts include soil and water conservation districts, watershed districts, lake improvement districts, and regional development commissions (League of Minnesota Cities, 1997: 10-11). The state legislature established soil and water conservation districts that geographically cover every part of the state. Their boundaries generally coincide with counties. These districts provide drainage and flood control, soil information and maps of wetlands. Local citizens create watershed districts by petition. The districts exercise land and water use regulatory authority. County boards or a combination of cities and townships may create a lake improvement district to undertake various projects to upgrade a particular lake and its shoreline. Regional development commissions contain several counties within their jurisdictions. They provide planning and technical assistance. At one time these thirteen commissions, including the Twin Cities Metropolitan Council, covered all territory in the state. Local governing bodies in three of the regions exercised a local option to dissolve their commissions. Governing bodies for these districts are chosen in a variety of ways. Voters elect some. Governing bodies for other local units appoint others. Delegates from other local units govern still others.

City Government

Minnesota law creates cities as public corporations. Unlike counties or townships, local citizens voluntarily create these units to provide urban services. The Minnesota legislature officially designates cities as a unit of government that can most efficiently provide governmental services in areas intensively developed for residential, commercial, and industrial purposes (League of

Minnesota Cities, 1997: 3). Based on expenditure levels, major city functions include police, fire, street maintenance, parks and recreation, water, sewer, economic development, and election administration. Basically cities may provide only those functions allowed by the state, and sometimes must provide services mandated by the state. Often they must provide those services in a manner prescribed by state law. Actual city services vary to a great degree because in some policy areas state law allows local option. The city may provide the service if it wishes. Also, the legislature classifies cities by population size and treats these classes differently for policy purposes. The four classes are: First Class (over 100,000), Second Class (20,000 to 100,000), Third Class (10,000 to 20,000) and Fourth Class (under 10,000). Three cities qualify as First Class, thirty-seven as Second Class, thirty-eight as Third Class, and seven hundred and seventy-five as Fourth class (League of Minnesota Cities, 1997: 4).

Minnesota allows for two basic types of municipalities, home rule and statutory. By far the larger number of Minnesota communities follow the statutory city mode. Almost 750 of Minnesota's 853 incorporated municipalities retain this default form. A uniform state code, Minnesota Statutes 412, specifies the basic governmental forms and powers for all statutory cities. This code provides local citizens three optional forms. Two versions would be considered forms of weak mayor and one a form of city manager (communities under 1,000 population may not choose this form). Cities automatically fall under Plan A. In this weak mayor version voters elect a mayor and four council members. The mayor acts as a voting member of the council and its presiding officer. The council appoints a clerk and treasurer (these offices may be combined). The code delegates broad authority to the council to create and appoint other appointed department heads and boards. By local vote a community may change to one of the other two plans. The Standard Plan differs primarily in that the voters elect a clerk who takes the place of one of the members on the council. The voters also elect a treasurer unless the council combines that office with the clerk position.   Plan B creates a city manger appointed by the elected council (a mayor and four council members).   These are the only elected officials.   The manager appoints all operating department heads and supervises day to day city administration.   Most cities follow Plan A.   Only 133 (6 percent) select the Standard Plan and a tiny 16 choose Plan B (See Table 1).

TABLE 1							
Forms of Minnesota Municipal Government							
	Home Rule			Statutory			Total
Size	Weak Mayor	Strong Mayor	Mgr.	Plan A	Std.	Plan B	
1st Cl.	1	2	0	0	0	0	3
2nd Cl.	4	1	15	8	0	9	37
3rd Cl.	16	1	7	10	1	3	38
4th Cl.							
5-10000	11	0	3	26	1	2	43
1-5000	38	0	5	155	4	2	204
< 1000	2	0	1	398	127	0	528
Total	72	4	31	597	133	16	853

Source: League of Minnesota Cities. 1997.

Any city may adopt home rule through procedures partially set by the constitution and partially by statute.   The move for a home rule charter may be initiated by a district judge, petition by local voters, or by city council resolution (for cities already incorporated).   The district court appoints the initial commission. This commission drafts a charter.   The charter must be approved by 51 percent of city residents voting at a general election.   The law provides various channels for amending the charter. A distinct minority of Minnesota Cities opt for home rule status. The one hundred plus cities that take this route make up only a little over 12 percent of the total (See Table 1). About 60 percent of cities over 10,000 population, including all cities of the first class, choose home rule status. Less than 8 percent of cities under 10,000 do. Observers put forth several attempted explanations for this lack of interest in home rule. The adoption process takes extensive time and effort. Home rule cities lose some advantage of legal certainty as they cannot rely on court interpretations that apply to all statutory cities. Most legislative provisions, both procedural and substantive policy, that apply to statutory cities also restrict home rule cities. Few real differences exist. Home rule communities can choose strong mayor or commission government in addition to weak mayor and manager. They can more clearly utilize wards as a basis for electing city council members. They may adopt initiative and referendum. They can impose tighter restrictions on city finances and franchises. Large communities may select this form more frequently because they perceive that their needs will be more unique. Home rule may also provide the psychological perception of greater local independence.

On the surface very few Minnesota cities appear to utilize a professional administrator. Only 5 percent employ the manager form. This seems inconsistent with the image of the state as following a moralistic culture. However, to some degree this obscures the actual practice. As is the case with counties, cities increasingly adopt some form of an administrator system through local council resolution. The cities variously designate these as administrators, coordinators, or clerk-administrators (see Table 2). Almost one-third of all cities use a central administrative position. One of the three forms can be found in 95 percent of the cities of the third class or larger. Nearly three-fourths of cities over 1,000 have some type of administrative position. Additionally, a number of clerks perform administrator functions without the formal title.

TABLE 2				
Administrators in Minnesota Municipal Government				
Size	*Manager*	*Administrator or Coordinator*	*Clerk-Administrator*	*Total*
1st Class	0	1	1	3
2nd Class	24	12	1	37
3rd Class	10	23	2	38
4th Class				
5-10,000	5	25	8	43
1-5,000	7	74	45	204
< 1,000	1	21	16	528
TOTAL	47	156	73	853

Source: League of Minnesota Cities. 1997.

CHANGING THE CONSTITUTION

Even the most basic and fundamental constitutional document cannot anticipate all issues that may arise. Nor can it anticipate future changes in a state's life. All constitutional documents, therefore, provide some legal means for formal change. The Minnesota constitution stipulates two alternative methods for revising the fundamental law. The legislature and voters may call for a new constitutional convention that could consider broad changes to several parts of the document at once. Or the same actors could use individual amendments. By practice, the system has twice used a constitutional commission, not found in the constitution itself, to advise on revisions.

Constitutional Convention

The Minnesota constitution provides for a constitutional convention. Since there is no stipulation that the call for such a convention can limit its actions, presumably that body could recommend far-reaching changes to several different parts of the document. First, two-thirds of the members of each house of the legislature must approve such a call, then a majority of votes cast at the next general election must approve the call. At its next session, the legislature then provides for convening the convention. Delegates are selected in the same manner as members of the house of representatives. That is, they would presumably be elected from single member districts. If the convention proposes changes, these must be ratified by three-fifths of all electors voting on the question at the next general election (Minnesota Constitution, Article IX, Sections 2 and 3). Changes become effective the next year after the election. Minnesotans never carried out this provision. In 1895 the legislature approved a convention call, however, the proposal failed to receive a majority of those voting at the next election (Kane, 1984: 38). After World War II pressure for a convention again surfaced. Instead the legislature created a Constitutional Commission in 1947 to study constitutional issues. The commission recommended thirty-four major changes and seventy-eight minor changes. It also proposed a constitutional convention to draft the changes (Harrigan, 1993: 37). The legislature debated a call over several sessions, but no convention materialized. Governor Wendell Anderson proposed a constitutional convention in 1971, but instead settled for another constitutional study commission. That commission made seventy-five recommendations for change, only four of which were implemented (Harrigan, 1993: 40).

G.T. Mitau argues that several factors lie behind the reluctance to use a constitutional convention. The constitutionally prescribed method discourages its use by being cumbersome and time consuming. Assuming no negative votes or major delays the process could normally consume five to six years from initiative to implementation (Mitau, 1977: 57). Even legislative approval of a call in the 1998 legislative would not lead to effective implementation until the year 2003. More importantly, because of its potentially open ended nature, many groups and participants view a convention as being politically risky.

Constitutional Amendment

The current amendment process provides for easy initiation. A majority of members in each house may propose amendments. However, a majority of all those voting at the election at which the proposal is on the ballot must approve in order to ratify (Minnesota Constitution, Article I, Section 9). Also, voters must vote on each amendment separately. Because some people may not vote on an amendment at all, but cast a votes for candidates on the ballot, the ratification process has often been difficult. In effect, not voting on the issue becomes a no vote.

Between 1858 and 1898 ratification was also easy. During that period a majority of those voting on the question itself guaranteed approval. The legislature proposed this change in part to slow down the large number of constitutional changes adopted under the old system. Some also contend that liquor interests, backed the change to head off a possible constitutional amendment requiring prohibition. (Kane, 1984: 38-39). Immediately the rate of constitutional amendment slowed considerably (see Table 3) Formal structure impacts the informal process, just as the political process (i.e. liquor groups) shape the formal structure for advantage.

The voters passed almost three-fourths of all proposed amendments under the simple majority rule before 1900. This dropped to under one-third after constitutional change implemented the absolute majority rule after 1900. If Minnesota had used the simple majority rule throughout its existence nearly three-fourths of

all proposals would have been implemented. Under actual rule a
little over half passed. However, formal procedures don't
completely control results. The absolute majority rule remained
effective after 1954. However, passage rates exceeded even the
success ratio under the old simpler rule prior to 1900. During the
last time period only eight more amendments would have passed
under the simpler rule. Most of these dealt with legislative
organization. A few involved basic political issues such as the
method for legislative reapportionment and initiative and
referendum. Again, informal political realities modified formal
structure. Mass media techniques made voters more conscious of
the consequences that followed failure to vote on an amendment
issue. Also, more interest groups became more actively involved in
campaigning for constitutional amendment changes (Kane, 1984:
40).

TABLE 3				
Constitutional Amendments: Frequency of Change				
Time Period	*Proposed*	*Adopted*	*% Adopted Under Constitutional Rule*	*% Adopted Under Simple Majority Rule*
1858-1898	66	48	73%	73%
1900-1952	92	28	30	63
1954-1996	50	39	78	94
Total	208	115	55	74
Source: The Minnesota Legislative Manual, 1997-1998: 47-54.				

CONCLUSION

Even a topic as pedestrian and dry as the state constitution and government form reveals the interplay between formal structure, social and economic change, and political forces.

Fundamental provisions of the Minnesota constitution, such as the Bill of Rights on the surface appear no different from that found in the national document. However, subtle differences, and state court interpretations different from that of federal courts, may lead groups to seek redress at the state level when national courts fail to provide a satisfactory interpretation. A constitutionally required plural executive creates potential political rivalries for the governor. Media attention to perceived scandals such as "phonegate" and criminal convictions for incumbent state legislatures assist revising the state constitution to allow for popular recall of public officials.

Constitutionally the Minnesota legislature virtually controls all aspects of local governments. Court interpretations tend to reinforce that control. Even constitutional protections such as home rule seem less attractive when the state legislature regulates many aspects of local finance and policy directly through statute. Few Minnesota cities exercise their constitutional right to home rule. However, some communities, because of population size and the socio-economic complexity of their citizens, still find some advantage in unique governmental forms to meet their unique circumstances. Counties also must bow to state constitutional dominance. However, the expanded population size and complexity of metropolitan areas lead the state legislature to expand options for both structure and services for metropolitan counties. Population size also seems to affect the form of government chosen by Minnesota cities. When the options, such as city manager, seem unappealing to city councils, they create their own structures through local designated administrators or coordinators.

Finally, the form of the constitutional amendment process encourages or discourages the use of that particular form. Minnesota decisionmakers avoid the constitutional convention route because it is difficult and time consuming. However, political calculations also play a role. The same decision makers have been reluctant to risk the more open ended and unpredictable nature of the convention method. Changing the legal requirements for the amendment process drastically affected, for a time, the success rate for passing constitutional amendments. However, changing technology, and a more active interest group role, increased the success rate without altering the legal form.

REFERENCES

Harrigan, John. 1993. "The Cultural and Constitutional Setting for Minnesota Politics." In C.M. Shrewsbury and H.E. Williamson, eds. *Perspectives on Minnesota Government and Politics*. 3rd Edition. Edina, MN: Burgess Publishing Group, Inc. Pp. 23-43.

Kane, Betty. 1984. "Constitutional Change in Minnesota." In M.L. Gieske, ed. *Perspectives on Minnesota Government and Politics*. 2nd Edition. Edina, MN: Burgess Publishing Group, Inc. Pp. 35-43.

League of Minnesota Cities. 1997. *Handbook for Minnesota Cities*. St. Paul, MN: Author.

Minnesota Constitution.

Minnesota Legislative Manual, 1997-1998. 1997. St. Paul, MN: Election Division, Secretary of State.

Mitau, G.T. 1977. "Constitutional Reforms in Minnesota - Change by Amendment, 1947-1977." In M.L. Gieske and E.R. Brandt, eds. *Perspectives on Minnesota Government and Politics*. 1st Edition. Dubuque, IA: Kendall/Hunt Publishing Company. Pp. 55-86.

Tesdell, Loren E. and Karl A. Obrecht. 1984. "Rural Government in Minnesota." In M.L. Gieske, ed. *Perspectives on Minnesota Government and Politics*. 2nd Edition. Edina, MN: Burgess Publishing Group, Inc. Pp. 271-287.

Vogel, Howard J. 1991. (May/June). "Remembering Minnesota's Bill of Rights." *Minnesota Bench and Bar*. Volume 33: 33-38.

Chapter 2

THE MINNESOTA GOVERNOR: POTENTIAL FOR POWER

Homer E. Williamson
St. Cloud State University

INTRODUCTION

The post World War II era in American politics witnessed a massive change in the position of U.S. state governors. Larry Sabato in *Good-bye to Good-Time Charlies* (1983) observed that governors and their settings have been transformed, gaining major new powers, both formal and informal. It should surprise no one, then, that the powers of the Minnesota Governor increased substantially during the same period. Thad Beyle, a leading specialist on state governors, ranked the Minnesota Governor's office among the top fourth in formal powers by the 1990s (1995). However, we must distinguish power defined as actual influence on governmental action, from other powers, particularly formal powers. As Donald Gross makes clear, power and success are not coterminous. An individual governor's degree of success or failure depends on her or his ability and willingness to exercise power, as well as on the influence of other important actors within the state. As is the case with presidential power, ultimately gubernatorial power is the power to persuade (Gross, 1991: 3).

This chapter explores two related themes. First, how have the powers available to Minnesota governors increased? Second, has the influence exercised by individual governors consistently increased as well? We could label the method used to explore these questions the "bargaining approach." Underlying it are four assumptions. First, separated institutions that share policymaking powers characterize state governments. Second, these separate institutions serve both different and overlapping constituencies, leading to institutional conflict. Third, the very nature of constitutional, political, and economic systems largely guarantees that neither a governor nor a legislature dominates the decision process. Finally, since many differences remain marginal, and long-term stalemates appear mutually unacceptable, the system inclines the participants towards compromise. Recognizing this, skillful governors both build coalitions and prepare to bargain.

The power resources available to the office of Minnesota's governor include: legal-constitutional, institutional, political, and personal. We examine eleven postwar governors from Edward Thye to Arne Carlson to see how these resources potentially grew.

LEGAL-CONSTITUTIONAL RESOURCES

Most legal-constitutional powers derive from a state constitutional base. These resources include military powers, special sessions, messages, the veto, and tenure power. Article V, section 3, of the Minnesota Constitution contains most of the Minnesota Governor's major constitutional powers. Additionally, control over the administrative branch and finances rests partially on statutory law.

Miscellaneous Powers

Miscellaneous grants of power noted in the preceding paragraph include the role of commander-in-chief and the right to present messages to the Legislature. Miscellaneous powers found elsewhere in the Constitution include the pardoning power and the executive prerogative of calling special legislative sessions. Generally, these powers remain stable.

The Minnesota Constitution limits the special session power of the Governor, who cannot control the session's subject matter or adjournment date. Between 1944 and 1996, governors called twenty-four special or extra sessions. Most sessions dealt with appropriations, taxation, reapportionment or other major unfinished business of the regular session. In no case did they add to an incumbent governor's prestige. In some cases they diminished the incumbent's political influence. Governor Quie's record setting seven special sessions in a four-year span is a case in point. The Governor called most of these sessions to deal with the state's ongoing economic and fiscal crisis. Although Quie managed to limit the scope of the sessions, never did the sessions enhance his public prestige. On the other hand, Governor Quie felt that his failure to call a special session in 1980 resulted in his shouldering the entire blame for initial budget cuts, and marked the downward point in his administration (Renner, 1982). Governor Perpich limited the negative impact of the four special sessions from 1983-1990 by refusing to call a session until he reached prior informal agreement on legislation with legislative leaders. Governor Carlson also largely followed this practice.

The message power, a minor constitutional resource, expanded to include not only the "state of the state" address but budgetary and special messages as well. These are largely political devices through which the Governor focuses attention on key issues. Possibly DFL legislators feel more bound to a DFL governor's proposals than is the case between Republican governors and legislators. In recent years, as with Governor Arne Carlson, budget messages have contained the major gubernatorial concerns. However, the real legislative programs are those initiatives introduced in bill form.

Veto Power

All legislatively approved bills go to the Governor for approval or rejection. The Governor may, under the veto power, return the bill to its house of origin. The Legislature, in turn, can override the rejection only by a two-thirds vote in each chamber. Through the "item veto" the Governor may select one or more separate items in an appropriation bill and reject only those while allowing the rest of the bill to become law. This item veto action also is subject to a two-thirds overriding vote. Finally, a bill passed during the last three days of the legislative session, but not signed within fourteen days following adjournment, does not become law. Through this "pocket veto" the Governor may reject bills without an opportunity for legislative override. The potential veto power has changed little since 1945. Formally, Minnesota ranks in the top group among all states in potential veto power.

In comparison to actual practice in other states, Minnesota governors rather infrequently use the veto power. On the average, a governor only vetoes eleven bills per session. Four governors have accounted for three-fourths of the total vetoes. Governor Carlson's 55 vetoes during the 1993-94 session stands as the record. He cast half the total vetoes in the post World War II period. Governors virtually ignored the item veto until 1979. Since then they have begun to utilize it with some frequency. Governor Carlson also stands out in this respect with forty-one item vetoes covering over 200 different items in the 1991-1996 sessions. The Minnesota Legislature rarely overrides a veto. The record shows only four such overrides (of 298 vetoes) in fifty years. Also Minnesota governors rarely use vetoes as an effective medium for political negotiation. Alan Rosenthal argues that frequent use of the veto denotes gubernatorial weakness since a veto would be unnecessary if a governor possessed other effective powers (Bernick and Wiggins, 1991: 79). The veto in Minnesota, therefore, appears mainly as a gubernatorial resource of last resort, primarily when the Governor faces opposing legislative party majorities.

Tenure Potential

Until 1963, the Minnesota Constitution granted a relatively short formal tenure in office. The traditional term lasted two years, with no restrictions on re-election. Such a short term potentially handicapped the Governor in dealing with the Legislature and mastering the administrative process. An incoming governor received just two months to prepare for the legislative session, to develop a program, to revise the budget, and to make numerous appointments. Further, veteran legislators, appointed administrators, and state-wide elected officials, often enjoyed a longer tenure, formally or in practice, and therefore felt more free to resist gubernatorial initiatives.

Finally, the Governor expended much time and energy in continually running for re-election. In 1962, voters adopted a four year-term with no legal limitation on the right to seek re-election. This provision made Minnesota governors (beginning with Karl Rolvaag) somewhat more secure in office.

In spite of this increased tenure potential, only 45 percent of recent Minnesota governors have served more than one elected term in office. Challengers defeated C. Elmer Anderson, Elmer Andersen, and Karl Rolvaag when they sought to succeed themselves. Harold Levander and Al Quie, partially for personal reasons and partially due to low public support, chose not to seek re-election. Luther Youngdahl and Orville Freeman both won three (two-year) terms, though Freeman was defeated for a fourth term. In 1974, Wendell Anderson won a second four-year term. Rudy Perpich served longer than any other Minnesota governor. In 1977-78 he completed the remainder of Anderson's term. He won election in his own right in 1982 and 1986, finally serving a full eight years. However, even Perpich proved vulnerable, losing close races both in 1978 and 1990. With both Perpich and Arne Carlson winning two consecutive terms, recent incumbents appeared more secure than those in the past.

Administrative Powers

Classical administrative theory considers a governor to be a state's chief executive officer. The theory prescribes that each department be headed by one individual, appointed and removed by the governor. There should be a chain-of-command from the chief executive down through the ranks. Administrative units should then actively serve the governor with advice on programs, legislative testimony, interest group support, and patronage cooperation. From the mid-1960s to the early 1990s two reform waves attempted to draw governors' powers closer toward this enhanced executive model. However, in Minnesota a strong control relationship between the Governor and the administrative branch remains problematic. The Constitution creates a plural executive with six elected officers. The other elected officers may have partisan or programmatic differences with the Governor. Offsetting this administrative separation is the fact that only the Attorney General's office wields very great power. Other, more potentially potent, gubernatorial weaknesses stem from lack of control over line agencies, the large number of agencies, long overlapping terms for multi-headed agencies, and program policy dispersion among many agencies.

Other than the constitutional elective offices, we may classify the agencies comprising the Minnesota administrative branch into several types: (1) administrative departments and agencies, (2) policy-making boards, (3) authorities, (4) adjudicative boards, (5) advisory boards, and (6) semi-state agencies. Departments and independent agencies carry out major policy programs. Generally, one officer directly appointed by the Governor heads each of these agencies. Approximately twenty 'cabinet' departments constitute the heart of the administrative system; examples include Children, Families & Learning and Natural Resources. The Legislature designed policymaking boards as multi-member headed entities that directly carry out responsibilities in a fairly limited functional area (e.g., Ethical Practices Board) or regulate specific professions (e.g., Medical Practice). Authorities designate agencies with the primary purpose of issuing bonds for financing, ownership, and development (e.g., Higher Education Facilities Authority). Adjudicative agencies, although not included within the court system, arbitrate or settle disputes between two or more parties (e.g., Tax Court of Appeals). Advisory boards primarily advise the Governor, administrative departments, or the Legislature on matters of specific concerns (e.g., Black Minnesotans). Finally, semi-state agencies (e.g.,Minnesota Historical Society) receive state funds, but a private membership not connected with state employment governs the agency.

State administrative structure changed markedly since 1945 (see Table 1). Some changes potentially weakened gubernatorial control. Agency numbers grew sharply. Legislative actions dispersed expanded state functions, notably in education, social services, and commerce, among many administrative agencies. Also, the Minnesota Legislature refused to increase the Governor's chain of command through single-headed agencies. In 1945, 26 percent of all units had an individual head as director; by 1996 this had actually declined to 14 percent. According to classical administrative theory, as agency numbers increase greatly, a governor's time and stamina impose limits on supervisory ability. Also, dispersed agency leadership responsibilities sustain independence from the office of the Governor.

In practice, however, the real thrust of Minnesota's administrative changes decreased the number of agencies, principally advisory boards, which the Governor must directly oversee, while consolidating influence over the major departments. In practice, the number of administrative units increased little, while the proportion of single-headed agencies in this group increased (see Table 1). Advisory and policy boards accounted for most of the functional dispersion, while incremental reorganization brought much of the functional operating responsibility under the administrative departments. Until quite recently, no conscious design fostered this pattern. Few Minnesota governors comprehensively pursued greater coordination. Freeman's 1955 and 1957 attempts at reorganization largely failed.

TABLE 1						
Minnesota State Administrative Structure: 1945 and 1996						
		Appointed by Governor				
		Number	*Single Head*	*Multi Head.*	*Longer Term*	*Same Term*	*Not by Gov.*
1945						
Constitutional		4	4	0	0	0	4
Administrative		26	13	13	17	4	5
Policy Boards/ Examining		25	0	25	20	0	5
Authorities		2	0	2	1	0	1
Adjudicative		3	1	2	2	1	0
Advisory		5	0	5	0	2	3
Semi-state		4	0	4	0	0	4
Total		69	18	51	40	7	22
1996						
Constitutional		4	4	0	0	0	4
Administrative		30	30	0	0	28	2
Policy Boards/ Examining		101	0	101	0	62	39
Authorities		5	0	5	0	3	2
Adjudicative		6	1	5	4	1	1
Advisory		97	0	97	0	28	69
Semi-state		10	0	10	0	0	10
Total		253	35	218	4	122	127

Source: Minnesota Legislative Manual. 1945 and 1995; Minnesota Guidebook to State Agencies Service. 1996-1999.

Since 1967, change has occurred through continuous piecemeal action. The Legislature increased gubernatorial authority over the Department of Public Services (Levander) and Department of Commerce (Perpich), and consolidated functions in the Pollution Control Agency (Levander), Department of Public Safety (Levander), Department of Transportation (W. Anderson), Department of Jobs and Training (Perpich-1977), and Department of Trade and Economic Development (Quie), and Department of Children, Families, and Learning (Carlson). During the 1975-76 session it also streamlined gubernatorial responsibility for advisory boards by providing definite termination dates for all such legislatively created bodies. On the other hand, the Governor acquired the power to independently establish personal advisory committees. Finally, with the passage of the 1969 Reorganization Act, Minnesota became one of the first states to grant the Governor power to initiative executive reorganization. However, although Rudy Perpich took some initiatives in his first full administration, no governor fully tested this provision's full potential in practice.

The Governor potentially exercises the greatest influence over the executive branch through the appointment power. Constitutionally, the Governor appoints all notaries public and other officials provided by law, the latter generally subject to senatorial confirmation. The Governor fills interim vacancies in the constitutional elective offices (except Lieutenant Governor), state and district offices, and judicial positions without Senate confirmation. Historically, agency policymaking independence is greatly reinforced by set terms, often longer than the Governor's, for agency heads, removal only "for cause," and appointment authority lodged with officials other than the Governor. One-third of agency heads in 1945 were independent of gubernatorial appointment; only 10 percent had the same term. Four- to six-year term administrators, or a board with staggered terms, headed the remaining nearly 60 percent. Also, after years of patronage abuse, 1939 civil service legislation isolated civil service employees from gubernatorial interference.

The greatest opportunity for actual control lies in agency head appointments. Senatorial confirmation has proved no check to this power. There has been a distinct trend away from agency head independence. By 1996, 48 percent of agency heads by law served the same term as the Governor. This trend appears to be even more dramatic for heads of administrative departments, policy boards, and authorities where congruence of terms reached nearly 70 percent. This change was wrought in stages, such as creating the four-year gubernatorial term (1963) and shortening department head terms in 1969. Between 1975 and 1978, the Minnesota Legislature promoted sweeping changes in the appointment process. Although the law reduced the Governor's direct appointing authority from over 900 positions to about 550, it considerably enhanced control over the remaining positions. These appointive positions included virtually all of the important policy areas. The Governor remains the appointing authority only for those *advisory* bodies directly responsible to that office. Department heads subject to the Governor's control appoint most other advisory bodies. The Senate no longer approves appointment to advisory bodies and examining boards. By a 1977 enactment, heads of twenty major agencies currently serve solely at the pleasure of the Governor (Minnesota, 1996: 1). Moreover, their terms end when an incumbent governor leaves office. The law staggers terms for multi-member boards subject to gubernatorial authority in such a way that a governor should be able to appoint a majority of the membership within two to four years. Therefore, by the beginning of the 1980s the Minnesota Governor possessed the opportunity to create and control a cabinet. Even though the expansion during the late 1980s of policy boards not subject to gubernatorial appointment modified this appointment power, it remains substantial.

Appointment of administrative department heads, potentially benefits the Governor because these administrators best know the programs they direct and, through bill drafting and testimony, they can be a valuable aid to the Governor in dealing with the Legislature. In practice, the degree of appointive control has varied depending both upon statutory prescription and upon how long the Governor served. Between 1945 and 1996, the Governor appointed a majority of agency heads before nearly 60 percent of the sessions. Only two governors had personal appointees heading a majority of agencies at the beginning of their first legislative session. Third-term governors (Youngdahl and Freeman) placed personal appointees in 90 percent of the offices. The actual average percentage of control by appointment over state administrative agencies for the following governors was:

Youngdahl, Freeman	75.0%
Wendell Anderson	73.0
Levander	69.5
Thye	56.0
Perpich (1983-90)	52.0
Andersen	49.0
Carlson	48.0
Quie	47.5
C. Elmer Anderson	37.5
Rolvaag	36.5
Perpich (1977-78)	12.5

However, only Elmer L. Andersen and Wendell Anderson stressed department head use in practice. By 1975, Anderson placed trusted department heads in most agencies, and they worked closely with advisors in the Governor's office. Although Governor Rolvaag received adverse publicity because of squabbles with department heads, only Rudy Perpich viewed administrative fragmentation as a long-run barrier to gubernatorial control (Perpich, 1982).

Although earlier Minnesota governors possessed only limited formal power, these powers increased after 1967. By 1995, they ranked at or near the top among all states (Dye , 1997: 199). The maximum potential gubernatorial appointment over department heads still extends to only 65 percent of the departments. The limits on gubernatorial appointment authority bothered most Minnesota governors very little. A strong-willed governor such as Youngdahl could bend the system to support his goals. Among very recent governors, only Governor Perpich (in 1983-84) and Arne Carlson pursued major administrative reform. Carlson's major stated goals included efficiency and cost saving, not increased power. In spite of legal restraints, the major limitation on gubernatorial power seems to be the personality and skills of an individual governor.

INSTITUTIONAL RESOURCES

Institutional resources tie closely into the Minnesota Governor's personal apparatus. These resources have some basis both in statutory law and in informal practices within the Governor's office. The Governor does not exercise these resources directly. The Governor works through others who have the powers including staff agencies as well as personal staff.

Staff Agencies

The strong executive budget system, originally assigned to the Department of Administration in 1939, stands foremost among staff agency functions. The Administration Commissioner, acting as the Governor's agent, reviewed all agency budget requests. Following agency hearings, occasionally with the Governor sitting in, the Commissioner coordinated all requests to achieve a balanced budget and emphasized gubernatorial priorities. Only after this review did the Governor send the final budget message to the Legislature. The Commissioner also established an allotment system thus controlling the rate of department spending. The Commissioner, with the Governor's approval, may permanently reduce appropriation allotments to compensate for revenue shortfalls. The Department of Finance, created in 1973, expanded the Governor's financial staff. The Department assumed all budgeting duties as well as responsibility for pre-auditing, accounting controls, and revenue-expenditure forecasts (Minnesota, 1996: 114). Although all Minnesota governors potentially draw on strong budgeting powers, some utilized it more than others. Youngdahl, Freeman, Wendell Anderson, Levander, Perpich, and Carlson became especially active in this regard (Williamson, 1971: 294; Scribner 1976; Montgomery, 1982). Arne Carlson also attempted to wield negative control through very active use of the item veto.

The Legislature, dedicated funds, and the unreliability of budget forecasts serve as three potential barriers to the Governor's budget control. The Minnesota Legislature long cultivated a tradition of being strong and independent (Esbjornson, 1955: 213). It relied heavily on the committee system, and its appropriation committees insisted on knowing past departmental expenditures and current requests, which are then compared to the Governor's recommendations. At the hearing, stage legislators may encourage department heads to challenge gubernatorial requests. The Legislature may even limit gubernatorial control over the spending process, as with the exemption of school aids from allotment reductions in 1981. Typically, the legislative committee begins by using the Governor's requests, but in the end it exercises its own judgment on details (Williamson, 1971: 300-1) . It can also write appropriations bills in such a way as to make item vetoes difficult. Compartmentalization of state revenues through dedicated trust funds further limits flexibility in executive control. The Minnesota Constitution designates five of these. This limit recently declined with over 70 percent of revenues now in the general fund.

The rather unpredictable nature of budgetary forecasts poses another problem for the Governor. This became readily apparent during the Quie administration when a declining national economy, among other factors, both continually disrupted state finances and damaged the Governor's political influence. The Legislature took steps to create more flexibility in the allotment and withholding system by establishing a reserve fund, greatly expanded during the Perpich administration in the 1980s. The size of the reserve fund continued to be an area of controversy during the Carlson administration.

Continued federal deficits, coupled with periodic recessions, and fluctuating economic forecasts, sometimes compel the Governor and the Legislature to revise the budget during the fiscal year.

Personal Staff Aides

Traditionally the Minnesota Legislature provided the Governor with very little staff assistance. In 1945 Governor Thye received but three non-clerical assistants. During the Freeman administration (1955-60) this number grew to seven, and only gradually increased thereafter. Staff peaked under Wendell Anderson with a total of about 60. The Anderson administration achieved this number by augmenting the Governor's normal complement with staff on assignment from administrative agencies. Upon replacing Anderson, the Perpich administration reduced staff size to 35 (half professionals), where it has remained. The most important staff functions include appointment scheduling, office management, correspondence, bill review, legal advice, public relations, and liaison with administrators and legislators. Prior to Anderson, most staff aides performed multiple functions. Governors drew other assistance, some semiofficial, where they could find it. Wendell Anderson developed by far the most elaborate staff, apparently an outgrowth of his own legislative career and a belief that it was crucial to the entire executive-legislative relationship in state government. Anderson assigned a particular staffer to contact every important legislator, and expected staff to discover a legislator's interests and requirements, including the need for information and campaign help when necessary. Although reduced in size, the staffs under Quie, Perpich, and Carlson retained a fairly specialized structure (Scribner, 1976; Montgomery, 1982; Renner, 1982; Riley, 1992).

Legislators often judge a governorship by the skill with which its staff deals with them. Most importantly, this means possessing an acute sensitivity to legislative style and being able to influence, without aggressively antagonizing, leaders and chairs. Due to legislative independence, staff inexperience, and staff aggressiveness, relations tend to deteriorate over time. From an institutional perspective, Minnesota legislators generally rate gubernatorial staffs at best ineffectual, at worst detrimental — usually the former. Legislators perceived Governor Rolvaag's staff as the most destructive, although Rolvaag disputed this judgment (Williamson, 1971: 308-11). Legislators viewed Levander's and Quie's staffs as inexperienced. Only two governors earned legislative praise for the quality of staff relations. Legislators considered Freeman's staff, with a couple of exceptions, skillful. Due to the high priority placed on legislative relations, Wendell Anderson's staff also maintained a very good working relationship with the House and, to a lesser degree, with the Senate (Williamson, 1971: 309; Scribner, 1976). Part of strained staff relations with the Legislature derives from the inherent institutional conflict between a governor and a legislature. Arne Carlson experienced unusually high turnover with seven chiefs of staff in seven years. This turnover may have resulted from the Governor's turbulent relationship with a DFL majority, despite the fact that three chiefs of staff boasted prior legislative experience (Wilson, 1994: 13-14).

POLITICAL RESOURCES

The basis for political resources stems not from constitutions or laws but from the political culture and customary practices of a particular state. Although these factors change more frequently than formal resources, they are still relatively stable over time. Especially where formal powers are lacking, political resources may form a crucial element in a governor's success. Public opinion and political party leadership remain the two most important political resources.

Public Opinion and the Governor

More than any legislator or other state public official, a governor can focus public attention on policy issues. Forcefully communicated public appeals can move an otherwise reluctant legislature into acting (Williamson, 1971: 321-3). However, such a tactic, to be successful, must be selective and not be harsh or appear demeaning to legislators. Not all governors succeed with it. Above all else, a governor must be genuinely popular with the public and the public must basically support the issue.

Early postwar governors generally enjoyed wide popular appeal. Popularity dropped during the 1960s. Since the 1970s most governors received a slight majoritarian support (see Table 2). However, although Anderson's popularity gradually increased, Quie experienced a substantial erosion. In the 1980s, Rudy Perpich built substantial support during his first full term, but that support declined during the second term. Arne Carlson reversed this pattern with low early support and nearly 60 percent approval during his second term. The reasons for the recent trend toward unstable support for governors remains difficult to pinpoint. In part it may be an outgrowth of weak public relations skills. It may result from the increased complexity of problems that government must solve. Part stems from conflicts between individual governors and the Legislature. Possibly it reflects the impossibility of living up to the leadership skills that the public expects (Stinnett and Backstrom, 1964, Chaps. 2-3).

Only three recent governors, Youngdahl, Freeman, and Wendell Anderson, consistently used the requisite skills to rally the public behind a gubernatorial program. More than any other, Luther Youngdahl mastered the direct public appeal for support of legislative issues. He formalized this approach through biweekly radio addresses during the session. Orville Freeman used a less direct approach; relying on near weekly press conferences, radio appearances, a weekly newspaper column, and frequent public speeches. Yet both Youngdahl and Freeman lost effectiveness as their administrations aged. This was especially the case with Freeman's sometimes aggressive legislative attacks, and the direct campaign he waged in 1958 against Conservative legislators. That campaign failed, and for Freeman the 1959 session ended disastrously, hurting him politically and in the public eye.

TABLE 2			
Popular Approval for Minnesota Governors: 1947-1997			
Governor	Years[1]	Average % Approval	Range of Approval
Luther W. Youngdahl	1947-51	82%	76-89%
C. Elmer Anderson	1951-54	67	64-72
Orville Freeman	1955-59	60	49-72
Elmer L. Andersen	1961-62	44	37-48
Karl R. Rolvaag	1963-66	38%	32-45%
Harold W. Levander	1967-70	40	41-59
Rudy Perpich	1977-78	54	45-63
Wendell Anderson	1971-76	51	41-59
Al Quie	1979-81	54%	34-67%
Rudy Perpich	1983-90	54	42-67
Arne Carlson	1991-97	51	34-62

1. Generally the approval score reflects the percent saying the individual is doing an excellent or good job as governor.

2. This probably overestimates Quie's popularity. The Minnesota Poll took no polls on Quie after June 1981. A local poll in January 1982 revealed a 23 percent approval rating.

Source: Minnesota Polls and Minneapolis Tribune. 1947-1997.

Although Wendell Anderson used direct public appeals for selected issues during the 1971 session, he seldom relied on this tactic when his own party controlled the Legislature. His effective use of television maintained general public support, which in turn positively affected his legislative support. Al Quie deliberately parlayed his initial high public approval into legislative passage of selected issues such as tax indexing and initiative and referendum. Such tactics fell flat later in his administration as his popularity dropped sharply. Rudy Perpich's unconventional, open style initially earned public favor. During his first full term he also directly elicited support for reform initiatives such as open enrollment in secondary schools. Again, during his second full term his impact slipped with declining popularity. Arne Carlson started out low due to the unusual circumstances surrounding his election and his highly adversarial relationship with the DFL legislative majority. His image as a cost-cutting governor, coupled with his very substantial 1994 election victory at least partially accounted for his later rise in popularity.

Party as a Political Resource

The Governor may first use the party organization to assist the election of party oriented legislators, in expectation of party cooperation during the session. Second, the greater the Governor's margin of electoral victory, the more likely it is that fellow party members will win legislative seats, and will appreciate the Governor's role in their success. Finally, during the session the Governor may directly appeal to the party loyalty of the legislative caucus for programmatic unity and support.

In Minnesota, party organizational support appeared to be largely inconsequential until recent years, a logical outcome of the nonparty Legislature. Before 1955 both parties lacked strong organization, and Republican governors dealt with loose personal organizations inside and outside the legislature. Republican governors often found themselves at odds with "old guard" party regulars. Only Harold Levander benefited from the party organization, a carry-over of the successful 1962 Republican effort to recruit legislative candidates. However, observers never regarded Levander as a spokesman or central leader of his party. Arne Carlson represented only one wing of the party (Koustorous, 1991: 31). When the state Republican convention denied him endorsement in 1994, he defeated the endorsed candidate in the September primary election.

Democratic governors relied only slightly more on the party organization. Freeman held the strongest organizational ties within the party, but this was still an emergent party not yet fully equipped to contest legislative elections. Though Rolvaag began with strong party contacts, these steadily deteriorated after the long 1962 re-count (Lebedoff, 1969: 59-63). Rudy Perpich often appeared as a "maverick" within the organization, defeating the endorsed party candidate in the 1982 gubernatorial primary.

Conventional political wisdom contends that legislatures are more likely to follow chief executives who carry large electoral majorities into office. However, few recent Minnesota governors claimed great popular mandates. Only four won even one term exceeding 60 percent of the popular two-party vote. Half the elections were won with less than 55 percent (see Table 3). Though landslide mandates remain rare, all governors carried a popular majority of House districts and (with one exception) Senate districts.

Not until the 1975 Session did the Minnesota Legislature formally organize itself into party caucuses as Democrats or Republicans (for caucus control see Table 4). However, the DFL (Liberal) caucus, especially in the House, usually lined up in rather close support of the DFL Governor (Williamson, 1971: 357-8; Anderson, 1982; Perpich, 1982). Caucus leaders met regularly with the Governor and more unified caucus voting seemed more common. Nevertheless, due to divided control, caucus loyalty failed to gain programmatic success for Freeman and Rolvaag. For Wendell Anderson, after 1971, and Rudy Perpich, DFL legislative majorities (except in 1985-86) appeared crucial to program passage. Rarely could Republican governors rely on Conservative caucus support. Both Youngdahl and Elmer L. Andersen built support around a coalition of party oriented Conservatives and Liberal caucus members.

TABLE 3		
Percentage of Two Party Vote for Minnesota Governor: 1944-1994		
Governor	*Year*	*Governor % of Two-Party Vote*
Carlson	1994	65.0%
Anderson, Wendell	1974	62.8
Thye	1944	62.0
Youngdahl	1950	61.3
Youngdahl	1946	59.8
Perpich	1982	59.6
Freeman	1958	57.3
Perpich	1986	56.5
Anderson, C.E.	1952	55.7
Anderson, Wendell	1970	54.3
Youngdahl	1948	54.1
Quie	1978	53.6
Freeman	1954	53.0
Levander	1966	52.8
Freeman	1956	51.6
Carlson	1990	51.1
Anderson, E.L.	1960	50.7
Rolvaag	1962	50.0
Source: The Minnesota Legislative Manual. 1995-96		

TABLE 4					
Caucus Control in Minnesota Legislature: 1945-1996					
		House		*Senate*	
Governor	*Year*	*Cons./IR*	*Liberal/ DFL*	*Cons./IR*	*Liberal/ DFL*
Thye (IR)	1945	107	24	57	10
Youngdahl (IR)	1947	105	26	55	10
	1949	86	45	57	10
	1951	87	44	51	16
C. E. Anderson	1953	85	46	52	15
(IR)	1955	65	66	49	19
Freeman (DFL)	1957	61	70	48	19
	1959	59	72	43	24
	1961	58	73	43	24
E. L. Andersen	1963	80	54	43	24
(IR)	1965	80	55	43	24
Rolvaag (DFL)	1967	93	42	45	22
	1969	85	50	45	22
Levander (IR)	1971	70	65	34	33
	1973	57	77	30	37
W. Anderson	1975	31	103	28	38
(DFL)	1977	31	103	18	49
	1979	67	67	20	47
	1980	66	68	20	47
Perpich (DFL)	1981	64	70	22	45
Quie (IR)	1983	57	77	25	42
	1985	69	65	24	42
	1987	51	83	20	47
Perpich (DFL)	1989	54	80	23	44
	1991	55	79	21	46
	1993	48	86	22	45
	1995	63	71	23	42
Carlson (IR)					

Sources: The Minnesota Legislative Manual. 1945-1996; Journal of the Minnesota House. 1945-81, Journal of the Minnesota Senate. 1945-81.

Senate Conservatives maintained the most independence from the Governor. Only the Levander administration relied on Conservative caucus members, based on common issue positions, in both houses for a rather sizable party base of support. During Quie's administration, party divisions in the Legislature became quite significant, but Quie never enjoyed legislative majorities for his own party. He never resolved the dilemma of satisfying Independent-Republican minorities while also negotiating with the DFL majority. The Carlson administration continued this pattern of divided control.

LEGAL-CONSTITUTIONAL RESOURCES

Legal-constitutional powers, staff, and political resources all set channels within which a governor must operate. The manner in which a governor chooses to operate, and how skillfully that governor actually performs, are functions of the individual who holds the office. Personal factors constitute the most variable element in a particular governor's success. Personal background and executive style represent two major examples of personal factors.

Personal Background

Excepting in ethnic heritage, recent Minnesota governors reflect personal backgrounds not uncommon to the nation's governors as a whole. All but one possessed a Norwegian or Swedish ethnic background and most followed occupations as lawyers or businessmen. A few worked as party officials and all previously participated in party campaigns. Most attained middle age (average 49) when first elected. All held some prior public office, 14 years being the average previous public experience. Governors follow mixed career paths. Earlier governors commonly served previously as Lieutenant Governor. After 1970, governors were more likely to have served in the state Legislature. Larry Sabato argues that extensive political experience, especially legislative experience, provides invaluable preparation for becoming an outstanding governor. More recent Minnesota governors, then, should be better prepared to function well in office.

Gubernatorial Style

Chief executives may adopt a variety of styles or roles. Table 5 classifies governors into five types. The classification scheme assumes that the program-politician would be the most "successful" as measured by policy impact. In Minnesota the public, press, and academic observers appear to favor this dynamic leadership type, while legislators, until recently, seemed more suspicious of this style (Fridley, 1966: 4; Stinnett and Backstrom, 1964: 12-20). There appear to be differences between caucuses, with the DFL more likely to favor activist governors.

No Minnesota governor perfectly fit the theoretical role types. Freeman and Youngdahl best reflect the pattern of bold, dynamic, and program oriented executives (yet their critics found them uncompromising and legislatively insensitive). We may also describe Wendell Anderson as program oriented. As a career politician he relied more on compromise and "soft-sell" persuasion. He first developed an extensive program, derived from many sources, then delegated day-to-day contacts to his staff. Elmer L. Andersen, Levander, and Quie most conform to the "executive" type. They stressed program change in selected policy areas. All used a rather soft-sell approach to the Legislature. Andersen rather carefully respected the legislative norm of separation of powers, considering excessive executive intrusion as improper. Levander's policies coincided with the majority legislative caucus views, but he avoided personal involvement in negotiations, reflecting an unfamiliarity with the legislative process and a distaste for political bargaining. Quie concentrated on a relatively few major policy issues making an unusually sharp distinction between "governor's initiatives" and departmental bills. Although open to receiving legislators in personal conferences, he left most legislative contact to staff. Neither Thye nor C. Elmer Anderson developed extensive legislative programs.Thye functioned primarily as a caretaker and hand-picked successor to Harold Stassen. C. Elmer Anderson stressed, and appeared to relish, his role as symbol of state government and greeter of visiting dignitaries.

TABLE 5				
Gubernatorial Role Styles				
Type	*Goals*	*Methods*	*Goals*	*Methods*
Ceremonial	Limited Symbolic No staff	Limited Personal Limited ability	Honest "Nice" No change	Small Positive
Caretaker	Maintenance	Limited bureau-cratic and pers-sonal contacts limited staff	Honest Dedicated "Nice"	Positive on short run maintenance
Reformer	Push middle-range change projects	Personalistic Some coalitions Limited staff	Strong willed Straight forward Hard-working	Moderate on some pro-gram areas
Executive	Middle range change	Moderate alliances; Heavy bureaucratic and staff use	Straight-laced Business like conser-vative	Fairly large on main-tenance; some pro-gram change
Program-Politician	Numerous Integrated Middle and long range change	Ideas from many sources; Through bureaucracy, groups, legislators; staff important	Talented Dynamic Gregarious Impatient	Change in large number of policy areas

Adapted from John P. Kotter and Paul Lawrence, *Mayors in Action*.

When Rudy Perpich succeeded Anderson, reform considerations motivated Perpich's role more than any other factor. Although he understood politics, Perpich wished to change the basic system, making government at the same time more accessible and more manageable. His unconventional style (appearing around the state unannounced) and vitality endeared him to the public while unnerving other governmental actors. After election in his own right in 1982, Perpich retained elements of the reform style both in his personalistic approach and in initiatives such as government reorganization and open enrollment in secondary education. However, his personal actions became more directed as he moved more toward the program-politician style. Perpich had held public office practically continuously since 1956, a mark of a career politician. He also developed a very extensive substantive legislative program throughout the period from 1983-1990. As Governor, Karl Rolvaag most defied role typing. Rolvaag steadfastly supported expanding major liberal social programs. As a self-proclaimed career politician, who saw politics as the "art of the possible," he maintained effective internal relations with the Legislature. His public image in no way matched that of a dynamic program-politician. Perhaps Karl Rolvaag exemplified the case of a governor who only imperfectly pursued a desired role (Naftalin, 1980-81).

Arne Carlson also remained difficult to classify, combining elements of the reformer and program-politician. As in the case of a reformer, he lacked close ties to the party organization and reflected an outsider image with a public attack style toward the press and the Legislature. He stressed more efficient government through administrative overhaul and changed service delivery. He advocated reforms in education, local government funding, and legislative process. However, as in the case of a career politician, he served virtually continuously in public office for twenty-five years before becoming governor. His legislative initiatives pursued a "no tax increase" policy and stressed state policies that encouraged business expansion (Wilson, 1994: 12-17). Since he has not completed his second term at this writing, a definitive judgment on Governor Carlson's style appears premature.

The legislative relationship often directly reflects a governor's styles and skills. How does a governor influence legislators? Some invite legislators to the governor's office for get-acquainted sessions or to discuss a specific bill. Some governor's regularly meet with groups such as the caucus leadership and key committee leaders. Other governors prefer phone calls and written messages. A few more daring governors may attempt to influence committee appointments and election of legislative leaders, a risky technique. A governor's program success may also be an outgrowth of how carefully it is integrated into the legislative system. This process includes program formulation, bill drafting, and careful selection of legislative authors. A bill's success frequently depends on selecting several influential legislators as official authors. Orville Freeman used the entire range of legislative techniques appearing to be the only governor to directly influence legislative assignments, including the house speakership and committee chairs. Youngdahl, on the other hand, relied upon a bipartisan bloc that crossed party lines. Rolvaag limited himself primarily to private individual conferences in his office, and occasional discussions with minority caucus leaders. As a former legislator, Rudy Perpich was more likely to work through the DFL speakers in the House, but he and his staff generally selected their own legislative sponsors for major bills. Other governors, except on the most crucial issues, downplayed direct private legislative contact, preferring to work mainly through their staffs or, increasingly, since 1967, through party caucus leadership.

A generally reliable conclusion is that Minnesota governors have traditionally avoided playing an open role in the legislative process. Only Youngdahl and Freeman played a more aggressive role. At the same time, a majority of governors pursue programmatic change. The concluding section evaluates which gubernatorial style, along with other factors, maximizes successful policy adoption.

GUBERNATORIAL PROGRAM SUCCESS

One major test of gubernatorial power is success in getting the Legislature to pass the major elements in the administration's program. Through program success we are able to evaluate which available resources most effectively contributed to gubernatorial power.

Ranking Power Potential

By using the previously discussed four dimensions of gubernatorial powers (legal-constitutional, institutional, political, and personal style), we can rank the eleven postwar Minnesota governors in order of potential power resources. Based on all four factors, from the most resources to the least, the governors rank as follows (Williamson, 1971: 382-92):

> Wendell Anderson (1971-76)
> Rudy Perpich (1983-90)
> Luther Youngdahl (1947-51)   *Moderately High*
> Arne Carlson (1991-)
> Orville Freeman (1955-60)
>
> Al Quie (1979-82)
> Rudy Perpich (1977-78)   *Moderate*
> Harold Levander (1967-70)
>
> Edward Thye (1943-46)
> Elmer L. Andersen (1961-63)
> C. Elmer Anderson (1951-54)   *Moderately Low*
> Karl Rolvaag (1963-66)

Wendell Anderson, Perpich, Youngdahl, Carlson and Freeman fall into the highest ranking group. A clear gap separates this group from the next three. A lesser gap exists between the second group and the last four governors. These composite rankings gloss over differences on each of the four dimensions. For example, Luther

Youngdahl would rank first on this ability to generate public support. Al Quie ranks higher on legal-constitutional powers. We would expect that gubernatorial success in gaining legislative acceptance of their program would be roughly in the order of this composite ranking.

To measure success, we compare the number of governor's proposals presented to the Legislature in bill form to the number that actually passed. This measure reveals Minnesota postwar governors as moderately successful in gaining legislative acceptance of their programs (see Table 6). Two early governors, Thye and Youngdahl, had good success. More recently Levander, Wendell Anderson, and Perpich had high averages. The remaining governors fell near or below 50 percent, some far below. In comparing program success with power potential ratings, we find the two factors are not identical. The resource rankings do predict a rough order of success, with two important exceptions. Thye was far more successful than his ranking would suggest. In contrast, Freeman was far less successful.

Factors in Success

Many variables, including economic conditions, the political climate, the match between gubernatorial style and legislative expectations, and how well a governor utilizes resources, all condition success (Beyle, 1995: 28; Ferguson, 1996: 14-15; Gross, 1991: 10). Combining all four resource dimensions modestly predicts program success. Of the four dimensions, political resources most closely relate to policy approval. And of those political resources, partisan control of the Legislature appears the best single indicator (Gross, 1991: 20; Herzik, 1991: 27). However, no simple relationship exists between a governor's power resources and programmatic achievement.

TABLE 6				
Minnesota Governor's Program Success: 1945-1996				
Governor	*Year*	*Passed*	*Failed*	*% Success*
Thye	1945	16	6	73.0%
Youngdahl	1947	28	19	59.6
	1949	43	24	64.0
	1951	47	30	61.0
C. E. Anderson	1953	19	34	35.5
Freeman	1955	41	39	51.5
	1957	28	39	41.8
	1959	16	46	25.8
E. L. Andersen	1961	27	32	45.8
Rolvaag	1965	19	30	38.8
Levander	1967	60	32	65.2
	1969	65	41	61.3
W. Anderson	1971	41	38	51.9
	1973-74	169	35	82.8
	1975-76	81	17	82.6
Perpich	1977-78	93	63	59.6
Quie	1979-80	130	113	53.5
	1981-82	130	127	50.5
Perpich	1983-84	60	38	61.0
	1985-86	25	22	53.0
	1987-88	87	63	58.0
	1989-90	58	48	55.0
Carlson	1991-92	45	45	50.0
	1993-94	62	46	57.4
	1995-96	90	83	52.0
Total		1478	1128	56.7
Average				55.6

Source: Computed from *Journal of the Minnesota Senate*, 1945-1990 and *Journal of the Minnesota House*, 1945-1990.
Note: This omits the 1963 session split between Governor Andersen and Governor Rolvaag.

Consider gubernatorial victory margins.   Carlson, Thye, Youngdahl, Wendell Anderson, and Perpich all won by wide margins; all but Carlson   had high program success.   However, Harold Levander won by a narrow margin.   He enjoyed high program success.   More importantly, those governors who won a majority vote in a large number of legislative districts experienced much greater program success.   Even that measure appears less than definitive. Orville Freeman won 57 percent of the vote in 1958, carrying 79 percent of the legislative districts.   During the 1959 session he suffered the lowest success ratio for the period covered.

Partisan control constitutes the key final political element to program success. This holds true even under the previously formally nonpartisan Legislature. Partisan orientation grew beginning in the mid-1950s. Governors who worked with their own party caucus majorities in both chambers achieved 63 percent success. Those forced to deal with an opposition party caucus in one or both houses averaged 47 percent success.

Legal-constitutional resources appear only modestly important. Among the formal legal powers, the appointment power stands out. Generally, trusted department heads help keep administrative agencies accountable to the Governor.   The departments refine and expand existing state programs.   Their employees explain and defend programs before the Legislature. Increases in the appointment power developed mainly since 1967. Youngdahl retained office long enough so that he appointed most department heads.   Governor Freeman's administration proved the major exception between controlling department heads and program success.

Public opinion support, available staff, and personal style produce no simple relationship with program success.   Little correlation exists between where a governor stands in public popularity and legislative success. Six governors' public opinion ranking accorded well with success ranking. C. Elmer Anderson and Orville Freeman received high public support, but low legislative success. Although Harold Levander enjoyed great legislative success, his popularity deteriorated the longer he held office.

Career experience very marginally predicts legislative success. Governors with prior legislative experience enjoyed slightly higher success than those with neither legislative experience nor state wide office. Style, by itself, also fails as a determining factor. "Program-politicians" succeeded only very slightly better than the other styles. C. Elmer Anderson as a ceremonial government may have succeeded within his own frame of reference. This did not lead to high program achievement. Of the most aggressive governors, Youngdahl succeeded, Freeman did not. After Freeman openly campaigned to defeat veteran conservative senators, he suffered at their hands at the next session. The best generalization seems to be that a particular style will be most successful when it suits legislative expectations, the program demands of the times, and a governor's skills.

Five Successful Governors

Luther Youngdahl, though an aggressive, program politician, enjoyed limited formal powers. He lacked organizational party links. No disciplined *party* caucus existed. Many Conservative legislative leaders remained unsympathetic to his rather liberal program. Youngdahl relied primarily on high popularity and his personal skills to fashion a successful program. By intense effort, he built a legislative following, using his prestige and effective news coverage to constantly pressure the Legislature. Over time his aggressiveness eroded positive legislative relations. Rather than continue the wearing battle, he resigned for the calm of a federal judgeship.

Ed Thye succeeded as a caretaker governor. His modest and noncontroversial program, during wartime when the state government's role diminished, demanded little. Both his style and program agreed with the inclinations of many senior Conservative legislative leaders.

Harold Levander, a "citizen politician," adopted an "executive style," stressing controlled change to solve moral social problems and to improve government efficiency. He relished problem solving. A personal aversion to legislative bargaining led him to work through others. Levander's program benefited from a Republican electoral revival that in the early 1960s successfully elected (non label) Republicans to the Legislature. The newer Conservatives were loyal Republicans. Many older, less party aligned Conservatives sympathized with his program. His low key style meshed well with traditional legislative expectations concerning the proper gubernatorial role.

As a governor who loved politics, who admitted political ambition, and who as a New Deal Democrat espoused an active role for government, Wendell Anderson closely fit the "program politician" model. He enjoyed more potential power advantages than any other governor. Recent laws had consolidated formal gubernatorial power. Administrative reorganization encouraged the development of a loyal administrative team. He employed a skillful staff. Legislative caucuses became organized on party lines and more disciplined. After 1973 for the first time the DFL controlled both chambers of the Legislature. Anderson's broad legislative program incorporated ideas from many sources. Initially the support of key Republican legislative leaders and outside interest groups for popular programs, coupled with direct public appeals, aided his program success. After 1973, large DFL majorities rendered direct public appeals less necessary. His relatively high public opinion support and landslide re-election added to his legislative successes. He normally worked through legislative leadership, especially House Speaker Martin Sabo.

When Rudy Perpich first became governor, political observers viewed him as both unusual and unconventional. His initial style most closely resembled the "reformer" approach. Perpich championed open government. He devoted much time to personally fighting political fires such as the power line controversy. Huge DFL legislative majorities were the keys to his program successes. High initial public popularity reinforced his legislative support. Perpich, along with many other DFLers, suffered election defeat in 1978. Upon his comeback in 1983 his style shifted more toward a program politician orientation. Although he eschewed close party organization ties, Perpich held public office virtually uninterrupted from the mid-1950s. He stressed issues such as education reform, property tax revision, and economic development. He still normally enjoyed substantial DFL legislative majorities. Republican control of the House from 1985-86 limited his legislative success during that period. Although legislative success continued after 1987, several factors limited Perpich's governorship. He suffered periodic strained relationships with activists within his own party. He quarreled with the press more over personal style than policy substance. His popularity fluctuated, then declined toward his term's end. Arne Carlson narrowly defeated Perpich in the highly unusual 1990 election.

CONCLUSION

The governorship of the 1990s and beyond is a potentially more powerful office than its predecessor. Lengthened terms, increased staff, growing budgetary consolidation, administrative reorganization, and reawakened partisanship all contributed to this change. However, increased power potential fails to guarantee increased actual power for individual governors. Uncertain popular support may undermine legislative successes. Divided party control in the Legislature presents a serious barrier for a program-oriented governor. No single gubernatorial style guarantees success. A successful governor must be blessed with favorable political circumstances, as well as formal powers. Then a governor must adopt a personal style compatible with prevailing political conditions.

REFERENCES

Bernick, E. Lee, and Charles W. Wiggins. 1991. "Executive-Legislative Relations: The Governors' Role as Chief Legislator." In Eric B. Herzik and Brent W. Brown, eds. *Gubernatorial Leadership and State Policy*. New York, NY: Greenwood Press. Pp. 73-92.

Beyle, Thad. 1995. (Winter). "Enhancing Executive Leadership in the States." *State and Local Government Review*. Volume 27, No.1: 18-35.

Dye, Thomas. 1997. *Politics in States and Communities*. 9th Edition. Upper Saddle River, NJ: Prentice-Hall.

Esbjornson, Robert. 1955. *A Christian in Politics: Luther W. Youngdahl*. Minneapolis, MN: T. S. Denison Co.

Ferguson, Margaret. 1996. "Gubernatorial Policy Leadership in the Fifty States." Paper presented at annual meeting of the Midwest Political Science Association. April 18-20.

Fridley, Russell W. 1966. *Evaluating the Governors*. St. Paul, MN: The Minnesota Historical Society.

Gross, Donald. 1991. "The Policy Role of Governors." In Eric B. Herzik and Brent W. Brown, eds. *Gubernatorial Leadership and State Policy*. New York: Greenwood Press. Pp. 1-24.

Herzik, Erik. 1991. "Policy Analysis and Gubernatorial Leadership." In Erik B. Herzik and Brent W. Brown, eds. *Gubernatorial Leadership and State Policy*. New York, NY: Greenwood Press. Pp. 25-38.

Koustorous, John. 1991. (February). "The Outsider Steps In." *Minnesota Law and Politics*: 31.

Lebedoff, David. 1969. *The 21st Ballot*. Minneapolis, MN: University of Minnesota Press.

Minnesota Legislative Manual, 1995-1996. 1995. St. Paul, MN: State of Minnesota.

Naftalin, Arthur (narrator). 1980-81. "Minnesota Governors." A video tape series produced by the University of Minnesota Media Resources Department.

Sabato, Larry. 1983. *Good-bye to Goodtime Charlies: The American Governor Transformed.* 2nd Edition. Washington, DC: Congressional Quarterly Press.

State of Minnesota. 1996. *Minnesota Guidebook to State Agency Services, 1996-1999.* St. Paul, MN: Department of Administration.

State of Minnesota. 1995. *Minnesota Legislative Manual, 1995-1996.* St. Paul, MN: Secretary of State's Office.

Stinnett, Ronald, and Charles H. Backstrom. 1964. *Recount.* Washington, DC: National Documents Publishers, Inc.

Williamson, Homer E. 1971. *Executive-Legislative Relations in Minnesota.* Ph.D. Dissertation. University of Minnesota.

Wilson, Betty. 1994. (October). "The 1,001 Faces of Arne Carlson, 1994." *Minnesota Law and Politics*: 10-17.

INTERVIEWS

Governor Wendell Anderson, July 21, 1982.

Terry Montgomery, Executive Secretary, Governor Perpich, June 21, 1982.

Governor Rudy Perpich, July 23, 1982.

Robert Renner, Legislative Assistant, Governor Quie, June 22, 1982.

John Riley, Chief of Staff, Governor Arne Carlson, August 11. 1992.

Duane Scribner, Special Assistant, Governor W. Anderson, July 23, 1976.

Chapter 3

THE MINNESOTA LEGISLATURE

Donald Ostrom
Gustavus Adolphus College

"The future will be very much like the past, only different."
Woody Allen

INTRODUCTION

In this chapter we will first take up the qualities that the members of the Minnesota Legislature share with most other U.S. state legislators—increasing professionalism, election on a partisan ballot, demographic characteristics, bicameral divisions, committee work, and relations with staff and lobbyists. Then we will discuss what makes Minnesota different from most other states—Democratic party dominance, strong media coverage, a moralistic political culture, and progressive outcomes. To paraphrase Woody Allen, the Minnesota Legislature is very much like the other state legislatures, only different.

MINNESOTA IS LIKE OTHER . . .

A Semi-Professional Legislature

Like most state legislatures, the Minnesota legislature has become more professional over the past generation. In 1973

Minnesota changed to annual sessions, increased the salaries, and added to the staff. It is not the full-time, professional legislature of New York, California and six other states larger than Minnesota, as well as the U.S. Congress (Kurtz, 1989). But the time demands in Minnesota of sessions lasting several months each year, occasional special sessions, interim sessions and committee meetings, as well as campaigns for office every two or four years take their toll. One educator in the House bemoaned the situation (Ostrom, 1980):

> You can't be a classroom teacher and a legislator. They take too much time. Mini-sessions held for two days each month in the fall are the key. If the legislature only went from January to March or May you could do it. But if in the fall you're going to be gone on Tuesday-Wednesday once or twice a month, then go out of state for a tax conference, it just becomes a pain in the ass for the principal.

Service in the Minnesota legislature requires far more commitment now than the amateur legislatures of neighboring states North and South Dakota, or Minnesota a generation ago. In 1967 no Minnesota member listed legislator as his or her only occupation. Since then 23-32 members, or 12 percent to 15 percent of the total membership of 201, classify themselves as full-time legislators (Table 1). The salary level of the legislature is modest (approximately $30,000 a year in the 1990s), and the energy level of the average legislator is high. Consequently, most members continue to have a second job, although in almost all cases a subordinate one. A 1978 survey showed the median amount of time House members devoted to legislative and political work was forty-one hours a week (some weeks less than five hours, other weeks over eighty). The workload if anything has increased since then. The result has been a limitation on their non-legislative careers, as one member explained (Ostrom, 1980):

While I'm in the legislature I can't get promoted, because I'm already in the highest non-supervisory rank. But I can't be a supervisor when I'm gone half the year. They don't promote me, and they're right.

TABLE 1			
Occupations of legislators in selected sessions, 1967-97			
	1967	*1977*	*1987*	*1997*
Attorney	55	25	23	30
Business	57	33	57	45
Educator	12	28	31	31
Farmer	39	31	42	20
Other	39	52	31	20
Full-time legislator	0	32	23	25
Source: Minnesota Legislative Reference Library.			

Getting Elected, Staying in Office

The Minnesota Legislature has 201 members, 67 in the Senate and 134 (down from 135 prior to 1973) in the House. Like all states except Nebraska, legislators run on a partisan ballot. Minnesota did go through a six-decade era, 1913 through 1972, when party labels were not on the ballot. But even during this period the legislators, once in the capitol, usually divided into caucuses of Conservatives, allied with the Republican party, and Liberals, who later took the name Democratic-Farmer-Labor (DFL), as the Democratic party is called in Minnesota. After party designation on the ballot was restored for the 1974 election, all winning legislative candidates except for an occasional maverick have run as Republicans or DFL.

If legislative candidates expect to win election handily, they must rely on their own resources and whatever local and other help they can muster. But in races expected to be close, and thus affecting the partisan lineup of the legislature, the legislative leadership of each party has increasingly become involved. Legislative leadership has been more able than the political party organizations to muster the resources, especially money and interest group support, needed to make a difference in marginal contests (Rosenthal, 1994).

As in other states, incumbency is a great help in winning election. Only a minority of incumbents get defeated. They may succumb because of losing touch with the district, changes in the constituency due to redistricting each decade, or the political tidal waves that periodically have swept out large numbers of one party. In 1978, 1984 and 1994 there were substantial Democratic losses in the House, and in the early 1970s and 1986 the Republicans lost heavily.

Despite the absence of constitutional term limits there is turnover. Between 1970 and 1996, an average of one-fourth of incumbents whose term was up did not return after the election (Table 2). At the opening of each two-year session in 1977, 1987 and 1997, the members had served on the average, only four to eight years (Table 3). Thus, service in the Minnesota Legislature has not been a lifetime career for members. Only one member reached thirty years of service since the legislature went to annual sessions in the early 1970s. The exception, helped by a sterling reputation, favorable district, and good genes, was Rep. Willard Munger of Duluth who by 1997, had set two House records by staying in office more than forty years, and serving beyond his 86th birthday.

Both the willingness of incumbents to seek re-election and their success rate have been increasing over the past generation (Table 4). Consequently, as Table 2 showed, the turnover rate has been declining, from an average of 32.4 percent in the 1970's elections, down to 20.1 percent in the 1990s.

TABLE 2			
Turnover in Minnesota Legislature, 1970-96			
Year of election	*Members elected*	*New members elected*	*Turnover*
1970	202	67	33.2%
1972	202	80	39.6
1974	134	52	38.8
1976	201	44	21.9
1978	134	40	28.9
Totals, 1970s	873	283	32.4
1980	201	46	22.9
1982	201	63	31.3
1984	134	29	29.6
1986	201	42	20.9
1988	134	15	11.2
Totals, 1980s	871	235	27.0
1990	201	39	19.4
1992	201	49	24.4
1994	134	27	20.1
1996	201	33	16.4
Totals, 1990s	737	148	20.1
Totals, 1970-1996	2481	626	25.2

Source: Minnesota Legislative Reference Library. "Turnover data: 1970-1996 elections."

TABLE 3		
Average (mean) years of service by members at beginning of selected legislative sessions		
Year	Senate	House
1977	4.1	4.3
1987	6.1	5.7
1997	8.2	6.5

Source: Minnesota Legislative Reference Library.

TABLE 4					
Incumbency success in average election, 1970-78, 1980-88, 1990-96					
Senate			House		
	Number of incumbents who ran	Number of incumbents who won	Incumbent success rate	Number of incumbents who ran	Number of incumbents who won	Incumbent success rate
1970s	53.3	44.0	82.6%	112.0	91.6	81.8%
1980s	55.3	49.3	89.2	116.0	105.6	91.0
1990s	57.0	53.3	93.6	117.0	107.3	91.7

Source: Minnesota Legislative Reference Library.

Demographics

As in all states, white males have dominated the Minnesota Legislature. As recently as 1971-72 only one of the 202 members then serving was a woman. The number of women steadily increased into the 1990s, with women comprising a higher percentage of the membership with almost every election. By 1997, 30% of the legislators were women with the Senate having a slightly higher proportion than the House (Minnesota, 1996).

Only a handful of legislators are minority members. In 1997 there were two Hispanics, one African-American, and one Asian-American, all in the House. The small percentages reflect not only societal bias, but also the small percentage of minorities in Minnesota's population. The 1990 census reported that the population of the entire state was only 2 percent Hispanic, 2 percent African-American, 1 percent Asian, and 1 percent American Indian. No Senate district and only one House district had a combination of minorities comprising a majority; and no Senate or House district had a majority consisting of a single minority group. Minnesota *is* near the top of the states in number of openly gay or lesbian legislators with two, but that population is also under represented.

The Minnesota Legislature is a well-educated group of people. All the members serving in 1997 had at least a high school degree, and all but 5 percent had further education. Indeed, half the legislators had post-college training (St. Paul Pioneer Press, 1997; Whereatt, 1997).

The one-person, one-vote decisions of the 1960s, along with population movements from rural areas to the Twin Cities, changed the basis of representation. There are fewer rural members than a generation ago. Although the two central cities of Minneapolis and St. Paul declined in population, the strong growth of their suburbs meant that a majority of the Legislature has represented the Minneapolis-St. Paul metropolitan area from the 1992 election onward. A generation ago when most members were from rural areas, they lived and socialized together in hotels when the Legislature was in session. Now, a substantial majority of legislators live at home and commute daily to the Capitol.

The occupations of legislators have changed in several ways over the past generation (Table 1). First, the number of farmers decreased due to the reapportionment toward the metropolitan area. Second, the number of attorneys dropped even more sharply, caused by the greater time demands of the Legislature after annual sessions were instituted in the early 1970s, and laws were strengthened in response to greater sensitivity about conflicts of interest. Third, the greater time demands and higher legislative salary led some members toward full-time service after the 1960s. Finally, the number of educators substantially increased, as teachers became more active in politics and the greater pay for legislators made public service more attractive. Although business, education, law and farming made up the largest occupational groups in the Legislature, none of them ever came close to having a majority of the membership.

Two Houses Like Other Legislatures;
Two Houses Different from Each Other

As in other states, with the exception of Nebraska, Minnesota has a bicameral legislature. The two chambers are equal in power, in that both bodies must approve a bill with exactly the same language for it to become law.

While the bicameral organization resembles other state legislatures, the Minnesota House and Senate do differ from each other. A Senate seat is more desirable than one in the House because of the Senate's smaller size (67 members, half the House size) and longer terms (four years instead of two). In 1997 there were no former Senators serving in the House, while 24 of the 67 Senators, or 36 percent, had previously served in the House. Most of them would say they had moved up.

The Senate and the House have different cultures. To overstate the differences, they are like the House of Lords and the House of Commons, respectively. The women in both chambers usually dress with some formality. Male Senators, however, always wear jackets and ties on the floor, although male Representatives sometimes show up without jackets, without ties, occasionally without socks. The Senators are polite to each other; if they are going to stick in the knife, they do it quietly. The House is a noisy place. Members are talking or out of their seats, or both. While heckling never reaches the level of the British House of Commons, there are times when members give a vocal reaction to provocative statements. The House is a more partisan body in its rules structure than the Senate, and Representatives of the minority party have more difficulty getting their bills passed or even considered than Senators of the minority party. In both bodies, issues of taxation and labor-management are likely to break along partisan lines, but the House is much more likely to carry partisanship into other issues.

The leadership of the two chambers also differs in structure and longevity. The Senate is presided over by its President, a respected member, but the most powerful member is the Majority Leader. In the House, the Speaker is the most powerful member and also presides. The House Majority Leader is only the second in command. As of 1997, Democrat Roger Moe, held the position of Majority Leader in the Senate, a role he has played for 16 years. During that period the House had seven different people serving as Speaker and nine different Majority Leaders. Some of the turnover was due to the Republicans having a House majority during the 1985-86 term. Most was due to House Democratic leaders leaving because of their own unhappiness with the job, or because of public or member unhappiness with them.

Minority party leadership in the two chambers shares one important characteristic, turnover. Partly due to frustration over their chronic minority status since the 1972 election, House and Senate Republicans have constantly chosen new leaders. During the 1973-97 period, the Senate Republicans had six leaders, the House Republicans had eight.

Committees

As in other legislative bodies with complex responsibilities and size, much of the work gets done in committees. The party ratio in each committee reflects the party ratio of the full membership, with the exceptions of certain committees such as the Ethics Committee where equal numbers of both parties served to promote a bipartisan handling of delicate issues. In the Senate, members receive committee appointments from a committee of the majority party, with strong influence by the Majority Leader. In the House, the Speaker alone traditionally has the power of appointment, although in 1997 Speaker Phil Carruthers announced he would follow the advice of an advisory committee. Committee chairs are chosen through the same process. The most senior members of the majority party without exception become the committee chairs. Because some committees are more important than others, the particular chairmanship given to a senior majority party member depends upon a combination of previous service on the committee, subject matter interest and knowledge, perceived ability, party loyalty, and alliance with the party leader.

The organization of the committees changes somewhat from term to term. In 1997 the House had twenty committees to make policy, the Senate had thirteen. Some had important policy jurisdictions, such as committees on the judiciary and environment. But most "policy" committees are less important than the "money" committees responsible for raising revenue and spending. The tax committees in each house raise most of the revenue; they also spend a good share of it through grants to local governments.

At the beginning of each term the major party leaders often reorganize the other money committees, the ones responsible for spending and bonding. Although the party leaders always have a strong influence over the major spending decisions—how much money will be allocated to K-12 (elementary and secondary) education, higher education, health care, etc.—there has usually been a committee in each chamber assigned this formal responsibility.

Allocations of money *within* the broad subject areas are the responsibility of committees called Finance Divisions in the House and Budget Divisions in the Senate. Thus, the House K-12 Education Finance Division and the Senate K-12 Education Budget Division wrestle with the formulas for funding public education, the single largest budget item. How much money should be allocated for basic education, special education, transportation, schools with high levels of students living in poverty, schools in areas of very sparse population? What should be the tax effort and financial contributions of school districts with great property wealth or little property wealth, great or lesser needs? What provisions should be made for extra local taxation and spending above the state allocations? The questions are endless, the formulas are complex, and reportedly the subject is fully understood by no members and only two staff people — and those two don't always agree.

Other finance and budget committees handle spending allocations within areas such as higher education, transportation, and state agencies. Although members serve on several committees, usually five or six in the Senate and three or four in the House, their committee assignment involving the raising or spending of money is the most important — as is true in most legislative bodies.

Not listed on the formal organization chart distributed at the beginning of each term are the most powerful committees, the conference committees. Legislation of any controversy usually passes the House and Senate in different forms, but a bill must pass both chambers in identical language before it can become law. To work out the differences, the majority party leaders of the House and Senate each appoint several members (usually three for minor bills, five for major legislation). Typically, the members will come from the parent committees for the legislation, and include one or two minority party members. The members of the conference committee are not supposed to approve provisions that are in neither bill, although they sometimes breach this rule. Otherwise they have wide discretion, which gives them great influence. Members of the Tax Committee, for example, say, "You're not really on the tax committee if you're not on the conference committee."

The negotiations between House and Senate members on a conference committee can feature posturing, game-playing, bluffing and serious bargaining, with each side ostensibly trying to uphold the position passed in their respective legislative chambers. Ideological preferences also enter into the decisions. With Democrats in charge in recent years, conservative amendments adopted on the floor of either chamber stand a good chance of being dropped in conference committee.

The Governor's role complicates the negotiations. The Governor has veto power over each bill. Occasionally legislators will deliberately pass a bill knowing that it will be vetoed, especially with a governor from the opposite party, in order to make a political statement on an issue of public policy. On the other hand, legislators who want to pass a bill that year have to take into account the position of the Governor and the Governor's staff, since it is nearly impossible to get the two-thirds vote needed in each chamber to override a veto. Consequently, the wishes of the Governor and his staff have to be considered by legislators seeking to enact a law.

Eventually, conference committee members make enough compromises for agreement on a common bill, although it sometimes takes until near the end of the session that year. Occasionally the policy and personal differences become so great that no agreement is reached. If the bill is important enough, a special session of the Legislature is needed. When a bill is approved by the conference committee it almost always will be approved by both the House and Senate and sent on to the Governor for signature.

Staff

The professionalization of the Minnesota Legislature has included the growth of year-around staff, matching changes seen in other states. In the early 1950s no one worked year-round in the Minnesota Legislature. From 1967 to 1997 the number of year-around staff grew from 33 to 652, with most of the growth occurring in the 1970s and 1980s. The staff includes everyone from entry-level employees to long-time professionals with substantial training, such as attorneys and accountants. In addition, there are about 200 employees hired for session-only service (Pinney, 1991; "Legislative staffing," 1978).

Each Senator has a secretary; in the House members usually share a secretary with one or two other members. Most staff serve more than one member. Generally, the year-around staff can be divided into two groups. One group is nonpartisan, serving all members, often for many years. In the 1990s Chief Clerk Ed Burdick reached his second half-century of House employment. This group includes researchers, attorneys, staff of the Chief Clerk, payroll, library, cable television producers, auditors and others. A second group includes employees usually hired on a partisan basis—leadership aides, partisan analysts and media staff, constituent service, committee administrators and analysts, secretaries, and others. Partisan personnel are chosen by the party leadership or, especially in cases of an employee such as a committee administrator who reports to only one member, by an individual member.

Given the responsibilities and complexity of state government today, it is impossible to believe that the tasks could be performed with as small a staff as a generation ago. Staff influences the outcomes of the Legislature. Many also directly and indirectly contribute to the re-election of incumbent members, although the Minnesota Legislature has resisted placing staff in individual districts, as occurs in a dozen other states, which would be the greatest help toward re-election. The highly professional staff also make legislators less dependent upon the executive branch and lobbyists for information.

Lobbyists

One scene in Minnesota that is typical of state legislatures is the ubiquitous presence of lobbyists. In the hours when the House and Senate are in session, they literally live up to their name, standing in lobbies outside the chambers, waiting for the members to come out so that they can be buttonholed. At other times, lobbyists can be found in the hallways and offices of members and staff, trying to activate supporters and, less frequently, convert or at least mollify potential adversaries.

During the 1990s, in an average year, figures from the Minnesota Ethical Practices Board showed that there were 1,336 registered lobbyists, or more than six lobbyists for each of the 201 members of the legislature. Lobbying organizations spent $3,850,837 annually, heavily weighted toward business.

... BUT THERE ARE IMPORTANT DIFFERENCES

Despite the many similarities with most state legislatures, the Minnesota Legislature is also unusual in some of its important features. Those features include dominance by the Democratic party, strong media coverage, a moralistic political culture, and progressive outcomes.

Democratic Dominance

Minnesota is a Democratic state. Nevertheless, since the 1960s the Republican party has been successful in some state-wide elections, winning a majority of the races for Governor, Auditor, and U.S. Senator since 1978. The other contests in Minnesota have consistently been dominated by the DFL. Statewide offices such as Secretary of State, Attorney General, and Treasurer, were consistently won by the DFL. The DFL regularly won six of the eight U.S. House seats from Minnesota in the 1990s. Democratic success can be seen most dramatically at the presidential level.   The Democratic presidential candidate carried Minnesota in nine of the past ten presidential elections, a record of success achieved nowhere else in the nation. In five of those elections a Minnesotan, Hubert Humphrey or Walter Mondale, was on the Democratic ticket as the presidential or vice-presidential nominee.

The Democratic party dominance appeared in state legislative races in the early 1970s. Prior contests for legislative seats did not list the partisan affiliation of the candidates, and the DFL had difficulty gaining a majority, especially in the Senate. But in the 1972 election, the DFL party, which already held the Governor's office, for the first time gained control of both chambers of the Legislature. They promptly enacted a law providing for party designation on the ballot for state legislative candidates, and the Republican party has had trouble winning ever since (Table 5).

In the House, Republicans held power only in 1979, when a 67-67 tie led to a compromise that included putting a Republican in the Speaker's chair, and 1985-86, when they had a small majority. In other years the Democrats held the majority, often by large margins. The Democratic dominance of the Senate has been even more thorough, consistently giving them advantages close to two to one. The margins achieved by DFL candidates in Senate elections were enhanced by a four-year term and fortunate timing which allowed them to avoid the bad Democratic election years of 1978, 1984, and 1994.

Minnesota Democratic success in the mid-1990s, maintaining majorities in both houses of the Legislature, was matched only in the southern and border states and in a handful of other states — Massachusetts, Rhode Island, and New Mexico.

TABLE 5				
Partisan control of legislature, 1961-97				
	Senate		House	
	Conservatives	Liberals/DFL	Conservatives	Liberals/DFL
1961	43	24	58	73
1963*	43	24	80	54
1965*	44	23	78	56
1967	45	22	93	42
1969	45	22	85	50
1971	34	33	70	65
1973	30	37	57	77
1975	28	38	30	104
1977	18	48	30	104
1979	20	47	67	67
1981	22	45	64	70
1983	25	42	57	77
1985	25	42	69	65
1987	20	47	51	83
1989	23	44	53	81
1991	21	46	54	80
1993	22	45	47	87
1995	24	43	63	71
1997	24	42	64	70

TABLE 5 (notes)

All figures are from the convening of the Legislature in January of that year. Prior to 1974 candidates ran without party designation on the ballot, but convened in caucuses as Republicans and Liberals (later DFL).
\# House had 135 members until 1972, 134 after that year.
* The House had one independent in 1963 and 1965, as did the Senate in 1975 and 1997. In January 1977, the Senate had one vacancy.

Strong Media Coverage

Most state legislatures receive little media coverage, partly because the capitals are located away from the major population/media centers — Sacramento instead of Los Angeles, Albany instead of New York, Madison instead of Milwaukee, Springfield instead of Chicago, even Pierre instead of Sioux Falls. Minnesota is different. The capital is located in the Twin Cities, the fourteenth largest metropolitan area in the nation, home to more than half the state's population. The state's major newspapers, television and radio stations are located just minutes from the Capitol.

Minnesota's political culture adds to the media coverage and has other profound effects on the behavior of the Legislature. Political scientist Daniel Elazar wrote about three political cultures that dominate the United States: traditionalistic, individualistic, and moralistic. The traditionalistic culture, found most frequently in the southern states, is concerned with preserving an existing, hierarchical structure. The individualistic culture, located originally in the middle Atlantic states, emphasizes individual freedom, with political officials regarding their position as a job in which they can enrich themselves.

The moralistic political culture originated in New England and upstate New York and spread west. In the words of Elazar (1984: 117-118).

Politics, to the moralistic political culture, is considered one of the great activities of humanity in its search for the good society — a struggle for power, it is true, but also an effort to exercise power for the betterment of the commonwealth . . . Both the general public and the politicians conceive of politics as a public activity centered on some notion of the public good and properly devoted to the advancement of the public interest.   Good government, then, is measured by the degree to which it promotes the public good and in terms of the honesty, selflessness, and commitment to the public welfare of those who govern.

[G]overnment is considered a positive instrument with a responsibility to promote the general welfare . . . Politics is ideally a matter of concern for every citizen, not just for those who are professionally committed to political careers.

[G]overnment service is public service, which places moral obligations upon those who participate in government that are more demanding than the moral obligations of the marketplace.   There is an equally general rejection of the notion that the field of politics is a legitimate realm for private economic enrichment . . . There is also much less of what Americans consider corruption in government and less tolerance of those actions that are considered corrupt.

[P]ublic officials will themselves seek to initiate new government activities in an effort to come to grips with problems as yet unperceived by a majority of the citizenry.

No state is an ideal type, including Minnesota. But Minnesota has the most moralistic political culture of any state in the union. On Elazar's map of the United States, with each state filled with the letters T, I, and M to illustrate the various locations of the three cultures, only Minnesota emerges with nothing but Ms within its boundaries (1984: 124-125). The values of the moralistic political culture — the good society, the public interest, government as a positive instrument, intolerance of corruption, government activities even when a problem is yet unperceived — these are not always achieved in Minnesota, but they do form the standard against which actions are measured.

So there is, first, considerable media attention to the state Legislature, because "politics is ideally a matter of concern for every citizen" (Elazar, 1984: 117-118). (Minnesota regularly finishes first or second in the nation in voting participation.) The major newspapers and commercial television stations have offices in the basement of the Capitol, and on major stories they can send reporters from their headquarters just a few miles away. When the Legislature is in session, there is steady coverage, especially in the Minneapolis and St. Paul newspapers and on the state's largest radio station, all of which reach most parts of Minnesota. Public television and especially public radio greatly add to the coverage. Minnesota along with the much larger state of California, has by far the largest number of public radio stations. Many public radio stations are dedicated to news and discussion over a network that can reach the great majority of residents in the state, and a good share of the coverage is devoted to state issues and the Legislature. In addition, in the 1990s the Senate, and later the House, began cable television coverage of floor sessions and the committee meetings of greatest interest to the public.

Second, there is little media tolerance of corruption. Several years ago Eric Black, a reporter for the *Minneapolis Star and Tribune*, wrote an article in *Washington Monthly* magazine entitled "Sweetheart, Get Me Re-Write. They've Indicted the Donut Dunker." He argued that incidents that wouldn't get any play at all in other states become front-page scandals in Minnesota, including park board officials golfing at reduced rates at the local municipal courses, an alderman who was allowed to illegally park at a baseball game, and a legislative candidate who served free coffee and rolls at a campaign gathering. "The Minnesota investigative reporter," Black wrote, "has the advantage of writing for a readership with an astonishingly low threshold for indignation."

The tradition continues. In January 1993, there was front-page coverage of legislators who spent a weekend in the city of Duluth staying at a local hotel, attending a hockey game of the local university or a play, skiing down a gentle hillside, and in general having fun, in addition to attending a presentation about how Duluth needed support for its university, dredging the harbor, and other municipal endeavors. The trip was paid for by the local Chamber of Commerce, not the taxpayers. Duluth in January is not a resort mecca; in fact, it's one of the nation's coldest locations south of Alaska. As Alan Rosenthal, a national expert on legislatures, said, "[W]ho would want to go to Duluth — in January?" (Coffman, 1993: 12B). Still, the Minnesota media and public indignation was fierce. The transgressing legislators were listed by name in the newspaper, and it was one of the incidents leading to the ouster of the Speaker of the House in 1993 and passage in 1994 of a strict ethics code making it illegal for legislators and other public officials to take anything of value (not even a cup of coffee or a doughnut!) from a lobbyist or anybody else with a stake in governmental outcomes.

Legislators are human, and their behavior does not always match the rhetoric of the moralistic culture. Some legislators still accept entire meals from lobbyists. More serious offenses in recent years included the use of legislative phones for personal calls, drunken driving, and alleged abuse of constituents. Most of the incidents involved personal problems more than government corruption. But almost all the offenders were soon gone from the Legislature, confronted by media and public indignation leading to their resignation, retirement or defeat.

Progressive Outcomes

A moralistic political culture is not synonymous with progressive politics. Utah, exceedingly Republican and conservative, has the second highest concentration of Ms on Elazar's map. But the political traditions of Minnesota, with its early population drawn from New England and later immigrants from Scandinavia and Germany, led to the Legislature enacting progressive policies.

One result was a government of high taxes and high services, only partly due to the dominance of the DFL in the Legislature since 1972. Well before that era, Minnesota was a high tax, high services state. Governors Harold Stassen and Luther Youngdahl were from the progressive wing of the Republican party, and even legislators who caucused as Conservatives were willing to support their policies. Later Republican governors did not match the liberalism of Stassen and Youngdahl, but none were conservatives; Governor Arne Carlson (1991-99) was probably the most liberal Republican governor in the nation during his terms in office.

Figures from the Minnesota Department of Revenue show that for more than thirty years the tax and spending levels of state and local governments in Minnesota, measured as a percentage of personal income, have been 12 percent to 15 percent above the average of the fifty states. In the 1990s Minnesota ranked approximately sixth among the fifty states in its tax levels. The Minnesota Legislature has also enacted tax policies that are close to proportional (i.e., high income people pay about the same proportion of their income in taxes as low income people), putting Minnesota among the half-dozen most progressive states (Citizens for Tax Justice and the Institute on Taxation and Economic Policy, 1997).

Where does all this money get spent? Education is the big item; state expenditures on K-12 and higher education, along with tax relief for local property taxes for schools, take up approximately half the state budget. Minnesota government also spends more than the national average on transportation and health care, including subsidized health insurance for low-income working people, that has helped Minnesota achieve second place among the states in proportion of population covered by health insurance.

One area where Minnesota spends less than the average is criminal justice. Its spending on police ranked below the national average, and the rate of incarceration was forty-ninth, with only North Dakota imprisoning a smaller proportion of its population. Minnesota is also one of only a dozen states without the death penalty. In recent years, when proposals to enact a death penalty came to a recorded vote before the Minnesota House, they failed by 3-1 margins.

Minnesota's spending decisions are accompanied by fiscal discipline. Due to the willingness to pay for expenditures through taxation, strong budget reserves, and limited borrowing, as well as a strong, diversified economy, Minnesota was one of only six states given a top-level AAA bond rating by all three of Wall Street's major bond houses (Baden, 1997).

In the moralistic political culture described above, "public officials will themselves seek to initiate new government activities in an effort to come to grips with problems as yet unperceived by a majority of the citizenry" (Elazar, 1984: 117-118). Hubert Humphrey, the most important political figure in Minnesota in the second half of the twentieth century, was sometimes accused of proposing more solutions than there were problems! In Minnesota legislators are constantly urged to "get ahead of the curve," and told that education, health care and other expenditures will save money in the long run. Perhaps this is correct. Despite constant warnings that the high tax levels contribute to a bad business climate, Minnesota's job growth has been strong for the past generation, with unemployment consistently below the national average. In the 1990s there was no sign of slowing down.

This made Minnesota the major exception to a general pattern of decline in the snowbelt states of the northeastern quadrant of the United States. For a generation these states have not kept pace with the job and population growth in the rest of the nation, going from more than half the nation's population in the 1960 census to less than half in 1990. Consequently, their representation in the U.S. House, which is based on population, also declined. All the states west of Vermont through North Dakota, and from the Canadian border down to the Mason-Dixon line, lost membership in the U.S. House. Minnesota, with its strong job and population growth, fought that trend, however.   It retained the same number of eight U.S. Representatives that it possessed in the 1960s.

A FUTURE VERY MUCH LIKE THE PAST, ONLY DIFFERENT

As this chapter is written, the Minnesota Legislature continues much as before. The Legislature has two chambers. One party, the DFL, continues its dominance since the early 1970s. Liberal social policies continue.   New legislation penalizing hate crimes and discrimination against gays and lesbians was enacted in the 1990s, and the death penalty was easily voted down. Major health care legislation was enacted in 1992, and the state is edging toward universal coverage. Tax and spending levels continue to be high. The citizenry seems to value their public services. The economy is booming, and unemployment is low.

But the future might be different, at least in some respects. The Minnesota news media, like media everywhere, are paying less attention to government and more to news about crime, entertainment, and "news you can use" to enhance your personal situation. Major figures such as Governor Carlson have campaigned for a unicameral legislature, although there is probably not enough support to change from the present bicameral structure.

The partisan and ideological posture is most subject to change. Minnesota elected a conservative U.S. Senator, Rod Grams, in 1994, and only some rather flukish events late in the 1990 campaign prevented the election of a conservative Republican Governor that year. The Republicans are within striking distance of a majority in the Minnesota House, and may gain it in a future election. Most, although not all, House Republicans are social and economic conservatives; if they gain control of the House leadership and committee chairmanships and a conservative Republican governor is elected in 1998 or a later election, the future might even be *quite* different from the past.

REFERENCES

Baden, Patricia Lopez. 1997. (July 25). "Wall Street Gives State Top Fiscal Rating." *Minneapolis Star Tribune*: B1+.

Black, Eric. 1982. (June). "Sweetheart, Get Me Re-write. They've Indicted the Donut Dunker." *Washington Monthly*: 23-26.

Citizens for Tax Justice and The Institute on Taxation and Economic Policy. 1996. *Who Pays? A Distributional Analysis of the Tax Systems in All 50 States.* Washington, DC: Citizens for Tax Justice and The Institute on Taxation and Economic Policy.

Coffman, Jack B. 1993. (September 2). "Expert: Long Hurt by Press, Not by Errors." *St. Paul Pioneer Press*: 12B.

Elazar, Daniel J. 1984. *American Federalism: A View from the States.* New York, NY: Harper and Row.

Hanson, Royce. 1989. *Tribune of the People: The Minnesota Legislature and Its Leadership.* Minneapolis, MN: University of Minnesota Press.

Kurtz, Karl T. 1989. *State Legislatures in the 1990s.* Paper prepared for the Public Affairs Council.

Minneapolis Star Tribune. 1978. (February). *Legislative Staffing: 1967-1977.*

Minnesota Commission on the Economic Status of Women. December 1996/January 1997. *Newsletter #217.*

Ostrom, Don. 1980. *Educators in Politics: The Rise of an Occupational Group.* Paper delivered at annual meeting of Minnesota Academy of Science, Mankato.

Pinney, Gregor W. 1991. (November 4). "More Going to Work at State Capitol." *Minneapolis Star Tribune*: 4B.

Rosenthal, Cindy Simon. 1994. "Where's the party?" *State Legislatures.* Pp. 31-37.

St. Paul Pioneer Press. 1997. (January 19). *Snapshot of a Legislature.*

Whereatt, Robert. 1997. (January 5). "Are Your Legislators True Minnesotans?" *Minneapolis Star Tribune:* A1.

Chapter 4

MINNESOTA COURTS: BASIC STRUCTURES, PROCESSES AND POLICIES

Philip Kronebusch
St. John's University

INTRODUCTION

While Minnesota's legislature enacts laws (subject to the governor's veto power) and the governor is charged with carrying out those laws, the decisions of courts determine how those laws are going to be interpreted in specific circumstances. State administrative agencies often interpret statutes in order to carry out their functions, but those agency interpretations can usually be challenged in court. No statute could ever specify how it should be interpreted in every possible case. By interpreting law and using those interpretations to decide specific controversies, courts play a critical role in the policy process. Those who doubt the importance of state courts need only consider a couple of recent cases.

In 1992, Dennis Linehan was nearing the end of a prison term of more than thirty years. In the 1950s and 1960s, Linehan had committed several sexual assaults and had kidnaped and murdered one of his victims. In 1975, he had escaped from prison and had assaulted a twelve-year-old girl before he was recaptured. Because Linehan was diagnosed as suffering from antisocial personality disorder and because Minnesota officials thought that he was likely to commit additional crimes upon his release, they sought to have Linehan committed to a state security hospital under the state's Psychopathic Personality Commitment Act. The Minnesota Supreme Court refused to support the commitment because, under that Act, the state needed to show that Linehan was "utterly unable" to control his sexual impulses. Following that decision, Linehan was paroled to a halfway house. Two weeks after Linehan's parole began, the Minnesota Legislature met in a special session in order to amend the civil commitment statute to include a category called "sexually dangerous persons." That category included persons who suffered from a mental disorder and were likely to engage in harmful sexual conduct. The standard of "utter inability to control" was therefore lowered to "likely to engage." Within days, Ramsey County successfully petitioned to have Linehan committed under the amended act. In 1996, the Minnesota Supreme Court decided that lowering the legal standard for commitment did not violate any of Linehan's rights (*In Re Linehan*, 557 N.W. 2d 167; 1996 Minn.).

The impact of the Minnesota Supreme Court on the policymaking process is also clear in a 1995 case in which the Court held that Minnesota could not deny Medicaid funding for abortions for poor women if Medicaid funds were available to pay childbirth expenses. The decision was based on the right to privacy found in the Minnesota Constitution (inferred from Article I, secs. 2, 7, and 10), and not on the U.S. Constitution. The decision explicitly challenged the decision of the U.S. Supreme Court in *Harris v. McRae* (448 U.S. 297; 1980), which held that the U.S. Constitution did not require Medicaid funding for abortion. According to Chief Justice A.M. (Sandy) Keith, writing for the majority, the Minnesota Supreme Court "has long recognized that we may interpret the Minnesota Constitution to offer greater protection of individual rights than the U.S. Supreme Court has afforded under the federal constitution." Chief Justice Keith based his argument, in part, on Minnesota's "long tradition of affording persons on the periphery of society a greater measure of government protection than may be available elsewhere"

(*Women of the State of Minnesota by Doe v. Gomez* 542 N.W.2d 17, 30; 1995 Minn.).

Each of these was a high profile case that made headlines in the state. In the first, the Minnesota Supreme Court's interpretation of a statute led to a special legislative session and a change in the law. In the second, an interpretation of the Minnesota Constitution protected a right beyond those protected by the U.S. Constitution. This Minnesota decision can only be changed by a later decision of the Court or by a state constitutional amendment. But courts have a significant impact on public policy even when they don't make headlines. Everyday in courthouses throughout Minnesota, judges make decisions on how to interpret words in state statutes, what sorts of evidence are admissible in trial, and whose arguments are more persuasive. Taken together, these decisions affect everything from how fast we drive to who gets custody of the children in a divorce to how well we have to shovel the snow off our sidewalks to avoid a lawsuit. Decisions made by courts affect the daily lives of citizens whether or not they set foot in a courtroom.

COURT ORGANIZATION AND STRUCTURE

Minnesota's court structure went through a period of dramatic change from the early 1970s through the 1980s. Before 1970, Minnesota's courts reflected Minnesota's history as a rural state. In a state where transportation and communication were difficult, county and municipal (city) courts developed a great deal of independence. In the nineteenth century and the beginning of the twentieth, the Legislature created numerous separate municipal courts, each by special legislative act. In 1937, the Municipal Court Act authorized a court for every city and incorporated village with a population over one thousand. The Act also called for each of these courts to have jurisdiction over the entire county where the court was located. This provided greater access to courts in rural areas of the state, but it created the problem of overlapping jurisdictions in those counties that had more than one city larger than one thousand. The jurisdiction of these courts also conflicted with the justice of the peace courts used by smaller villages (Elazar, 1989: 333). While each of these courts decided cases involving statutes passed by the Minnesota Legislature (as well as county and city ordinances), the courts themselves were organized and the judges were paid by the local county boards or cities. Courts were more often perceived as entities of county or city government, rather than as agents of state government. Legally, counties and cities are created by the state, but for much of Minnesota's history, county and city governments have been political forces often at odds with the Legislature and the Governor.

By the 1960s, Minnesota had nearly 700 courts with varying geographic and subject matter jurisdictions (Klaphake, 1993: 205). Many towns made use of justice of the peace courts for minor offenses. Frequently, these justices of the peace did not have law degrees and their salaries depended on the collection of the fines the court assessed. One study of the courts in all fifty states at this time ranked Minnesota's system as the third most complex on a scale of court consolidation and simplification. Only the courts of Delaware and Arkansas were ranked as more complex (Glick, 1973: 123).

Trial Court Reform

The first step in major reform occurred in 1971 with the passage of the County Court Act. This Act created two levels of trial courts in the state: county courts and district courts. Each county had a single county court which consolidated the powers of the previously existing county courts, municipal courts, reconciliation (small claims) courts, and justice of the peace courts. Justice of the peace courts were abolished and the costs and salaries of these county courts were paid by the local counties. Counties were organized into judicial districts of (except in the cases of Hennepin and Ramsey Counties) several counties each (see Figure 1). More serious crimes involving a charge of a gross misdemeanor or felony were heard in district courts, by judges elected on a district-wide basis and paid by the state.

Minnesota's Ten Judicial Districts

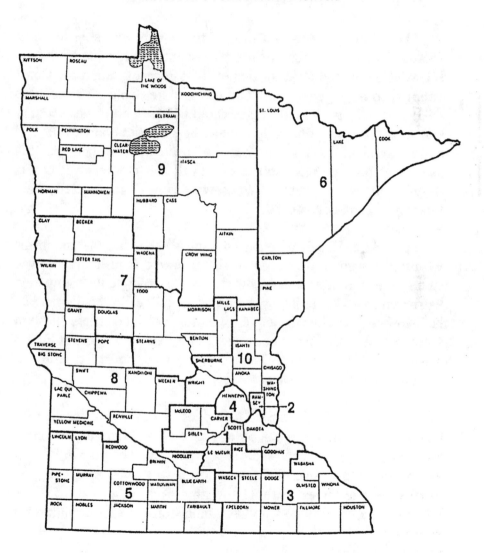

Cases involving petty misdemeanors and misdemeanors were heard at the county court level. Those cases could be appealed to the local district court. Cases heard by the district courts could be appealed to the Minnesota Supreme Court.

The County Court Act proved to be only one step in court reform. In 1977, the Legislature passed the Court Reorganization Act, which gave the Chief Justice of the Minnesota Supreme Court authority to manage the workload of the state's courts (Klaphake, 1993: 206). District court judges could be assigned to hear county court cases; county court judges could hear district court cases; and judges could be assigned to hear cases outside of their election districts. This Act was another step in the development of courts away from local control and toward more centralized state organization and control.

In 1982, the Legislature passed a law which led to the end of the two-tiered system of trial courts. In that year, the Legislature allowed each of the state's ten judicial districts to consolidate its county and district courts voluntarily, by a vote of the judges in the district. In the following five years, the judges of all ten judicial districts chose to consolidate and all county court judges became district court judges (Klaphake, 1993: 207). The resulting trial court structure is essentially what exists today (see Figure 2).

Currently, 252 district court judges from ten judicial districts hear cases involving all areas of law, except workers' compensation law and tax law, for which separate courts exist. The Fourth District (Hennepin County) has the most judges with 54 and the Eighth District has the fewest with 11. Within each judicial district, the judges elect a chief judge who has administrative responsibilities for the district.

While the system of county courts is gone, the system of county courthouses remains an important part of the organization of these courts. Nearly all counties in the state have at least one judge who

Minnesota Court System

SUPREME COURT
7 judges
Appeals from:
Court of Appeals
Tax Court
Workers Compensation Court of Appeals
District court first degree murder convictions
District court cases involving legislative elections
Other duty:
Reviews charges of judicial and attorney misconduct

COURT OF APPEALS
16 judges who hear cases in three-judge panels
Appeals from:
District court
(except first-degree murder convictions and cases involving legislative elections)
Administrative agency decisions
(except Tax Court and Workers Compensation)

DISTRICT COURT
252 judges in ten state judicial districts
Original trial court for:
Civil Actions
Criminal Actions
Family
Juvenile
Probate
Ordinance Violations
Appeals from:
Conciliation Court,
by trial de novo

Conciliation Division
(Civil disputes up to $7,500)

keeps his or her "chambers" or office in that county's courthouse (now sometimes called a "government center"). In the more populouscities of a judicial district, several judges will keep their chambers in that county's courthouse. In the Seventh District, for example, 7 judges have chambers in the Stearns County Courthouse and 15 judges have their chambers in the remaining nine counties. While judges may be located in what are still often called "county courthouses," this does not affect the fact that they are district judges who may be assigned to a trial in any courthouse in the district, as well as outside the district. In the Second and Fourth Districts (Ramsey and Hennepin Counties), all district judges have offices in the county government centers, though judges are also assigned to conduct minor cases in suburban trial centers.

Within each judicial district, there are organizational divisions for different areas of law. These are: criminal, civil, probate (wills and involuntary commitment), juvenile, conciliation (small claims), and family (divorce, child custody and adoption). Except for juvenile courts in the Second and Fourth Districts (Ramsey and Hennepin counties), these divisions exist for administrative and scheduling purposes. A single trial judge in a rural district may hear several different types of cases (e.g., probate, civil, and traffic) in a single day. The chief judge in each district is charged with making assignments in order to process the waiting caseload most effectively. In the Second and Fourth Districts, a set of judges serve exclusively as juvenile court judges for a minimum two-year assignment.

Appellate Courts

Minnesota's appellate court structure also has undergone considerable change in the past twenty years. Through the 1970s, the number of appeals to the Minnesota Supreme Court from county and district trial courts increased dramatically. This caseload pressure had the effect of limiting the ability of the Supreme Court to provide uniformity in the interpretation of state law at the trial court level. One former chief justice wrote: "For many years, the Minnesota

Supreme Court worked under an oppressive caseload . . . [and] was so burdened that appellate review was likely to be insubstantial or virtually nonexistent in many cases" (Amdahl, 1984: 623). In 1973, in order to relieve some of the caseload pressures and reduce delays in issuing decisions, the Legislature increased the size of the Court from seven to nine justices to enable the Court to hear appeals in panels of three justices. For several years, the caseload pressures continued to increase and problems with a backlog of cases continued, so the Legislature proposed a constitutional amendment that authorized the creation of an intermediate court of appeals. That amendment was adopted in the fall of 1982 and the Legislature created the Minnesota Court of Appeals in the legislative session of 1983. At that time, the Legislature also returned the size of the Supreme Court to seven members.

The composition of the Minnesota Court of Appeals is established by statute and currently consists of 16 judges, including one chief judge. All judges are elected to six-year terms on state-wide ballots, though eight positions are reserved for a judge from each of Minnesota's eight congressional districts. The Governor appoints people to fill any vacancies and any judge thus appointed must run for re-election in the next state-wide election that is at least one year after the date the judge takes office. The Governor also appoints the chief judge who has administrative responsibilities for the Court.

In nearly all cases, the losing party at the district court level has a right to appeal to the Court of Appeals, where the case will be considered by a three-judge panel. A "right to appeal" means that the Court of Appeals is required to issue a decision on the appeal, though the Court may choose to issue only a brief summary decision rather than an extensive written opinion in the case. The right to appeal a case beyond the Court of Appeals to the Minnesota Supreme Court is limited. Thus, the Court of Appeals issues the final decision in 95 percent of the cases it hears (National Center for State Courts, 1995: Table 2). The state Supreme Court exercises discretionary review, meaning that the Court chooses cases because of their importance to the development of the law or to correct an error made by a lower court.

The process of an appeal requires each party of the district court case to file briefs which present arguments why, on one side, the decision of the district court was incorrect, and why, on the other side, the decision of the district court was correct. The judges decide whether or not to schedule oral arguments in the case or whether to base their decision entirely on these written briefs. If oral arguments are scheduled, each side is allotted an equal amount of time to present an argument and to respond to questions from the panel of judges. Court of Appeals cases are frequently heard at the Minnesota Judicial Center, located next to the state Capitol building, but panels of judges also conduct hearings in courthouses throughout the state. Appellate judges are likely to defer to the jury or trial judge on questions about the reliability of evidence or the credibility of witnesses, but when an issue presents a question of law (concerning the appropriate interpretation of a statute, for example) the Court of Appeals panel is likely to examine the issue without deferring to the earlier decision of the lower court judge (Klaphake, 1993: 210). Thus, most appeals concern questions of law rather than questions of fact.

After oral arguments, if scheduled, the judges of the panel confer in private and vote. A majority may sustain the district court decision, reverse that decision, or remand the case back to the district court for further proceedings in accordance with the decision. A member of the majority is appointed to author the written opinion of the panel and any dissenting member can write a dissenting opinion. By law, the Court of Appeals must issue a decision within 90 days after consideration of a case (Klaphake, 1993: 210).

The Minnesota Supreme Court

According to the Minnesota Constitution, "the supreme court consists of one chief judge and not less than six nor more than eight associate judges as the legislature may establish." Currently, the

Legislature has established that there are seven members (called "justices" as a matter of convention) including one chief justice. Each justice is elected to a six-year term, and vacancies are filled by the Governor. As with other judges in the state, a judge appointed to a vacancy must run for re-election in the next election at least one year after taking office.

The Minnesota Supreme Court hears appeals from the state Tax Court and Workers' Compensation Court of Appeals; it reviews all first degree murder convictions made by the district courts; and it hears appeals from district court cases involving challenges to legislative elections. It also accepts, for discretionary review, cases from the Court of Appeals where the losing party has filed a petition for further review. In 1990, the Supreme Court heard 297 cases appealed from the Court of Appeals, 79 cases appealed from the Workers' Compensation Court of Appeals, and 7 cases appealed from Tax Court. Under statutory guidelines, the Minnesota Supreme Court accepts cases for discretionary review that meet one or more of the following criteria: 1) the legal question is "an important one which the court has not, but should rule;" 2) "the court of appeals has held a statute to be unconstitutional;" 3) "the court of appeals has decided a question in direct conflict with applicable precedent of the supreme court;" or 4) "the lower courts have so far departed from the accepted and usual course of justice" (Minn. Stat. 480A.10, subd. 1). These criteria allow the Supreme Court substantial control over its own calendar.

The creation of the Court of Appeals has succeeded in reducing the caseload pressures that the Supreme Court experienced in the early 1980s. Filings, which had numbered nearly 1800 before the creation of the Court of Appeals, have fallen to just under 1000. In addition, the average time the Supreme Court takes from initial filing to final disposition of a case has fallen from 420 days in 1984 to 122 days in 1989 (Popovich and Miller, 1990: 120).

Non-judicial Branch Courts

In the Minnesota court system, two courts decide cases within specific subject matters: the state Tax Court and the Workers' Compensation Court of Appeals. These courts, however, are part of the executive branch rather than the judicial branch. They are designed to bring uniformity and accountability to the administrative decisions of the state Department of Revenue and the Workers' Compensation Division of the Department of Labor. The Tax Court consists of three judges appointed by the Governor and confirmed by the Senate. It hears appeals in non-criminal cases involving state or local taxes. The Workers' Compensation Court of Appeals consists of five judges appointed by the Governor. It hears appeals concerning claims for workplace injuries made under the state's workers' compensation law. The decisions of these courts can be appealed to the Minnesota Supreme Court, as a matter of right, meaning that the Supreme Court cannot refuse to hear those appeals.

FEDERAL COURTS IN MINNESOTA

The federal government operates a court system that extends into every state, but which is separate from the state court system. The federal and Minnesota state court systems both have courts named "district courts," a "Court of Appeals," and a "Supreme Court," so people often confuse the two court systems. In the federal court system, Minnesota constitutes the U.S. Judicial District of Minnesota, and this district has seven U.S. district judges who conduct trials in federal courthouses in Minneapolis, St. Paul, and Duluth. Appeals from federal district court in Minnesota are made to the U.S. Court of Appeals for the Eighth Circuit. The Eighth Circuit consists of Minnesota, North Dakota, South Dakota, Iowa, Nebraska, Missouri, and Arkansas. The Eighth Circuit is based in St. Louis, but the Court of Appeals sometimes schedules hearings in one of Minnesota's federal courthouses. After a case is decided by the U.S. Court of Appeals, the losing party may seek review by the U.S.

Supreme Court. All federal judges are appointed by the President, with the consent of the U.S. Senate, and hold life tenure.

Whether a case is heard in the state or federal court system is generally a matter of whether the case involves federal or state law. Counterfeiting, for example, as a violation of federal law, is always prosecuted in federal court. Assault, except assault of a federal agent, is prosecuted in state courts. Some areas of law provide for overlapping jurisdiction. The possession of illegal drugs, even fairly small amounts, can be prosecuted under either federal or state law. The federal prosecutor in Minnesota, called the "U.S. Attorney," makes the decision whether to prosecute a case under federal law. Another category of overlapping jurisdiction is civil lawsuits that involve citizens (or businesses) from different states and that have more than $75,000 in dispute. These lawsuits may be heard in state court, but plaintiffs can chose to have them heard in federal court under the court's "diversity" jurisdiction.

A case that begins in one court system almost always ends in that court system. Only if a case raises a federal question (for example, a defendant's rights under the U.S. Constitution) can the losing party at the level of the state supreme court attempt to have the case heard by the U.S. Supreme Court. Fewer than one case per year from the Minnesota state court system is heard by the U.S. Supreme Court.

STRUCTURAL REFORM: PAST, PRESENT, AND FUTURE

In stark contrast to the system of the early 1970s, Minnesota now has what court reformers call a unified court system because it has a simple hierarchial structure. Nearly all cases begin in the district courts and the entire system is overseen by the Minnesota Supreme Court. There is little doubt that Minnesota's court system has increased in clarity of organization, efficiency in the disposition of appeals, and statewide uniformity in the application of laws in the past decades. But no important political change comes without some costs. In the case of court reform, one cost has been a decrease in the power of city and county governments to tailor courts to the specific interests of their localities. There is less room for variation in a system that makes use of multi-judge districts and an effective system of appeal. While some citizens, attorneys, and local officials worried, as Minnesota courts changed, that courts and judges would become less accessible (Klaphake, 1993: 207), there is little or no evidence that has occurred. What is most remarkable is the speed with which change took place, once reform began. With three major legislative acts (one requiring a prior constitutional amendment) over the course of two decades, Minnesota's court structure changed dramatically. While Minnesota's court system was one of the most complex and least consolidated in the early 1970s, as noted earlier, a 1993 U.S. Department of Justice report on state court organization listed Minnesota as tied with five other states for having the most consolidated trial court system (Rottman, 1995: 6).

TRIAL PROCESS

Minnesota's district courts, as the state's trial courts of general jurisdiction, handle approximately two million cases per year. The state Court of Appeals hears about 2,500 cases in a year, so the trial courts provide for the final resolution of more than 99 percent of legal cases in a year (National Center for State Courts, 1995: Tables 2 and 8).

In Minnesota, as well as in other states, there are two general categories of law. Criminal law concerns actions, described in state statutes, that threaten the welfare of society. Civil law concerns legal disputes between individuals, businesses or other legal entities. A typical case in criminal law is prosecuted by a county attorney, while a typical case in civil law is a lawsuit between two individuals or businesses. There is some overlap between these two categories. The killing of a person may be the subject of a criminal prosecution in one trial, and the subject of a civil wrongful death lawsuit in another trial. A criminal prosection may lead to penalties involving fines and imprisonment, while a civil case generally involves the awarding of monetary damages to whomever wins the lawsuit or the issuance of a court order requiring the losing party to do something, like return a piece of property.

Criminal Cases

Within its criminal code, Minnesota distinguishes among four levels of crime. The first of these is felony, which is defined as a crime that is punishable by more than a year in prison. The second level is gross misdemeanor, which is a crime punishable by up to one year (usually in a local jail rather than a state prison) or a fine of up to $3000, or both. The third level consists of misdemeanors, which are punishable by up to 90 days in jail or up to $700 fine, or both. The fourth and lowest level is petty misdemeanor, a violation of which, according to statute, is not defined as a "crime." The violation of a petty misdemeanor (in many cases, these are city and county ordinances) may be punished by a fine of up to $200, but not by time in jail.

Within a category of crime, like "assault," for example, different elements of the crime allow the prosecutor to charge the crime at a number of different degrees. Assault is prosecuted as a felony if the action involved "great bodily injury," for first degree assault; involved the use of a dangerous weapon, for second degree; involved "substantial bodily harm" for third degree; or involved "demonstrable bodily harm" of a peace officer, for fourth degree. The maximum penalties for the different degrees of assault range from up to twenty years for first degree assault to two years for fourth degree. Fifth degree assault includes the infliction of bodily harm, the attempt to inflict bodily harm, and an act intended to cause someone to fear immediate bodily harm and it is generally punishable as a misdemeanor (Minn. Stat. 609.221).

The initial decision to charge someone with the violation of a crime is generally made by the county attorney. A city attorney, appointed by the mayor or city council, may also charge someone with misdemeanor and gross misdemeanor violations committed within the city. Only rarely is the state attorney general involved in a criminal prosecution. Each county in the state elects a county attorney, who serves for four year terms. Each county attorney operates with a staff of assistant county attorneys, who are county civil service employees. The county attorney is not only the county's chief prosecutor, he or she also provides legal advice to the county board in its decisions on land use planning, the drafting of ordinances, and legal disputes involving the county. As a result, county attorneys generally supervise the work of their assistant county attorneys and they limit their personal involvement in cases to those involving more serious crimes. Many county attorneys in rural counties serve part-time and have a private law practice as well, often creating the potential for conflicts of interest.

In nearly all cases, a criminal case begins when the prosecuting attorney files a complaint or indictment with the district court. Those documents must demonstrate to the judge that there is probable cause that the accused person has committed the stated crime. If that standard is met, the judge issues a warrant or summons if the accused is not already under arrest. The only exception to this process is that indictments for first degree murder can only be issued by a grand jury. As a matter of practice, when someone is arrested for murder, he or she is initially charged with second degree murder (which the county attorney can do by filing a complaint) in order to hold the accused in custody while the grand jury is meeting. During that time, the prosecuting attorney presents testimony and other evidence in a closed meeting of a grand jury of 16-23 members. The grand jury issues an indictment by a vote of at least 16 members. The defense does not, at this stage, have an opportunity to rebut the prosecution's case. Infrequently, grand juries are also used in Minnesota to investigate charges of the corruption of government officials, but their use is often seen as clumsy and inefficient, so the trend in court reform is to make less use of grand juries.

Following indictment, criminal cases in Minnesota proceed in a manner that is typical among state courts. While the details of every state court system are different, the general pattern is for a case to proceed from indictment, to arraignment and the setting of bail, to pre-trial procedures, and finally to trial. While the details of this process are critically important to practitioners within the system, scholars who study courts frequently emphasize that cases are much more likely to be resolved through the informal practice of plea bargaining than through formal trial procedures.

Plea Bargaining

As is typical among the states, more than 95 percent of criminal prosecutions in Minnesota are resolved with a plea of guilty.   A Minnesota State Court Administration study of 1995 felony cases (the type of case most likely to go to trial) showed that 4 percent went to trial (Minnesota Supreme Court, 1996: 26). This does not mean that all of the remaining cases were plea bargained, because a defendant can plead guilty without receiving any reduction in the charges, but there is no doubt that plea bargaining is a regular feature of criminal prosecutions in Minnesota courts.

Under plea bargaining a defendant agrees to plead guilty in exchange for a reduction in charges against him or for a reduced recommended sentence. While a defendant might have been initially charged with 1st degree assault because, in the view of the prosecutor, "great bodily harm" was inflicted, the charge might be reduced to 3rd degree assault ("substantial bodily harm") in exchange for a plea of guilty. Before a case is scheduled to come to trial, the prosecutor (usually the assistant county attorney) and the defense attorney will usually discuss under what terms the case might be resolved without going to trial. The defense attorney communicates any offer the prosecutor makes to the defendant. If the defendant agrees, he or she must still appear in court to plead guilty. Technically, the judge must approve the reduction in charges, but it is rare for a judge to interfere with a plea bargain.

The factors contributing to a high rate of plea bargaining are complex. Court scholars have frequently noted that all courtroom actors may derive some benefit from the process. Prosecutors obtain convictions which help them maintain a high conviction rate. Plea bargaining also saves the time it would take to prepare for a trial and the challenge of proving the more serious charge. Judges are spared the time a trial would take as well as the difficulty of ruling on various motions regarding the admissibility of evidence and other matters. Defense attorneys (often public defenders) are also able to handle their caseloads more easily if a substantial number of defendants plead guilty. Defendants probably receive lower sentences by pleading guilty, but this is a subject of some debate. Some studies show that prosecutors may "overcharge" at the indictment stage in anticipation of a later plea bargain. Thus, a plea bargain may often be close to the maximum charge the defendant's actions warrant. While some people criticize plea bargaining for being "soft" on defendants, others criticize plea bargaining because a defendant's plea of guilty relieves the state of having to prove its case in court.

Juries

If the defendant pleads "not guilty" and the judge does not dismiss the charges in a pre-trial procedure, the case goes to trial. In all criminal and most civil cases heard in district court, defendants have a right to trial by jury, though a defendant may waive that right and be tried before the judge (called a "bench trial"). In a jury trial, the members of the jury determine the facts of the case and the judge explains the law to the jury. In a bench trial, the judge determines both facts and law in issuing a decision. In both jury and bench trials, the legal standard for conviction in a criminal trial is guilty "beyond a reasonable doubt."

There is state-by-state variation on the size of juries as well as the requirements of unanimity. In Minnesota, juries for felony trials must be twelve persons and the verdict must be unanimous. For non-felony criminal trials, six-person juries are used, but the verdict must still be unanimous. In a civil trial, a six-person jury is used and five of the members must agree on a verdict. In a civil trial, a jury decides based on a "preponderance of the evidence."

Civil Cases

In Minnesota, civil cases follow a process that is typical among state courts. Though the term "civil law" includes areas of law such as probate (dealing with wills and estates) and family law (dealing with divorces and child custody), what most people think of as a civil case is a lawsuit between individuals or businesses. These lawsuits generally may be classified as either a contract dispute or a tort. A contract dispute involves allegations that one party has not fulfilled the terms of a contract. A tort is a lawsuit that involves the allegation of an injury, usually to a person or property caused by the negligent act of the defendant. Within the category of torts, a broad exception are injuries at the workplace. These are covered under workers' compensation rules and are processed through the Workers' Compensation Division of the Department of Labor and Industry, subject to review by the Minnesota Supreme Court.

Civil lawsuits begin when one party (the plaintiff) has a complaint served on the defendant. The defendant then serves an answer on the plaintiff. Before the trial takes place, motions to dismiss the case may be heard by the judge as well as motions for discovery. In the discovery phase of the pretrial process, each side is given access to evidence and witnesses for the other side. A defendant's attorney in a tort lawsuit, for example, may seek a deposition from the person who is alleging the injury as well as access to medical records from the doctors who have treated that person. The purpose of discovery is to allow each side the opportunity to be fully informed about the testimony and other evidence that will be presented at the trial. If both sides are fully informed, it is less likely that the outcome of the trial will depend on last minute legal maneuvers.

At the conclusion of the discovery phase, when the evidence has been examined, the plaintiff (in consultation with his or her attorney) may conclude that the case is too weak to pursue to trial, or the defendant may conclude that the case is so strong that it would be prudent to settle the case before the trial begins. Just as more than 95 percent of criminal cases are resolved by either a plea of guilty or a dismissal of charges, close to 95 percent of civil suits are resolved by the parties themselves before trial, either by the plaintiff dropping the lawsuit or by the two parties reaching a settlement. In District 4 (Hennepin County), only 31 out of 613 civil cases that reached final disposition in the month of September, 1997 were concluded by a trial (Hennepin County, 1997: 1). Given that settlements are going to occur, the efficient functioning of state district courts requires that cases be settled as long before the scheduled trial date as possible. If a case is settled "on the courthouse steps" on the day that trial is scheduled to begin, the court administrator will already have scheduled a judge and courtroom for a trial that won't take place. Thus, Minnesota and several other states have adopted policies that authorize judges to require parties to a civil case to attempt to resolve their dispute before trial through a process of alternative dispute resolution.

Alternative Dispute Resolution (ADR)

In 1991, the state Legislature required the state Supreme Court to establish an alternative dispute resolution program to be used for civil cases filed in district courts and to adopt rules and procedures governing alternative dispute resolution (Minn. Stat. 484.76). These procedures were promulgated by the Supreme Court in 1994 as Rule 114 of the General Rules of Practice for District Courts.

Under Rule 114, parties to a civil case must meet within 45 days of the filing of the case to discuss the selection of an ADR process. Within 60 days, the results of this meeting are communicated to the judge. If either party believes that the case is an inappropriate one for the use of an ADR process, that is also communicated to the judge. Ordinarily, the judge will approve the ADR process that the parties have selected, but if the judge does not approve the ADR process selected or if the parties cannot agree on a process, the judge can order the parties to use one of several non-binding processes. The judge can also determine that the case is inappropriate for ADR and allow the case to proceed to trial.

There are numerous ADR processes and Rule 114 encourages flexibility and innovation, but the most widely used types of processes are mediation and arbitration. Both of these processes make use of a "neutral" who is someone trained in ADR and on whom both parties have agreed. A neutral can be a retired judge, an attorney, or a non-attorney who might have specialized knowledge about a subject matter (the practices of the construction industry, for example). Minnesota has established minimum training requirements that must be met in order to serve as a qualified ADR neutral.

In a typical mediation process involving a civil case, the two parties to the lawsuit and their attorneys meet with a neutral mediator who has no decision making authority. The neutral listens to each party, asks them what they are seeking, and helps the parties find common ground. In some variations of mediation, the parties and their attorneys sit in separate conference rooms and the neutral moves between the separate rooms, listening to each party and providing his or her analysis of the strengths and weaknesses of each side's case. The neutral's actions are focused on improving communication between the parties, reducing the level of conflict, and fostering a negotiated agreement that is acceptable to both sides, rather than on ferreting out the truth of what happened. If both sides agree on a resolution to the case and they sign a legal agreement to that effect, the lawsuit is ended. If no voluntary resolution is reached, the case then proceeds to trial.

Under arbitration, the neutral becomes a decision maker. Each side presents its case to the neutral, relying on physical evidence, written depositions, and witnesses who appear in person. The neutral then issues his or her decision based on the law of the state and the evidence. Under non-binding arbitration, the two parties can then accept the decision and end the case, or continue to a formal trial in court. Under binding arbitration, the two parties agree in advance to abide by the decision of the neutral arbitrator and to waive their right to demand a formal trial. A judge cannot order parties to enter into binding arbitration unless the parties have already agreed to it, for example, by the terms of a written contract.

There are several other types of ADR and there are numerous possible variations on mediation and arbitration. There is so much flexibility in ADR processes because the parties themselves can adapt the process they choose to their own circumstances. A common element is that ADR processes (with the exception of binding arbitration) yield voluntary settlements. If either side rejects the settlement proposed by the process and the plaintiff does not drop the suit, the case proceeds to trial. A second common element is that these processes are private. The proceedings are not public and the neutrals are paid by the parties themselves, not by taxpayers.

Because Rule 114 was adopted only a few years ago, systematic evaluation of the effects of the movement to increase the use of ADR is only now taking place. The goals of ADR include earlier settlements, lower legal fees, and greater satisfaction of the parties to the case. Several studies have shown that ADR processes, because they are oriented more to voluntary settlement rather than the adversarial conflict of a trial, lead to greater satisfaction of the parties to the case, but whether ADR saves money for the parties to a case is an open question that requires continued research (McAdoo and Welsh, 1997: 376-7).

Conciliation Court

In all counties, the district courts have created what are formally called "conciliation courts," which are more popularly referred to as "small claims courts." If a civil suit involves a claim of less than $7500, the plaintiff can bring the case initially to conciliation court.

Conciliation court provides a less formal environment for the settlement of cases than the regular court structure. Typically, the plaintiff and defendant represent themselves rather than use attorneys, and the judge allows each party time to present their arguments, followed by an opportunity to refute the argument on the other side and questions from the judge. Evidence is also presented and witnesses can be called. After the presentation of the case, the judge usually issues a written decision within ten days. There is no jury in conciliation court. If the losing party to the conciliation court case chooses to, he or she may appeal to the regular district court, where the case will be heard *de novo*, meaning that the entire case is heard again as a new trial.

JUDICIAL SELECTION

Researchers on state courts usually classify judicial selection procedures according to five basic models. They are (1) appointment by legislature, (2) appointment by governor, (3) election with political party endorsement, (4) election without party endorsement, (5) appointment by non-partisan panel, then retention elections (often called the "Missouri plan"). Minnesota's system is usually classified as one based on election without party endorsement. As a matter of political practice, however, Minnesota's system currently combines elements of #2, #4, and #5.

All state court judges serve for a specified number of years and must be re-elected to continue to serve. District court judges are elected by voters within their districts and Supreme Court justices and

Court of Appeals judges are elected on a state-wide basis. Incumbent judges who seek re-election and their challengers file for election in the same way as candidates for other state offices, except that candidates for judicial office are forbidden from listing or seeking any political party endorsement. Candidates for judicial office must also restrict their campaigns to discussions of their qualifications for the position and general topics like the need for crime control. Candidates are prohibited from directly criticizing an opponent and from commenting on how they would rule on a specific case.

More than 90 percent of incumbent judges who seek re-election are re-elected. Some judges, though, have recently argued that the campaigning rules are overly restrictive. In 1996, two Supreme Court justices, Edward Stringer and Paul Anderson, survived challenges by opponents who were endorsed by Minnesota Citizens Concerned for Life (MCCL), a major anti-abortion organization. Justices Stringer and Anderson had voted with the majority in a case that is summarized in the introduction of this chapter. The decision in that case held that the State of Minnesota could not eliminate abortion coverage for Medicaid patients, under the individual privacy guarantees of the state Constitution. While the challengers did not seek any political party endorsement, there is nothing in Minnesota law that prohibited the MCCL, in its own campaign literature, from endorsing judicial candidates. Despite what the MCCL was doing, Justices Stringer and Anderson could not directly challenge the organization's arguments without violating the prohibition on discussing specific cases.

Those interested in judicial reform face a dilemma. On one hand, it may not be constitutionally permissible to restrict the free speech rights of a political organization like the MCCL. On the other hand, if judges are allowed to discuss specific cases, judicial elections are likely to become more politicized. Such campaigns are also likely to require judicial candidates to engage in more fundraising. This, in turn, will raise questions of conflicts of interest because many wealthy contributors, in their business dealings, are likely to have cases pending before state courts.

While elections play an important role in the Minnesota judiciary, most judges first achieve their office through appointment by the Governor. In Minnesota, more than 95 percent of sitting judges first achieved their office through gubernatorial appointment to a judgeship that became vacant because of the resignation or death of a judge (*Minneapolis Star-Tribune*, 11/20/97, A17). The remaining judges first achieved their position through election against an incumbent or, more frequently, for an open seat that had no incumbent. On the current Minnesota Supreme Court, only Justice Alan Page was not originally appointed to the Court by a governor, and even Justice Page's initial election to the Court in 1992 occurred only after a failed attempt to prevent an election for the seat from taking place. In 1992, Page's predecessor on the Court, Justice Lawrence Yetka was coming to the end of a term in office and Alan Page, a former Minnesota Vikings football star who is now a lawyer, planned to file for the seat. Governor Arne Carlson then acted to extend Yetka's term for two years, at Yetka's request, so that the justice could retire at age 70 and receive full retirement benefits. Page sued and, because the case involved a current member of the Supreme Court, all seven members of the Minnesota Supreme Court removed themselves from the case. In their place, a special ad hoc Minnesota Supreme Court consisting of seven retired judges heard the case and ruled in favor of Page, requiring an election for the seat to take place. In the meantime, the deadline for filing for the seat had passed and only Page and two other attorneys had filed. Yetka did not file because he believed that his term had been extended (*Minneapolis Star-Tribune*, 6/23/92, 7D). When the election took place, Page won handily.

Different procedures are used for filling vacancies at the district court and appellate levels. For district court vacancies, the Commission on Judicial Selection, recommends to the governor a list of 3-5 candidates from which the Governor chooses the person to fill the vacancy. The Commission consists of nine members (seven chosen by the governor, two by the state Supreme Court) plus four members from each judicial district (two chosen by the governor and two chosen by the Supreme Court). When the Commission meets for a specific vacancy, the nine state-wide members are joined by the four members from the district where the vacancy exists. When these 13 members meet, then, nine are gubernatorial appointees and four have been appointed by the Supreme Court. While the Commission is sometimes called a nonpartisan commission, slightly more than two-thirds of the members who meet to fill a vacancy are gubernatorial appointees. According to statute, the Commission evaluates candidates on the basis of their "integrity, maturity, health if job related, judicial temperament, diligence, legal knowledge, ability and experience, and community service" (Minn. Stat. 480B.01, subd. 8). In the end, the appointment is the Governor's decision.

When a vacancy occurs in the state Supreme Court or the Court of Appeals, the Governor makes the appointment and is not required to consult any commission. Governor Carlson used ad hoc committees to advise him on appointments in a way that is similar to the way the Commission on Judicial Appointments operates. The use of this process, however, was Governor Carlson's choice. According to statute, he could have filled vacancies in those courts without the use of any advisory body.

Women and Minorities in the Judiciary

The statute creating the Commission on Judicial Selection for district court judges requires the Commission to "actively seek out and encourage qualified individuals, including women and minorities, to apply for judicial office" and to solicit recommendations "from organizations that represent minority or women attorneys." A 1994 publication of the American Bar Association's Task Force on Opportunities for Minorities in the Judiciary notes that Minnesota had 14 African-American judges, 3 Hispanic judges and none who were either Native American or Asian-American (American Bar Association, 1994: 3). These 17 judges comprise 6 percent of Minnesota's 275 judges at all three levels of courts. This compares to

7.4 percent of Minnesota's population who are members of racial and ethnic minorities (Minnesota Planning, 1997).

A 1993 Supreme Court Task Force on Racial Bias in the Judicial System reported that racial bias permeates the state's legal system. The study found, among other things, that minority defendants in Hennepin county were less likely than white defendants to have charges against them dismissed.   Included in the study's recommendations is cultural diversity training for all employees in the judicial system, the hiring of more members of racial and ethnic minorities within the judicial system,   increasing minority representation on juries, and better data collection practices (*Minneapolis Star-Tribune*, 6/11/93, 1A).

The Minnesota Supreme Court received national press coverage in 1991, when it became the first state supreme court in the country to have a membership that was a majority women.   In 1994, when Edward Stringer was appointed to replace retiring Justice Rosalie Wahl, the Court returned to a majority of men, with four men and three women. Justice Wahl had been the first woman appointed to the Minnesota Supreme Court in 1977.   In 1997, when Governor Carlson promoted Associate Justice Kathleen Blatz to the position of chief justice, she became the first woman to serve as chief justice of the Minnesota Supreme Court, and the tenth woman in the country to serve as a state supreme court chief justice (*Minneapolis Star-Tribune*, 10/9/97, A18).

Minnesota's record for women serving on the state's highest court is not repeated in appointments to the state's lower courts. A 1990 study by The Feminist Majority showed that Minnesota ranked 21st out of the fifty states and the District of Columbia in the percentage of women on state courts. Approximately 14 percent of Minnesota judges are women, although women make up 51 percent of the state's population and, according to the Minnesota Bar Association, about 24 percent of the state's attorneys.

Whether women judges decide cases differently from men judges and whether the decisions of the Minnesota Supreme Court were distinctive during the years it had a majority of women are current subjects of research.   When Minnesota Associate Justice Jeanne Coyne was asked whether women judges decide cases differently by virtue of being women, she replied that, in her experience, "a wise old man and a wise old woman reach the same conclusion" (Ginsburg, 1994: 5).   Or it may be, as U.S. Court of Appeals Judge Alvin Rubin said, in a case involving the service of women on juries, that women bring "a distinctive medley of views influenced by differences in biology, cultural impact, and life experience" (*Healy v. Edwards*, 363 F. Supp. 1110, 1115; 1973).   Commenting on the years that the Minnesota Supreme Court was a majority women, U.S. Court of Appeals Judge Deanell Reece Tacha wrote: "I doubt that the outcomes were affected at all by the gender of the members of the court . . . I suspect that business went on as usual, but that the landscape for young women looked a bit different; opportunities seemed more real, and perhaps justice seemed a bit more equally shared between men and women" (Tacha, 1995: 690).

Politics in the Selection Process

While several features of the judicial selection process push overt partisanship to the margins, judgeships in Minnesota generally go to lawyers who have been active in the political party of the governor.   Several judges have been state legislators.   The Supreme Court's Kathleen Blatz, initially appointed as an associate justice in 1996 by Republican Governor Carlson and promoted to chief justice by Carlson a year later, was a Republican legislator from 1979-94.   Court of Appeals judge Fred Norton, appointed by Democrat Rudy Perpich, had been a longtime Democratic legislator and, for two short periods, speaker of the Minnesota House of Representatives.

Politics can also influence a judge's decision on when to leave his or her position.   The resignation of a judge gives the Governor an opportunity to fill the vacancy.   If, on the other hand, a judge allows his or her term of office to end without filing for re-election, the office will be filled by an election for the "open" seat. Because there isn't a vacancy at the end of the judge's term under the latter scenario, the position is filled by the voters rather than by the Governor.

The system of judicial selection in Minnesota cannot be understood as one that relies only on nonpartisan judicial elections. In practice, the Governor is a powerful actor in the selection process, and the use of the Commission on Judicial Selection also incorporates principles that many states have adopted as part of a nonpartisan merit selection system. Minnesota's complex system of judicial selection reflects the dual demands that judges should be independent from partisan politics, but also responsive and accountable to the public. Minnesota takes a middle position between these demands. Minnesota's system allows for more partisanship than the systems of merit-based selection and retention elections (where voters do not chose between candidates for the judgeship, but only whether or not to retain the sitting judge) that several states use. But Minnesota's system is less partisan than those systems that vest the appointment power exclusively in either the Governor or the state Legislature.

CONCLUSION

Among Minnesota's three branches of government, Minnesota's courts have gone through the most dramatic change over the past three decades. In 1970, Minnesota had a confusing array of justice of the peace courts, as well as city and county courts. The state Legislature, by statute and constitutional amendment, simplified the court structure and brought it clearly under the administrative control of the state Supreme Court.

The current system is operating effectively. A 1996 study by the Minnesota Supreme Court shows that Minnesota district courts have case clearance rates of close to 100 percent, which means there is little developing backlog of cases in the system (Minnesota Supreme

Court, 1996: 13). In 1995, the Minnesota Conference of Chief Judges adopted timing objectives for the trial courts. The purpose was to establish a timetable for how much time it should take for a case to move from initial filing to final disposition. Minnesota trial courts are currently meeting those timing objectives 96 percent of the time (Minnesota Supreme Court, 1996: 15).

Minnesota courts have achieved these successes at a time that the number of cases filed has increased significantly. Since 1986, the number of cases handled by the trial courts has increased 44 percent, while the number of judges has only increased 12 percent (Minnesota Supreme Court, 1996: 11).

While the court system is operating efficiently, it will face pressure from several sources in the future. The costs for the Minnesota prison system are increasing dramatically, and a political climate in which politicians eagerly support increased penalties for crime will continue to put pressure on that system. Increased funding for the operation of the court system is unlikely. Any increase in cases may be accommodated by even greater increases in efficiency, but some means of improving efficiency may be controversial. District judges in rural parts of the state would not need to spend time traveling to individual courthouses if all hearings and trials were held in a few "trial centers" in each judicial district, but some citizens (including prosecutors and attorneys) may find that such a system would weaken a judge's ties to local communities. District judges could also save time if they were permitted to conduct simple hearings (like the setting of bail) through audio/video links between local jails and courthouses. This proposal might save money, but it would certainly encounter legal challenges.

Efficiency is only one of the values of a legal system. Some gains in efficiency may be offset by reduced accountability of judges, as connections between individual judges and local communities weaken. Due process is another value that may be compromised when further gains in efficiency are made. The disposition of a rapidly growing caseload by a number of judges that is increasing only slightly almost certainly means that judges are able to spend less time on each individual case. The likely result is that the court system will become more dependent on plea bargaining and the decisions of prosecutors. Currently, there is little public demand for more judges to make sure that the legal rights of defendants are being protected.

Political pressures are also building on the state judiciary. The 1996 election of two Minnesota Supreme Court justices saw a campaign where an interest group actively campaigned for the opponents of the incumbents. Because of current campaign rules, these incumbent justices could not directly challenge those interest groups. Although the incumbents won re-election, judges are increasingly calling for rules that allow them more freedom to campaign, or else a system of retention elections where a judge would not have a challenger and voters would simply choose whether or not to retain the judge in office.

A final challenge facing Minnesota courts is the accessibility by the poor to the legal system. Poor defendants charged with a crime have a right to a court appointed public defender, but the state funding for public defense has not kept pace with the increased caseload. In civil matters, the poor often have little access to attorneys. Legal service providers offer help to those meeting strict income criteria, but even with their help, a poor person seeking a divorce will likely spend a year on a waiting list.

Minnesota's court system has improved dramatically in clarity and efficiency over the past few decades. The system's greatest challenge may be to provide citizens seeking justice with improved access to its benefits.

REFERENCES

Amdahl, Douglas. 1984. "Appeals to the New Minnesota Court — Foreword." *William Mitchell Law Review*. Volume 10: 623.

American Bar Association. 1994. *Directory of Minority Judges in the United States*. Chicago, IL: Author.

Elazar, Daniel J. 1989. "A Model of Moralism in Government." In Clifford E. Clark, Jr., ed. *Minnesota in a Century of Change*, ed. St. Paul, MN: Minnesota Historical Society Press. Pp. 329-359.

Ginsburg, Ruth Bader. 1994. "United States Supreme Court Justice Ruth Bader Ginsburg Address: Remarks for California Women Lawyers." *Pepperdine Law Review*. Volume 22:1.

Hennepin County, Hennepin County District Court. 1997. *Civil Automated Tracking System: Final Civil Dispositions by Case Type for September, 1997*. Minneapolis, MN: Author.

Glick, Henry Robert and Kenneth N. Vines. 1973. *State Court Systems*. Englewood Cliffs, NJ: Prentice Hall, Inc.

Klaphake, Roger M. 1993. "The Minnesota Court System." In Carolyn M. Shrewsbury and Homer E. Williamson, eds. *Perspectives on Minnesota Government and Politics*. 3rd Edition. Edina, MN: Burgess Publishing Company. Pp. 205-221.

McAdoo, Barbara and Nancy Welsh. 1997. "Does ADR Really Have a Place on the Lawyer's Philosophical Map?" *Hamline Journal of Public Law and Policy*. Volume 18: 375-392.

Minnesota Planning. 1997. *Racial Populations by Age*. (October 29). http://www.mnplan.state.mn.us/demography/demog_3a.html.

Minnesota Supreme Court. 1996. *Statistical Highlights—1995; Minnesota State Courts*. St. Paul, MN.

National Center for State Courts. 1995. *State Court Caseload Statistics, 1994*. Williamsburg, VA: Author.

Popovich, Peter S. and Erin Leigh Miller. 1990. "Obtaining Review in the Minnesota Supreme Court." *Hamline Law Review*. Volume 14: 117-149.

Tacha, Deanell Reece. 1995. "'W' Stories: Women in Leadership Positions in the Judiciary." *West Virginia Law Review*. Volume 97: 683-701.

Rottman, David B., et al. 1995. *State Court Organization, 1993*. U.S. Department of Justice, Bureau of Justice Statistics. Washington, DC: U.S. Government Printing Office.

Chapter 5

PUBLIC BUREAUCRACIES: DOING THE STATE'S WORK

Kay G. Wolsborn
College of Saint Benedict

INTRODUCTION

Each of the state's three constitutional branches is staffed by elected or appointed officials and by administrative staff who perform the duties and responsibilities assigned to that branch. These public servants are held responsible for the day-to-day work that Minnesota citizens have asked of their government in the Constitution, in legislative statute, and in the administrative regulations of the State of Minnesota. The popular conception of the state's bureaucracy may be as broad as to include all persons paid by the state to do state work, elected or not. However, this chapter directs the reader's attention in particular to the roles and significance of nonelected staff.

From the Accountancy Board to the Zoological Garden, public servants together with citizen advisors are charged with implementing and coordinating the policies of the State of Minnesota, making rules, and adjudicating conflicts about those policies and rules. Nonelected government officials are often criticized, rarely understood, and even more rarely praised. The challenge of an overall review of Minnesota's public bureaucracies is to describe how the state's bureaucracies are organized, who does the state's work in those organization structures, what are those public servants asked to do, and who is accountable for the results? The chapter responds to these questions respectively in sections below, beginning with the section on organizational variation. The chapter concludes with a call for citizens to take seriously their responsibility to hold state government accountable and to recognize the contributions public servants make to the lives of Minnesotans.

ORGANIZATIONAL VARIATION

Max Weber is given credit for providing the first and best description of what bureaucracies are for and how they are organized for the efficient achievement of their goals. To accomplish the objectives set for them by leadership, units are organized according to Weber's classic principles of structural hierarchy, chain of command and span of control, with authority flowing down from superiors to subordinates to maximize accountability and to define responsibilities. Some one hundred years after Weber's articulation of these and other principles of authority, most large organizations, whether public or private, are likely to conform to some extent to the characteristics of traditional bureaucratic structures. The administrative units of the State of Minnesota do not challenge that conventional wisdom. Once you get past the complexity of three branches of government, and multiple constitutional officers, the principle organizational units of state government are similar to other public and private bureaucratic structures, with an important exception. The vehicles for citizen input, participation, and accountability are extensive, including a dazzling array of boards, councils, commissions, committees, and task forces.

Three Branches

Each branch of state government is dependent upon staff, but the numbers of employees and organizational structures vary greatly among the legislative, executive, and judicial branches. As is the norm throughout U.S. state governments, powers are separated among the three branches. At the same time, checks and balances make the branches interdependent and accountable to each other in policy development and implementation. The Weberian ideal of a single unified hierarchy does not apply at the level of branches of government.

According to 1996 information from the Minnesota Department of Employee Relations, the fewest number of state employees are officially assigned within the legislative branch. Among the many professional services provided by a relatively small staff are the revision and publication of bills and statutes, maintenance of the Legislative Reference Library, public information and media services. Approximately 1,600 employees are employed in direct support of the judicial branch. Professional staff administer trial and appellate courts throughout the state, the Supreme Court in St. Paul, the State Law Library, the State Public Defender's Office, and the Workers' Compensation Court of Appeals. In addition, the work and records of several law related state boards are supported by judicial branch staff. Most of the nearly 51,000 state employees, however, work in the departments and agencies of the state's executive branch. Consequently, the remainder of the chapter focuses specifically on the structures and characteristics of administrative units in the executive branch.

Multiple Constitutional Executive

Unlike U.S. national government bureaucracies, Minnesota's administrative structures are not unified in a single hierarchy, even within the executive branch, with one only executive answerable to the electorate. In addition to the Governor and Lt. Governor, four other constitutional officers are separately elected statewide to direct the operations of their respective constitutionally defined sections of the executive branch. As indicated by their numbers, size, and variety, the departments and other units under the Governor's leadership are responsible for the largest proportion of the state's work. Before proceeding to the structures subject to gubernatorial leadership, however, a brief review of the administrative units under the authority of the other four constitutional officers is in order.

The Office of the Attorney General is the largest employer of the constitutional officers outside the Governor's authority with approximately 500 employees.   Six major divisions roughly correspond to the jurisdictional scope of departments and agencies under gubernatorial direction in order to facilitate the attorney general's responsibility to advise and represent state government units on legal matters.   In contrast to the Attorney General's focus on government at the capital, the seven divisions of the Office of the State Auditor direct their attention throughout the state to assure fiscal accountability within some 4,300 units of local government.

Nine divisions of the Office of the Secretary of State are responsible for a wide range of missions. Authentication of official state documents, registration of business incorporations, and public access to Uniform Commercial Code records are a few of the services provided by this office to the citizens of the state. It is the Office of the Secretary of State that services and protects Minnesota's election processes, administering state laws concerning, for example, candidate filings, political party recognition, voter registration, certification of results, and recount procedures. Of particular importance with respect to public accountability throughout administrative bureaucracies is the Secretary of State's role in the open appointments process. Citizens interested in volunteering service on a state board, task force, commission, council or committee are provided information and application materials upon request. Information on vacancies is published monthly and an "Annual Compilation of State Agencies" is published each November by the Office of Secretary of State.

The fourth constitutional officer outside gubernatorial authority is the State Treasurer. Its Treasury Operations Division includes a small staff divided into three sections in support of financial checks and balances on the collection and disbursement of state funds. In this office as with the other independently elected officials, coordination and liaison are the best descriptors of the relationship to the state's chief executive officer.

Although the model of a unified hierarchy does not fit the state's government structures overall, Weberian principles fit better within the departments and agencies under the Governor's administrative span of control, though not without many variations.

Gubernatorial Administration

A newcomer to the administration of state government is immediately struck by a complex array of structural designations — a complexity that may confirm the worst images of meaningless bureaucratic red tape. The meaning or significance in titles of administrative units appears obscure, however, because protocols for naming have evolved throughout the history of the state and the changing administrative visions of its governors and legislatures. Units created or reorganized at a particular period reflect the titles that were preferred during that period. Consequently, although there are general protocols currently in place as described below, conformity to current protocols is still not uniform throughout all state administrative structures.

The portion of state government within the executive branch and subject to the Governor's leadership currently includes twenty Departments, 113 boards and other agencies, plus the State Colleges and University systems. The Departments comprise the core structures of state government directly under gubernatorial leadership. Each is headed by a Commissioner designated by the Governor and approved by the Minnesota Senate.

A review of Minnesota's Departments is tantamount to a review of the services Minnesota populations have come to expect from their government. A brief summary of each Department's mission and structure is adapted below from the *Minnesota Guidebook to State Agency Services, 1996-1999,* and the *1998 Legislative Manual.* Rule-making authority is designated with an asterisk (*) and discussed later in the chapter in the section that responds to the question, What work are Minnesota's public servants asked to perform?

Department of Administration*
- 7 major units, 4 consultant agencies.
- directs the state government's information, real property, management and material resources.

Department of Agriculture*
- 3 major units, 6 consultant agencies.
- encourages and promotes agricultural industries, assists in the marketing of farm products, and exercises regulatory powers to ensure the continued high quality of agricultural production.

Department of Children, Families and Learning*
- 18 major units, 21 consultant agencies.
- serves local school districts and other educational agencies, and state and local family service providers, through a program of planning, research, consultation, coordination, communication, and in-service education.

Department of Commerce*
- 3 major units, 16 consultant agencies.
- responsible for the regulation of all financial institutions organized under the laws of the state.

Department of Corrections*
- 6 major units, 10 correctional facilities, 5 consultant agencies.
- has the responsibility to accept persons committed by the courts for care, custody and rehabilitation and to administer state correctional facilities.

Department of Economic Security*
– 6 major units, 6 consultant agencies.
– has responsibility for income and employment policies and for linking those policies with veterans' programs, post-secondary education and training, insurance programs, economic development and rehabilitation services.

Department of Employee Relations
– 6 major units, no consultant agencies
– represents overall personnel and labor relations management for the executive branch of state government.

Department of Finance
– 9 major units, no consultant agencies.
– in charge of the financial affairs of the state and keeps the general books of account for the state.

Department of Health*
– 3 major units, 13 consultant agencies.
– responsible for the development and maintenance of an organized system of programs to protect, maintain and improve the health of the citizens.

Department of Human Rights*
– no major unit subdivisions, 1 consultant agency.
– administers and enforces the Minnesota Human Rights Act, exercises leadership in the development human rights policies, and mitigates discrimination through public education and awareness.

Department of Human Services*
– 10 centers, 9 consultant agencies
– administers programs for citizens whose personal or family resources are not adequate to meet their basic needs; persons with disabilities; and persons with chemical dependency,

developmental disabilities, and mental illness, plus one center for geriatric patients.

Department of Labor and Industry*
– 3 major units, 8 consultant agencies
– administers the laws relating to workers' compensation, working conditions and wages.

Department of Military Affairs
– 1 major unit, no consultant agencies.
– responsible for military forces and reservations of the state, i.e., the Minnesota National Guard.

Department of Natural Resources*
– 7 major units, 2 consultant agencies.
– coordinates management of the public domain and serves the public in developing a long-range program to conserve the natural resources of the state.

Department of Public Safety*
– 15 major units, 5 consultant agencies.
– coordinates and directs the functions and services of the state relating to the safety and convenience of its citizens.

Department of Public Service*
– 6 major units, 1 consultant agency.
– responsible for enforcement of Public Utilities Commission rules, regulation of gas and electric public utilities, energy conservation standards, telephone and telegraph companies, and enforcement of standards for weighing and measuring devices used in commerce.

Department of Revenue*
– 6 major units, no consultant agencies.
– supervises the administration of Minnesota tax laws.

Department of Trade and Economic Development*
– 4 major units, 7 consultant agencies.
– maintains a balanced and competitive statewide economy through partnerships with communities, commercial, industrial and agricultural sectors; labor; education and consumers.

Department of Transportation*
– 9 major units, 1 consultant agency.
– responsible for development, implementation, administration, consolidation and coordination of transportation policies, plans and programs.

Department of Veterans Affairs*
– 7 major units, 1 consultant agency.
– furnishes services and benefits to veterans and their families.

Comparisons based on "major units" from one Department to the next are complicated by interdepartmental (as well as intradepartmental) variations in naming protocols. The newest Department, Children, Families and Learning, for example, designates most of its units as "offices" and "teams." The Department of Economic Security identifies its major units as "branches." The largest Department, Human Services, on the other hand, designates several units as "operations" or "services," but for the most part employs no standardized naming protocol throughout the Department (although descriptive information about various units typically refers to them as "divisions"). When standardized unit naming is employed, the Minnesota Guidebook advises that the order from most comprehensive to most specific would be Bureau, Division, Section, Office, Unit, and Activity or Program. Terminology referring to services, branches, operations, teams, groups, etc. may mean one type or size of unit in one part of state government and another type or size of unit elsewhere.

"Consultant agencies" in the list of Departments above refers to a wide variety of regulatory and advisory entities with whom a department can be expected to work. Agencies generally are charged with advisory or regulatory powers and specifically include a portion of membership appointed by the Governor; semi-state agencies are not under gubernatorial authority. Included under the broad rubric of "agencies" are over 170 state boards, commissions, councils, committees, task forces, and other multi-member bodies designated in statute or by executive order to perform some governmental responsibility. Again, the Minnesota Guidebook is helpful in explaining the distinctions.

> *Boards* engage in rule-making, license-granting, adjudicatory, or other administrative tasks.

> *Authorities* are agencies whose task it is to issue bonds for financing, ownership, and development.

> *Commissions* are agencies composed of legislators, with the exception of those established by interstate compacts.

> *Committees* are advisory agencies.

> *Councils* are advisory agencies with at least half of their membership designated from specific areas of expertise, from political subdivisions, or from among other affected stakeholder groups.

> *Advisory task forces* can be designated to study a single topic and have a duration of two years or less.

> *Governor's agencies* are created by executive order to advise or assist the state's chief executive on matters related to state law. They may be titled as the Governor's Task Force on ..., or the Governor's Council on ..., or the Governor's Committee on ...

In addition to the Departments under gubernatorial authority, the *1997-1998 Legislative Manual* identifies several other units for which gubernatorial leadership is particularly important:

Minnesota Pollution Control Agency *
– 5 major units, 5 regional offices, 2 consultant agencies.
– administers laws relating to preservation of the environment and protection of the public health consistent with the economic welfare of the state.

Office of Strategic and Long Range Planning
– no major unit subdivisions, 2 consultant agencies.
– keeps Minnesotans focused on the future, provides policy-makers and the public with accurate information and analysis on the emerging and critical issues, and influences public policy decisions through long-range planning.

Minnesota State Colleges and Universities (MnSCU)
– governing board of trustees
– 37 state universities, community college campuses, consolidated community and technical colleges, and technological campuses.

Minnesota Historical Society
– 22 historical sites statewide, no consultant agencies.

University of Minnesota
– governing board of regents.
– campuses in the Twin Cities, Crookston, Duluth, and Morris.

The development of Minnesota's institutions, administrative departments, regulatory boards, and other agencies has reflected the response of state legislators and gubernatorial executives to the evolving needs and values of the state's populations. Increasingly, programmatic initiatives from the federal government have necessitated assessment and sometimes reformulations of state agency missions. The most recent structural reconfiguration that produced the Department of Children, Families and Learning was the result of efforts to improve citizen access to a wide variety of programs at unified services locations.

Even the very brief summaries of state services provided above are likely to raise more questions than they answer. Fortunately, technologies old and new make it easier than ever to find out more about state government organizations and services. Three sources are especially helpful. For those who work with state government offices on a regular basis, the *Minnesota Guidebook to State Agency Services* (published every three years) is detailed and thorough enough to be a crucial investment in reference resources. The Guidebook is available in print or on CD ROM from the Minnesota Department of Administration.

The *Legislative Manual* is issued biennially by the Secretary of State's office. The Manual focuses especially on the membership of the current legislature, but provides less comprehensive, but very helpful, up-to-date descriptions of the state's administrative units and identifies the current appointees to leadership positions. It is usually available in the fall of the year following biennial legislative elections.

A third source is the World Wide Web site for the North Star — Minnesota Government Information and Services, created by the Government Information Access Council to facilitate a two-way communication between Minnesota units of government and the citizens they serve. Requiring only computer access to the World Wide Web, citizens can go to *http://www.state.mn.us* for user-friendly accessibility to information on branches, departments and agencies of state government, as well as linkages to other politically useful sites. The particular advantages to this source include its economy (no charge), its convenience, and its timely maintenance. Even more important is that most sites provide email access directly to that agency, or put more precisely, to some person who will try to answer questions — perhaps a faceless way to communicate with a bureaucrat, but helpful nonetheless. Discussion of communication with persons (rather than with agencies or offices) is a good lead into the next three chapter sections that consider the people who serve in the state's workforce, what they do, and who cares.

WHO DOES THE STATE'S WORK?

Political appointees, members of the classified civil service, members of unions and professional associations, managers, scientists, corrections specialists, social workers, librarians, attorneys — this entire section would be necessary to list the variety of skills and credentials encompassed in the state's employee workforce. Data reported in 1996 by the Minnesota Department of Employee Relations reported the number of state employees in the executive branch at 48,805, including 17,063 employees in the MNSCU system (but excluding the University of Minnesota because it is separately designated in the Constitution and not considered within the executive branch).

In many ways, bureaucratic officials in all large organizations — both public and private — share characteristics identified a century ago by Max Weber: hierarchy of authority, written specifications of the qualifications for a position, expertise, duty to the position and its responsibilities (rather than to a person). Weber presupposed that officials would remain in their positions for life, except for movement "from the lower, less important, and lower paid to the higher positions" according to "a mechanical fixing of the conditions of promotion" (Gerth and Mills, 1958: 203). Such characteristics are not unknown in modern administrative structures. Public sector bureaucracies, however, are different from private sector bureaucracies by virtue of the constraints and complications imposed by constitutional and legislative definitions of missions and allocations of resources, as well as by public expectations of neutral competence and responsiveness to the needs of society. This section addresses in particular these public expectations as they are reflected in

Minnesota's civil service employee system, political appointments, collective bargaining organizations, and policies directed toward representativeness.

Civil service

The largest proportion of state employees is included within the state's merit system. Minnesota has one of the oldest state systems of civil service, a system initiated in 1939. Excluding the MNSCU system, approximately 79 percent of state employees are within the classified system. Classification of positions according to job related skills and qualifications provides for hiring and promotion based upon merit as determined by applicants' credentials and by open competitive examinations. The Minnesota Department of Employee Relations regularly publishes notice of examinations as well as positions and classifications open for application in *Minnesota Career Opportunities*, available in Job Service centers throughout the state or by subscription.

Political appointments

Minnesotans want public servants to be competent to do their jobs without regard to political affiliation. However, in a democracy, citizens also expect government to be responsive to the will of the voters. Changes in the administration elected to lead the executive branch are expected to produce corresponding changes in the values and policies that define the work of the state. As gubernatorial leadership changes from one administration to the next, the values and policies of each new governor are integrated into the work of state agencies by means of his or her appointments to leadership positions over Departments and other state agencies, as is the case in the federal executive branch. However, unlike the federal executive where department secretaries come and go exclusively at the pleasure of the President, Minnesota designates four-year terms for Department Commissioners and for appointments to most other agencies, except for agencies that function in quasi-judicial roles where terms are set at six years.   Again unlike the federal bureaucracies where all appointments to administrative positions are available for each newly elected president to fill immediately, openings in Minnesota's appointive positions are staggered. Staggered openings and specific terms provide for continuity between successive administrations and for a less hectic round of gubernatorial appointments at the outset than is the case for newly elected U.S. Presidents. On the other hand, the flexibility and extent of the Governor's influence on state policies is diminished accordingly.

Collective bargaining

The culture of Minnesota has traditionally been supportive of collective bargaining and has recognized its value in state employment. Most state employees are covered by the sixteen collective bargaining units established by the Legislature in 1980. Managing and supervising are especially challenging tasks in large units of government in which there may be several different contracts in place, all subject to periodic and separate negotiation.

Six bargaining units (approximately 24,000 state and university workers in 70 local unions) are represented by the American Federation of State County and Municipal Employees. The Minnesota Law Enforcement Association represents employees in the law enforcement unit and encompasses three separate associations. Four organizations represent faculty in various Minnesota state institutions for post-secondary education.   Other collective bargaining organizations represent nurses, engineers, and residential school teachers respectively. The Minnesota Association of Professional Employees represents professionals in over 400 career specialities, and the Middle Management Association represents over 2,700 supervisory employees throughout state government (Minnesota Guidebook). In addition to negotiating contracts, all of these organizations include in their missions activities directed toward influencing the development of legislative policies of significance to their membership. Thus, although individual state employees are expected to refrain from overt political activities, their organizational representatives engage in lobbying, candidate endorsements, and policy advice on political issues related to their professional specialties.

Representativeness

One healthy indicator for a democracy is that a government's workforce approximates the distributions of gender and people of color in the population it serves. As is the case with the elective legislative branch, Minnesota is slowly making progress with respect to the demographic representativeness of its employees, although that progress varies widely between the metropolitan and outstate areas and from one agency to the next. Due to gubernatorial appointments at the level of agency leadership and the process of open competitive examinations at other levels, progress has been most evident in new hiring for entry positions.

A newsworthy example of the reduction in gender barriers occurred with the appointment in 1995 of Patt Adair as the first female warden of the Minnesota Correctional Facility at St. Cloud. The appointment was notable following as closely as it did on a series of disruptions at the facility and an out of court settlement to former guards who based their claims on sexual harassment and retaliation from a previous warden (deFiebre, 1995).

One might well ask, however, what evidence there is that gender inclusivity makes any difference in the administration of public policies. Drawing on the results of an extensive investigation that extended over six states and included surveys of 1,289 respondents in managerial positions, Mary Guy's summary noted that even when researchers held constant "the homogenizing influences of socialization and similar job experiences, a consistent pattern of differences showed up on all the states over most of the issues" (1992: 206). Guy concluded that (1992: 206):

> [I]f women were to hold decision-making posts in
> proportion to their representation in the work force (to
> say nothing of their representation in the population),
> many decisions now being made would be made
> differently. Even if the end result were to be the same,
> the inclusion of women in the decision-making process
> would enfranchise a currently disenfranchised majority
> of the population.

In upper level career civil service management and supervisory
positions, however, inclusiveness and responsiveness to demographic
changes in the state's population may occur slowly due to the
emphasis at those ranks of training and development, retention, and
promotion from within pools of candidates experienced in state
government. Yet such generalizations are risky in light of differences
in professional culture from one department or agency to the next.

Offices located outside the metropolitan area have been slower
to adapt to demographic changes due to strong social networks that
filter information on openings, hiring procedures, training and
promotion opportunities along well established community patterns of
communication. Increased professionalization of human resources
management procedures concerning testing and information
dissemination has been helpful in continuing to open up recruitment
processes. These are responsibilities located in the Department of
Employee Relations (referred to as DOER). Although the
Department acts as the state's official clearinghouse for state
employment (other than political appointments), state agencies behave
somewhat like a confederation with respect to their respective hiring
and promotion protocols. Gubernatorial leadership can provide
powerful encouragement in its demonstration of commitment to a
diverse workforce. The voices for a governor's bully pulpit include
two particular divisions within DOER: the Office of Diversity and
Equal Opportunity and the Office of the State ADA/Disability
Coordinator. Although their authority does not include sanctions,
these divisions are able to promote inclusiveness in state government

by establishing goals, providing consultation and technical support for agency diversity plans, reviewing state policies and procedures, monitoring and reporting on progress.

Progress toward an inclusive state government workforce has been laudable in Minnesota, yet may not even be keeping up with population trends. A leading indicator of continuing demographic changes in the state's population is enrollment in early education. Current enrollments in K-12 education show twice as many children of color as compared to the overall population (Larson, 1997). Consequently, the current modest rate of improvement in this area is likely to be a concern for some time.

Competitors

Before the discussion moves away from those who do the state's work, it is important to comment on those not directly employed by the state, but who nevertheless help (or compete) to accomplish the state's objectives. In 1988, Donald Kettl described how the national government had begun to hold down the number of government employees by increasingly relying on "government by proxy." As demands on state governments have increasingly pressed for services and facilities cut from federal budgets, states too have found government by proxy to be both a useful resource as well as a challenge of coordination and management (Thompson, 1993). As a result of carrots and sticks (financial incentives, contracts, regulations and mandates), private sector contractors, nonprofit organizations, local governments, and even individuals contribute to the goals that Minnesotans have asked their political leadership to hold dear. A thorough treatment of nongovernmental delivery systems is not possible here. Suffice it to note that the challenge of competing and/or cooperating with the private or nonprofit sectors is alive and well in Minnesota. The challenge of competition is particularly sharply felt by state employee professionals, their agencies, and bargaining associations who must work under tighter constraints and more diverse (and watchful) stakeholders than those who operate outside of state government.

As a consequence of employment on the basis of merit, a good deal of professional expertise and experience is resident in the departments and agencies. Public policy analyses in the legislative branch would be deficient if they did not include input from present and former public servants. An illustration of this point and of the competition presented by the private sector to public sector agencies occurred in the 1997 legislative session. Plans for building a new state correctional facility at Rush City bogged down in the face of a proposal offered by the private Corrections Corporation of America (CCA) to house more inmates with lower construction costs, within an earlier time frame, and for lower ongoing costs per inmate. State corrections officials and unionized state prison guards contributed arguments and evidence strongly against the privatization of corrections for medium security inmates citing issues of construction quality, public safety, and constitutional values (deFiebre, 1997a). Meanwhile, former corrections commissioners were reported to be offering endorsements for an even less costly nonprofit alternative to reduce early on the need for increased prison space by developing group home residential options (Inskip, 1997: A13).

Max Weber did not envision competition from other sectors that would so greatly complicate an understanding of the question discussed in this section: Who does the work? It is also likely that he would not be pleased to learn of the political activities and influence of state employees and their professional associations on legislative policymaking. It is clear that public servants themselves seek representation of their concerns in policymaking decision processes. Also important to a representative democracy is a public service sector that models an approximation of the people of color and of women and men that it serves. The next section surveys the work expected from the state's public servants and the extent to which that work is likely to match the intent of those who define its goals.

WHAT WORK ARE BUREAUCRATS EXPECTED TO DO?

It is the responsibility of state bureaucracies to administer the laws and policies assigned to them, to make rules and regulations as authority is delegated to them to do so, to respond to various constituencies, and to maintain public accountability. Characteristics of administration, rulemaking, and responsiveness are addressed in the following paragraphs. Accountability in a democratic system of governance is a central topic that deserves a section of its own late in the chapter.

Again Weber's analysis is illuminating. In his observations of bureaucratic officials he noted among other essentials the importance of written records, the division of tasks into job specific categories, and documented management procedures. He regarded with disdain any role for public opinion as it is likely to reflect ignorance and the effects of demagoguery rather than the expertise that is the most valuable tool of the bureaucratic machine (Gerth and Mills, 1958). It fell to later theorists to raise concerns about quality, performance assessment, client satisfaction, collaborative work processes, competition, and continuous improvement within the federal bureaucracies (Stillman, 1996). In 1993 the National Commission on the State and Local Public Service published *Revitalizing State and Local Public Service,* summarizing these and other challenges that have continued to confront state governments even as their resources and authority expand.

Administrative powers

Departments and agencies receive their mission directives from a variety of sources, sometimes over a lengthy period of history. In 1897 a single Board was responsible for all of Minnesota's correctional and charitable institutions, including institutions for the deaf, blind, mentally ill, criminals, and old veterans. At that time, it made some sense to group all state institutions together for administrative purposes. Today institutional remedies are no longer the policy of choice to address many of these continuing social problems. Contemporary wisdom expressed in subsequent legislative decisions allocates responsibilities in these areas quite differently from the state's initial response, distributing them in the late twentieth century across several agencies with more specific and suitable mission definitions. Evolution in agency missions has followed changing public attitudes. Yet even as it evolves, if an agency's mission is all there is to the work of an agency, goals and tasks might be simple enough to define. Rarely is the work of public servants that simple.

The mission of an agency may be defined in one legislative session and expanded, curtailed or modified in subsequent sessions. In the context of divided governance, a particular governor may not be supportive of programs assigned to that agency by a legislature dominated by the opposing political party. Funding may or may not be adequate to accomplish the goals represented in the mission. If funding is insufficient, the agency may be compelled to make decisions that influence the degree and definition of "success" with respect to the intent of those who originally framed the agency's program focus. Interest groups representing agency clientele supportive of its mission may clash with interest groups representing opposition. Opposition groups may bring court cases to halt, modify or eliminate objectional programs from an agency's agenda.

With the smell of controversy in the air, media investigators may demand records and reports that require a substantial effort to assemble, material that in the framework of a constitutional democracy should be publicly accessible but is difficult to interpret to an unsophisticated public. A 1995 editorial praised the idea of regular performance reports by Minnesota agencies, but chided some of the results as inadequate or unfocused, noting that such limitations may have been why little attention was paid to them — even in the Legislature (*Star Tribune*, November 3, 1995). In this fishbowl of public scrutiny surrounded by a climate of hostility toward government, the life of a public servant is not easy. And if the agency's responsibilities include program reporting and coordination with a federal agency (e.g., on Medicare, environmental regulations, welfare reform policies), all of the pressures described above are intensified by regulatory federalism, which incorporates influence from Congressional legislation, federal funding issues, and more framers' intentions into the mix of influences over agency work.

An administrative function common to most departments and agencies is the work of gathering, processing and regularly reporting statewide data on issues of concern to Minnesotans. These tasks may not seem like exciting stuff, yet information is the fuel on which a healthy democracy must run. Concerns that arise from individual experiences or specific events reported in the media acquire meaning and significance for society as a whole only when properly grounded in the context of statewide patterns. Is a murder in the neighborhood evidence that crime is on the rise and therefore more law enforcement and correctional facilities are needed? If a major employer lays off workers, is there an economic crisis? What kinds of preventive or remedial measures should be applied at what levels to address the problems associated with the state's AIDS cases? Answers to questions like these require credible research and data collection over time to determine patterns, evaluate policies, and contribute to public discourse.

Throughout the 1980s and 1990s, for example, there was widespread (though not unanimous) agreement on the importance of improving education performance. How to accomplish that goal remained a source of intense and complex disagreement at federal, state and local levels of government. In an effort to document and improve education achievement by Minnesota students, revised graduation standards and testing policies were implemented at the direction of the Minnesota Board of Education statewide during the second term of Governor Arne Carlson. Information can now be released annually by the Department of Children, Families and Learning on each district's progress, or lack of progress, in student performance in mathematics and science. The prominence of media coverage and level of data available permits district-to-district comparisons of achievement.   The information offers evidence to advocates for change and focuses the spotlight of public vigilance on defenders of the status quo (Hotakainen and Smith, 1997: A-1, 18).

Agency reports are not, however, always greeted with applause by various audiences.   A report issued in February 1997 from the Department of Agriculture on the mixed blessings of ethanol additives to automobile fuel was met with disappointment by concerned parties on all sides of that controversy.

Rulemaking authority

Rulemaking represents the delegation to an agency by the Legislature of authority to make rules that carry the force of law. Rules developed by administrative agencies exemplify most clearly the "red tape" problems laid at the feet of bureaucratic officials. So why would legislative bodies at the state and national levels continue to write laws so vaguely specified that complex rules are the inevitable outcome? Cornelius Kerwin's extensive analysis of rulemaking at the national level provides some answers (1994). Although members of Congress (as well as their electoral competitors) are all too quick to add to a climate of criticism of bureaucratic over-regulation and incompetence, they are themselves left free of criticism concerning the vagueness, inadequacies, or contradictions of the legislation that assigns rulemaking on any particular issue. A public administrator is not likely to go public with criticism of those in legislative bodies who have the power to make decisions on budget and oversight of executive branch agencies. In addition, having passed statutes that require rules for implementation, legislators can leave the details (wherein devils may lie) to the special expertise of appropriate professionals.   If everything works out as intended, credit for sponsoring successful legislation goes to the lawmaker. If the rules turn out to be burdensome to constituents or ineffective, lawmakers have administrative officials (the experts, no less) to hold responsible for the consequences.

The authority to make rules is not granted without subjecting the rulemaking process itself to rules. The Minnesota Administrative Procedures Act was first passed in 1945 and has been subject to frequent amendment. According to the Minnesota Guidebook, the Act provides for enhanced public participation in the rulemaking process, agency adherence to statutory authority, demonstration of the need and reasonableness of the proposed rules, protection of individual rights in the adjudication of any dispute or violation, and the assurance of due process (1996: 2).

The Minnesota Guidebook summarizes the procedures established for the rulemaking process (1996: 2-4). According to Minnesota's Administrative Procedures Act, an agency directed to formulate a rule must comply with the following abbreviated list of requirements:

– Provide the public with notice that details the authority directing establishment of a new rule. (Notice and reporting requirements are generally understood to be met with the agency's publication of the relevant information in the weekly *State Register*.)

– Respond with "a specific and detailed reply" to any petition requesting "the adoption, suspension, amendment, or repeal of a rule."

– Solicit public comment at least sixty days prior to the initiation of a rulemaking process, and maintain a rulemaking docket that tracks each proposed rule throughout the period of its active consideration.

– Provide a "statement of need and reasonableness" that establishes the justification for the proposed rule and provides a cost analysis.

– Publish a notice of intent to adopt the particular text of the proposed rule.

– Provide a copy of the proposed rule at no charge to anyone requesting it, and maintain a list of persons who have requested notification of the proceedings.

Noncontroversial rules may be adopted without public hearings. However, hearings are held if requested in writing by 25 or more persons. Public hearings are conducted by administrative law judges not affiliated with the agency and must follow strict protocols for recordkeeping. A publicly available report is issued by the administrative law judge on the facts, conclusions and recommendations resulting from the hearing. As a result of a hearing, there may be changes in the proposed rule and further procedures may apply. Rules adopted must once again be published in the *State Register*.

This edited summary of state rulemaking procedures is provided to illustrate a point. The remedy for one problem, the potential for regulatory abuse, can present unintended consequences, and produce additional bureaucratic complexity. On the other hand, granting rulemaking flexibility to nonelected administrators without public input, open procedures, adequate notice, etc., runs the risk of arbitrary use of authority by officials and agencies not subject to democratic safeguards. Democratic governance is not simple governance.

Responsiveness

Commissioners are at the front edge of public response and interaction with the state's print and broadcast media in the presentation of Department reports, responses to criticisms, defense of gubernatorial initiatives, etc. They serve the dual role of representing the political positions of the current administration as well as the policies and professional expertise of the Department. There is a symbiotic relationship between regional media and government agencies, a relationship that serves both the media as it endeavors to cover the work of agencies and the agencies seeking to raise public awareness on matters of concern to state governance.

An important response to agency constituencies has been the systematic and uniform codification of all rules issued by state agencies.   Only since 1983 has the state begun to issue comprehensive summaries of existing state regulations in odd-numbered years, with supplements in even-numbered years. Before 1983, individual agencies were separately responsible for providing public notification in their own agency-specific format concerning new or revised rules. According to the 1980 directive that responded to the public need, biennial publication of *Minnesota Rules* is a compilation of all the state's permanent and temporary rules "in a manner convenient for public use" (Minnesota Guidebook, 1996: 2). By 1993, publication of rules information had come to require a total of 13 volumes and represents an important companion to information in *Minnesota Statutes*. Both compilations are available in libraries designated as "state depositories" throughout the state.

The expectation that the state's administrative agencies will not only perform the tasks assigned by legislative, executive and judicial directives, but respond as well to interest group and citizen initiatives is addressed further in the final section of the chapter.

HOW ARE STATE BUREAUCRACIES HELD ACCOUNTABLE?

Following on the dramatic growth of federal bureaucracies during the administration of President Franklin Roosevelt, concerns arose that administrative agencies were proliferating beyond the capacity for elected leadership to maintain control and accountability. The resulting series of reform efforts have continued over the subsequent decades, periodically calling for improved management practices and increased public scrutiny of administrative agencies

(Stillman, 1996). Similarly, as state governments grew larger and more professionalized in the fourth quarter of the twentieth century, management reforms and calls for accountability grew out of a climate of public criticisms of costly and complex "bureaucratic" governmental agencies, rules, and processes (Thompson, 1993). Labeling the relationships between state bureaucracies and their various stakeholders as "battles," William Gormley observed that (1996: 161):

> State bureaucracies have paid a price for their growing
> importance, and that price is a loss of discretion . . .
> They are subject to a growing number of controls, as
> governors, state legislators, state judges, presidents,
> members of Congress, federal bureaucrats, interest
> groups, and citizens all attempt to shape administrative
> rule making, rate making, and adjudication at the state
> level.

The strength and effectiveness of influences exerted by various stakeholders varies from coercive to hortatory.

Stakeholder influences

One of the amazing things about the state's public servants is that they can function at all in light of the many stakeholders who lay claim to holding public employees accountable. Although a specific list would vary from one state agency to another, a generic list would have to emphasize legislative oversight and gubernatorial management. Throughout the 1970s, the traditional tools of statutory language and budget control were used more frequently as increasingly professional legislators attached sunset limits to statutes and made provisions for legislative review of administrative regulations, held investigative hearings, and assigned staff to track agency implementation (or not) of state statutes (Gormley, 1996: 162). Within the executive branch as well, the 1970s and 1980s saw dramatic changes in the ability and the willingness of governors nationwide to exert authority over administrative agencies. Nowhere was this initiative more evident than in Minnesota. Between 1970 and 1988, reorganization orders were issued on 155 occasions throughout the terms of five governors (Beyle, 1990: 76).

Interagency accountability may be collaborative or something more adversarial. The Minnesota Department of Natural Resources (DNR) and the U.S. Corps of Engineers collaborated for over three years on a study of proposed flood plane projects in the northwestern part of the state. In 1996, however, ten regional watershed agencies unhappy with the results brought suit against the state agency asking that it be blocked from using the study to make decisions on permits for flood control projects (Rebuffoni, 1996: B2). This example of intergovernmental relations illustrates cooperation across agencies of national and state government, and also indicates the use of the courts in addressing challenges to state agency accountability by agencies of regional jurisdiction.

The DNR is also an example of an agency often caught between a rock and a hard place due to scrutiny from a variety of interest groups. Although environmentalist groups were supportive of the flood plane report mentioned above, in March 1997 environmentalists were divided on support for logging agreements on public lands containing stands of white pine. Some groups made agreements with the Department and others protested (Rebuffoni, 1997: B5).

While the exposure of public employees to public scrutiny leaves a public official no corner in which to hide, public attention to the work and accomplishment of state agencies and their employees is fickle and sporadic. Cheers are rare. Jeers are frequent and often unenlightened by evidence. Scandal or ridicule is most likely to draw the attention of the media and its audiences. The problem of unanswerable criticisms constantly plagues employees in the public sector. In light of restrictions on political activity by state employees, rules of confidentiality, and the risk of displeasing various stakeholders, public employees are afforded few opportunities to respond to public criticism — and therefore are easy (and virtually voiceless) targets.

Citizen influence

Years before he was elected to the Presidency, Woodrow Wilson the political scientist urged that public administration courses ought to be an integral part of the college curriculum for all citizens in a democracy (in Woll, 1996: 34). He believed that demagogues who direct criticisms against those who do the state's work deserve no less than the response of educated citizen critics who could evaluate the merits of such claims and allocate responsibility carefully and appropriately.

In a democracy, public accountability is no small matter, yet public accountability is inhibited by the low visibility of administrative agencies. In comparison to the Office of the Governor, the Legislature, and other elected officials, bureaucratic officials below the level of political appointee are rarely interviewed. Elections bring political candidates before the public at regular intervals for public affirmation or rejection. Although no such systematic process affords the public with information and opportunities to choose those who do the work of the state, never before has it been easier for a citizen anywhere in the state to obtain information, identify responsible officials, and even contact state agencies directly.

Traditional sources of information continue to be useful, and have been considerably enhanced by internet technologies. The state's major newspapers, the *St. Paul Pioneer Press* and the Minneapolis *Star and Tribune,* regularly observe and report on the work of administrative agencies. Commercial broadcast sources originating within the state provide little comprehensive or systematic coverage of the work of state agencies, generally limiting their reporting to the occasional release of major reports or allegations of scandal. Not surprisingly, public television's *NewsNight Minnesota* is better than commercial broadcasters in presenting state matters, often including direct interviews. Most of these print and broadcast sources also maintain informative and interactive computer Web sites. Such ease of communications access allows the transformation of every citizen with a computer into a potential lobbyist.

How can ordinary citizens influence decisions of state agencies and make the contributions hoped for by democratic idealists? The following brief list is suggestive rather than inclusive.

1. Seek out and monitor reports on state agencies, their work and accomplishments no less than their scandals and critics.

2. Ask news media for more coverage of public servants and their work.

3. Identify and apply for positions on State Boards, Commissions, Committees, Task Forces.

4. Use the World Wide Web to monitor rule changes, budget requests, appointment processes.

Accountability in the state's public sector is not a one-way responsibility. Minnesota's nonelected public officials recognize that the spotlight of public scrutiny is ever present in a democratic system of governance and continue to expand the ways in which citizens can observe, inquire, and even contribute to public service.

CONCLUSION

It is helpful perhaps to confront the cultural baggage of the term "bureaucratic." The first "challenge" listed on a web site for one of the state's departments is: "Government is 'bureaucratic.' Even 'experts' have trouble." No reader is likely to regard the term "bureaucratic" as a positive descriptor in a climate in which the traditional American distrust of government has been exacerbated by public rhetoric. Even Minnesota's own government uses the term as a self-deprecating example of public distrust. But do public servants really deserve such unremitting negativity? Charles Goodsell wrote persuasively that our public bureaucracies are better than popular myths would indicate. In *The Case for Bureaucracy*, Goodsell marshaled convincing evidence that attitudes measured on the basis of specific individual experiences with public bureaucracies are generally favorable in terms of citizen satisfaction. He concluded that (1994: 3):

> Whereas public bureaucracy, in the U.S. at all levels of government, inevitably involves individual instances of breakdown, it does, *on the whole and in comparison to most countries,* perform surprisingly well.

A 1993 report assembled by the National Commission on the State and Local Public Service included a collection of essays setting forth an agenda for addressing many of the issues mentioned throughout this chapter. The volume editor identified the following challenges (Thompson, 1993: 309):

> (1) leadership that shuns micromanagement; (2) an approach to the workforce challenge rooted in deregulating the public sector, customer orientation, the involvement of front-line workers, and a performance or bottom-line emphasis; (3) the quest not only to attract and retain the talented but to engage them in life-long learning; (4) a balanced approach to information technology issues; and (5) understanding the private delivery of government programs, especially by nonprofits, as a partnership.

This agenda for "strengthening performance, accountability, and citizen confidence" deserves not only the attention of those directly involved in public service, but the vigilance and respect of the public served thereby. With an attentive and educated citizenry and technologies to facilitate interactivity, Wilson's ideal (rather than Weber's) may be a possibility after all (in Woll, 1996: 36):

> A civil service cultured and self-sufficient enough to act with sense and vigor, and yet so intimately connected with the popular thought, by means of elections and constant public counsel, as to find arbitrariness or class spirit quite out of the question.

REFERENCES

Beyle, Thad L. 1990. "The Executive Branch: Organization and Issues, 1988-1989." In *The Book of the States, 1990-91*. Lexington, KY: Council of State Governments. P. 76.

deFiebre, Conrad. 1997a. (March 13). "Public vs. Private issue stalls prison project at Rush City," *Star Tribune*: A1,12.

_____. 1997b. (February 7). "Ethanol boosts rural economy, fuel prices, report says," *Star Tribune*: B1.

_____. 1995. (October 23). "Changing of the guard comes during challenging time at St. Cloud prison." *Star* Tribune: B1,3.

Gerth, H. H. and C. Wright Mills. 1958. *From Max Weber: Essays in Sociology*. New York, NY: Oxford University Press.

Goodsell, Charles T. 1994. *The Case for Bureaucracy: A Public Administrator's Polemic*. 3rd Edition. Chatham, NJ: Chatham House Publishers, Inc.

Gormley, William T., Jr. 1996. "Accountability Battles in State Administration." In Carl E. Van Horn, ed. *The State of the States*. 3rd Edition. Washington, DC: Congressional Quarterly Press. Pp. 161-178.

"Grading state agencies: Make better use of performance reports." 1995. (November 3). *Star Tribune*: A16.

Guy, Mary E. 1992. "Summing Up What We Know." In Mary E. Guy, ed. *Women and Men of the States: Public Administrators at the State Level*. Armonk, NY: M. E. Sharpe, Inc. Pp. 205-224.

Hotakainen, Rob and Maureen M. Smith. 1997. (March 20). "Schools get more bad news." *Star Tribune*: A1,18.

Inskip, Leonard. 1997. (April 1). "Agency working to build lives instead of prisons." *Star Tribune*: A13.

Kerwin, Cornelius M. 1994. *Rulemaking: How Government Agencies Write Law and Make Policy*. Washington, DC: Congressional Quarterly Press.

Larson, Mark. 1997. Strategic Planning Specialist, Office of Strategic and Long-Range Planning. Interview, January 8, 1998.

League of Women Voters of Minnesota. 1997. *How to Make a Difference: A Citizen's Guide to State Government*. St. Paul, MN: Author.

Minnesota Guidebook to State Agency Services, 1996-1999. 1996. St. Paul, MN: Department of Administration.

Minnesota Legislative Manual, 1997-98. St. Paul, MN: Election Division, Secretary of State.

Rebuffoni, Dean. 1997. (March 21). "Environmentalists lambast state, federal forest plans." *Star Tribune*: B5.

_____. 1996. (October 26). "Red River agencies sue DNR over flood-control projects." *Star Tribune*: B2.

Stillman, Richard II. 1996. *The American Bureaucracy: The Core of Modern Government*. 2nd Edition. Chicago, IL: Nelson-Hall Publishers.

Thompson, Frank J., ed. 1993. *Revitalizing State and Local Public Service: Strengthening Performance, Accountability, and Citizen Confidence*. San Francisco, CA: Jossey-Bass Publishers.

Wilson, Woodrow. 1966. "The Study of Administration." In Peter Woll, ed. *Public Administration and Policy, Selected Essays*. New York, NY: Harper and Row, Publishers. Pp. 15-41.

SECTION II

THE INPUT CHANNELS OF MINNESOTA GOVERNMENT AND POLITICS

Donald Ostrom
Gustavus Adolphus College

Government in Minnesota is complex. Charles Backstrom points out that at any one time there are approximately 20,000 elected officials in Minnesota. But there is even great complexity in the organizations and activity surrounding the elected officials, including political parties, campaign contributors, election officials and voters, and lobbyists.

Joseph Kunkel III describes the political parties. The major parties are competitive. The Republican party dominated in the generations after the Civil War. In the 1920s and 1930s their main competition was the Farmer-Labor party, born of protest. In 1944 the Farmer-Labor party merged with the Democratic party to form the Democratic-Farmer-Labor party, or DFL. Although currently the major parties are competitive, especially in races for governor and U.S. senator, in other contests for offices such as president, U.S. House, and state legislature the state leans toward the DFL. An unusual feature of the parties in Minnesota is a system of preprimary endorsements at party conventions. This system allows party activists to dominate the nominations for office, although there has been some weakening of the power of endorsement in recent state-wide contests.

The parties take issues seriously, with the Republicans taking a consistently conservative stance and the DFL backing liberal positions.

Candidates for Minnesota state offices receive help in their campaigns from the nation's most extensive public financing system, analyzed by Patrick Donnay and Graham Ramsden. Candidates get substantial support from an income tax checkoff, and also a unique rebate program in which the state government reimburses citizen contributions up to $50. Almost all the candidates for the state legislature use public financing.   In return they must accept contribution limits, spending limits, and disclosure of their finances. Although incumbents usually win, the Minnesota public financing has helped achieve more competitive races and fewer uncontested elections than in the neighboring state of Wisconsin.

Backstrom outlines the election system in Minnesota. Except in Minneapolis, local elections are conducted without party designation on the ballot. Most of the local elections are held in November of odd-numbered years. Candidates for state and federal office run in November of even-numbered years on a partisan ballot. Minnesota always ranks near the top of states in voting participation. Voting is encouraged by "every means imaginable to facilitate registration," including registration by mail, by candidates, by government agencies actively soliciting their clients, even registration at the polling place on the day of election. Twenty thousand local election judges under the overall direction of the Secretary of State conduct the elections fairly.

Finally, Craig Grau discusses the work of lobbyists. Lobbying is extensively regulated in Minnesota, more than at the national level. It is done by professionals and amateurs, public and private organizations, individuals and groups. Their methods include direct contact, grass roots efforts, and electioneering. Success and failure are difficult to measure. In other words, contrary to the image of a lobbyist as "a lawyer in an expensive suit walking the halls of the legislative chamber," lobbying is many faceted and complex — like the other input channels.

Chapter 6

POLITICAL PARTIES IN MINNESOTA

Joseph A. Kunkel III
Mankato State University

INTRODUCTION

In the past Minnesota's parties seemed to fit the ideal of the responsible party (Jewell, 1984: 87). They were open to citizen participation so a wide base of activists shared in shaping contrasting platforms for each party. The voters thereby had a clear choice on election day. The parties were evenly balanced and both could compete in many elections. The grass-roots party organizations were effective in getting their message out to the voters. The preprimary endorsement system allowed them to control candidate selection and ultimately hold public officials accountable to the party platform. When elected to government, key platform planks became law.

Parties in Minnesota, like those nationally experienced a complex transformation since the 1960s. In many respects they have declined. Party organizations involved fewer people. Voter attachment and loyalty waned. Parties began to lose control of the nomination of candidates. Interest groups and individual candidates played more important roles in election campaigns. Still in other ways parties revived in the 1980s and 1990s. National and state-level party organizations raised enough money to establish professional headquarters and provide candidates with modern services such as polling, telephone banks, direct mail and help in using the media.

161

Party caucuses in state legislatures played a larger role in elections and in organizing government.

This chapter describes the transformations of Minnesota's political parties. First, we evaluate the historic and more recent competitive balance of the state's parties. Second, we describe the structure of the official party organizations. Third, we discuss a few findings about the effectiveness of these organizations. Fourth, we analyze the parties' attempt to control nominations through preprimary endorsements. Fifth, we return to the issue of party effectiveness and examine campaign finance. Finally, we look at issues; the differences between the parties, and the differences within each party.

THE PARTY SYSTEM: PATTERNS OF COMPETITION

American electoral history is usually divided into five eras, or systems with different parties or different "competitive relationships" (Flanigan and Zingale, 1987: 4). Each system is separated by a "realignment" of the partisan relationships.

Republican Domination 1858-1920

After the Civil War Republicans dominated the northern states, including Minnesota, through the 1920s. In Minnesota this dominance persisted into the 1950s. Nationally Democrats became the majority party in 1932 but except for presidential elections this realignment did not occur until after 1948 in Minnesota.

Two different third party movements challenged Minnesota Republicans. The Populists, a farm protest movement with a radical anti-monopoly platform, rose as a result of economic hard times in the 1880s and 90s. In 1890, the Democrats and Farmers' Alliance gained control of the Minnesota legislature for one session. Nationally Populists joined Democrats when they both nominated William

Jennings Bryan for president in 1896. This alliance led to a realignment but one that only increased Republican strength nationally. The Democratic-Populist fusion was more successful in Minnesota, electing a governor in 1898. But Republicans controlled the legislature and elected governors in 1900 and 1902 (Lass, 1977: 174). A popular Democrat, John A. Johnson, served as governor from 1904-1910 but was opposed by a Republican legislature. After this interlude, Republicans regained control until 1930.

Populists and progressives demanded economic and political reform in the early 1900s. The progressive reform impulse affected both major parties but especially the majority Republicans. Progressive reformers eventually dominated the Minnesota Republican party, and they reshaped state government in their image. Progressives distrusted concentrated power, whether economic or political. Thus, progressive reform usually meant weakening party organizations that were viewed as corrupt "machines." Momentum for reform accelerated after Theodore Roosevelt won Minnesota on the Progressive or Bull Moose presidential ticket in 1912 (Lass, 1977: 178-9). The direct primary (1912) and a nonpartisan legislature (from 1914-1972) were legacies of progressivism that challenged the influence of party organizations.

Republican vs. Farmer-Labor (1920-1940)

While national politics were conservative or reactionary after World War I, radical movements grew in the upper Midwest. In North Dakota, the Nonpartisan League used the direct primary to nominate populists and socialists on the Republican ticket. When League organizers in Minnesota were unable to take over the Republican party in 1918, they launched the Farmer-Labor Party (FLP) (Lass, 1977: 180). By 1923 both Minnesota senators Henrick Shipstead and Magnus Johnson were Farmer-Laborites. For most of the next twenty years the Farmer-Labor Party was the major party providing opposition to the dominant Republicans. Democrats were strong only in a few areas, primarily where Catholics and Irish predominated.

The FLP represented a conception of a political party quite different from the progressive ideal. Progressives envisioned weak parties with skeletal or "cadre" organizations. These parties could be checked and limited by ordinary voters through the open primary. In contrast, behind the FLP stood a mass membership organization, the Farmer-Labor-Association (FLA), whose purpose was as much educational as electoral. The FLA took issues very seriously and endorsed candidates prior to the primary as the North Dakota Non-Partisan League had done. While the open primary was a legacy of progressivism, the Farmer-Laborites gave Minnesota the preprimary endorsement system.

The Great Depression of the 1930s and a new generation of voters gave Democrats under Franklin Roosevelt the opportunity to build a new majority coalition. The Farmer-Labor Party in Minnesota, with its strong organization and appeals to the working class and poor, also rode a protest movement against the economic depression. Floyd B. Olson was elected governor in 1930, but he faced a conservative (Republican) legislature for most of his tenure.

Competitiveness: DFL vs. Republican (1944-present)

After Olson's death the FLP was torn by factionalism and hurt by Communist activity. In 1938 a liberal or progressive Republican Harold E. Stassen won the governorship over radical Farmer-Laborite Elmer Benson. Revived Republican strength and FLP friendliness toward Roosevelt for president moved the two opposition parties to merge. In 1944 they formed the Democratic-Farmer-Labor Party (DFL).

From the start DFL leaders believed endorsements were necessary to build a united party committed to liberal principles (Jewell, 1984: 44-5; Mitau, 1960: 70). Liberal Democrats used the endorsement system in 1948 to purge radical Farmer-Laborites and elected Hubert Humphrey to the U.S. Senate. In 1954 the election of Orville Freeman as DFL governor with a liberal (DFL) caucus in the

House (but not the Senate) completed the realignment of Minnesota's parties. Minnesota was finally a state with two competitive parties.

The two parties differed primarily on the economic issues that originated in the depression: the role of government in the economy, labor-business issues and the social-welfare state. In the 1950s, 1960s and 1970s new issues emerged that eventually divided both parties. Civil rights, Vietnam and militarism, feminism, abortion, and gay rights were added to the traditional economic controversies. In 1968, the DFL was split over the Vietnam War as one DFL leader, Minnesota Senator Eugene McCarthy challenged another, Vice President Hubert Humphrey for the presidency. Two factions battled for control of the DFL organization. Minnesota Republicans remained competitive, having elected Harold LeVander governor in 1966. In 1975 after the Nixon presidency they tried to distance themselves from the national party by renaming themselves the "Independent Republican" Party, a name they retained until 1996. The Minnesota Republican Party had its own liberal heritage, and resisted the conservative take-over that began with the Goldwater campaign in 1964. But during the Reagan presidency in the 1980s Christian conservatives and anti-abortion activists succeeded in controlling the party organization.

Recent Election Results

Contrary to Minnesota's national image as a Democratic stronghold, political scientists classified the state as having a competitive two-party system in elections for governor and legislature between 1989 and 1994. Minnesota had a ranking of .608 on a scale that ranged from 1.0 for one-party Democratic to 0.0 for one-party Republican. Nineteen states were more Democratic and thirty states were more Republican (Beck, 1997: 37). While competitive the state clearly leans Democratic.

TABLE 1		
Major Parties' Percentage of Vote (Average of 1978-1996 Elections)		
	DFL	*REP*
President	47.3%	42.4%
Governor	48.3	49.7
U.S. Senate	45.2	50.6
U.S. House	54.4	44.6
Sources: Legislative Manual, 1979, 1981, 1983, 1985, 1987, 1989, 1991, 1993, 1995, and Secretary of State [Online].		

Democrats did not dominate elections for governor or U.S. Senator (see Table 1). Between 1930 and 1997, Republicans held the governorship for 33 years, Democrats for 28 years and the Farmer-Labor Party for eight years. In five gubernatorial elections between 1978 and 1997, Republicans won three while Democrats won two. The two U.S. Senate seats were held by Republicans from 1978 to 1990, when Paul Wellstone, the DFL populist, upset Rudy Boschwitz. As the decade closed each party held one U.S. Senate seat.

Democrats won most elections for state legislature, for U.S. Congress and also carried the presidential elections. DFL majorities controlled the state legislature almost completely after the 1970s. Democrats formed large majorities in the state senate throughout this period. In the state house Republicans were closer but only managed a majority for one session and a tie for another (Gray and Spano, 1996: 10). The Republican share of Minnesota's eight U.S. House seats dwindled from five in 1980 to only two throughout the 1990s.

Minnesota's national image as a Democratic stronghold was true of presidential elections. Since 1928 the only Republicans to win

Minnesota were Eisenhower in 1952 and 1956 and Nixon in 1972. Minnesota was the only state carried by Democrats in every presidential election between 1976 and 1996.

Party Identification Among Voters

Since the 1940s the Minnesota Poll surveyed ordinary voters on their party identification.   Table 2 shows that for thirty years, Democrats outnumbered Republicans. Toward the end of the 1980s, Republicans pulled virtually even and in later polls overtook the DFL (Minnesota Poll, 1981, 1986, 1994).

TABLE 2			
Party Identification of Minnesota Poll Respondents			
Includes Independents who "lean" toward a party			
	DFL	*REP*	*Independent/ other*
1956	44%	36%	20%
1968	46	29	25
1976	40	32	28
1986	33	23	44
1994	28	30	42
Source: Minnesota Poll, 1981, 1986, 1994.			

Even more important however, the number of independents increased in recent years, consistent with national trends. One-third to one-half of Minnesotans claimed to be independents (Wright, Erikson and McIver, 1985; Minnesota Poll, 1994.).   Thus despite Minnesota's image as a partisan state, independents held the balance of power. However most of the independents leaned to one or the other party. Table 3 shows the Minnesota Poll results when these "independent leaners" were grouped with the party they preferred. A slightly larger share sided with the Republicans. No matter how the independents were classified, the DFL and Republican parties were quite close in voter loyalty in the 1980s and 1990s.

TABLE 3			
Party Identification of Minnesota Poll Respondents			
Does NOT Include Independents who "lean" toward a party			
	DFL	*REP*	*Independent/ other*
1980	51	30	10
1986	48	42	10
1994	41	48	11
Source: Minnesota Poll, 1981, 1986, 1994.			

It is important to note that this state-level balance did not mean the parties were close in every area of the state. At more local levels, the competition was more one-sided. Compared to a whole state, a county, legislative district or precinct was more likely to overrepresent certain social characteristics. Since people with different social and economic characteristics tended to support different parties, one party domination was found in local constituencies. This was true of Minnesota's eight congressional districts, three of which were one-party DFL, one of which was one-party Republican and four of which were competitive in varying degrees. State districts were even more one-sided. The close competition between the parties at the state level was built on many geographic areas that leaned or were safe for one party.

Competitive parties tend to have strong organizations (Patterson and Caldeira, 1984). Minnesota's party organizations were strong and open to citizen participation. But involvement declined, leaving the few who participated less representative of the general public. Pundits and politicians criticized the party organizations as elite-dominated and made periodic attempts to limit party influence.

Legal Regulation

Beginning in the progressive era, state laws regulated parties as if they were public utilities (Epstein, 1986: 155). In some states this regulation was detailed and very restrictive. Minnesota progressives imposed the direct primary on the parties, but state law only lightly touched the parties' internal organizations. Minnesota election law set the date and time for the local precinct caucuses and ensured that they stayed open to participation, but beyond this, parties were free to design their own organization (Beck, 1997: 67-68.).

Despite this freedom, both parties developed similar organizations that paralleled election districts. DFL party officers were elected for each level at conventions that met in election years. While Republicans met in the election year, they also met in non-election years to elect county and district officers (Mitau, 1960: 46). This probably enhanced the impact of the most active in the party.

Precinct

Grass roots precinct caucuses met on a March evening in most of the state's nearly 4,000 precincts. Caucuses elected precinct officers, selected delegates to conventions at the next level, and adopted platform resolutions. Any person who lived in the precinct, who would be eligible to vote at the next election and who signed a loose declaration of party support could participate.

The caucuses were very open. It was rather easy to be elected as a delegate or party officer. But spending several hours at a political meeting was not for everyone, so attendance was usually low and declined recently. In the 1970s perhaps 6-11 percent of eligible voters attended precinct caucuses (Marshall, 1980: 146). But in the 1990s the turnout dropped off. Table 4 shows that the number attending caucuses amounted to only 3-9 percent of those voting in the subsequent general elections. This means that in the 1990s probably fewer than 2 percent of the state's eligible voters attended precinct caucuses.

TABLE 4				
Estimated Precinct Caucus Attendance and Voters in Election				
	DFL	*REP*	*Total*	*Primary*	*General*
1988	103,000	92,000	195,000	311,145	2,125,119
1990	65,000	36,500	101,500	998,156	1,843,104
1992	48,000	25,000	73,000	560,659	2,355,796
1994	21,000	30,000	51,000	901,002	1,794,618
1996	36,000	40,000	76,000	450,120	2,211,161

Source: Caucus estimates for 1980-90: Minneapolis Tribune 2/28/80: 28; 2/23/88: 1A; Minneaplis Star Tribune 2/24/88: 1; 2/28/90: 1A; St. Paul Pioneer Press 2/24/82: 1. For 1992: Joel Hedlund, Minnesota DFL 5/1/92; Mike Triggs, Minnesota Republican Party, 5/1/92. For 1994 and 1996: Republican Party of Minnesota.   Election totals to 1994: Legislative Manual; 1996: Minnesota Secretary of State [Online].

A study of caucus attenders in the 1970s found them to be somewhat better educated and more middle class than nonattenders. DFL attenders tended to be somewhat more liberal than nonattenders. At that time Republican attenders had views similar to nonattenders (Marshall, 1984: 91). As turnout continued to drop differences between these party activists and the general population became greater. It was a common complaint that DFL caucuses were dominated by ideological liberals while Christian conservatives had taken over the Republican caucuses.

After the 1960s the DFL used a proportional voting system known as subcaucusing to elect delegates from precinct caucuses and conventions. Any candidate or issue group larger than a minimum threshold could form a subcaucus to elect delegates in proportion to their numbers. Republicans used plurality voting which allowed the largest group to elect all delegates. The DFL system allowed the factions within the party to survive at higher level conventions. Republican liberals and moderates in many areas were defeated at the precinct or county level, rendering higher level conventions more cohesively conservative.

Besides electing delegates to the next level, caucuses chose precinct officers. The parties gave these officers an impressive list of responsibilities, including building the precinct organization, canvassing voters, distributing literature and getting out the vote. However most officers served in name only. There was not much organization in the precinct after the caucus adjourned (Agranoff, 1967: 87-89). In most precincts, willingness to serve was sufficient to win election. Those few active precinct officers quickly found themselves involved in the county or higher level party organization.

County and Legislative District

In most states "the county has been the strongest unit of party organization" (Jewell and Olson, 1988: 81). At this level some organized activity usually took place. In Minnesota, DFLers called it a County Unit (CU) while Republicans named it the Basic Political Organizing Unit (BPOU). In metropolitan areas, the state senate district usually served as this unit. In rural areas and small towns the county was used. Delegates elected from precincts attended the County Unit or BPOU conventions. These conventions elected delegates to congressional district and state conventions, adopted resolutions, and elected party officers such as the county or district chairman (or chair) and the central committee. Where the CU or BPOU was a state senate or house district, the convention was responsible for endorsing preferred state legislative candidates before the primary. Where the CU or BPOU was a county, a special senate or house district convention was held.

Congressional District

The parties built what organization they could in each of the state's eight congressional districts. The most important responsibility of the congressional district convention was to endorse and support a candidate for the U.S. House. They also elected district and some state party officers, approved resolutions, and in presidential years elected some national delegates.

State Organization

The state convention was formally the supreme authority of each party. The DFL state convention was composed of about 1,200 delegates, and the Republicans of 2,220 delegates. Most were elected at the CU or BPOU conventions. The state conventions endorsed candidates for statewide offices such as governor and senator, and in presidential election years also chose some national convention delegates. The state conventions also built each party's platform by voting on resolutions passed up from lower level conventions.

Between conventions each state party was run by a central committee of 200-300 members, a smaller executive committee, and the state officers who direct some paid personnel. The members of the state central committee were elected from CU or BPOU conventions. While the state central committees were officially the governing party authority between elections, they meet only a few times each year and only rarely decided important issues.

A 1975 study observed that both parties' central committees, like the precinct caucus attenders, differed from the general population. They overrepresented males, college-educated, middle-age and middle-class persons compared to the general population. But there seemed to be a balance between newcomers and veterans. Most members said they had faced little competition in their election to the central committee (Shrewsbury and Shrewsbury, 1984). The overrepresentation of certain types of persons was due in part to the unwillingness of most people to commit the time and energy to extensive political involvement.

Between meetings of the central committees, a state executive committee governed each party. Both parties' committees were composed of the top state officers and leaders from congressional district organizations. They influenced which issues were brought before the central committees (Agranoff, 1967: 101-7).

Republican state officers were elected by the state central committee while DFL officers were elected by the state convention. The DFL and Republican state chairs were the most important officers. Typically both were full-time salaried chief executives who directed paid staff and volunteers. The DFL departed from this pattern after 1995 by utilizing a part-time chair as public spokesperson and a full-time executive director to manage the staff. Both parties maintained modern offices, using phone banks, computers, printing and other operations to assist candidates, conduct surveys, raise funds, generate publicity, persuade voters and maintain contact with their local and national organizations.

PARTY ORGANIZATIONAL STRENGTH

It is one thing to describe the formal party structure and quite another to determine the effectiveness and influence of these party organizations. There was not much hard evidence about the real impact and effectiveness of party organizations in Minnesota. One study evaluated the strength of party organizations in nearly all the states. Minnesota's *local* parties' organizations showed only average strength. Out of fifty, the Minnesota DFL ranked twenty-first and Republicans eighteenth (Cotter, et al., 1984: 52-3). Minnesota's local parties, like those elsewhere, were volunteer organizations, not complex professional bureaucracies.

In contrast at the *state* level the Minnesota Republicans were ranked as the second strongest state party in the nation. The DFL ranked only forty-seventh out of 100 state parties (Cotter, et al., 1984: 13-29). This partially explained Republican success in statewide elections for governor and U.S. senator. Because of its more middle-class support, better funding base, and ties to the business community, the Republican party nationally and in Minnesota modernized earlier and developed a professional organization to provide services to candidates. At the local level, where volunteers worked more frequently than paid staff, the DFL and Republican parties differed little in effectiveness.

Frank Sorauf has pointed out that the "American political party" as a singular noun was an "elegant fiction" and that rather than a "single organization with a single set of goals" the major American parties were actually "loose coalitions of individuals and groups" (1988: 136). Besides the layers of party organization described above, the members of each party caucus in each chamber of the state legislature formed their own organizations. A recent study of ten state legislatures ranked the Minnesota caucuses third highest in terms of influence over legislation, party unity and leaders' resources (Jewell and Whicker, 1994). These caucuses were also involved in elections but with a clearer focus than other party units. They sought only to gain or hold a majority of legislative seats.

PARTIES AND THE NOMINATION PROCESS

In the United States the main goal of parties is to "capture public office" (Beck, 1997: 14). In pursuing this goal, the first and sometimes most crucial step was for the party to choose its candidates. No introduction to Minnesota parties is compete without a discussion of preprimary convention endorsements. The endorsement system was one of the most distinctive and important features of Minnesota's parties. Traditionally endorsements gave the parties effective control of nominations. More recent failures of the party endorsement system have weakened the influence of party activists over candidates and public officials.

Primaries

Before the 20th century, party conventions or committees of party leaders nominated candidates. In the Progressive era states adopted the direct primary, allowing ordinary voters, not convention delegates, to nominate candidates. Minnesota was one of only nine states using an "open" primary to nominate candidates (Jewell and Olson, 1988: 89-92). Under the open primary voters did not register or declare their party preference to vote in the primary, as required in "closed" primary states. Voters still needed to choose between the candidates of only one party, but the choice of party was secret. Midwest progressives pushed the primary, and especially the open primary, to weaken political parties' influence over nominations (Kunkel, 1988b: 211).

Political scientists blamed the direct primary for the weakening of party organizations in the twentieth century (Key, 1956: 271). Primary elections threatened party organizations because the voters might nominate candidates who disagreed with the party platform, or who were unacceptable to party leaders. To respond to this threat the parties in Minnesota and in about one-third of the states developed preprimary convention endorsements.

Preprimary Endorsements

Endorsement systems came in two basic forms, legal and extralegal. In some states, endorsement was "mandated or authorized by law" but in others, it was purely a party activity and was not legally recognized (Jewell, 1984: 34). Eleven states had legal or statutory endorsements where candidates might be required to try for convention endorsement.   In these states endorsed candidates automatically qualify for the ballot while others must gather signatures on petitions. The words "party endorsed" might appear behind the candidate's name on the ballot.   In contrast, endorsements in Minnesota were extralegal.   The convention endorsement was basically a recommendation from the party convention as to who should be supported in the primary. The endorsement gave no ballot advantage (Kunkel, 1987: 4).

The DFL party endorsed candidates since it formed in 1944; Republicans began the practice in 1959 (Jewell, 1984: 44-5; Mitau, 1960: 70).   State conventions endorsed candidates for statewide offices such as governor and senator, congressional district conventions endorsed for the U.S. House, and CU or BPOU (county or legislative district) conventions endorsed for state legislature. In some cities parties endorsed for city and county offices. Both parties required a 60 percent vote for endorsement. Thus, when two or more candidates competed, there might be several suspenseful ballots as candidates hung in or dropped out and their support went to a surviving candidate.

Bluntly put, the endorsement system tried to make the primary a mere formality. The party tried to prevent intra-party contests from spilling out into the primary. If the endorsement system worked "perfectly," all candidates, other than the endorsee, would drop out after the convention.   But primary contests did occur when a convention loser, or someone who skipped the convention, ran in the primary. In those cases the aim of the system was to see that the endorsee won the primary. When this occurred, the party activists and leaders who were convention delegates determined which candidate represented their party.

Effect of Endorsements

Since selecting candidates was a basic party function, successful endorsements were evidence of strong party organizations.

Traditionally endorsement in Minnesota almost always meant nomination. But in 1966 the DFL suffered its first endorsement setback for a statewide office. The party endorsed Lieutenant Governor A.M. "Sandy" Keith rather than incumbent governor Karl Rolvaag. Rolvaag did not drop out and won the primary, but lost the general election (Lebedoff, 1969). In 1978 the party's endorsed candidate for the U.S. Senate, Representative Donald Fraser was defeated in the primary by businessman Robert Short. In 1982 Rudy Perpich became governor after winning first the primary over Warren Spannaus, the DFL endorsed candidate, and then Wheelock Whitney, the Republican candidate. Whitney himself won nomination by defeating the Republican endorsed candidate in the primary. In 1994 the Republican state convention endorsed Allen Quist, a favorite of Christian conservatives, over the more moderate incumbent governor Arne Carlson. Carlson easily defeated Quist in the primary and won the general election. These endorsement fights usually originated in issue-based factionalism within the parties. Defeats of endorsed state-wide candidates were exceptions, but created a widespread perception that the endorsement system was in serious trouble.

Party endorsements were most shaky at the state-wide level because the desirability of the offices encouraged more competition. State legislative endorsement contests were rare, and unendorsed candidates were more disadvantaged. In 1986 for example, there were endorsement fights at only 14 percent of the legislative district conventions compared with 40 percent at the state conventions (Kunkel, 1987: 23). Primary contests were also more likely at the higher levels. Between 1976 and 1986, contested primaries occurred in 65 percent of the races for state wide office, in 44 percent for U.S. House but in only 13 percent for the legislature (Kunkel, 1988b: 216). Overall, the number of primary contests in Minnesota was low compared to other states. Contested primaries for state legislature were as rare in Minnesota as in states that had legally binding endorsements (Kunkel, 1988b: 215).

In the few contested primaries that occurred, endorsed candidates were only rarely defeated. In 1986 for example, of all the candidates (statewide, Congress, state legislature) in races where there was an endorsement, 382 endorsees won (99 percent) and only 5 lost (Kunkel, 1987: 36). So the endorsement system worked in the vast majority of cases. But when endorsed candidates for governor or senator were defeated the endorsing system failed visibly and dramatically. If these failures continued Minnesota could resemble other states where party organizations have only very limited influence over candidate selection.

Reasons for Endorsement Success

Why were endorsements usually successful and why did they become less effective? Some observers think that voters were initially favorable but became hostile to endorsement. But scholars doubted that voters were informed enough and so inclined to deliberately vote for, or against, endorsed candidates (Jewell, 1984: 140-1, 153). Tangible resources were sometimes thought to give a big advantage to the endorsees. While it is true that party funds, volunteers, technical help and publicity only went to the endorsed candidate, there was little reliable evidence of the extent of this help. The local party organizations tried to provide assistance, and the state parties did have resources that could make a difference. The direct financial help was certainly rather modest. In the 1986 primary elections, endorsed DFL legislative candidates received only about 5 percent of their funding from party organization sources. Republican candidates received about 19 percent from the party (Kunkel, 1988a: 18).

Intangible factors such as the perception that endorsees were invulnerable and norms supporting the endorsement system may actually have been major reasons for past endorsement success and current decline. The amount of tangible party assistance might be exaggerated but if candidates believed that the endorsee had a big advantage, they might act as if the help were real. The power of endorsement might rest on a belief that was rarely tested. Also, the effort required to mount a state legislative campaign is so great and resources so scarce that any help the party can give might be significant.   The low pay, long hours and other disadvantages discouraged many citizens from running for the state legislature. There was usually an incumbent running, either in your party or the other, and the difficulty in defeating an incumbent discouraged potential candidates.

At the state-wide level it was a different story. The attraction of power and prestige were strong. Through big spending on media, by capitalizing on a famous name, and by exploiting internal party factionalism, some unendorsed candidates emerged victorious. Each time a major endorsed candidate was defeated the power of the myth of endorsee invincibility weakened.

Besides tangible resources and exaggerated perceptions of such resources, the endorsement system always rested on a norm or custom.   Activists in both parties had an almost moral belief that competition should end with the convention endorsement. Many simply believed that supporting the endorsed candidate was the right thing to do for party unity (Agranoff, 1967: 276). As it became apparent that unendorsed candidates could win, this norm itself probably weakened. Despite this weakening, the endorsement system remained an important feature of Minnesota's parties and its demise was frequently exaggerated.

Parties and Campaign Finance

In trying to win elections parties provided assistance to their candidates, both in the primary and in the general election. Money was always a major campaign resource. In past U.S. history and in other democracies parties monopolized the raising and spending of money (Sorauf, 1988: 123). But in more recent elections parties were only one source of funds.   Individual donors and political action committees sponsored by interest groups became increasingly important. The role of the parties in raising and spending money in elections was another indicator of organizational effectiveness.

Minnesota was known nationally for a "moralistic" political culture, intolerant of any political corruption. Consequently the campaign finance system was probably more tightly regulated than anywhere else in the nation. The size of contributions was limited. The vast majority of candidates agreed to voluntary spending limits in exchange for partial public funding of their campaigns.

While these regulations were strict, parties enjoyed greater freedom of action. There were no limits on the size of contributions to political parties, and party committees could give ten times more to candidates than could individuals or political action committees (Weiss, 1996: 7). National elections were regulated by different federal laws. Nationally too, the finance regulations were looser for parties. Through the so-called soft money loophole, parties received unlimited amounts from private contributors for get-out-the-vote activities (Wayne, 1996: 46). Much of this money was passed on to state and local party units to pay for basic campaign expenses. Minnesota's major parties received substantial amounts of this soft money in recent elections.

While party control of nominations seemed to be weakening, Minnesota's parties were playing an increasing role in financing elections. In the 1994 election contributions to DFL and Republican state parties and house caucuses were over $5.5 million, an increase of 58 percent over 1992 and 45 percent over 1990. The second largest source of party money, after contributions from business sponsored committees was other party units, mostly the national party (Weiss, 1996: 3, 12, 19). In 1994 national party committees transferred almost $1,000,000 in "soft money" to Minnesota's parties. Both parties benefited substantially from these transfers but Republicans received somewhat more. In 1996 the amount of national party money increased to nearly $2,000,000. Most of this was spent on television advertising for presidential and U.S. Senate candidates.

In 1996 DFL party committees raised $4,421,217 from all sources, while Republican committees raised $4,955,254. This was 27 percent of the $34,530,748 raised by all party and political committees combined (Ethical Practices Board, 1997).

Party caucuses in the state legislature assumed a major role in providing funds and other services to candidates. While much of the money raised by legislative party caucuses was from special interest political action committees (PACs), interest groups could not legally "earmark" caucus contributions for specific candidates (Gray and Spano, 1996: 21). The caucuses targeted this money carefully to candidates in races where it would do the most good.

These developments in campaign funding were significant for several reasons. First, while parties seemed to be declining in control of nominations and more voters considered themselves independents, parties became more important in funding campaigns. More party money meant more effective campaign operations could be purchased. The parties in Minnesota became more professionally sophisticated in contesting elections. Second, it seemed that party office holders, especially state legislators were able to exercise increasing influence within the political party. Since a party is a coalition of groups and individuals, the increased financial clout of the state legislative caucuses made them major players in intra-party politics. Candidates and state legislators looked more to their legislative caucus, and less to their state or local party unit for money and modern campaign help. These state and local party units thereby lost some influence over public officials after the election, compared with the caucuses.

PARTY ISSUES AND FACTIONS

In the past many were involved in parties for personal material rewards such as political jobs. But since the 1960s party activists were increasingly recruited because of their concern over issues and ideology (Beck, 1997: 112). This was particularly true of Minnesota's parties.   Compared to other states, Minnesota's parties were "extraordinarily issue oriented" (Jewell, 1984: 86). Activists became involved in the party endorsement system and worked on campaigns because they hoped to influence candidates' stands on issues and thereby affect government policies.   This resulted in sharp issue differences between Minnesota's parties.

Consequently voters usually faced a clear choice between DFL liberals and Republican conservatives, something many political scientists considered good for democracy. However some citizens with moderate opinions were discouraged from participation in the parties which they, and many editorialists, saw as too radical. Party activists' concern about issues sometimes was criticized as a desire for ideological purity that fueled factionalism within both parties and led to primary fights, election losses and long term divisions in the party.

Differences Between Parties

Any recent platforms of the state DFL and Republican parties clearly showed stark distinctions on issues. A few examples from 1996 demonstrated this contrast (Republican Party of Minnesota, 1996; Minnesota DFL Party, 1996). The parties differed in their attitudes toward the role of government in the economy. Republicans wanted to reduce the size and scope of government and in particular to reduce taxes.   In contrast, Democrats advocated a variety of government regulations of private sector activity. The DFL platform expressed support for organized labor, for a progressive tax structure where the rich would pay more and for ending requirements that welfare recipients must work. Republicans wanted to reduce taxes and regulatory burdens on business, cut taxes 10 percent and require welfare candidates to work.

The parties also differed sharply on so-called moral and social issues. Republicans wanted a constitutional amendment outlawing abortion, while the Democrats opposed such restrictions. Republicans favored a referendum on capital punishment while Democrats opposed capital punishment.   Democrats wanted to prohibit discrimination based on race, creed, sex, sexual or affectional orientation preference, marital or homemaker status, disability or age, while Republicans opposed recognition of homosexuals as a protected class. Republicans attacked affirmative action as a form of discrimination, while Democrats advocated such a program for Native Americans. The parties differed on many other issues.   Republicans advocated a strong defense and a missile defense system, while Democrats called for cuts in military spending.   Republicans were suspicious of the United Nations, while Democrats called for expanding the U.N. role in international peacekeeping.

Differences Within Parties

Despite these differences, internal factionalism was a constant challenge in both parties (Hathaway and Gieske, 1984: 68).   The heavily DFL but more socially conservative northeastern part of the state was often pitted against Twin Cities liberals on noneconomic issues.   This split contributed to endorsement defeats in 1978 and 1982.   Factionalism in the DFL was probably perpetuated by the proportional voting system at caucuses and conventions.   If the DFL failed to bring its factions together, victory became very difficult. When economic, labor and welfare issues were primary the party stayed united.

Republican conventions were overwhelmingly conservative and not so bitterly divided.   Less than one-third opposed the party position against legalized abortion.   Despite the near consensus, there were differences in emphasis.   As Christian fundamentalists and social conservatives flooded Republican caucuses and conventions in the 1980s traditional economic conservatives felt out of place in a party increasingly focused on issues of sex and morality.   But the Republican rules did not allow proportional representation at caucuses and conventions so the moderate minority faction did not advance to higher conventions.

CONCLUSION

The transformation of Minnesota's parties reflects both national trends and regional differences. The parties became weaker in some ways and more effective in others. Recently Democrats replaced Republicans as the majority party but Republicans still benefited from the large number of independents, the stronger Republican state organization, and sometimes from Democratic factionalism. Despite the openness of the caucus-convention system, declining participation left those few involved subject to criticism as an unrepresentative elite. Until recently the parties' strong endorsement systems enabled them to dominate the open primary. The parties' role in nominations for state legislature and U.S. House continued strong. But party intervention in statewide primaries to help endorsed candidates win modern media campaigns was not always sufficient to overcome factionalism, well-known candidates or personal wealth. While party influence over nominations weakened, the parties' role in campaign funding increased. Voters in Minnesota often faced a choice between candidates whose party platforms differed clearly and whose party organizations helped provide modern campaign services.

Minnesota politics has been shaped by competitive, well organized, strong, and issue oriented parties. Complex forces challenged the political parties nationally and in Minnesota. Minnesota's parties certainly were not as dominant in the past but they continued as major influences on state and national politics.

REFERENCES

Agranoff, R. 1967. *The Minnesota Democratic-Farmer-Labor Party Organization: A Study of the 'Character' of a Programmatic Party Organization.* Doctoral dissertation, University of Pittsburgh. Dissertation Abstracts, 28, 2742-A.

Beck, P.A. 1997. *Party Politics in America.* 8th Edition. New York, NY: Longman.

Cotter, C. P., J. L. Gibson, J. F. Bibby, and R. J. Huckshorn. 1984. *Party Organizations in American Politics.* New York, NY: Praeger Publishers.

Epstein, L.D. 1986. *Political Parties in the American Mold.* Madison, WI: University of Wisconsin Press.

Ethical Practices Board, State of Minnesota. 1997. *Ethical Practices Board Issues Summary of 1996 Campaign Finance Reports for State Candidates, Political Committees, and Political Funds.* St. Paul, MN: Author.

Flanigan, W. H. and N. H. Zingale. 1987. *Political Behavior of the American Electorate.* Newton, MA: Allyn and Bacon, Inc.

Gray, V. and W. Spano. 1996. *The Minnesota Legislature: Pretty Good and Now Purer Than the Rest.* Paper prepared for the meeting of the American Political Science Association, San Francisco, CA.

Hathaway, W. and M. Gieske. 1984. "Minnesota Political Parties and Politics." In M. Gieske, ed. *Perspectives on Minnesota Government and Politics.* 2nd Edition. Minneapolis, MN: Burgess Publishing Company.

Jewell, M. 1984. *Parties and Primaries: Nominating State Governors.* New York, NY: Praeger Publishers.

Jewell, M. and D. Olson. 1988. *Political Parties and Elections in American States.* 3rd Edition. Chicago, IL: The Dorsey Press.

Jewell, M. and M. Whicker. 1994. *Legislative Leadership in the American States.* Ann Arbor, MI: University of Michigan Press.

Key, V.O. 1956. *American State Politics: An Introduction.* New York, NY: Knopf.

Kunkel, J. A. 1987. *Organizational Effectiveness in an Era of Weakened Parties: Preprimary Endorsements in Minnesota, 1986.* Paper presented at the meeting of the Midwest Political Science Association, Chicago, IL.

Kunkel, J. A. 1988a. *Financing Nominations: Campaign Contributions and Party Endorsement of Minnesota Legislators.* Unpublished manuscript.

_____. 1988b. "Party Endorsement and Incumbency in Minnesota Legislative Nominations." *Legislative Studies Quarterly.* Volume 13: 211-23.

Lass, W. E. 1977. *Minnesota: A Bicentennial History.* New York, NY: W.W. Norton and Company, Inc.

Lebedoff, D. 1969. *The 21st Ballot: A Political Party Struggle in Minnesota.* Minneapolis, MN: University of Minnesota Press.

Marshall, T.R. 1980. "Minnesota: The Party Caucus Convention System." In G. M. Pomper, ed. *Party Renewal in America.* New York, NY: Praeger Publishers. Pp. 139-158.

_____. 1984. "Representation in Minnesota's Precinct Caucuses." In M. Gieske, ed. *Perspectives on Minnesota Government and Politics.* 2nd edition. Minneapolis, MN: Burgess Publishing Company. Pp. 82-91.

Minnesota Democratic-Farmer-Labor [DFL] Party. 1996. *Ongoing Platform 1996.* St. Paul, MN: Author.

Minnesota Poll. 1981. (August 23). Republican-Democratic gap narrows in state. *Minneapolis Tribune*: 1A

_____. 1986. (May 27). "Voters without party label lean more toward IR." *Minneapolis Star Tribune*: 1A.

_____. 1994. (September 26). "Carlson holds commanding lead over Marty." *Minneapolis Star Tribune*: 1B.

Mitau, G. T. 1960. *Politics in Minnesota.* Minneapolis, MN: University of Minnesota Press.

Patterson, S .C. and G.A. Caldeira. 1984. "The Etiology of Partisan Competition." *American Political Science Review.* Volume 78: 691-707.

Republican Party of Minnesota. 1996. *1996 State Platform*. St. Paul, MN: Author.

Secretary of State. 1997. *Minnesota State General Election Results*. [Online] available: http://www.sos.state.mn.us.

Shrewsbury, S. and C. Shrewsbury. 1984. "The Organizational Elite of Minnesota's Political Parties: Perspectives on Representation." In M. Gieske, ed. *Perspectives on Minnesota Government and Politics*. 2nd Edition. Minneapolis, MN: Burgess Publishing Co. Pp. 115-122.

Sorauf, F. 1988. *Money in American Elections*. Glenview, IL: Scott, Foresman and Company.

Wayne, S. 1996. *The Road to the White House 1996: The Politics of Presidential Elections*. New York, NY: St. Martin's Press.

Weiss, E. 1996. *Money in Minnesota Politics: 1994 Contributions to the Minnesota DFL and Republican State Parties and House Caucuses*. St. Paul, MN: Minnesota Alliance for Progressive Action.

Wright, G. C., R.S. Erikson, and J.P. McIver. 1985. "Measuring State Partisanship and Ideology with Survey Data." *Journal of Politics*. Volume 47: 469-89.

Chapter 7

THE HISTORY AND PERFORMANCE OF MINNESOTA'S PUBLICLY FUNDED LEGISLATIVE ELECTIONS

Patrick D. Donnay
Bemidji State University

Graham P. Ramsden
Creighton University

INTRODUCTION

Concerns about the role of money in American politics are always present. We in political science approach the subject from a variety of perspectives. We wonder about the effect of moneyed interests on public policy, we worry about money's effect on our electoral processes, and we worry about the implications of the role of money for democratic theory.

Everyone agrees that challengers have trouble attracting the money they need to run competitive campaigns. And most researchers agree that incumbents have a great advantage in attracting contributions from the variety of organized interests that seem to dominate our politics. Public funding is one proposed solution to this dilemma.

Another proposed solution is to give political parties a greater role in campaign finance. According to some, party money should make legislative elections more competitive because a political party's primary goal is to win elections. Party money in campaigns, in this view, will go to candidates who need money to hold on to, or seek, an elected office. This is a different motivation from most interest groups or Political Action Committees (PACs). Moneyed interests are most fundamentally motivated by access to winners, not by concerns for competition or ideology.

To examine more closely the link between money, elections, and political parties we look at state legislative elections in Minnesota. Minnesota's system of campaign finance is based upon a unique mixture of public financing, private contributors and party funds. By looking more closely at the Minnesota campaign finance system we can assess the relative role of money from political parties, public financing, individuals, interest groups and PACs in Minnesota's elections. Minnesota has a reputation for "clean" politics and a progressive legacy. These elements of political culture mixed with DFL dominated politics in the early 1970s set Minnesota on a course for innovative, and some would say radical, ideas for campaign finance. In this chapter we will trace the origin and evolution of the Minnesota campaign finance system with all its partisan twists and turns, and then assess the consequences of this complicated system in terms of whether it makes elections competitive or not.

CAMPAIGN REFORM IN MINNESOTA

Minnesota's Reformist Culture

Deservedly or not, Minnesota's reputation for "clean" politics earns the state praise from conservative and liberal alike. This reputation comes out of a legacy of progressive populist reform that saw its high water mark during the era of the farmer-labor coalition in the first half of this century. The farmer-labor movement was based upon an incongruous mix of socialist thinking and traditional progressive reform. It appeared in the 1910s as the Democratic party in Minnesota failed to embrace the progressive agenda.

The progressive agenda took root in Minnesota with an organization called the North Dakota Nonpartisan League (NPL). In addition to the traditional ideas of political reform like primary elections, the Australian ballot, and city-manager forms of local government, the Nonpartisan League also had a collectivist side. It advocated public ownership of railroads, banks, grain terminals and communications centers. The Nonpartisan League was, as the name suggests, explicitly not a political party. In North Dakota the Nonpartisan League largely operated within the Republican party. In Minnesota the same forces formed their own party, Farmer-Labor, which was the main opposition to the Republicans in the 1920s and 1930s. It elected members of Congress, governors, and other officeholders.

These forces have had an enduring effect on politics in Minnesota. The Farmer-Labor party merged with the Democratic party in 1944. Thus there is the contemporary Democratic-Farmer-Labor, or DFL, party in Minnesota. While the history of the Republican party is somewhat less turbulent, part of what remains of the influence of the progressive era is a sense of independence from national and other centralizing forces. Minnesota Republicans in 1975 renamed themselves the Independent Republicans (Gieske, 1977; Kunkel, 1993). Only in 1995 did Minnesota's Republicans vote to drop the "independent" portion of the their name.

This progressive history makes it clear why Minnesota was so quick to adopt electoral reform in the 1970s. In the heat of the Vietnam War and Watergate, the public's distrust of government rose dramatically. In this atmosphere, it was not surprising that Minnesota, with its reformist bent, would be one of the first places to adopt important political reforms. Additionally, in 1972 one of Minnesota's leading newspapers, *The Minneapolis Tribune,* added to the pressure for reform by exposing Minnesota's own campaign finance scandal. The *Tribune* reported a dominant source of campaign money for Minnesota legislators was an industry consortium called the Good Government Committee. Its major members were the central industries of Minnesota, including such big corporations as Minnesota Mining and Manufacturing (3M), General Mills, and Honeywell.

The Good Government Committee prioritized giving their funds to conservative voices in Minnesota politics. These voices included the "conservative caucus" in the Minnesota legislature, aligned with the Republican party during the six decades (1913-72) when party designation did not appear on the ballot for legislative candidates. The 1972 elections would fundamentally change the nature of the Minnesota legislature. The DFL legislative victories in 1972 put liberal Democrats in control of the legislature while DFLer Wendell Anderson was governor. This DFL-controlled legislature restored partisan labels to legislative elections and began rewriting the rules of campaign finance in Minnesota — doing all they could to minimize the role of conservative-leaning organizations like the Good Government Committee — while at the same time hoping to restore trust and a sense of fairness in Minnesota politics by lessening the importance of big money in politics.

The Incremental and Partisan Evolution of Campaign Finance Reform

As a result of the Watergate scandals the Republican party was in national and local disarray. The Minnesota DFL, in control of both chambers of the legislature for the first time in history, felt it had a strong hand to change the way state campaigns are funded in Minnesota. The ideas under discussion were controversial then and remain so. Public financing for campaigns had not been tested nor did the parties agree that there was a fair way to raise the money needed to subsidize campaigns. Spending and contribution limits were novel ideas as well. As early as May of 1973, it was clear that the reform of campaign finance would have a strong partisan tone. Ironically Arne Carlson, a central player in the reforms of 1993 as governor, was at that time a state representative. He declared after a House committee session, "I don't think we any longer have an ethics bill. I think you've just attempted to abolish one political party" (Talle, 1973: 14B). Elements of the early reform legislation to which Republicans objected included limitations on the amounts political parties could contribute to campaigns, the $1.00 tax check-off for political campaigns, the general notion of publicly funding campaigns, and several provisions regarding the role of labor unions that seemed to get protected status from the DFL (Dornfield, 1974).

Both parties believed the $1.00 check-off on tax forms, where people could declare which party would receive their $1.00, would greatly advantage Democrats. The Democrats had more difficulty raising private funds, so the absence of public financing benefited the Republicans. Also, at that time there were approximately twice as many people in the state who identified themselves as Democrats, and so the Democrats could expect more public financing from the check-offs. Hence Republicans were eager to kill the proposal, but were unsuccessful despite several attempts (Shellum, 1974). When Republicans were unable to stem the check-off scheme they made many efforts to amend the formulas by which it would be distributed. One innovative idea was to allow challengers to have spending limits 10 percent greater than those for incumbents, a proposal not adopted until 1993. Of course, as the minority party Republicans were eager for provisions to help them be effective challengers (Ackerberg, 1974).

As is typical, many policy ideas that were floated in the 1974 legislative session had clearly partisan implications, but they also could be justified on policy grounds as well. For example, while the $1.00 check-off mechanism would advantage the DFL, a strong case was made that public financing of campaigns was an important part of the reform movement and the money needed to come from somewhere. It is arguably just as partisan to have collected the revenues via the check-off and redistributed them equally. Republicans, as the minority party, would have jumped at the opportunity to receive subsidy amounts equal to the majority. Indeed, they proposed this approach in 1978 (Wilson, 1978). It is relatively easy to find partisan motives behind most reform ideas. It is much harder to find reform ideas that are absolutely nonpartisan. As the political parties have worked over the past 25 years to re-shape and fine tune the Minnesota campaign finance system, both sides had sound justifications intermingled with partisan motives.

While DFL control had much to do with the passage of the initial reform in 1974, so did the events of Watergate. The front page of the *Minneapolis Tribune* on Sunday, March 10, 1974 made the linkage. Two parallel headlines read "State disclosure, public funding bill passes Senate" and "58 percent surveyed think Nixon broke the oath of office." Sagging trust in political figures guaranteed that some form of reform would become law. The public sentiment was so strong that even Republicans felt compelled to vote for the legislation on final passage. The only votes in opposition came from just five Republicans. The core of our present system took shape with the legislation passed in 1974, titled "The Ethics in Government Act." These core elements include public financing generated primarily from a check-off on state tax forms, spending limits for campaigns, limitations and disclosure provisions on contributions, and the establishment of the Ethical Practices Board to implement and oversee the administration of campaign finance law in Minnesota.

Of course Minnesota law is not immune from the U.S. Constitution. Republican forces in Minnesota and the nation quickly challenged in the courts various provisions of the 1974 campaign finance reform bill. Regulations on what organizations of different types are allowed to do with their political resources can easily run headlong into our constitutional rights of free speech and association. A U.S. District Court *Bang v Chase* (1977) ruled unconstitutional the limits on a candidate's personal expenditures and independent expenditures (these are expenditures by people or organizations that are "independent" from a candidate's campaign funds). So those limits were struck down in the Minnesota law. Only in recent years have new efforts been made to restrict independent expenditures (Smith, 1993a).

The court also found fault with the check-off mechanism. In the 1974 law the amount of the public subsidy that went to legislative candidates was based on the amount each party raised statewide by the check-off. The court said this violated principles of speech and association in the case of legislative candidates. The decisions of the District Court were appealed to U.S. Supreme Court in *Bang v Noreen* in 1978 where they were upheld. Legislative candidates, the court said, needed to be awarded public subsidy based upon the check-off within their districts. The court argued that it is inappropriate, for example, that DFLers in Republican areas of southwestern Minnesota should get a greater subsidy than Republicans in those areas. Basically the court said the money should return more closely to the area from where it came.

The Republican party, now renamed the Independent-Republicans or IR, offered in January of 1978 to accept an equal distribution of the public subsidy (Wilson, 1978). DFLers in the legislature rejected this proposal. They instead set out to amend the check-off mechanism to provide more local geographical units and indicators of partisan preference. In this way the public subsidy could be directed back more efficiently back to where it came from and meet constitutional tests. Senate DFLers proposed collecting the check-off funds by county and using county boundaries as the determinant of local control. For House members county boundaries were too large; they preferred to rely on the party support members have in their legislative districts. The final compromise between the two chambers involves a complicated mix of both ideas. The money for the public subsidy is now collected by county but returns to candidates in those counties according to how well their party has done in previous legislative elections. While this plan was good for some Republicans who hail from predominantly Republican areas, it was a solution to the constitutional faults of the law that Republicans did not anticipate or approve. Sen. Nancy Brataas (IR-Rochester), a plaintiff in the legal challenge, remarked, "It makes a mockery of the court decision. It's a thinly veiled attempt to circumvent the district court decision." DFL sponsor Steve Keefe said in defense of the reform, "[What we do is exactly what the court said. Those candidates who will benefit more are those where the local parties are encouraging members to use the check-off" (Phelps, 1978: B2).

Whatever the merits of the partisan arguments, one fact is indisputable. This solution was — and remains — incumbent friendly. As you will see later incumbents, DFL and Republican, have gotten a disproportionate share of the public campaign subsidy in Minnesota.

By 1980 a new issue was on the agenda. The original Ethics in Government Act included fixed expenditure limits on how much candidates could spend in their campaign if they accepted the public subsidy. These limits had not changed since their creation in 1974. The late 1970s were marked by rapid inflation so the limits imposed in 1974 were very restrictive already by 1980. Participation in the public financing mechanism, which had always been voluntary, was dropping dramatically and candidates from both parties found they could not run an effective campaign with such sharp constraints on spending. We will look at this more closely later in the chapter.

By this time the Republicans had regained their footing in Minnesota politics and Republicans nationally were gaining momentum as Ronald Reagan was on his way to the presidency. Al Quie, a Republican, had become Governor in 1979. The DFL still controlled the legislature in 1980. Quie and the Republicans were looking for an opportunity to end the system of public financing. Quie generally opposed public financing, and had rejected the public subsidy in his bid for Governor. DFLers were losing out to the Republicans in raising money from other sources and wanted to maintain the system of public financing ("Senate Overrides Veto...", 1980). The political field was set for an extended battle over adjusting the spending limits of the Ethics in Government Act.   The DFL legislature tried several tactics to induce the signature of Governor Quie (Salisbury, 1980b). Quie exercised his veto power. The debate became so partisan that two Representatives had to be restrained from coming to blows as the rhetoric grew in intensity (Salisbury, 1980a).

The resolution of this confrontation was classic compromise. The issue would be settled with state constitutional referenda on two issues: public financing and the Governor's proposal for initiative and referendum. The initiative and referendum effort failed to pass, but the spending limit reform was approved.   Hence since 1982 the spending limits in Minnesota's campaign finance system have been adjusted upward and continue to be adjusted for inflation each election year. Participation by legislative candidates has grown to nearly 100 percent since 1982.

With the new rules of campaign finance settling down, the decade of the 1980s saw many familiar patterns return. Unions learned how to play by the new rules and continued to be especially strong supporters of the DFL. The Minnesota AFL-CIO consistently ranked as the single biggest giver to Minnesota campaigns and the majority of their resources went to the DFL. Other big interests consistently appearing toward the top of contributors include the Minnesota Education Association, American Federation of State, County and Municipality Employees (AFSCME) and the Teamsters union (Wilson, 1982; Wilson, 1985). Not to be outdone the IR party was just as aggressive at attracting resources to itself and its candidates ("IR Donations to..", 1983). The Minnesota Leadership Council, made up of business leaders, replaced the Good Government Committee (Sturdevant, 1984).   They began the practice of "bundling" contributions as a way around the limits on contributions in the campaign finance law. In bundling individual contributions are grouped or bundled together so as to magnify their impact but still remain individually relatively small contributions. The DFL later took the Leadership Council to court over the practice (Zack, 1986). They lost the lawsuit, but took control of the House again in 1986 and rewrote the law to disallow bundling (though Republicans charge that some unions do very similar things) (Pinney, 1990). Another important change occurred in 1987 to insure continued revenues for the public subsidy: the tax check-off amount was increased to $5.00 (Pinney, 1988).

The DFL strength of 1974 slipped so dramatically in just a decade that by 1984 they lost the majority in the Minnesota House. The Republicans in the House quickly attempted to scrap the system of public funding for campaigns (Salisbury, 1985). It was largely a symbolic effort because the Senate was still solidly in DFL control and DFLer Rudy Perpich was Governor. No major changes came from the effort, but it was a reminder of the strong partisan feelings about public financing.

Incremental reform continued through the late 1980s and into the 1990s. One particularly significant reform occurred in 1990. With the DFL in control of both the legislature and the governor's office, an innovative expansion of public financing occurred. The Contribution Refund Program was initiated. With this program contributors to campaigns or party organizations are refunded up to $50.00 from the state treasury. For example, if Mary Smith gives $75.00 to candidate Jones, then Mary will receive $50.00 back from the state. DFLers were interested in this concept for a variety of reasons: it would expand the number of people who could participate financially in politics, and it raised money from a larger number of people. Ironically, by 1996 Republicans were gaining more money from this program than were Democrats ("Republicans benefit most...", 1997). This contribution refund program is available only to those candidates who participate in the public subsidy program. The money for the refunds comes from the state general account and is independent of any check-off amounts.

The presidential candidacy of Ross Perot got the reform ball rolling again with more momentum in 1993. A thorough and critical analysis of the Minnesota system of campaign appeared in the *St. Paul*

Pioneer Press in 1992 (Coffman and Collins, 1992). By this time Arne Carlson, the outspoken critic of the early DFL reform proposals, had moved from his position as State Auditor to become Governor of the state in 1991. The DFL continued in control of the legislature. As the criticisms grew, both Governor Carlson and DFL leaders in the legislature promised reform (Smith, 1993b).

Reaching agreement on the nature of the reform, however, was not without its predictable confrontation. As this history would suggest, at least one veto would be used by the Governor to force the legislature to meet some of his demands (Smith, 1993a). In the end, however, the two sides found much to agree on and enacted a long list of reforms in 1993. Some of these changes include: lowering contribution limits to $500 per year ($100 in nonelection years) from most campaign contributors, banning leadership or "friends of" committees, restricting bundling, addressing the impact of independent expenditures, raising the spending limit for first time candidates, and requiring that matching funds be raised in contributions of $50 or less in order to qualify for the public subsidy.

Thus, Minnesota's system of campaign finance evolved incrementally with a mixture of good and self-interested motivations. While the DFL has clearly been the driving force behind campaign finance reform in Minnesota, no one party or individual can claim total ownership of the system. The campaign system that emerged is very complex. Everyone involved in campaigns in Minnesota — political parties, candidates, interest groups, political consultants and campaign workers — needs to be well versed in the intricacies of this system. Unfortunately, sometimes these professionals are not fully informed and most of the time the average voter is left confused as well (Wilson, 1988).

MAJOR FEATURES OF CAMPAIGN FINANCE

Public Financing

Campaign finance in Minnesota is unusually complex and its evolutionary history tells us how we got the system we have. Minnesota is one of only a few states that have a system of public financing for legislative elections. The public financing component of the Minnesota law is probably one of its most progressive and controversial elements. In this portion of the chapter we set out to explain how the system of public financing for Minnesota legislative elections operates.

The public financing system has two basic components. First, voters in Minnesota have the option of allocating $5.00 to fund elections in their state by checking a box on their state income tax form. Voters can earmark that money to either the general account fund, the Democratic-Farmer-Labor party, or the Republican party. Minor parties, if they show enough strength, are also included; in 1996 the Reform, Libertarian and Grassroots parties qualified for the check-off. These accounts are kept separate. The money allocated to the party accounts is collected by county, and then returned to the legislative candidates of the parties.

The amounts of party account money given to each candidate can vary dramatically. The number of taxpayers exercising the check-off option varies by party and popularity across the counties. In addition, the precise amounts awarded to candidates are determined in part by a complicated formula incorporating proportions of the same party vote candidates received at the district level in the last general election. To illustrate how these amounts can vary, look at some examples from 1994. In District 5A, a highly Democratic area, incumbent DFLer Tom Rukavina had a public subsidy of $10,788 for his campaign while his Republican challenger only received $6,863. Similarly incumbent DFLer Mike Jaros in District 7B got $10,252 while his Republican challenger only received $7,310. In recent years as Republicans have regained popularity, Republican incumbents can be advantaged by this mechanism. For example Republican Eileen Tompkins in District 36A received $10,615 to her DFL challenger's $8,734 (State of Minnesota, Ethical Practices Board, 1994). The party account funds are awarded to the winner of the party primary prior to the general election.

The second component of public financing is the general account fund, which is quite different. The money that taxpayers check-off for this account is allocated to all candidates for state elected office according to a legislated proportion. In recent years the formula specified that 21 percent of this money would go to the governor and lieutenant governor races, 23.3 percent to state senate races and 46.6 percent to races for state representative. This money is awarded equally to all candidates shortly after the general election regardless of location or party so long as they achieve a threshold percentage of the popular vote.

Additionally, the reforms of 1993 added still more variables. The public subsidy a candidate can receive depends on whether their opponent is supported by any organizations doing independent expenditures, and whether their opponent agrees to participate in the public funding system and abide by its spending limits.

Contribution Refund Program

The Contribution Refund Program created in 1990 offers yet another fund raising opportunity to legislative candidates. As described above, in this program contributors to campaigns or party organizations are refunded up to $50.00 from the state. This form of a public subsidy mechanism exists in no other state and appears to have many positive attributes. It has the likelihood of increasing participation by lowering the hurdle to contributing financially to campaigns. It offers challengers who are aggressive and systematic a mechanism to access campaign funds in a way that insures their commitment to the campaign. This program appears to be especially significant for challengers who find money raising from individuals much easier when they are able to promise the giver that they will get $50.00 of that money back.   Some candidates fail to take great advantage of this program.   On the other hand, several candidates in 1996 were able to raise over $15,000 through this program. Nonetheless, it is too soon to say who is really using this program effectively and what kinds of consequences it is having on Minnesota's elections, but is definitely worth more study.

Finally, the Contribution Refund Program appears to be gaining some momentum relative to the public financing based on the check-off. In 1995, there were 21,101 contributors to campaigns who were refunded $1,251,212. In 1996 there 41,510 contributors to campaigns who were refunded $2,423,182. Of course 1996 was an election year and we would expect the amounts to be significantly higher than in 1995, but $2.4 million is a significant share of the total spent on state elections in 1996. When combined with the refunds for contributions to party organizations a total of $4.5 million was refunded in 1996, a figure greater than the $4.1 million that year in direct public subsidy from the check-off ("Republicans benefit most...", 1997).

Spending Limits

Another central component of Minnesota's campaign finance system is the spending limits that are attached to the public subsidy. There is a delicate balance between the amount of public subsidy that is offered to candidates and their allowable spending limits. Frequently a key goal of rewarding candidates public dollars is to get their commitment to reduce their spending. These spending limits were the crux of the political battle in 1980. As Table 1 reveals one out of three legislative candidates were opting out of the public financing mechanism in 1980. And as other researchers have found, those who were most likely to accept the spending limits and the public money were either safe incumbents who did not need to worry about spending limits, or long shot challengers who desperately needed the public subsidy (Jones and Borris, 1985). This essentially means that where the limits and the subsidy are not balanced appropriately, those expecting competitive, expensive campaigns opt out of the system. Unfortunately, however, these are precisely the kinds of campaigns where one might like to see the spending reduced. In short, the adjustments of 1980 that allowed the spending limits to

TABLE 1			
Election Year Spending Limits and Rates of Participation Minnesota State Legislative Elections, 1976-96			
Election Year	*House*	*Senate*	*Percent Participating*
1976	$7,500	$15,000	92%
1978	7,500	*	87
1980	7,500	15,000	66
1982[a]	15,885	31,770	90
1984	16,775	*	78
1986	17,728	35,326	77
1988	18,597	*	89
1990	20,335	40,669	93
1992	21,576	43,150	95
1994[b]	21,576	*	92
1996	22,784	45,568	96
* no election for Senate			
[a] Spending limit adjusted for CPI per adoption of state constitutional amendment in 1980 election, beginning in this year and continuing in succeeding election years.			
[b] Spending limit for 1994 frozen at 1992 level by reform of 1993.			
Source: State of Minnesota, Ethical Practices Board.			

increase with inflation and the later reforms enabling first time challengers a greater limit were a healthy step for insuring broad participation in the Minnesota system.

Contribution Limits

Also tied to the system of public financing are tight limitations on contributions that candidates can accept. These vary by the type of giver. In particular, there is a distinction made between political party organizations and non-party sources. Since 1993 non-party contributors are limited to $500 in election years, $100 in other years. Because of the unique role of political parties, they have contribution limits ten times these amounts. Political party funding is that expressly linked to a political party at any level. For example, money from the Rice County DFL and the House DFL Caucus counts as party money, whereas that from the Minneapolis Police Relief Association does not. In 1994 there were 378 non-party organizations that contributed $7,202,575 to Minnesota campaigns. In addition, there were 166 Democratic party organizations that contributed $538,930 to Democratic campaigns and 140 Republican party organizations that contributed $457,433 to Republican campaigns (State of Minnesota 1994).

Disclosure of Contributions and Spending

Lastly, and perhaps the most non-controversial element of campaign finance in Minnesota, are tight regulations regarding the disclosure of political contributions and expenditures. Almost everyone agrees that disclosure is a necessity for keeping the relationships between money and politics exposed. Hence in Minnesota every contribution over $100 must be documented with the contributor's name and address and be included in campaign reports submitted to the state's Ethical Practices Board (renamed in 1997 the Minnesota Campaign Finance and Public Disclosure Board). Likewise every expenditure over $100 must be documented with the recipient's name and address and be submitted to the Board. With some of these basics now explained, we can begin to look at the impact of this complicated system of campaign finance on election results.

EVALUATIONS

General Observations of Public Financing: Mixed Results

The professional literature on the public financing of elections reflects uncertainty about the effectiveness of public funding. Kenneth Mayer and John M. Wood (1995) finds Wisconsin's system failing on nearly all counts, while Donnay and Ramsden (1995) find Minnesota's system to have some merit. Earlier efforts to assess the effect of public financing also yield mixed conclusions. After surveying the literature, Herbert Alexander (1991) concluded that the various systems around the country have had only mixed success and are becoming increasingly unpopular with voters and taxpayers. Sorauf's review of the literature led him to conclude, "[The complexity of the subject defeats all but the experts, and even they do not easily come to consensus judgments" (1992: 157). While conclusions about the overall effectiveness of public financing can be only tentative at best, there is growing recognition that systems of public finance vary dramatically from one another and so does their effectiveness. Minnesota's system of public finance for its state legislative elections, despite the sometimes less than pure motives of its creators, shows some promise for making elections more competitive.

The Importance of Money and Where It Comes From

As challengers are able to spend more they are able to pull down the incumbent's share of the vote. Challenger spending in Minnesota House elections explains over 40 percent of the variance in the incumbent's share of the vote. The same pattern is evident in Senate elections although the picture is not quite as strong as in House elections. There is always a complicated mix of things going on in any individual campaign, and there is important research about what kinds of challengers seem to get money to spend (Herrnson, 1996; Jacobson, 1992). Nonetheless, it is hard to refute the basic point that challengers need money to wage effective campaigns.

The challenge for a system of campaign finance is to achieve some semblance of financial viability for challengers. It is difficult to find a way to support challengers financially in an environment where so many potential contributors would prefer to back incumbents. At the moment, there exists a vicious circle: incumbents attract more money because they are most likely to win and because most special interests want access to lawmakers, and because they attract more money, they are still even more likely to win. The only way for challengers to escape this "Catch-22" is for them to get enough money and momentum in their campaigns to convince potential donors of their viability and chance at winning the election. Getting to that threshold is a significant barrier to many candidacies. Designing an equitable and constitutional campaign finance system that enables challengers to achieving this threshold is a complicated policy task. Some elements of the Minnesota system accomplish this goal, some work against it.

In Table 2 we learn that incumbents in Minnesota's legislative elections have considerable financial advantage over challengers. In both the House and the Senate incumbents have received approximately 65 percent of the total contributions. Put crudely that means incumbents get roughly two dollars for every dollar a challenger is able to raise. Of course this situation is not unique to Minnesota. What is unusual, however, is that this state of affairs exists despite Minnesota's system of public financing. While public financing does put important campaign money in the hands of challengers, it also gives a lot to incumbents. Table 2 also confirms the significant advantage incumbents have in contributions from PACs and individuals. In both the House and Senate elections, approximately 70 percent of PAC and individual money went to incumbents, and only 30 percent to challengers.

		TABLE 2		
		Campaign Finance Sources		
	Candidates for the Minnesota House of Representatives: 1980-1994			
Actual Dollars	*Public Subsidy*	*Political parties*	*Individuals, Groups, and PACs*	*Total*
Challengers	2,300,548	991,167	5,078,252	8,369,967
Incumbents	3,173,376	717,608	11,597,094	15,448,078
Total	5,473,924	1,708,775	16,675,346	23,858,045
Constant 1994 Dollars				
Challengers	2,767,311	1,298,439	6,332,846	10,515,955
Incumbents	3,820,835	951,015	14,559,568	19,469,964
Total	6,588,146	2,249,454	20,892,414	30,012,889
Means				
Challengers	4,386	2,019	10,100	16,457
Incumbents	5,344	1,321	20,478	27,117
Range				
Challengers	0-11,687	0-8,670	0-64,632	0-69,286
Incumbents	0-21,227	0-6,746	0-290,444	3,974-299,979
Standard Deviation				
Challengers	2,569	1,756	8,418	9,425
Incumbents	3,273	1,576	14,631	14,704

TABLE 2 (con't)				
Candidates for the Minnesota Senate: 1980-1994				
Actual Dollars	*Public Subsidy*	*Political parties*	*Individuals, Groups, and PACs*	*Total*
Challengers	865,134	397,052	2,041,321	3,303,507
Incumbents	1,274,827	245,619	4,821,770	6,342,216
Total	2,139,961	642,671	6,863,091	9,645,723
Constant 1994 Dollars				
Challengers	1,091,667	585,550	2,769,537	4,434,312
Incumbents	1,608,445	364,352	6,343,569	8,343,049
Total	2,700,112	949,902	9,113,106	12,777,361
Means				
Challengers	7,182	3,778	18,464	29,173
Incumbents	9,808	2,169	38,918	50,872
Range				
Challengers	0-23,908	0-20,596	0-235,430	0-235,429
Incumbents	0-35,312	0-13,493	7,407-316,591	15,865-327,010
Standard Deviation				
Challengers	5,307	4,021	24,185	24,840
Incumbents	7,269	3,259	29,887	14,869
Note: Excluded are open seat races and, because of redistricting, all races from 1982 and 1992				
Sources: Data collected by authors from *Campaign Finance Summary*. State of Minnesota, 1980-1994.				

As Table 2 further indicates, between 1980 and 1994, 58 percent of the total direct public subsidy went to incumbents and only 42 percent went to challengers in House races. In the Senate 59.6 percent of public funding went to incumbents and only 40.4 percent to challengers. Meanwhile the average incumbent received $5,371 in House races and the challenger $4,392. In the Senate the disparity was even greater. The average incumbent received $9,808 and challengers only $7,182. Hence, the rule of the public subsidy system as they emerged out of the conflict in the mid 1970s — where the party account money is collected by county and party preference on tax forms, then redistributed by previous party performance — works very heavily to the advantage of incumbents.

The contributions of party organizations, unlike the public subsidies or the money coming from individuals and PACs, go disproportionately to challengers (Table 2). In House elections, 58 percent of the money from party sources went to challengers. In the Senate, 61.8 percent went to challengers. This is the only source category where challengers do better than incumbents.

The mean contribution amounts from the respective sources in Table 2 are also telling. On average, incumbents receive more from public subsidies as well as from PACs and individuals. Curiously though, both house and senate challengers received more money on average from political parties than did incumbents. This is crucial, because it shows that party organizations prioritize differently than other givers and do a better job of directing money to challengers than does Minnesota's system of public financing or other contributors. One researcher (Jones 1984: 196) explored the priorities of party leaders in state politics and found this rule of thumb for recruiting and aiding candidates; "first to provide strong competition for open seats, then create strong challengers, then support vulnerable incumbents, then support regular incumbents and finally give a token nod to the 'unwinnable' seats. In other words giving money to incumbents, especially safe ones, is a relatively low priority. This point is also made by Loftus (1994). Importantly, this is exactly the opposite of the preferences of individual donors and organized interests, and it suggests that a significant role for political parties in campaign finance would be sound policy.

Competitiveness

Perhaps the most important test of a system of campaign finance is whether it helps to create more competitive campaigns. There are numerous ways to assess competitiveness and regrettably they do not all point in the same direction. One seemingly simple way to determine whether Minnesota's public funded campaign system has created more competitive elections is to look at how well incumbents did before and after the advent of public financing. This analysis is presented in Table 3. Supporters of public financing will not be encouraged by the results in Table 3. Incumbents have tended to get a greater share of the vote in the 1980s and 1990 than the did in the years before 1976 and the beginning of public financing. The average House incumbent received 55.19 percent of the vote before public financing in 1976, and 60.86 percent of the vote since then. This is an increase of over 5 percent. In the Senate the increase was nearly 4 percent.

Unfortunately, however, for those who are looking for simple answers there are likely to be other explanations for why incumbents have increased their share of the vote over these years. For example Squire (1992) has pointed out that state legislators are gaining the tools of professionalism — acquiring more staff, putting in more time, and thinking of politics as a career. Or perhaps the dramatic party realignment that occurred in Minnesota in the early 1970s contributed to incumbents receiving a lesser share of the vote during that time than in later years.

All of these developments among others could be part of the explanation for incumbents receiving an increased share of the vote. These possible alternatives complicate a simple before and after test such as Table 3. Consequently, more sophisticated studies of the

TABLE 3				
Average Vote Share for Incumbents in Minnesota State Legislative Elections, 1966-96				
	State House		*State Senate*	
Election Year	*Average Vote Share*	*Number of Incumbents*	*Average Vote Share*	*Number of Incumbents[a]*
1966[b]			56.37	35
1968	54.05	90		
1970	53.20	85	57.53	49
1974	58.22	90		
1976	63.10	103	60.78	48
1978	56.31	110		
1980	61.80	94	60.55	45
1984	57.58	117		
1986	60.02	120	61.31	60
1988	63.51	120		
1990	63.81	120	61.10	53
1994	59.42	106		
1996	62.23	106	61.14	56
All Years	59.43		59.83	
Before Public Financing (1976-96)	55.19		57.05	
After Public Financing (1976-96)	60.86		61.00	

TABLE 3 (con't)
[a] Incumbents who ran unopposed are excluded from the analysis.
[B] In 1966 House elections are not included because redistricting in 1965 altered the labeling of House legislative districts. Redistricting also reduced the number of incumbents running in unchanged Senate districts.
The years 1972, 1982, and 1992 are excluded because redistricting significantly altered district boundaries.
The difference between average incumbent vote shares before and after public financing is significant at the .05 level in both the House (T=-6.78, p<.0000) and the senate (T=-3.11, p<.001).
Source: Authors own data.

competitive success of the Minnesota system have been done. One of these studies (Donnay and Ramsden, 1995), through the use of various statistical techniques, finds that the public subsidy in Minnesota is very important in moving challengers to the viability threshold that is so important in the early stages of a campaign. Every dollar of public subsidy moves a challenger closer to competitiveness with an incumbent. This study also finds, however, that incumbents benefit significantly from their generous public subsidies as well their advantages in attracting money from PACs and individuals. So while public subsidies are important for challengers, Donnay and Ramsden conclude that it is unfortunate so much of the public subsidy goes to incumbents. In their view, the Minnesota system shows much promise but needs to address the incumbent friendly design of the public subsidy mechanism (Donnay and Ramsden, 1995; 1996).

Another study that is statistically more accessible is a recent comparison of the Minnesota and Wisconsin system done by Kenneth Mayer (1997). Wisconsin has a much less comprehensive and far less generous system of publicly financing elections. And according to Mayer, compared to Wisconsin's system, Minnesota's campaign finance system is doing much to create more competitive elections.

A summary of Mayer's findings is presented in Table 4. Table 4 reveals that Minnesota's campaign finance system has been successful in dramatically reducing the number of incumbents who go unopposed. Only 7.8 percent of Minnesota incumbents went unchallenged in 1996 compared to nearly one-third of Wisconsin legislators having that luxury. Likewise Wisconsin legislators are far more likely to have only weak challengers. Nearly 80 percent of Wisconsin legislators get over 60 percent of the vote in their elections. In Minnesota the comparable number is around 33 percent. Minnesota incumbents tend on average to get a lower share of the vote in contested races and the re-election rate of Minnesota Representatives is consistently lower than those in Wisconsin.

The results in Table 4 offer convincing evidence that Minnesota's system of campaign finance creates more electoral competition than exists in Wisconsin's system. It provides further evidence that the systems for publicly financing elections can have very different designs and corresponding results. We can conclude from Table 4 that the combined elements of Minnesota's campaign finance create an environment in which viable candidates can emerge to successfully challenge incumbent legislators. In particular, challengers are encouraged to enter the electoral contest because they are guaranteed a significant sum of money through the public subsidy program, and they can add to this sum relatively easily with the Contribution Refund Program. And further, incumbent legislators will be held to rather constraining spending limits if they accept the attractive public subsidy agreement. The interaction of the subsidies and the spending limits works to encourage electoral competition while lessening the importance of money in Minnesota politics.

CONCLUSION

Money in the hands of challengers helps their electoral prospects. Public subsidies have the potential to equalize campaign resources, and the Minnesota model moves towards achieving that

TABLE 4		
Competitive Legislative Elections, 1990-96 **Comparing Minnesota and Wisconsin**		
Percent of Incumbents Unopposed, Lower House		
Year	*Wisconsin*	*Minnesota*
1996	32.6%	7.8%
1994	51.1	10.5
1992	44.3	8.5
1990	43.0	16.8
Percent of Incumbents in Non-Competitive Races (>60% of vote)		
1996	78.3%	N/A
1994	78.9	33.3%
1992	75.9	30.6
1990	78.2	40.3
Average Incumbent Vote Share, Contested Races		
1996	62.6%	N/A
1994	61.9	58.8%
1992	61.0	58.1
1990	63.5	60.2
Incumbent Re-election Rate, Lower House		
1996	96.7%	94.8%
1994	96.7	90.4
1992	96.2	91.5
1990	97.7	92.4
Source: Mayer, 1997.		

goal. Several studies document the promise of generous and equitable public financing. Minnesota's system of public financing would be greatly improved if it stopped using district location and previous performance as its criteria for allocating funds. Money from political parties also has the potential to make elections more competitive. So too does the Contribution Refund Program.

We think that political parties ought to be a central part of any campaign finance system — if only because the priority they assign to winning elections makes them more inclined to support challengers, and less inclined to funnel money to secure incumbents. Admittedly, giving parties a greater role in campaign finance may not be politically popular, but such a move would enhance competitiveness, and by implication, the democratic process. Such a reform might also produce stronger and more unified parties. If party leaders controlled a significant chunk of campaign money, they could use it to discipline their candidates, and enforce a coherent party platform. Candidates would no longer be quite so beholden to special interests, and candidates would no longer have to spend all their free time fund raising. All these changes, we think, would improve a system that despite its partisan history, actually does make legislative elections in Minnesota more competitive.

REFERENCES

"58 Percent Surveyed Think Nixon Broke Oath of Office." 1974. (March 10). *Minneapolis Tribune*: A1.

Ackerberg, P. 1974. (February 13). "Challengers May Get Vote Edge." *Minneapolis Star:* C12.

Alexander, Herbert E. 1991. *Reform and Reality: The Financing of State and Local Campaigns*. New York, NY: Twentieth Century Fund Press.

Bang v. Chase (1977). D.C., 442 F. Supp. 758, affirmed 98 S. Ct. 2840. U.S. Supreme Court decision is listed as *Bang v. Noreen*, 436 U.S. 1 (1978).

Coffman, Jack B. and Thomas J. Collins. 1992. (April). *Bankrolling the Legislature*. Special reprint section of the St. Paul Pioneer Press.

Donnay, P. and Graham Ramsden. 1996. *Party Money and Public Money in Minnesota Campaigns: Making Elections Competitive*. Paper presented at the 1996 meeting of the Midwest Political Science Association.

_____. 1995. "The Public Financing of Legislative Elections: Lessons from Minnesota." *Legislative Studies Quarterly*. Volume 20: 351-364.

Dornfield, S. 1974. (March 10). "State Disclosure, Public Funding Bill Passes Senate." *Minneapolis Tribune:* A1.

Gieske, M. 1977. "Minnesota in Midpassage: A Century of Transition in Political Culture." In Millard Gieske and Edward Brandt, eds. *Perspectives on Minnesota Government and Politics*. Dubuque, IA: Kendall/Hunt. Pp. 1-30.

Herrnson, Paul S. (1996). *Congressional Elections: Campaigning at Home and in Washington*. Washington, DC: Congressional Quarterly Press.

"IR Donations to Statewide Candidates Tripled DFL's." 1983. (May 12). *Minneapolis Star and Tribune:* 8b.

Jacobson, Gary C. 1992. *The Politics of Congressional Elections*. 3rd Edition. New York, NY: Harper Collins.

Jones, Ruth S. 1984. "Financing State Elections." In Michael Malbin, ed. *Money and Politics in the United States*. New Jersey: Chatham House. Pp. 172-213.

Jones, Ruth S. and Thomas J. Borris. 1985. "Strategic Contributing in Legislative Campaigns: The Case of Minnesota." *Legislative Studies Quarterly*. Volume 10: 89-105.

Kunkel, Joseph A. 1993. "Political Parties in Minnesota." In Carolyn Shrewsbury and Homer Williamson, eds. *Perspectives on Minnesota Government and Politics*. 3rd Edition. Edina, MN: Burgess Publishing Company. Pp. 109-126.

Loftus, Tom. 1994. *The Art of Legislative Politics*. Washington, DC: Congressional Quarterly.

Mayer, Kenneth. 1997. *Campaign Finance Reform in the States*. http://ps.polisci.wisc.edu/`kmayer/campaign.htm.

Mayer, Kenneth and John M. Wood. 1995. "The Impact of Public Financing on Legislative Competitiveness: The Case of Wisconsin, 1964-1990." *Legislative Studies Quarterly*. Volume 20: 69-88.

Phelps, D. 1978. (February 17). "DFLers Guide Bill Through Senate to Repair Campaign-Financing Law." *Minneapolis Tribune*: B2.

Pinney, G. 1990. (August 30). "DFL Shows Hypocrisy in Raising Funds, IRs Claim." *Minneapolis Star Tribune*: 1B.

_____. 1988. (July 4). "House Campaign Sources Shifting." *Minneapolis Star Tribune*: 3B.

"Republicans Benefit Most from Campaign Refund Program. 1997. (August 3). *The Pioneer*: 16A.

Salisbury, B. 1985. (April 23). "House Votes to Scrap Public Campaign Fund." *St. Paul Pioneer Press*: C1.

_____. 1980a. (April 13). "Referendum Bill Approved." *St. Paul Pioneer Press*: M1.

_____. 1980b. (April 9). "DFL Tries Squeeze Play to Raise Campaign Limits." *St. Paul Pioneer Press*: 14.

"Senate Overrides Veto of Bill on Campaign Funds." 1980. (March 21). *Minneapolis Tribune*: B2.

Shellum, B. 1974. (February 8). "GOP Senators Criticize $1 Campaign Check-off." *Minneapolis Tribune*: 2B.

Smith, D. 1993a. (May 12). "Carlson Vetoes Campaign Reform." *Minneapolis Star Tribune*: B1.

_____. 1993b. (May 9). "Demands for Campaign Reform Proving to be Just Empty Rhetoric." *Minneapolis Star Tribune*: B1.

Sorauf, Frank J. 1992. *Inside Campaign Finance: Myths and Realities*. New Haven, CT: Yale University Press.

Squire, Peverill. 1992. "The Theory of Legislative Institutionalization and the California Assembly." *Journal of Politics*. Volume 54:1026-1054.

State of Minnesota. Ethical Practices Board. 1980-1994. *Campaign Finance Summary*. St. Paul, MN: Ethical Practices Board (now called the Minnesota Campaign Finance and Public Disclosure Board).

State of Minnesota. Secretary of State Election Division 1980-1994. *Legislative Manual*. St. Paul, MN: Author.

Sturdevant, L. 1984. (May 4). "$100,000 IR Campaign Fund Far Outweighs DFL's." *Minneapolis Star Tribune*: B3.

Talle, J. 1973. (May 4). "Campaign-bill Tempers Rise." *Minneapolis Star*: 14B.

Wilson, B. 1988. (March 2). "Campaign Finance Check-off Confuses 80% of Taxpayers." *Minneapolis Star Tribune*: B4.

_____ 1985. (August 6). "AFL-CIO Top State Political Contributor." *Minneapolis Star Tribune*: 8C.

_____. 1982. (September 26). "PACs Giving More Money This Year." *Minneapolis Star Tribune*: A1.

_____. 1978 (January 4). "IR wants $1 Check-off Donations Shared Evenly." *Minneapolis Star*: A19.

Zack, M. 1986. (September 6). "Suit Says IR Fund-Raisers Violated Law." *Minneapolis Star Tribune*: B3.

Chapter 8

CONDUCTING ELECTIONS IN MINNESOTA[1]

Charles H. Backstrom
University of Minnesota/Twin Cities

INTRODUCTION

The fundamental criterion of democracy is that the government be answerable to the people. The goal of democracy is easy to state, but it is not easy to achieve. While various means are available to keep government officials aware of popular desires, the ultimate sanction is periodic elections. The people then have the opportunity to decide who should be installed in a given office and, later, whether that person should be continued in office for subsequent terms. Minnesota spends a good deal of time and effort in its election processes. Perhaps 20,000 Minnesotans serve in elected office at any one time, counting all levels of government. It costs approximately $3 million per year to choose them.

State law regulates all election aspects, some in excruciating detail. In part these regulations seek to keep elected officials answerable to the voters through a fair, accurate process. But, as in

---

[1] The author is solely responsible for the content, but wishes to thank Joe Mansky, Director of Elections in the office of Secretary of State, for assistance with this and many other projects.

sports, where the rules of the game actually favor persons with one kind of skill over another, election laws are not really neutral. They affect how much power certain kinds of people and particular political interests can exert. Thus election rules and practices are worthy of political science study.

This chapter begins with basic election structures (terms of office, election districts). Then it covers nominations and elections for special situations (local government and issue voting). Election mechanics (voting methods and ballot structure) and election administration may seem esoteric, but they do structure choicemaking. At many points in the chapter we discuss how the system of elections both shapes and is influenced by Minnesota government and politics.

BASIC ELECTION STRUCTURES

Both term lengths and district configurations affect political power. Term lengths differ considerably from office to office both to divide power and to differentiate among constituencies. Legislators in most large legislative bodies run from geographical districts to represent discrete population groups.

Terms of Office

Minnesota holds a state general election Tuesday after the first Monday in November — thus between November 2 and 8 — every even year. Presidential elections fall in years divisible by four (such as 1996). In the other general election (sometimes called "off-year") voters choose state executive officers: governor-lieutenant governor (they run as a team just as the president-vice president), secretary of state, treasurer, auditor, and attorney general.

Different lengths of terms for other offices, however, blur the neat division between timing for national and state elections. United States senators have six-year terms, and thus one of the state's two senators normally runs for office two elections out of three. If a senator resigns, the governor appoints someone to fill the vacancy until the next election. At that point the voters elect someone to fill the remainder of the original six-year term, keeping Minnesota's seats on schedule. Resignation or death can result in having both senate seats up for election in the same year, as occurred in 1978.

United States congressmen and Minnesota state representatives, with two-year terms, must all stand in each general election, thus being contemporaneous with president one year and governor two years later. Minnesota state senators have four-year terms. Because they never divided themselves into two classes as the state constitution intended, they are all elected together.   Without redistricting requirements they could always run in off-year elections. Since legislative seats must be redistricted after each decennial United States census to restore nearly equal population, however, state senators had to run in 1992 although they had been elected just two years before. They were then back on the presidential year schedule until the post-2000 census reapportionment gives them another two-year term.   That change will place senators on an off-year schedule until the end of another decade. If an incumbent vacates a legislative or congressional seat, and a legislative or congressional session will be held before the next general election, the state holds a special election in that district.

Length of terms can affect the results of elections. The presence of highly visible candidates, such as for U.S. president, on the ballot substantially increases election turnout and therefore presents a somewhat different electorate than in off-years. The particular appeal of certain of these candidates and the ideological tinge of their campaigns may also differentiate turnout. This may affect the election of other candidates far down the ticket. Elected officials with longer terms are believed to be more free to choose positions on difficult issues early in their term, because they will not have to face the voters again right away. Thus Minnesota state senators are somewhat more insulated from opinion pressures than Minnesota house members.

Minnesota judges serve a six-year term. Deaths and resignations seldom come at the end of judicial terms, so most judges initially take office by virtue of being appointed by the governor. They then run for the first time at the next election that falls more than a year from the interim appointment, and then at six-year intervals thereafter.

County commissioners serve four-year terms, some expiring in one general election year and some in the other. Voters select county "row offices," such as sheriff and county attorney, and often auditor, treasurer, recorder, and even coroner, assessor and surveyor, in the off-year for four-year terms.

Redistricting

Officials other than those elected statewide run in geographical areas called districts. Each decade, after the United States census, states are apportioned a certain number of congressmen based on the state population as compared to that of other states. In the last decade Minnesota grew faster than adjacent states, but not as fast as the nation as a whole. Minnesota had lost a congressional seat in 1930, and another in 1960, decreasing the state total to eight. It barely kept this number after 1990.

Even with the same number of seats, uneven population growth around the state meant that the congressional district lines had to be redrawn to correct the 55 percent disparity between the largest district (Third — west metro) to the smallest (Second — southwest Minnesota). The courts require that districts be as equal as possible, with differences of only one person in more than half a million. Redrawing of congressional lines is the job of the state legislature and governor through a regular statute. In 1991, however, the governor vetoed the legislature's plan, so the United States District court drew the boundaries. This was a repeat of events of the previous decade, when the state house and senate disagreed on how to do the job, and the court had to draw the districts. At that time the judges then departed radically from the previous districting scheme. Before, the legislature had kept five of the eight districts mostly rural, and three metropolitan. Since half the population of the state was in the metropolitan area, four of the "rural" districts had to extend into the metropolitan area to get enough population. The federal court instead took the Sixth district from central Minnesota and made it a north and east suburban district, giving a "four-and-four" plan. The federal court in 1992 continued this arrangement by imposing only minimum boundary adjustments among the other districts in order to make the populations equal.

The legislature is also supposed to redistrict its own seats. The Minnesota state constitution has always required population equality among both senate and house districts. The constitution even mandated an interim state census to redesign the seats between United States censuses, although this was never done. Urban areas of the state began rapid growth in the 1900s. Rural interests, wanting to keep control of the legislature, simply ignored the mandate of the constitution and failed to redistrict the state after the 1920, 1930, 1940, or 1950 censuses. In 1959 a suit was brought in Federal Court in Minnesota, contending that the legislature's inaction violated the Fourteenth Amendment's "equal protection of the laws" stricture. The Court agreed, and ordered the legislature to redistrict, which it did. Because the legislature complied, the case was not appealed to the U.S. Supreme Court, leaving another state — Tennessee — to make judicial history later with a similar successful challenge.

The legislature used 1950 census data, and did not strive for exactitude. Since the new districts did not go into effect until 1962, Minnesota was open for another suit after the U.S. Supreme Court defined "one person/one vote" as the standard. After Governor Karl Rolvaag had vetoed a new effort of the legislature that left one district twice as large as another, the federal district court drew new districts for 1966. In 1971 under pressure of another suit the legislature and governor successfully drew a plan. In 1981, however, failure of the legislature and governor to come to an agreement meant that the federal court had to draw the districts again.

Further complications ensued in 1991, when the DFL-controlled legislature passed a plan. Republican Governor Arne Carlson vetoed it, but he failed to get the message on that (and thirteen other measures) back to the legislature on time. A state court judicial panel ordered the legislative redistricting act into effect, while correcting some drafting errors. In the meantime Republicans brought a suit in federal district court. This court issued a plan of its own, saying there was no valid state plan. The legislature appealed to the U.S. Supreme Court, which temporarily voided the federal court intervention and allowed the state plan to be used for 1992. The full Supreme Court ultimately ruled that the federal district court must give preference to a valid state-drawn plan, if it meets judicial guidelines, before taking on the job themselves. Thus the legislature-drawn redistricting plan went into effect for 1992. For congressional seats, which the legislature had not finished redistricting before adjourning, the federal court drew a plan that was used for 1992. But when the legislature did pass a plan of its own, the U.S. Supreme court ordered that it superseded the federal court plan. It went into effect for 1994 and subsequent elections in the decade.

In contrast to congressional redistricting, population-equality guidelines are not quite as strict for state legislative districts. State districts typically aim for a maximum plus or minus 2 percent deviation from ideal size. The net result of several decades of court-ordered redistricting has been the continued geographical expansion of district size in Greater Minnesota where population has fallen. Conversely, the growing outer ring of metropolitan suburbs gains new seats. The effect of redistricting is that when some areas of the state are in economic decline, they cannot hold their population, so they also lose political power to effect state policies they need.

Besides keeping the numbers of constituents each member represents nearly equal, redistricting can impact the election possibilities of individual members and have broader partisan consequences. Changing the boundaries of a district can give sitting members substantial numbers of new constituents not familiar with their names, making their campaigns more difficult, or even throwing two incumbents into the same district. Also, parties may engage in gerrymandering. This involves the party in control of the legislature at redistricting time designing a plan that concentrates or spreads their supporters into adjacent districts in such a way to advantage more of their own candidates.

NOMINATIONS

In early state history, Minnesota political party organizations controlled which candidates ran under the party banner in the general election. Party activists exercised this control through conventions limited to party members. Reaction against this party control in the early twentieth century resulted in state laws that gave voters more direct control over the nomination process, through primary elections.

Primary Elections

Before each general election the state holds a primary election the Tuesday after the second Monday of September, thus falling between September 9 and 15. A primary is an elimination contest to get the number of candidates down, usually to two, a number insuring that the winner of the general election will likely be the choice of the majority.

Candidates for U. S. Senate, U. S. House of Representatives, state constitutional officers, and legislators are designated by party on the general election ballot. Their names go on the partisan primary ballot. The plurality of voters choosing to vote in a party's primary pick one person for each office to bear that party's label on the general election ballot. Thus the voters officially nominate that candidate.

State endorsements

Major parties in Minnesota commonly "endorse" candidates for their party's nomination. Convention delegates at the appropriate level — legislative district, congressional district, or state — vote on the endorsement. The law does not recognize this designation; therefore no indication of endorsement appears on the primary ballot. Parties must communicate their recommendation by other means, such as a party produced "sample ballot" listing the endorsees' names. If an unendorsed candidate wins the primary he or she becomes the official nominee of that party and bears its label in the general election. This happened in gubernatorial primaries in both parties in 1982, when Rudy Perpich beat Democratic-Farmer Labor-endorsed Warren Spannaus and Wheelock Whitney beat Republican-endorsed Lou Wangberg, and in 1994 when Arne Carlson beat Republican-endorsed Allen Quist.

State primaries

No test exists for voters' party "membership" before being allowed to vote in a party's September primary. Voters do not register by party at the polling place, and do not have to state their party choice at the polls to get access to the proper ballot. In the privacy of the voting booth, the voter decides in which party's primary, if any, he or she wishes to participate. All the candidates for nomination of one party are listed in a single column, however, and a voter must pick only among candidates for the nomination of one party. This restriction is based on the reasoning that only those who have some kind of commitment to a party should have anything to say about who will bear its banner in the coming election. Since nothing stops voters who identify with one party from crossing over to vote in the primary of another party for all offices, however, Minnesota is said to have an "open primary." Party activists often blame the defeat of their endorsed candidate on such crossing over, although proving this is difficult.

It is generally argued that the open primary weakens political parties. But one could make the case that without the advantage of a ballot label the parties must become even stronger organizationally to try to control their nominations.   Also, the effort factional candidates must put in to draw in all possible supporters ultimately increases the pool of party voters.

The lateness of the primary impacts the chances of certain candidates. Formerly the primary was in June. If there was a factional fight in the primary, there was time for wounds to heal before the general election five months later. During the era of great party strength that suppressed challengers to endorsed candidates, the primary was moved to September, when it was hoped vacations would be over, and more people would be likely to vote. Now, however, there are only seven or eight weeks to try to heal serious factional splits, stirring sentiment to move the primary to earlier in the year.

To try to strengthen the parties, a recent study commission on elections recommended that the names of several endorsed candidates be automatically placed on the ballot, with their endorsement so indicated. Other prospective candidates would face greater barriers to ballot access. The public's ambivalence toward parties appears to foreclose such change.

A primary is held only for those parties getting at least 5 percent of the vote in the last general election, which means that most of the time only the DFL and Republican parties have primaries. But in 1976 Paul Helm, the American party's candidate for United States senate, received 6 percent of the votes, and therefore the American party had a column on the primary ballot in 1978. In the general election of that year, their candidate for state treasurer received 5.7 percent of the vote, so the American party was entitled to have a primary column in 1980. In that year, however, there were no statewide offices open, and the American party fielded only one candidate for Congress in the Eighth district. Since this person received less than 10 percent of the previous American party vote, he was not certified to run in the general election. Without any candidates in the 1980 general election, therefore, the American party lost its primary ballot column for the next year. In 1994 the U.S. senate candidate of the Independence party (Dean Barkley), who filed by petition, received 5 percent of the vote. This qualified them as a major party for 1996. They changed their name to Reform to indicate connection with Ross Perot's presidential campaign in 1996. They once again qualified as a major party for the next election by receiving more than 5 percent of the vote in the presidential and U.S. senate contests.

If only one candidate files for a party-designated office, the name appears on the primary ballot anyway, apparently to find out if party voters approve. In this case, no write-ins are permitted. Each candidate getting a plurality wins the party's nomination. A losing candidate for one of the major parties cannot later file with some other party designation or as an independent in the general election — called a "sore loser" law.

If a partisan primary winner dies or withdraws, the appropriate party committee is supposed to designate a new party candidate for the general election. In 1990, however, John Grunseth, the Republican party endorsee and nominee, withdrew as a candidate for governor after facing charges of personal impropriety. Party officials asserted that they could not legally convene their state central committee in time to select a new nominee. The Minnesota Supreme Court then declared Arne Carlson, the runner up in the Republican primary, to be the party's candidate in the general election.

On primary election day, a "nonpartisan" primary election is also held for the offices without party designation, such as judicial and county offices. Here the primary eliminates all but two candidates for a single office. If no more than two candidates file, their names do not appear on the primary ballot, but go directly onto the general election ballot. If a nonpartisan primary winner vacates, the next highest candidate in the primary becomes the nominee.

To get a place on the primary ballot (or directly on the general ballot if no primary is to be held), candidates must file with the secretary of state if they run in more than one county. Otherwise they file with the county auditor.

A candidate can file in only one party. This usually means one of the two major parties. People with views not accommodated by the major parties oppose this legal duopoly. They can of course form a third party of their own liking, but this is a long shot. Recently a third party's supporters sued to allow them also to endorse the candidate of a major party, known officially as "simultaneous" nomination or popularly as "fusion".

In 1996 the U.S. Appeals court ruled that there was a constitutional right for fusion. The state legislature implemented this ruling by directing that to avoid confusion, a candidate's name would appear on the ballot only once, rather than separately for each party. This allowed minor parties to show their contribution to the total vote. The legislature also permitted the candidate or political party concerned to refuse the fusion. Several DFL candidates refused fusion in 1996. In 1997 the U.S. Supreme Court overturned the Appeals Court, ruling that to protect the integrity of parties, the state could after all prohibit fusion. Thus, the present system inhibits the growth of third parties.

Candidate qualifications

Candidates must be at least 21 years of age (25 years for governor or U.S. representative, and 30 years for U.S. senator) by the time they take office, and must reside in the district. The only test of a candidate's party membership is that they must have participated in that party's precinct caucus, or intend to vote for that party's candidates in the next election. This minimal test allows for party switching between one election and the next.

Candidates pay "filing fees" of $50 for county office, $100 for legislature, $300 for state offices and United States representative, and $400 for United States senator. A candidate who wishes can instead file by petition, which requires 500 signatures for the legislature or county office, 1,000 for congress, and 2,000 for statewide office. Candidates who change their mind after filing can withdraw within three days after filings close, but after that their name stays on the primary ballot. After the primary a candidate for a constitutional office may withdraw no later than 16 days before the general election.

Minor parties get their candidates put directly on the general election ballot by "petitions" bearing like numbers of voters and signatures, as do candidates not affiliated with a party but merely specifying a political principle. A court ruling allowed the use of the word "independent" by such candidates despite a party name-protection statute that would seem to restrict the use of that word to the Independent-Republicans of Minnesota, the name used by the GOP from 1976 to 1994. Some independent candidates believe that not being on the primary ballot is a publicity disadvantage, and confuses their supporters.

Presidential nominations

The national political parties nominate their presidential candidates at a national convention, not a primary. Each national party allocates a number of delegate slots to the state, based on how many electoral votes the state has, whether the state was carried by that party in the last election, and (in the case of the Democrats) how many total votes were cast for the party in the last election.

Minnesota parties choose their delegates to national conventions at congressional district and state conventions. This process starts with the precinct caucuses, held the first Tuesday in March. Caucus attendees choose delegates, in the Republican party by majority rule (if there is a contest), and the Democrats proportionate to the number present who support each presidential candidate. These delegates go to the county-unit conventions, which use the same process to select people who will serve as delegates for both the congressional and state conventions. The congressional district convention elects most of delegates to the national convention, with the remaining at-large delegates elected at the state convention.

Most states now have a presidential preference primary that influences in some way the choice of national convention delegates. Various participants have urged that Minnesota change to a presidential primary.

Minnesota had presidential primaries before, in 1916, in 1952-56, and in 1992. In the 1950s former governor Harold Stassen thought a certain win in Minnesota the week before the Wisconsin primary would propel him to the Republican nomination. A write-in campaign for Dwight Eisenhower did not top Stassen, but the 100,000 votes won the publicity battle. Regular Republicans blamed independents and crossovers of Democrats for their embarrassment. Four years later the tables were reversed. Eisenhower had no contest on the Republican side; on the DFL side challenger Estes Kefauver beat Adlai Stevenson, whom Hubert Humphrey and other party leaders were backing. Disgruntled leaders from both parties thereupon repealed the primary.

But pressures to join the now-typical state process continued, and the state legislature mandated that the state hold a presidential preference primary in April, 1992. Most DFL party leaders did not want the presidential primary reinstituted in Minnesota. But Republican legislators wishing to dilute the influence of the religious right in their caucuses were joined in support of the measure by DFL legislators. It passed in the last days of the legislative session without even a committee hearing.

Many states use a primary to elect the actual delegates who will go to the national convention, but in 1992 in Minnesota the primary was not for choosing delegates. This was still to be done by the caucus/convention system. The presidential primary was supposed only to determine relative support for various candidates within the party. The party at its convention would use the primary figures to apportion the delegates. For example, in the Republican party George Bush got 64 percent of the votes in the primary, and so got 22 of the 32 delegates; Pat Buchanan got 24 percent of the votes, and got 8 delegates; Harold Stassen and uncommitted got 3 percent of the votes and 1 delegate each. Observers reported that some of the delegates elected for Buchanan actually did not wish to vote for him.

In the DFL caucuses Tom Harkin won about 27 percent of the delegates, Paul Tsongas 19 percent, Bill Clinton 10 percent, Jerry Brown 8 percent, Bob Kerrey 7 percent, and 28 percent were uncommitted. After the DFL primary a month later, the secretary of state certified that Bill Clinton with just over 31 percent of the votes was entitled to 29 of the 87 delegates; Jerry Brown with just under 31 percent, 28; Paul Tsongas with 21 percent, 20; Tom Harkin and Ross Perot 2 percent each, 2 each; Eugene McCarthy under 2 percent, 1; and "uncommitted" 6 percent, 5. The DFL, however, had decided not to use the primary results to allocate their delegates, instead allocating them by the process they had always used. This procedure allocated delegates proportionately to the number of delegates pledged to the several candidates that made it to the congressional district and state conventions. Following this method, the DFL sent to the national convention 92 delegates, including 13 percent for Clinton and 5 percent for Brown, while 82 percent were uncommitted. (At the convention, however, the delegates voted 66 percent for Clinton, 11 percent for Robert Casey, 9 percent each for Brown and Pat Schroeder, 2 percent each for Tsongas and Larry Agran, with 1 percent uncommitted.) The DFL could get away with defying the state presidential primary law because the U.S. Supreme Court has ruled a number of times in recent years that political parties are private organizations that can follow their own procedures, although the specifics of the Minnesota presidential primary law have not been tested.

A unique aspect of the presidential primary law was that potential voters had to ask for the ballot of the party in whose primary they wished to vote, and the voter registration file records this party choice. This is a "closed primary." As mentioned, this is the first time Minnesota had any kind of registration by party. Many potential voters, used to the open primary for state purposes, expressed distress over this feature. There was also no way for independents to participate without at least temporarily declaring membership in one of the two major parties. The law imposed this restriction because the national Democratic party declares that it will not seat any delegates chosen by a state unless the choice is restricted to Democrats. Party leaders also welcomed the possibility of getting lists of voters by party identification for further contact. Since only 12 percent of registered voters participated in the 1992 presidential primary, most voters' party preference is still private.

There was great dissatisfaction over the primary's "meaningless" results for the Democrats, the lack of national attention, and the minuscule turnout (although it outstripped the usual caucus attendance of less than 5 percent). The Legislature in 1995 considered requiring the parties to follow the law in order to receive state subsidies. Another proposal was to schedule the primary in March on a common date with other midwestern primaries. Instead, the legislature voted to abolish the primary, but the Governor vetoed the bill. Instead, they finally just postponed any presidential primary to after 1999. Therefore, while the law is still on the books, there was no presidential primary in 1996.

The effect of Minnesota's system is to concentrate the presidential nominee selection in relatively few, usually party-loyalist hands. These tend to be the more ideologically pure people compared to all party-identifiers among the public. This tension means that the struggle to reinstitute the presidential primary will likely continue.

Presidential Electors

The president is elected not by the people directly but by electors chosen in each state. The state political parties, therefore, each nominates slates of ten electors who vie for election at the state general election in presidential years. The electoral nominees are chosen by congressional district and state conventions, and their names filed with the secretary of state under the party and presidential and vice-presidential candidates' names. The names of the elector candidates do not appear on the ballot, but that slate is elected whose party's candidates are marked by the most voters. These ten people gather at the state Capitol in mid-December and cast their individual votes for President and Vice President. They are constitutionally free to vote for whomever they wish, but since they were selected by their party, presumably they will loyally vote for the nominee of their party. Minnesota has never had a "faithless elector," but one of the DFL elector candidates in 1972 announced that, if elected in November, he would not vote for George McGovern to be President. This intention was never tested, because the Republican electors were elected, and they all voted for Richard Nixon. Likewise in 1992 the DFL elector for the First congressional district said that he would consider voting for Independent Ross Perot if he won a plurality in that district.

SPECIAL ELECTORAL SYSTEMS

Decisionmakers sometimes find that certain elections require special treatment. Past reformers, for example, believed that national and state elections should not influence local election results. They established times for those elections different from the state. The following section considers two special cases: local elections and issue elections.

Local Elections

City Offices Elections for city office now must be held either on the same day as the state general election or in November of odd numbered years.   The largest cities hold primary elections in September.   Only Minneapolis has party designated mayors and council members. Candidates appear with the party-designation they choose. The highest two vote-getters in the primary go onto the city general election ballot, regardless of party. This can result in two DFLers facing off against each other in the general election. This was the solution devised to try to insure significant contests in the general election even in a ward overwhelmingly dominated by one party.

Other cities have no party designation, but parties can and sometimes do endorse for offices like St. Paul Mayor. Smaller cities may have a primary no later than six weeks before their general election.

Towns The 1800 governments of rural townships (not to be confused with what many people call small cities) are ruled by direct democracy.   That is, the voters hold a mass meeting the second Tuesday in March.   All people attending directly make the governmental decisions such as adopting a budget. The same day a regular ballot election chooses one or more (up to five) supervisors who act for the town during the year, and the clerk and treasurer, who have previously filed for office.

School districts Minnesota has 356 school districts, all of which are independent units of self-government in Minnesota that elect their governing boards of six or seven members. Starting in 1998 school elections are held at the same time as the city general election.

This discussion demonstrates that Minnesota places a tremendous burden on its citizens to select officials. In Minneapolis, for example, in a four-year election cycle every voter will be faced with over seventy offices to be filled, only five of which will be the same office. Turnout for separate municipal elections is far lower than for state elections, meaning a small active group is in effective control of the governments geographically closest to the citizens.

Initiative, Referendum, and Recall

About half of the states allow their citizens to enact legislation directly, that is, without going through the legislature. In a "statutory initiative", a proposition is placed on the ballot by voter petition, and if a majority of voters voting on the measures support it, it becomes law. If a state allows a "constitutional initiative," a group proposes a constitutional amendment that appears on the ballot in the exact wording suggested. Subsequent voter approval automatically amends the constitution. In a "referendum," the legislature passes a bill, but refers it to the people by putting it on the ballot to see if it meets with voter approval.

Minnesota does not have statutory or constitutional initiative. Three different times a constitutional amendment to allow statutory initiative was proposed, but it did not receive support of a majority of voters. Minnesota does, however, have constitutional referendum. The legislature proposes amendments from time to time, and they are adopted or not by a majority of all people voting at a general election — not just a majority of those voting on the question.

Home-rule cities can have initiative and referendum if their charters provide it. State law requires school districts to utilize a referendum if the school board wants to issue bonds for buildings or raise new operating revenue by increasing the tax levy beyond certain limits.

Until 1996, Minnesota allowed no recall of state officials — a special election to remove elected officials during their term. Before that, citizens could petition for recall of county officials, and of city officials where provided in about half of the home rule charters. The governor and several groups had been pressing for term limits, which legislative leaders opposed. Then, as a number of legislators were revealed to have been involved in illegal activities, legislative leaders proposed recall. A constitutional amendment approved in 1996 authorizes a group of 25 citizens to petition for removal of a statewide executive officer, legislator, or judge.

The charge can be either malfeasance or nonfeasance. Malfeasance is acting outside the official's power, or commission of a gross misdemeanor or certain misdemeanors. Nonfeasance is failure to do a required task. Note that recall cannot be pursued merely for differences over the programs an official supports. The accusation is sent to the Chief Justice of the state supreme court. If he deems the accusation proven and sufficient to warrant removal, he puts the matter before a "special master" — a sitting or retired judge — for a hearing. If the master finds the facts warrant removal, the Supreme Court can approve the petition. The petition is then circulated among voters, and if it can obtain the signatures of 25 percent of the number of voters who voted for that office, a recall election is held. If a majority of the voters agrees, the official is removed. It should be clear that the recall procedure is so burdensome that it is unlikely to see much use.

ELECTION ADMINISTRATION

As mentioned at the outset democracy is a simple idea, but it is not simple to structure and record people's wishes. A vast bureaucracy, hundreds of procedures, and extensive machinery are required to stage an election. To give the claim of democracy credibility, election procedures must be fair and accurate.

Voting Methods

Voting is done by "precinct." A precinct is simply a geographical area defined by a municipality where citizens come to vote. It is not a unit of government that elects any government officials. The whole of a rural township typically constitutes a single precinct. Likewise, all voters in a small city vote in the same place. But for voter and administrative convenience, larger municipalities divide themselves into several precincts for election administrative purposes. All voters living within the precinct boundary vote at one designated polling place, usually some public property accessible to the handicapped. If there is no suitable voting place within a precinct, the municipality designates a nearby place outside the boundaries. Votes are counted and reported by precinct. This makes it possible to study past voting patterns to guide campaign strategists.

Each municipality chooses whichever type of voting apparatus it desires. Virtually all of the cities use optical-scan systems. A machine in each precinct draws the large ballot card out from the secrecy sleeve and into the machine. The machine then reads the marks voters have placed with a pen beside the names of candidates they favor. After the polls close, the machine prints out the totals for each candidate. In some jurisdictions the machine is located at a counting center to which ballots are transported from the polling places. By 1996 such machines tabulated nearly 95 percent of the vote.

The remaining state voters cast paper ballots by marking X's in a box opposite the names of candidates they favor. Election judges must count these by hand. In a precinct of any size, this takes considerable time, annoying the news media who want instant complete results early on election night.

A voter voids his vote for an office by voting for more than one candidate per office (if only one can be elected). The optical-scan machines at the precincts reject ballots marked in this way and print out a notice of error. This allows the voter to get a substitute ballot and correct the error, unless he or she wants to vote this way. On central-count systems, the system will not count the double votes, but it is too late for the voter to correct his or her ballot.

Write-in votes for persons not on the ballot are permitted in the general election (not the primary). About 0.1 percent of the voters in the presidential election avail themselves of this opportunity, but larger numbers write in names elsewhere, especially for unopposed judicial candidates. Sometimes such votes are cast for Prince or Mickey Mouse or "none of the above."

Ballot Structure

Minnesota law requires the "office group" ballot form. This means that all candidates for president are listed first. All candidates for United States Senate appear below them, followed by all candidates for United States Representative, then those for Minnesota senate and representative, and finally all candidates for state constitutional officers. Within each office group, candidates are arranged by party, with the party whose candidates received the fewest votes in the previous general election appearing first. There is no rotation of candidate names within one office group.

Candidates on the "nonpartisan ballot" (and all party primary ballots) are supposed to be rotated. Under this method, in paper ballot precincts, the first ballot handed out would list the names for each office alphabetically, and the next ballot would have the second name first. On each subsequent ballot, the names would move up one notch. In voting machine precincts, all voting machines in a single precinct use the same name order. This decreases confusion in recording the totals from several machines at the end of the day. Instead, the names are rotated among the precincts of the city.

Between 1913 and 1973 legislative candidates were not party-designated but appeared on the nonpartisan, rotated ballot. In 1974, when legislative candidates again became party-designated, they moved back to the partisan, unrotated part of the ballot. A group of Republicans and an independent filed suit to force rotation. The trial judge ruled that evidence of bias was not sufficient to overrule a legitimate legislative desire to make it easy for voters to discover the party affiliation of candidates.

This author's research on the effects of rotation in party-designated city elections (covering mayor and council members in Minneapolis and St. Paul) showed no significant differences in positional effect. Apparently the party-identification is sufficient clue for voters to find the candidates they want no matter where they appear on the ballot. In nonparty-designated races, however, such as for county office and judgeships, voters have no cues to what frequently appear to be unfamiliar names. Ballot position appears to significantly affect election outcome, with the advantage to being first. This may be at least part of the explanation for unknown, even notorious, candidates for judgeships receiving as much as 20 percent of the vote. Ballot rotation adds administrative headaches.   In Hennepin county, for example, officials in 1992 prepared more than four hundred separate ballot designs because of the different combinations of candidates to be voted on and the requirements of rotation.

Judicial candidates run under an "alley" system. That is, each judgeship has a separate numbered slot on the ballot. A challenger for, say, the district court must file against a specific sitting judge of a specific open seat, rather than running against the entire group of district court judges up for election.   Sitting judges have the significant advantage of having the word "incumbent" beside their names.

County auditors prepare all state and county ballots. In some years the state reimbursed counties for part of the cost of this effort, but the budget crunch of the 1990s resulted in no state money going to the counties for this purpose. Municipalities understandably must pay the cost of providing ballots for their own elections, provide the polling places, and employ election judges to run the election. Thus the state election is actually conducted largely at local expense.

The present largely automated system certainly reduces the number of mistakes in vote counting. While the famous 1962 statewide recount for governor uncovered no proved fraud or dishonesty, it revealed frequent instances of sloppy procedure and technical violations of the law by election judges. And the hand-counting of votes was error prone. The elimination of the old lever machines also eliminated the problem of presenting the voters with a different ballot face. Because of space limitations, constitutional amendments were shown off to the side or on a line above the candidates. More voters missed seeing them than in paper or punch-card precincts. This excess fall-off probably resulted in the defeat of some proposed constitutional amendments that narrowly failed to receive support by a majority of all voters at the election. Ironically this occurred with the so-called "gateway amendment" in 1974 that would have changed the amending process to require a majority only of those voting on the question. Although the proposal gained 57 percent support from those voting on it, the measure failed because one out of seven voters passed up the question, making the overall approval only 49.2 percent.

Election administration and personnel

Minnesota has a somewhat decentralized election system. The secretary of state exercises responsibility for election administration, with statutory power to define and enforce legal requirements on lower units of government. The actual work is done by the 87 county auditors, usually elected and with differing administrative and clerical skills, and municipal local election judges in some 4000 precincts. The auditors prepare and distribute the ballots to the voting precincts, appoint and instruct the election judges (the largest cities do their own training), receive the vote count from the election judges, and enter the results into the statewide vote reporting system. This system prepares the official abstract of vote showing the counts certified by the county canvassing boards, as well as the statewide totals. A state canvassing board officially accepts and certifies (in effect, rubber stamps) the totals.

Election judges

To first recruit and then train at least 20,000 individuals to be efficient election judges is not easy. After all, the work is occasional, perhaps only two days every two years at a time when most capable adults now have full-time jobs. The pay is low — about $6 an hour in Hennepin County (although judges may now receive time off from work without loss of pay to serve). The work day of 16 hours is long for anyone. In some areas it is difficult to meet the requirement that no more than half the judges be of one party. County chairs of political parties are supposed to certify names for these positions, but they cannot always find sufficient volunteers.

Polls are open from 7 a.m. to 8 p.m., except in certain small non-metropolitan area townships, where the governing body can decide to open as late as 10 a.m. Any voter in line at closing time may vote. Employers must allow a worker time off in the morning to vote in state elections without pay being docked.

During the day, the election judges check the registration of those who come in, hand out ballots, receive back and deposit the paper ballots in the boxes or supervise the voter submitting his ballot to the counting machine, open and deposit absentee ballots that arrive in the mail, and register new voters. After the polls close they ascertain the number of voters, count the paper ballots (by piling all ballots by candidate), enter the totals on the summary sheets that go (in state elections) to the county auditor and secretary of state. In some optical-scan system precincts, no totaling is done at the polling place. In some jurisdictions all absentee ballots are counted centrally.

The county or state canvassing board (where a district involves more than one county) conducts an automatic recount of votes in legislative or district judge races where a precinct's vote is in "obvious error," such as a transposition of figures, or if a candidate wins by fewer than 100 votes. Other losing candidates can have a recount only if they pay the costs.   Apart from counting errors, any other disappointed candidate can contest the election in court if they believe other election statute violations occurred.

In cases alleging unfair campaign practices, the disputing legislative candidates may narrow down a list of all district court judges available until one remains to try their case. The surviving judge decides the case on the facts, but submits this finding to the legislative house, which retains its constitutional right to ultimately decide election contests. In providing a strong judicial role in the settlement of contests for legislative seats, the legislature hopes to avoid party-line caucus votes which typically result in victory for the majority caucus's candidate. The legislature thus becomes involved relatively late in the disagreement, if at all. In congressional contests the judge can make findings only on who received the most votes; other evidence must be sent to the proper house of Congress for final determination.

VOTER PARTICIPATION

States regulate voter participation in many ways. Originally the laws sought to prevent fraud. More recent reformers seek to encourage higher participation levels.

Voter eligibility

To vote in Minnesota, a person must meet the following requirements: (1) United States citizenship, (2) at least eighteen years of age, (3) 20 days residence in the precinct, (4) no felony conviction (unless rights have been restored), (5) not under guardianship or adjudged mentally incompetent. Persons in jail for misdemeanors and persons in mental hospitals by voluntary commitment may vote by absentee ballot.

Registration

State law requires registration as a prerequisite to vote. The Secretary of State maintains a statewide computerized registration system, which is accessible to county auditors who actually enter the names into the system. The secretary of state provides printed registered voter rosters for each precinct. On election day, the voter signs in and then is permitted to vote. Lists of registered voters are available to political parties, candidates for office, and federal jury selection officials. The lists cannot be used for commercial purposes.

Minnesota uses every means imaginable to facilitate registration. People can register in person or by mail in an application up to 20 days before an election. Counties provide branch locations to register voters. Party organizations and candidates are allowed to go door-to-door with applications, and even help people fill them out and return them to the county auditors. In addition, Minnesota provides for "motor voter," a blank on driver license applications for registering to vote (done before the federal requirement). Moreover, state income tax booklets include registration cards. All state and local agencies, as well as private agencies operating programs with public money, that provide services to people must actively solicit their clients to register to vote. Colleges must ask students if they desire to register as voters when paying tuition.

Beyond all this, people can register to vote at the polls on election day. In 1996 nearly 15 percent of the voters registered on election day. Prospective registrants must provide a driver's license or Minnesota identification card with the current address, or student identification card or fee statement to show that they live in that precinct. They can also have a voter who is already registered there to vouch for their residence. Within ten days after the election the county auditor must sample 3 percent of the new registrants to verify their address. The auditor must supply any evidence of wrongful voting to the county attorney for prosecution. County attorneys seldom bring such prosecutions; it would be difficult to get a felony conviction. Minnesota simply chooses to facilitate voting even at the risk of a few possible violators.

By voting at least once in four years, and not moving or having their name changed, a voter maintains permanent registration. Each year, the secretary of state removes the names of those who have not voted in four years to an "inactive" file. Registration is legally canceled by death after notification to the secretary of state by the commissioner of health or publication of obituaries. When someone moves and registers in a new precinct elsewhere in the state, officials cancel their previous registration through the statewide computer system. It is not easy to cross-check registrations, because the forms do not record social security numbers, relying only on voluntary date of birth to help in distinguishing between people with the same name. Despite these heroic efforts to ease registration only about 80 percent of the voting age population is registered.

Voting

The law also permits "absentee" voting. Formerly, a voter had to certify a reason for being unable to vote in person on election day. In 1992, however, Ramsey county was authorized to continue an experiment to let people vote by mail for any reason, to further encourage voting.

Minnesota also authorizes counties and municipalities to have everyone vote by mail on ballot questions (referenda), which might otherwise have to be presented at special elections that typically draw a very light turnout. The law also authorizes non-metropolitan cities and towns with fewer than 400 registered voters to conduct regular elections by mail. In 1996 161 precincts (out of 4000) voted by mail in the state general election.

Finally, the secretary of state proposed to conduct the new presidential primary in 1992 entirely by mail, to save local units the expense of setting up the entire election structure for an expected maximum turnout of 20 percent. The estimated $3 million cost to the state was off-putting, however, and the proposal was not enacted. Obviously provisions that allow voting by mail would reduce the assurance that people cast only their own ballot.

The result of no bureaucratic bars to voting shows up in Minnesota's turnout rate. That rate usually tops the nation in presidential years. In 1996 Minnesota was second to Maine. Slightly less than 65 percent of age-eligible people voted, compared to the national average of just below 50 percent. In off-year elections Minnesota is usually not first, but within the top five states; other factors than ease of access to the ballot motivate voters to participate in elections. Minnesota officials brag about its high participation rate, but one should not forget that fully one-third of eligible voters in Minnesota do not take part even in presidential elections.

CAMPAIGN CONDUCT

State law regulated campaign conduct minimally for many years. Over the past twenty years efforts intensified to make campaigning fair while at the same time not unduly restricting free expression.

Unfair Campaign Practices

State election laws specify some (but not all) unfair campaign practices. Provisions restrict false advertising, false claim of party support, failure to show the name of the candidate and the author on campaign literature, spreading false information about a candidate, failure to indicate when a paid advertisement is for the benefit of a particular candidate. Others prohibit material rewards, such as promising any candidate a job for running (or not running), or giving anything of value in a campaign (not even useful campaign trinkets such as refrigerator magnets or oven mitts, as are common in other states). The law no longer prohibits snack foods or beverages, after Minnesota received derisive national publicity for the indictment of a candidate who served Twinkies at a residence for the elderly. Related restrictions govern coercion, such as promising or threatening any employee with economic reprisal based upon the outcome of the election, or betting on an election to influence it.

People cannot influence voters during voting itself. The law forbids campaigning within 100 feet of a polling place, wearing political buttons to the polls, hiring people (except challengers) on election day to perform work that affects the election, having campaign materials in a car or soliciting votes from anyone while transporting them to the polls. A few regulations protect candidates; they cannot be denied access to an apartment building to campaign door-to-door, or blackmailed into charitable contributions. Using corporate contributions other than for general promotion of participation in elections is forbidden.

Some former statutory restrictions have been found to violate the U.S. or state constitutional guarantees of free speech. A state statute barring campaigning on election day, and a local ordinance banning commercially-made lawn signs provide two examples.

Limitations on campaign contributions and expenditures and public financing of election campaigns are discussed elsewhere in this book.

CONCLUSION

Election laws, intentionally or unintentionally, shape political behavior. Basic structural features such as terms of office may separate national, state, and local elections. Local option provisions that allow municipal, township and school district elections at special times promote the same end. This results in a somewhat different electorate in these elections. Voting methods speed up or slow down vote tabulation. They also occasionally affect election outcomes by influencing voter choices. Not all structural features operate as

intended. Legally the state legislature determines boundaries for both
U.S. house and state legislative districts, but partisan, personal, and
regional differences have often caused legislative deadlock, requiring
the courts to complete the actual districting process.

Informal behavior sometimes modifies legal provisions. Primary
elections narrow the general election to two candidates, attempting to
ensure the victorious office holder represents a clear majority.
Primary regulations strive to balance popular influence with party
influence over the nominees. The open primary limits official party
impact, but an extra-legal pre-primary endorsement system generally
results in a candidate acceptable to party activists. The resurrection
of the presidential primary in 1992 and the struggles over fusion
reawakened the tension between party influence and more direct voter
participation and choice.

Reacting to perceived popular cynicism over election and
declining voter turnout, reformers attempted to open up the system
through legal regulation. Minnesota utilizes most means imaginable
to facilitate turnout, including "motor voter" provisions and election
day registration. The state recently experimented with voting by mail
in some elections. Minnesota regularly ranks among the top states in
voter turnout, but large numbers of people pass up the opportunity to
participate in the most basic political process — choosing their
leaders.

REFERENCES

Minnesota Secretary of State. 1995. *Minnesota Election Laws, 1995.* St. Paul, MN: Author.

Secretary of State. *Minnesota Legislative Manual "Bluebook". 1997-98.* St. Paul, MN: Author.

Stinnett, Ronald F. and Charles H. Backstrom. 1964. *Recount.* Washington, DC: National Documents Publishers.

Chapter 9

INTEREST PERSUASION IN MINNESOTA

Craig Grau
University of Minnesota, Duluth

INTRODUCTION

The image we have of a person who articulates an interest to a maker of public policy is likely to be a lawyer in an expensive suit walking the halls of the legislative chamber. Then again, in 1996 a picture appeared in the Star Tribune ("Protests of the pocketbook," 1996) of students who gathered in Minneapolis at a rally for lower college tuition. The students had listened to speakers that included members of the state legislature. These students were lobbying as were students the following month who urged lawmakers in the state capitol to support funding for a library on their campus (Broekemeier, 1996).

In this chapter, we will examine individuals and groups who try to persuade public officials to their views. To accomplish this they may use direct contacts or indirect contacts including becoming involved in the electoral process. Concern about their undue influence in the political process has led to regulation and mandatory disclosure of activities. All of this is very important to understanding the operation of the political system in Minnesota.

WHY THE EMPHASIS ON LOBBYING?

For quite some time, those who study politics have been interested in those who try to influence public officials to their public policy preferences. Since David Truman's *Governmental Process* was first published (1951), the study of interest groups has become an important part of the study of politics. The study of those who articulate interests is not only important in identifying some very important political actors, but is crucial to an understanding of the making of public policy and the operation of each political system.

An advantage of studying the articulation of interests in Minnesota is that it increases our   understanding of those that influence the making of policies that affect our daily lives and the lives of others. We need to look no further than taxes, expenditures, standards and penalties.

The state of Minnesota raises and spends billions of dollars every two years. These actions affect every resident. The state legislature with concurrence of the governor sets income and sales tax rates. They may also consider items less familiar to us such as tax credits and local government aid. If a locality wants to raise money through a special sales tax it needs state approval as well. Taxes on specific products such as gasoline and tobacco are set by the state.

State expenditures are of many types, too many to describe here. Education, health, welfare and criminal justice are important and affect large numbers of people. Other expenditures may be as specific as a business asking for financial help. In addition the state may through a bonding process borrow money to aid building projects such as those on college campuses.

The government also sets standards of many types.   The definition of criminal activity and their penalties are set by the state government. So are standards such as those for certain professions and for high school graduation.

Because the state makes so many important decisions, a large number of people have chosen to make their views known to public officials. Indeed it is useful when examining any issue to ask which groups have an interest in it. For instance, when reviewing some of the major issues in the 1997 regular session of the Minnesota legislature what groups might have an interest in the following: abortion restrictions, drunken driving laws, fishing license increases, gay marriage ban, minimum wage increase, a St. Paul hockey arena, access of tobacco to non-adults, welfare, white pine regrowth and the University of Minnesota steam plant (Legislative Roundup, 1997)?

THOSE WHO LOBBY

Those that articulate political interests try to influence governmental action.   This activity has sometimes been called lobbying.

If one surveys widely those things that influence governmental decisions, weather and other physical factors would have to be included. If we narrow our focus to more social influences, we still have a variety of structures that may be discovered. Among these are individuals, groups and movements. Although movements have had important impacts on our culture and political system, they are sporadic, hard to describe and nearly impossible to predict. Movements such as those promoting civil rights and taxpayer concerns have had national impacts and consequences on decisions made in the state. They will not be detailed here, but should not be forgotten.

We focus here on private and public individuals and groups that attempt to influence decisions of state officials. Political scientists have traditionally emphasized organized private political interest groups that attempt to influence public policy, such as the Minnesota AFL-CIO and the Minnesota Chamber of Commerce. Groups in the public sector such as school teachers and school boards are also represented in the capitol. From time to time even private individuals not inspired by a group may suggest policies to legislators. While not usually included by political scientists as lobbyists, various individuals in the public sector may also try to influence other public officials to their policy goals. Such an individual may be as famous as the Attorney General, Governor or Secretary of State.

Somewhere along the continuum of individual to group are other lobby voices such as an individual corporation like Northern States Power or a single city such as Minneapolis. Additionally there are coalitions that are formed from time to time to support or oppose policy alternatives.

In Minnesota the best source to find individuals and groups that lobby is the Minnesota State Ethical Practices Board (MEPB) which on July 1, 1997 changed its name to the Campaign Finance and Public Disclosure Board. It receives lobby registrations and periodic reports. For the year July, 1996-June, 1997 the board reported that 1380 lobbyists for 1361 individuals and groups had submitted disbursement reports. These numbers were similar to those reported in the previous two years (State of Minnesota, MEPB, September, 1997: 1 and 5). To put this in perspective there are 201 legislators and six elected officials in the executive branch.

Individuals and organizations become active in the governmental process as their interests are affected. This may result in strong involvement during a short period followed by less activity, while other organizations appear more regularly. Examples used here are from the top spending lobby groups during the 1995 and 1996 sessions (State of Minnesota, MEPB, September, 1995, section D; September, 1996 (b), sections A and D, and September, 1997: 25-28).

Various types of business groupings are usually evident ranging from single corporations to more general organizations. Single corporations may decide to lobby the state government. Utility issues, for example, bring corporations such as Northern States Power, Minnegasco and Otter Tail Power to the state government to try to influence decisions in their interest. Other corporations have included Amoco, First Bank System, and the Minnesota Twins. Some like RJ Reynolds Tobacco and Philip Morris Inc. are not identified with Minnesota, but lobby on issues that affect products they sell in the state.

Business trade associations often lobby. These organizations represent companies that specialize in a particular product area. Among the major lobby organizations in recent years has been the Insurance Federation of Minnesota that receives contributions from over one hundred insurance companies in the state (State of Minnesota, MEPB, September, 1996b: 3-4). Other examples of trade associations are the Minnesota Licensed Beverage Association, the Minnesota Forest Industries, Minnesota Association of Realtors, the Minnesota Retail Merchants Association, the Minnesota Trucking Association and the Iron Mining Association of Minnesota.

Some business groups try to represent a wide variety of businesses. Two groups of this type are the Minnesota Chamber of Commerce and the Minnesota Business Partnership. The Chamber of Commerce is probably well known due to its local organizations in many cities throughout Minnesota and the United States. The Minnesota Business Partnership represents many of the larger corporations in the state while the National Federation of Independent Business focuses on small businesses.

It might surprise some how many governments and those who work for governments lobby the state government. Most obvious are teachers, professors and school boards, but it is true of others. An individual city such as Minneapolis may lobby, but so too may cities that band together such as the League of Minnesota Cities and the

Coalition of Greater Minnesota Cities. Other governments such as the Association of Minnesota Counties and the Metropolitan Council have a presence in the state capital, as do public employee unions such as the American Federation of State, County and Municipal Employees (AFSCME) and some of its subunits.

Professional organizations such as the Minnesota Trial Lawyers Association, Minnesota Dental Association, Minnesota Medical Association, Minnesota Society of Certified Public Accountants also try to influence particular governmental decisions.

There are a wide variety of other groups that articulate interests in Minnesota, as one might guess given the large number that participate. There are groups that stress moral issues such as the anti-abortion group Minnesota Citizens Concerned for Life, and the Joint Religious Legislative Coalition which is supported by some Christian and Jewish groups as well as the Minnesota Council of Churches (State of Minnesota, MEPB, September, 1995a: 4). Minnesota Citizens for the Arts has been active in lobbying, as have groups associated with those afflicted with diseases including the Minnesota AIDS Project and American Diabetes Association. Allied Charities of Minnesota has also been active. Some senior citizens have coalesced in the Minnesota Senior Federation and some Minnesotans who favor term limits have had an organization. These organizations and hundreds of others try to affect the outcomes of legislative and administrative decisions.

Even though there are over a thousand groups that lobby in Minnesota some may feel all is not fair. Homemakers, migrants, consumers and taxpayers do not have organizations representing them equal to their size. Political scientist E.E. Schattschneider saw an upper class bias in the interest group system (1975: 31, 32). Small groups seemed to dominate (Schattschneider, 1975: 34). Mancur Olson Jr. agreed, arguing that "the larger the group, the less it will further its common interests" (1968: 36). According to Olson, the smaller the group the less expensive it is to organize it; the larger the group the smaller the individual benefit (1968). In other words, interests that have a large potential may never realize it because of a tendency to "let George do it." To overcome this, large potential groups rely on positive or negative selective incentives such as coercion or inducements (Olson, 1968: 51). Such activities may take away from the time the group spends on its political goals and raise questions as to whether members support the political goals or simply are in it for the selective benefits.

There are arguments in support of those active in articulating interests. Individuals and groups that lobby provide information to governmental officials. The more information decisionmakers can receive the better the decisions they will make. In addition expressing policy views provides a way to "let off steam." Doing so through presenting information is better for a society than doing so through violent actions. In addition, and very importantly, the framers of the Bill of Rights felt the right to assemble and ask for redress of grievances was so important that these freedoms were placed in the first amendment to the Constitution of the United States.

Lobbying

What political interest individuals and groups are trying to do on any level of government is best described from part of the definition of lobbyist in the State of Minnesota, Revisor of Statutes, Minnesota Statutes (1996): "[A]ttempting to influence legislative or administrative action . . . by communicating or urging others to communicate with public . . . officials" (10A.01 Subd. 11-1). The goal is to persuade public officials to make decisions in the group's or individual's interest. The lobbyist can make direct contact such as talking with a state legislator in her office, or indirect contact such as running an advertisement in a newspaper urging readers to contact their elected officials.

Lobbying is similar to sales. A group's position, for example, is the product, the public official is the customer and the group is the company. The lobbyist is the person trying to convince the public official of the product's worth. In lobbying as well as sales, gaining access to the customer, tailoring the message to the customer and making the product appealing are important. Some would argue that the whole process is made easier if the customer is predisposed to make the purchase. Being assigned to a good territory makes the life of a salesperson a whole lot easier. Selling air conditioners in International Falls, Minnesota may be tougher than in Atlanta, Georgia. Similarly a group promoting a socially conservative idea should have an easier time if the public officials lobbied are socially conservative. This is an important reason why some interest articulators become involved in the elections of public officials.

Elections

Although some individuals and groups who have interests to articulate may wait until after voters have made their choices, others may feel they can increase the odds for their success by influencing the selection process. Certain candidates for public office may be predisposed to the group's positions. That can be discovered through contact prior to an election. If the candidate can be persuaded to support an important position of the group during the electoral process, so much the better.

Even if a candidate is not an active supporter of its interest, a group may choose to give electoral support. The general idea is that in order to present one's position access to the official is necessary (Truman, 1951: 264). The official will more likely give access to a friend, the logic goes, and as proverbial grandmothers have often reminded us: "A Friend in Need is a Friend Indeed." Candidates for public office need friends at election time. Some groups choose to show that friendship if for no other reason than insuring access following the election.

Since the mid-1970s, the most famous way that interest groups aid candidates is through campaign contributions made through political action committees, better known by their acronym PAC. PACs were encouraged nationally following the campaign activities revealed during the Watergate scandals. The focus of many upset with the way campaigns were being funded at that time was huge individual donors called "fat cats." It was felt that a few individuals donating huge amounts of money could gain undue influence and distort the electoral process. A goal was to urge small contributions. One way to do this was to set up political action committees as had been done by the AFL-CIO labor organization and a few others. Individuals identified with an interest group, for example, could urge its members to each make a small contribution to a fund. The group would then decide which candidates would receive contributions from the fund. When reforms were made in the mid-1970s on the national level, PACs were seen as a way to gather small donations for elections. The idea became very popular and today many interest groups use political action committees to support candidates for elective offices. Today though some have criticized PACs as giving too much influence to interest groups.

Once again many of the statistics described here come from the Minnesota State Campaign Finance and Public Disclosure Board, formerly known as the Minnesota State Ethical Practices Board (State of Minnesota, MEPB, June, 1997, Sections A & D). One may interpret statistics in various ways and it should be stressed that there are other ways than the ones presented here. The reader is urged to look at the raw material which is easily obtained.

A problem that can occur when looking at donations to candidates is to look only at total donations by groups to all candidates. These totals are large amounts that border on the incomprehensible to those who deal with small daily budgets. What might be more useful initially is to focus not on all group donations or even totals by groups but instead to describe typical campaign costs and compare them to political committee donations. It should be emphasized that we are examining campaigns for state not national office. What is typical in an election, for example, for the Minnesota

House of Representatives is not typical for someone running for United States House of Representatives.

Two points should be noted.   First, most of the state governmental elective offices are for the legislature.   Very important officials in the executive and judicial branches are elected, but the 134 state house members elected every two years and 67 state senators selected every four years receive the largest number of donations from interest groups.

Second, the campaign finance laws in Minnesota affect not only donations by interest groups, but the entire electoral process. Public subsidies of elections have a major effect on state elections in Minnesota. In 1996 nearly all candidates for the state legislature (99 percent) agreed to state spending limits (State of Minnesota, MEPB, June 10, 1997 news release: 2).   Those limits in 1996 were $45,568 for the state senate and $22,784 for the state house of representatives. Average actual campaign expenditures were $25,180 for the state senate and $14,713 for the state house (State of Minnesota, MEPB, June 10, 1997 news release: 2-3).

Averages of all candidates do not always give an adequate picture. As calculated by the author, the average winning candidate for the state senate spent $34,239, with $7,612 coming from political committees and funds that are separate from the political party category.   The winning candidates spent 56 percent of the total expenditures. They received 92 percent of the donations from political committees and funds, and 87 percent of the donations (an average of about $800) from lobbyists. The house of representatives elections show a similar pattern.   The winning candidates spent an average of about $19,000, or 58 percent of the total expenditures. They received nearly 70 percent of the donations from political committees and funds (an average of $3325), and 75 percent of the donations by lobbyists (an average of about $280).

Minnesota law limits donations from a political committee or fund to legislative candidates to no more than $500 in an election year, $100 in non-election years. Lobbyists help candidates, especially incumbents.   However, their influence is limited.   No single contribution amounts to more than 3 percent of the total for a victorious candidate. A campaign's total donations from lobbyists, political funds and large donors cannot exceed 20 percent of its cost limits (Chapter 10A.27, Subd. 1 and 11).

On the other hand, money given early in a campaign, as PACs can do, is more helpful than money given later. Early money allows more accurate campaign planning, such as for media buys. Even if one agrees that donations do not swing votes they can aid access and certain groups still have an advantage. Some lawmakers, aided by the generous public financing of campaigns in Minnesota, have stopped taking PAC money because of the appearance of favoritism.

One could argue that if access is really what is important then choosing candidates who are on the same political wavelength is not as important as choosing the candidate that will be the winner. It may not even be that difficult.   In the 1996 election 82 percent of the incumbent state legislators who served a full term sought re-election. Of those 97 percent were successful.

Interest groups also give money to candidates for other offices, political parties and party related groups. For the six constitutional offices in 1994 political committees and funds provided $42 thousand, or 1.5 percent of the campaign expenditures for all candidates and 1.6 percent for the winners (statistics based on State of Minnesota, MEPB, July, 1995: C1-2). For Minnesota Supreme Court races in 1996 they gave about $30 thousand, or 8 percent of the total expenditures; all the funds went to the two incumbents (State of Minnesota, MEPB, June, 1997: E1).

Political action contributions to political parties are more striking. The Democratic-Farmer-Labor Party received just over $94 thousand from the Minnesota Education Association (MEA) political action committee and another $24 thousand plus from the Minnesota Federation of Teachers.   The Trial PAC (lawyers) gave over $16 thousand and another five PACs gave a total of over $58 thousand. In addition the DFL Central Committee received $167 thousand from the MEA, $72 thousand from the AFL-CIO, $30 thousand from AFSCME, and almost $30 thousand from the Shakopee Mdewakanton Sioux. The Senate Majority Caucus (DFL) also received over $39 thousand from the MEA, $41 thousand from the Trial PAC, $31 thousand from the Minnesota Federation of Teachers, and $15 thousand from the Minnesota Realtors PAC (State of Minnesota, MEPB, June, 1997: 1-4). Some groups, seeking access, gave to both parties; the House Republican Campaign committee received nearly $20 thousand from the MEA, over $12 thousand from the Trial PAC, and over $25 thousand from Minnesota Realtors (State of Minnesota, MEPB, June, 1997: 7-9)

In addition to giving money to a candidate's campaign, there are other means of supporting candidates. Providing campaign workers has been viewed nearly as important as monetary contributions in a survey done in the mid-1980s of lobbyists and legislators (Grau, 1993: 153). Since then additional public financing and limits on interest group and lobbyist financial contributions have made the other help even more valuable. State legislative campaigns are often run by only a few people, and help is gratefully received. A group can contact its members, letting them know which candidates to support. Groups that go beyond their own membership and try to reach the larger public by pounding in lawn signs, distributing literature, and engaging in the other endless tasks of political campaigns are especially valued.

An interest group need not support or oppose all government officials. The most important are those involved with issues important to the group. Education groups, for instance, are interested in the members on the education finance committees of each chamber of the state legislature. Legislative party leaders may also be of interest for their influence at crucial stages of the legislative process.

There are certain groups that donate more money than others to campaigns. The Minnesota Education Association contributed over $388 thousand dollars in 1996. The Minnesota AFL-CIO, Minnesota Realtors, Trial PAC, and the Minnesota Federation of Teachers each contributed over $100 thousand (State of Minnesota, MEPB, June, 1997, Section C). Also among the top donors are law firms and others that supply contract lobbyists.

Indirect Lobbying

Because public officials are concerned with representing constituents, which affects their own job security, some interest articulators try to persuade public officials that the articulator's position is also the position supported by their constituents. Time spent lobbying constituents, sometimes called grassroots lobbying, and getting the constituents to communicate their views to their legislators have become important aspects of the persuasion process of interest articulation.

Members of an organization or the more general public are informed of the importance of an issue and the position that should be supported. Members can be informed when to contact officials, how to do it, and the best arguments support the preferred position. This information can be transferred to the membership through letters, phone trees, FAX machines, e-mail, newsletters and other means. Contact with public officials can be made through letters, telephone calls or e-mail.

Some groups may even decide to contact their members and the general public through advertisements. Hrebenar categorizes interest group advertising into three self-explanatory categories: goodwill ads, offensive ads and defensive ads. More than one strategy can be used in an ad (1997: 120). Observers of the major media during a state legislative session in Minnesota will no doubt be able to fill the categories.

In 1993 and 1994 Northern States Power ran a multi-media advertising campaign to persuade the public of the need to increase nuclear storage. An opposing campaign was set forth by Minnesotans for Nuclear Responsibility, a coalition of thirty environmental groups. A description of the campaigns in the Star and Tribune was entitled "Power play: Dueling ads try to sway public on nuclear waste" (Meersman, 1994). These advertisements had a specific focus. In contrast three years later, an ad in the Saint Paul Pioneer Press entitled "Lakes, Loons, Lights", also paid for by Northern States Power, was much more of a goodwill ad. It noted how Minnesota in partnership with NSP had made energy efficiency a symbol of the state as were lakes and loons (Northern States Power, 1997). While such an advertisement may not seem as focused on a result as many offensive or defensive ads, the goodwill developed may make issue advancement at a later date an easier task. A combination of goals can be seen in an advertisement paid for by the Minnesota Education Association that appeared in the Star and Tribune entitled "An Investment in Public Education is an Investment in OUR FUTURE" (1997). It set forth good news of how Minnesota students were learning but bad news about funding, what was needed for the future and how to contact state legislators (March 23, 1997: A13).

Yet another way to involve the grassroots individuals in lobbying is to bring them to St. Paul to talk with decisionmakers. It may be that many groups that employ this tactic already have a spokesperson there, but hearing concerns from constituents is an effective supplement. Buses and cars filled with constituents regularly descend on the state capitol during a legislative session. These may not only be interest groups in the traditional sense. In 1997 one hundred and fifty Duluth citizens went to St. Paul for what they called Duluth Days. In the past they had brought legislators to the city to show them the city's attributes and needs, but when ethic law changes made that impossible they borrowed an idea from Superior, Wisconsin and sent representatives to the capitol (Bretts, 1997).

Another method of convincing legislators of support among the public is a public opinion poll. Happiness for an interest group is a major public opinion poll reflecting its public policy views and carried in the major media outlets to which all decisionmakers will be attuned. Failing that, organizations with their own resources can commission their own polls. In 1997, for instance, three different groups ran polls on aspects of the controversy surrounding an attempt by the Minnesota Twins to build a new baseball stadium. A proposal had been made to place slot machines in the Canterbury Downs race track to help pay for the stadium. The "Inside Talk" feature of the Star and Tribune pointed out that a poll had been commissioned by the race track. The favorable results were handed out at the state capitol. So too were the results of a poll with different results commissioned by the Minnesota Indian Gaming Association (Whearatt, 1997). A short time later Minnesota Wins, an organization supporting a new stadium, commissioned a poll. The results indicated that a majority of those polled opposed the stadium, but it was a smaller majority than a poll run two months previously. Therefore, according to Minnesota Wins, the opposition was fading (Sweeney, 1997).

Prior to direct lobbying, coalitions may be created to maximize resources and broaden support. Some coalitions seem quite natural such as the coalition of environmental groups mentioned earlier that opposed the Northern States Power nuclear waste expansion. Other coalitions seem more complex. Those supporting Governor Arne Carlson's tax credit proposal for private and public school students included the Minnesota Business Partnership, the Minnesota Chamber of Commerce, the Minnesota Realtors Association as well as Minnesotans for School Choice (Smith, 1997). Opposition included the Minnesota Education Association and the Minnesota Federation of Teachers. In the 1996-97 reporting year Minnesotans for School Choice and the Minnesota Education Association were among the three groups reporting the highest legislative lobby expenses in the state (State of Minnesota, MEPB, September, 1997: 26). Minnesota Wins, formed to promote a new baseball stadium, included seventeen corporations, a leader of the Minneapolis Building and Construction

Trades Council, a former Republican legislator, and public relations experts from one of DFLer Paul Wellstone's senatorial campaigns (Weiner, 1996b).

Letters to legislators, advertisements, public opinion polls and coalitions of groups are ways that interest articulators attempt to impress on public officials that large numbers of people support their position on the issue. This is not done separately from direct lobbying, but in conjunction with it.

Direct Lobbying

The goals and targets of interest articulators may vary. A piece of legislation may be supported or opposed. Likewise an amendment to a bill, a governor's veto or a court ruling may be the focus. Whatever the goals or targets, generally the articulator needs to convince the public officials to the desired viewpoint. While this is similar to sales, as noted earlier, it is also somewhat similar to the job of a lawyer presenting a case. Public officials seem to understand and expect that, as in a courtroom, a lobbyist is presenting the policy position of the group, one-sidedly but honestly.

As has been noted many times, information is power and transferring information persuasively is the job of those articulating an interest. The packaging of the information is important. Public officials have limited time and an avalanche of information. Information therefore needs to be presented as succinctly as possible. Brevity, though, should not reflect superficial knowledge by the presenter. A compromise might be a report on an issue prefaced with a list of major arguments so that succinctness and thoroughness can be combined.

It may also be useful to package the proposal in popular political themes of the times. John Kingdom in his book on public policy agendas and alternatives noted that sometimes there is a national mood (1995: 146-147). In the 1990s, for example, the themes of budget control, decentralization and family values seemed popular. It is no accident, for instance, that a supporter of a new baseball stadium for the Minnesota Twins made references to families and a clean environment (Weiner, 1996a). Themes may change over time, however, so interest articulators must be agile.

Targets of those urging policy positions vary depending on the specific goal. If the goal is a legislative enactment, asking legislators to sponsor legislation is an important early step. While bipartisanship may be important, it is very important to have sponsors of the majority party. It can be useful for those opposed to legislation to also talk with sponsors of legislation. The sponsors may discover that the opponent's position is important; even if a bill is not dropped, important amendments may be added. Members on the committees handling the issue are often crucial contacts. Building majorities at important steps in the legislative process requires support from legislative committees and party leaders. Members of the executive branch who deal with the topic of interest can also be of assistance. It is very useful if a public official is so supportive that he or she helps to convince others of the preferred position. When that occurs, the group has an "inside lobbyist" (Hrebenar, 1997: 89). They may not only be important in the legislative branch but also when decisions are made in the executive branch. Various methods can be used to make the case. It is important that representatives of an interest speak formally with elected officials at hearings and informally in one-to-one conversations, for example, in a public official's office. It may be that when time is very short a conversation may occur in the lobby near a legislative chamber.

Interests are articulated in the judicial branch as well as the other two branches, although different means are used. As on the national level, groups can litigate or file *amicus curiae* (friend of the court) briefs. Such activity is allowed by Minnesota Rules of Court, State and Federal, 1997 (Rule 129: 399). An example is the State of Minnesota Court of Appeals case *U.S. West Communications Inc v City of Redwood Falls* (No. C6-96-1765). *Amicus curiae* briefs were filed by the Minnesota Business Utility Users Council, the Minnesota Department of Public Service and the Public Utilities Commission as well as the cities of St. Paul and Minneapolis.

Lobbyists

Those who make the direct contact with public officials are usually called lobbyists. They can be categorized is various ways. One set of categories, based on their employment status, is volunteer, in-house and contract.

A volunteer lobbyist represents the group without pay. The organization may not be able to hire a full-time lobbyist so they may pay a member's expenses to lobby in the capital. If the organization has a Twin Cities area chapter, the volunteer can live at home. A logical advantage of a volunteer is that the lobbyist reflects the membership and is believable because she or he is "not in it for the money." A disadvantage may be that the lobbyist is only part-time at a job that can require constant vigilance..

An in-house lobbyist represents the company or group as part of his or her employment. One may assume that as part of the organization the lobbyist "knows what she is talking about." As an employee there may be a better chance that she can spend more time on the tasks than a volunteer.

A contract lobbyist is hired to lobby for a specified task or time. These lobbyists are generally viewed as having contacts in the political process that are useful in achieving the group's goals. Contract lobbyists in Minnesota may have more than thirty clients. A disadvantage may be that they are viewed as "hired guns."

Direct lobbying is clearly a form of interpersonal communications. Knowing those who need to be persuaded makes the task easier. In his book *The Third House*, Alan Rosenthal examined lobbying in seven states (one of which was Minnesota)

(1993). He wrote a whole chapter on the importance of building relationships. Some of the lobbyists with whom he had contact felt that they spent more time in developing the relationships than they did actually lobbying for their issues (1993: 112). He noted that relationships that began before the time spent around the legislature tended to be closer (1993: 113).

Lobbyists come in all shapes and sizes. Some work in groups, others as individuals. With thousands of them working in St. Paul at some time during a year, it is difficult to describe a normal lobbyist. A profession traditionally dominated by men now has a growing number of women, matching the increase in the number of women legislators. In 1997 33 percent of the registered lobbyists and 30 percent of the legislators were women. As Dane Smith wrote, "[I]ncreasingly, the prototype of today's lobbyist is young, highly educated, often female, relatively professional and apolitical and of average weight" (1995b). A poll named the eight most influential lobbyists. Six were contract lobbyists: Ted Grindal, Ron Jerich, Tom Kelm, Ross Kramer, Bob Renner and Wy Spano. The others were Judy Cook of the Minnesota Retail Merchants Association and Glenn Dorfman of the Minnesota Association of Realtors (Smith, 1995a).

Some lobbyists are former public officials. These included in 1997 former state legislators such as Winston Borden and Lona Minne Schreiber, former governor Wendell Anderson and former attorney general Warren Spannaus. Former public officials know the process, but now they are asking favors, not granting them, which may not be an easy role reversal.

POWER AND SUCCESS

For all the claims, resources and boasts about lobbying and lobbyists, when all is said and done it is difficult to determine success in the interest articulation business. The system of separation of powers and checks and balances makes passage of policy more difficult than killing a policy change. Those interests that favor change, it would follow, need more power to be a success than those who want to keep the status quo. Success itself is difficult to determine. The old saying that one can win a battle and yet lose a war can indeed occur. The engagements may go on for years.

Furthermore, interest groups are not the only actors in the governmental process. A good example was the agreement passed in a 1997 special session on funding for kindergarten through twelfth grade education. The DFL leadership in the two houses of the legislature and the governor made the agreement. The Minnesota Education Association, the Minnesota Federation of Teachers and the Association of Metropolitan School Districts opposed it (Hotakainen, 1997). These are powerful groups if one looks at campaign contributions, members located most likely in every legislative district and a major presence in direct lobbying. They lost this one. Political interest groups are major actors in the political process in the state of Minnesota, but so are elected officials and caucuses of the political parties. In Minnesota, compared with other states, interest groups seem more subordinate or complementary to others in the political system (Thomas and Hrebenar, 1996: 152). It is not always easy to predict success in the Minnesota political system, which makes the study of politics in the state interesting.

LOBBY DISCLOSURE

Over the years, interest groups and lobbyists have not usually been referred to in terms of praise. Images of vote buying, wining, dining, and arm twisting probably come to mind when one thinks of lobbyists. Interest groups are referred to as "special interests" or "pressure groups." Some are called "single issue" groups. None of these are positive images. Many citizens feel that public officials do not represent their constituents when they get down to the capital and start associating with special interests. These special interest groups are viewed as selfish, trying to persuade those in government to give the interests money from the pockets of hard working taxpayers.

A counter view is that citizens of the United States have a right to bring their grievances to the attention of their public officials. If this right is curtailed, liberty is lessened. Without information supplied by interest articulators, public officials will make decisions more in the intellectual dark and become more dependent on government bureaucrats for information.

Regulating lobbying must therefore weigh the negative aspects with the positives of liberty. In the 1970s and 1990s the pendulum swung towards more regulation. The Watergate investigations and media coverage of related scandals in the 1970s provided an opportunity for those wishing more regulation of lobbying. In the 1990s, a feeling that government was out of touch with the general public and captive of narrow interests provided another opportunity. Regulations in Minnesota focused on the disclosure of lobby activity, restrictions on gifts, and limitations on campaign funding.

The definition of lobbying and lobbyist was broadened to cast a much wider net than the law then being used by the national government. As noted earlier, Minnesota passed a law to cover communicating with legislative and administrative decisionmakers as well as urging others to do so. Much of what we considered direct and indirect lobbying was therefore covered.

A lobbyist is defined for legal purposes in the Minnesota Statutes as a person "engaged for pay or other consideration or authorized to spend money by another individual, association, political subdivision, or public higher education system who spends more than five hours in any month or more than $250, not including the individual's own travel expenses and membership dues in any year" (1996, Chapter 10A). Also covered are individuals who spend more than $250 and nonelected public officials who spend over 50 hours a month. Lobbyists in periodic, public reports must disclose their activities, including money spent on advertising, mailing, and dissemination of information.

In the 1996-97 reporting period, 850 associations and individuals (of the 1361 represented) made disbursements totaling over 6 million dollars. This does not cover lobbying salaries (State of Minnesota, MEPB, September, 1997: 5, 29).

In the 1990s gift bans became popular (Rabinovitz, 1996). Following the lead of Wisconsin, Minnesota in 1994 banned gifts of value to public officials, including tickets to athletic contests, cocktails or even a cup of coffee. Only minor exceptions were tolerated, such as food and beverage if the official is giving a speech or answering questions as part of an organizational program (10A.071). The restrictions cut down on interactions outside normal business hours between lobbyists and public officials.

To monitor the ethics requirements the state of Minnesota in 1974 established an Ethical Practices Board, renamed the Campaign Finance and Public Disclosure Board in 1997. This six member bipartisan board is appointed by the governor and confirmed by three-fifths of both legislative houses. The board had a staff in 1995-1996 of nearly nine full time employees. If one wishes information on lobby disclosure or campaign finance reports the board is the place to go. They not only collect the reports on campaign finance and lobbying, but make sure they are filed on time. They put out publications on the topics with which they deal, do training and education, and investigate violations. One of their important tasks is to give advisory opinions, for instance clarity on the gift ban. With limited resources the board has a large mandate, one crucial to the enforcement of government ethics in Minnesota (State of Minnesota, MEPB, September, 1996a: 1-17).

CONCLUSION

To understand how government operates in Minnesota (or elsewhere in the United States) comprehending interest articulation is important. Those who articulate interests may be individuals or groups in either the public or private sector.

The interest groups and individuals may decide to become active in choosing the public officials. They may influence these decisionmakers indirectly or directly. In lobbying indirectly a group may notify its members or the general public about issues important to the group and suggest they let their public officials know their opinions. An interest group may sponsor a public opinion poll to the same end. Prior to such activity they may place advertisements to build goodwill with the public. The goal is to convince decisionmakers that ordinary people favor the viewpoint of the interest articulator.

Direct lobbying occurs when an individual or interest representative contacts a decisionmaker. Lobbyists narrow their focus to the key decisionmakers on issues important to the group. Such a lobbyist may work as an employee of a group or represent it on a volunteer basis. Another alternative for those wishing to articulate an interest is to hire a lobbyist on a contract basis. Lobby power and success are not easy to determine

Because of its poor image lobbying has become the subject of regulation. Gifts have been banned and money spent to directly or indirectly influence decisionmaking must be reported. The organization in the state of Minnesota that monitors these disclosures is the Minnesota Campaign Finance and Public Disclosure Board.

REFERENCES

Bretts, Ann. 1997. (February 23). "Duluth lobbyists hope for Superior results." *Duluth News-Tribune*: 1B.

Broekemeier, Heidi. 1996. (February 15). Library in reach. *UMD Statesman:* 1,2.

Grau, Craig. 1993. "Minnesota: Labor and Business in an Issue-Oriented State." In Ronald J. Hrebenar and Clive S. Thomas, eds. *Interest Group Politics in Midwestern States*. Ames, IA: Iowa State University Press: 145-164.

Hotakainen, Rob. 1997. (June 27). "It's a one-day deal: K-12 funding bill sails through final approval." *Star Tribune (State Edition)*: A1 and A28.

Hrebenar, Ronald J. 1997. *Interest Group Politics*. 3rd Edition. Armonk, NY: M.E. Sharpe.

Kingdom, John W. 1995. *Agendas, Alternatives and Public Policies*. 2nd Edition. New York, NY: Harper Collins College Publishers.

"Legislative roundup." 1997. (May 20). *Star Tribune (State Edition)*: A12, A13.

Meersman, Tom. 1994. (March 14). "Power play: Dueling ads try to sway public on nuclear waste." *Star Tribune (State Edition)*: A1.

Minnesota Education Association. 1997. (March 23). "An Investment in Public Education in a Investment in OUR FUTURE." (advertisement). *Star Tribune (Minneapolis Edition)*: A13.

Minnesota Rules of Court, State and Federal. 1997. St. Paul, MN: West Publishing Company.

Northern States Power. 1997. (May 21). "Lakes, Loons, Lights." (advertisement). *Saint Paul Pioneer Press*: 3B.

Olson, Mancur, Jr. 1968. *The Logic of Collective Action*. New York, NY: Schocken Books.

"Protests of the pocketbook." 1996. (January 25). *Star Tribune, (Minneapolis edition)*: B 1. Photo by Tom Sweeney.

Rabinovitz, Jonathan. 1996. (May 5). "States Tighten Rules on Lobbyists' Gifts." *The New York Times (National Edition)*: 17.

Rosenthal, Alan. 1993. *The Third House.* Washington, DC: Congressional Quarterly Press.

Schattschneider, E.E. 1975. *The Semisovereign People.* Hinsdale, IL: The Dryden Press.

Smith, Dane. 1997. (May 16). "Groups mobilize over tax credits." *Star Tribune (State Edition)*: A1, A10.

_____. 1995a. (May 5). "The Lobbyists: The most influential lobbyists in Minnesota." *Star Tribune (State Edition)*: A20.

_____. 1995b. (May 4). "The Lobbyists: A new breed takes up the art of persuasion." *Star Tribune (State Edition)*: A1.

State of Minnesota Court of Appeals. 1996. *U.S. West Communications Inc. v City of Redwood Falls.* (No C6 - 96 - 1765). *Amicus Curiae* Brief, Minnesota Business Utility Users Council. *Amicus Curiae* Brief, Cities of St. Paul and Minneapolis. *Amicus Curiae* Brief, Minnesota Department of Public Service and Public Utilities Commission.

State of Minnesota, Minnesota Ethical Practices Board [MEPB] 1997. (September). *Lobby Disbursement Summary*: July, 1996 through June, 1997. St. Paul, MN: MEPB.

_____. 1997. (June). *Minnesota Campaign Finance Disclosure: Campaign Finance Summary: 1996.* St. Paul, MN: Author.

_____. 1996a (September). *Annual Report: July 1, 1995 — June 30, 1996.* St. Paul, MN: Author.

_____. 1996b (September). *Lobby Disbursement Summary: July, 1995 through June, 1996.* St. Paul, MN: Author.

_____. 1995a. (September). *Lobby Disbursement Summary*: July, 1994 through July, 1995. St. Paul, MN: Author.

_____. 1995b. (July). *Minnesota Campaign Finance Disclosure: Campaign Finance Summary: 1994.* St. Paul, MN: Author.

State of Minnesota, Revisor of Statutes. 1996. *Minnesota Statutes.*

Sweeney, Patrick. 1997. (April 19). "Opposition to new Twins stadium fading: Poll shows majority think it's inevitable." *Duluth News-Tribune:* 3C.

Thomas, Clive and Ronald J. Hrebenar. 1996. "Interest Groups in the States." In Virginia Gray and Herbert Jacob, eds. *Politics in the American States: A Comparative Analysis*. 6th Edition. Washington DC: Congressional Quarterly Press. Pp. 122-158.

Truman, David. 1951. *The Governmental Process*. New York, NY: Alfred A. Knopf.

Weiner, Jay. 1996a. (September 15). "Push for new Twins stadium has created unlikely pitching staff." *Star Tribune (Sunday First City Edition)*: A 1.

_____. 1996b. (September 15). "Lineup to sell new stadium has heavy hitters, savvy pitchers." *Star Tribune (Metro edition)*: A 1.

Whearatt, Robert. 1997. (March 24). "Inside Talk: Got a Position? Get a Poll." *Star Tribune*: B3.

More Information

In addition to the sources listed in the references more information can be found on lobbying on the State of Minnesota Campaign Finance and Public Disclosure Board website at *www. cfboard.state.mn.us*

SECTION III

PUBLIC POLICIES IN MINNESOTA

Steven M. Hoffman
University of St. Thomas

This first two sections of this volume have explored the institutions and processes that characterize Minnesota state government. This final section will examine some of the results generated by the interactions among the various elements of the political system.

Jo Beld begins the section by assessing the status of health care and welfare reform in Minnesota. Beld argues that both of these policies demonstrate a continuous interplay between state and national social policy making and that they are both shaped by a wide variety of factors: the economic environment of public policy; the inclusiveness of the process by which policies are crafted; the values and commitments of policy makers in both the legislative and executive branches; and the precedents established by previous programs. This chapter also demonstrates that policy choices at the state and federal level are inextricably linked. Either may inspire, parallel, or constrain the other; but neither can be fully understood in isolation from the other.

Energy policy is the second area of public policy examined in this section. Similar to Beld, Steven M. Hoffman argues that energy policy in Minnesota closely parallels national developments. He locates the historical development of energy policy within a number of larger social issues, including debates about the desirability and social implications of public versus private power; the problems associated with the regulation of private companies who must satisfy a larger "public interest"; and the interplay between a competitive economics and a federalist system of regulation. Hoffman also considers a number of important policy debates that bear upon related environmental and health issues. The chapter concludes with a review of the debate over the anticipated "restructuring"of the electric industry.

Patricia Wagner and Steven Bodelson's chapter expands upon Beld's discussion of health care policy by reviewing the emergence of managed care as a model for the delivery of health care. The authors argue that recent public policies have focused on controlling the ever-increasing costs of health services. A major consequence of this effort has been the evolution of managed care, a type of health care delivery system which was pioneered in Minnesota in the mid-1980s. Since at least the adoption of the HMO Act of 1973, the HMO model of health care delivery has become an archetype for the formulation of several innovative programs, one of which is the subject of the chapter: the Minnesota Prepaid Medical Assistance Program (PMAP).

The problems discussed by both Beld and Bodelson and Wagner will only intensify as Minnesota's population ages, a subject taken up by Carolyn Shrewsbury in her discussion of the politics and policies of aging. According to Shrewsbury, a special focus on the needs and concerns of older persons would have had a very small audience at the beginning of this century. Few lived to old age and families cared for most of the elders needing assistance. Poorhouses, usually run by municipalities, served to warehouse the rest. Now, however, issues surrounding old age have entered center stage. Furthermore, the problems of the aged cannot be considered in isolation from many other areas of public policy, including long-term care, work force policies, health care, housing, transportation, and criminal justice. As Shrewsbury points out, old age policy is no longer a concern just for the old and our ability to resolve them satisfactorily will have a major impact on American politics far into the 21st Century.

In the final chapter of this section John Harrigan takes up an issue of increasing importance to more and more of the state's resident's — how to govern the Twin Cities Metropolitan region. Harrigan demonstrates that political actors such as the state legislature established and refined a special bifurcated governing structure as a result of social and economic changes in the 1960's and 1970's. The structure solved many of these issues resulting from physical changes fairly well, including sewage treatment, solid waste disposal, recreation opportunities, and land use planning. However, he also demonstrates that more recent social and economic changes such as a global economy, central city disparities relative to the suburbs, and suburban sprawl, created growing dissatisfaction with the old structural framework. Political forces moved the state legislature to abandon the bifurcated structure and also place the Metropolitan Council more closely under gubernatorial supervision. Harrigan expresses some skepticism whether the new formal arrangements can resolve the problems without a new political regime to sustain it.

Chapter 10

"MINNESOTA LEADS THE NATION . . ." HEALTH CARE AND WELFARE REFORM IN MINNESOTA[1]

Jo Beld
St. Olaf College

INTRODUCTION

If you've taken a course in basic US government, you know that it's common to characterize the states as "laboratories for democracy." States, it is said, can experiment with policy innovations on a smaller scale and then pass along the lessons they learn to policy makers at the national level. Many federal programs are explicitly designed to promote state-level creativity in solving public problems and promoting the public interest.

While any state is, in principle, a possible testing ground for large-scale social policy, few states can claim the kind of policy leadership presently exercised by the State of Minnesota. Minnesota

[1] The author gratefully acknowledges the following individuals for their assistance in the preparation of this chapter: Ellie Garrett, Minnesota Council of Health Plans; Michele Evans, Rice County Social Services; Kay Olson Fischer, Rice County Public Health Nursing Service; Chuck Johnson, Minnesota Department of Human Services; and Karen Gervais, Minnesota Center for Health Care Ethics. Any remaining errors of fact or interpretation, however, are the responsibility of the author.

really *has* served as a laboratory for public policy; innovations and reforms in a wide range of policy arenas have made their way into the national debate and, more often than not, into national legislation. At the same time, like all states, its decisions are often shaped by policies developed at the federal level. This chapter illustrates the interplay between state and national social policy making through a close examination of health care and welfare reform in Minnesota.

HEALTH CARE

Minnesota has long been a leader in the national policy debate over health care. In fact, President Clinton's 1993 health care reform package included a number of provisions that strongly resembled what Minnesota was already doing in making affordable, high-quality health care available to its citizens. Indeed, had the *process* of policy reform at the national level also resembled the reform process in Minnesota, President Clinton's Health Security Act might very well have been successful.

Minnesota's health care policy reforms were preceded by some dramatic changes in the state's health care market. The most significant of these was a marked shift from "fee-for-service" health care systems to "managed care" systems. A "fee-for-service" arrangement is somewhat analogous to an a la carte meal plan, in which health care consumers, or their insurance companies, pay a separate fee for each "menu item" (health care service) they choose. This arrangement creates incentives for health care providers to get consumers to spend more (by increasing their fees, seeing patients more often, or using more expensive treatments) and for health care consumers to find ways to spend less, largely by avoiding preventive care, with no mechanisms for quality control.

By the 1970s, as health care costs began to mount, a number of policy analysts and physicians (notably Paul Ellwood, a Minnesota pediatric neurologist) began to advocate replacing the "fee for service" arrangement with pre-paid package deals that have come to be known as "managed care" (Belkin, 1996; Ellwood, 1988). Under managed care, health care consumers ("members") can receive a basic set of health care services (a "benefits package") from an approved list of clinics, hospitals, and health care professionals ("participating providers") for a single comprehensive fee (a "premium"), usually paid on a monthly basis to a participating insurance company (Minnesota Department of Health [MDH], 1995: 179). Managed care systems attempt to hold down health care costs without jeopardizing quality of care by including many preventive services, such as well-baby visits and immunizations, in the basic package of services covered by the comprehensive fee; by giving members financial incentives to use participating providers; and by standardizing and regulating many of the treatment options for patient care to make optimum use of limited resources for medical care. By the early 1990s, approximately three-quarters of Minnesota's population was covered by some form of managed care (MDH, 1995: 155).

Although managed care can be provided under a variety of organizational arrangements, the best-known "vehicle" for the delivery of managed care is the Health Maintenance Organization, or HMO. HMOs, colloquially known as health plans, bring health care consumers, insurance carriers, insurance purchasers (often employers) and health care providers into a single integrated system. HMOs have a long history in Minnesota; the first one was established by railroad workers in Two Harbors in 1944, and the second (Group Health) in 1957. Encouraged by federal legislation and the work of activists like Ellwood, HMOs have commanded a larger and larger share of Minnesota's health care market, particularly in urbanized areas; by 1993, over one-quarter of Minnesota's population, and over 40 percent of the Twin Cities population, was receiving its health care services from an HMO (MDH, 1995: 155).

These changes in the state health care market have been important influences on health care policy making. They also reflect some important objectives in the delivery of health care, objectives which have guided public policy as well as private sector decision making.   Among these objectives are *high quality, accessibility, affordability,* and *consumer choice.*

The health care policy arena attempts to address these objectives through a complex mix of distributive, redistributive, and regulatory programs, funded by a combination of federal, state, local, and private dollars. Together, this mix of policies affects the distribution of both benefits and costs associated with health care. Specifically, they help to determine who receives health care services; what kinds of services they receive; who provides the services; how much the services cost; and who pays for the services. The following programs are among the most important components of health care policy in Minnesota.

MinnesotaCare

This program is widely regarded as the cornerstone of health care reform in Minnesota. Initiated in 1987, MinnesotaCare (or MNCare, as it is commonly called) began as an effort to guarantee health care to poor children, and it has gradually expanded to include their parents and low-income adults without children. The development of MNCare illustrates how policy innovation can emerge from an incremental political process emphasizing broad-based participation and consensus-building.

The forerunner to MNCare, known as the Children's Health Plan, was passed in 1987. As its title suggests, this program served needy children under age 8 and low-income pregnant women; participants could receive basic health care services for an annual "premium" (the health care version of a membership fee) of just $25 per child. Two years later the state legislature expanded the Children's Health Plan to include needy children up to age 18. The 1989 revisions also established a fifteen-member health care advisory commission to study the larger problem of health coverage for *all* Minnesota residents, adults as well as children, in the context of steadily rising health care costs. The advisory commission developed a set of recommendations to the state legislature which included a modest plan for state-subsidized health care coverage for Minnesota's working poor and several provisions to help make HMOs more competitive in the health care market. The legislature passed a bill in 1991 incorporating many of the advisory committee's recommendations. Then-Governor Arne Carlson vetoed the bill, however, arguing that it was unworkable and too costly.

This did not spell the end of health care reform. Following Governor Carlson's veto, a bipartisan group of legislators (informally branded the "Gang of Seven") met over several months to craft a revised version of the 1991 bill. This time the reform advocates were successful, and the act known as HealthRight was signed into law in April 1992 (McMenamin, 1994). The HealthRight legislation attempted to make health care more widely accessible and affordable, without compromising quality or choice. Key features of the bill included:

• *state-subsidized health insurance* to uninsured families (parents as well as children) whose income was at $26,000 per year or less for a family of four; a *2 percent tax on health care providers* (physicians, clinics, pharmacies, hospitals) to help pay for the state-subsidized insurance;

• the creation of a permanent 25-member *Health Care Commission*, including representatives of health care consumers, providers, insurance companies, employers, labor unions, and state agencies, charged with providing ongoing health care policy recommendations to the state legislature;

• *growth limits* on both public and private health care spending, tied to the Consumer Price Index, with accompanying requirements for statewide *standardized data collection* on expenditures from both providers and insurance companies;

• *regulatory reform* to make affordable insurance more readily available to people who would otherwise have to pay higher insurance rates, such as consumers with high-risk health conditions; and

• the creation of six *regional coordinating boards* to "facilitate local collaborative efforts to improve access, quality, and affordability of health care services" (MDH, 1995: 104).

Since the passage of the 1992 HealthRight Act, the legislature has continued to revise and expand its key provisions. In particular, changes in the eligibility rules for MinnesotaCare (the new name for the HealthRight program) have dramatically increased the number of program participants. Like most programs for lower-income people, MNCare's eligibility rules are tied to the official poverty level established by the federal Department of Health and Human Services.

As of 1997, a family of four is considered to be in poverty if their annual household income is $16,050 or less (Federal Register, 1997: 10856-10859). In order to be eligible for MNCare, the income of a Minnesota family with one or more children must not exceed 275 percent of the federal poverty level (just over $44,000 per year, an amount which is above the median Minnesota income), and the family must not have access to private, employer-funded health insurance. Adults without children can also qualify for MNCare if their earnings do not exceed 135 percent of the federal poverty level, or $21,668 per year (Chun, 1997). Because MNCare operates with a generous "percent of poverty" eligibility requirement, many lower-income families whose incomes are too high for them to qualify for other social programs (even some college professors!) still qualify for MNCare if they have no access to employer-funded insurance. The annual premium a family must pay in order to enroll in the MNCare program is determined by a "sliding scale," so that those with lower incomes pay a smaller premium. In 1996, these premiums ranged from $48 to $295 per year (Chun, 1997).

These changes in eligibility and requirements and premium rates have resulted in a dramatic increase in enrollment. The original 1989 Children's Health Plan enrolled 7,850 children; the 1992 HealthRight legislation covered more than 27,000 participants (MDH, 1995); and as of October 1997, nearly 100,000 Minnesota residents were enrolled in the MNCare program (Office of the Governor, October 1997). Moreover, MNCare now covers more kinds of medical services, such as in-patient hospitalization. Not surprisingly, in view of these changes, MNCare expenditures have risen over time. The state spent approximately $9 million on MNCare in 1992 (MDH, 1995) and will spend an estimated $117.8 million in the 1997 fiscal year (Chun, 1997).

Although MNCare is not without its critics, it is now an accepted component of state health care policy. Minnesota's efforts were widely regarded as a potential model for federal health care reform; consequently, several of the state's key players (notably Lois Quam, chair of the legislative advisory commission whose work led to the passage of the 1992 HealthRight bill) were tapped for the President's health care reform task force. The result was a federal proposal that resembled Minnesota's health care reforms in many respects. In President Clinton's words, the 1993 Health Security Act "reaffirm[ed] an American principle: that our high-quality health care system should be rooted in the private sector and should respond to market forces" (US Department of Commerce, 1993: I).

Both the state and federal reforms assumed that the first place people should turn for health care coverage was to their employers. In fact, the proposed federal reform was even stronger on this point than the 1992 Minnesota reform, because the federal reform *mandated* that, except for smaller firms, all employers had to provide an affordable, basic package of health insurance benefits, even to individuals with pre-existing conditions; the Minnesota reform retained the voluntary nature of employer-provided insurance. Like MNCare, the federal reform relied on a publicly-subsidized health insurance plan to cover those who could not get coverage from an employer (which meant, for all practical purposes, primarily those who were unemployed). Like MNCare, the proposed federal legislation emphasized both managed care and "managed competition" among large networks integrating health care providers, insurance carriers, and "purchasing pools" of health care consumers. Both reform packages emphasized preventive care; both attempted to control health care costs by establishing spending limits; and both created a broadly-representative health care board to develop future policy recommendations and to monitor the achievement of cost containment and coverage objectives (Sherer, 1993; U.S. Department of Commerce, 1993; Patel and Rushefsky, 1995).

With so many programmatic similarities, why did the federal Health Security Act go down to defeat only one year after Minnesota's HealthRight was signed into law? Opinions on this point vary widely. Some fault the closed nature of the President's task force proceedings and power imbalances among the stakeholders. Others note that Minnesota's private market, having already begun a shift toward managed care, was much more conducive to policy reform than the national health care market, which was still largely dominated by fee-for-service arrangements.

The resulting federal policy was castigated by its opponents as too complex, too highly regulated, and too costly, despite a valiant lobbying effort by President Clinton and the bill's advocates. Had the details of the President's plan been developed in cooperation with members of Congress (as the Minnesota HealthRight legislation was crafted by the "Gang of Seven" in the state legislature) rather than by a Presidential task force which conducted much of its business behind closed doors, a version of the President's proposal might very well have passed (Patel and Rushefsky, 1995, ch. 8). It is also possible that a different time line would have enhanced the bill's chances for success. As the *New York Times* puts it, "Managed care is no longer a model *proposed* for the American health care system. It *is* the American health care system. Nearly 60 million people are enrolled in managed care insurance plans and three in four doctors participate in at least one managed care program" (Belkin, 1996: 68). Thus, had Clinton waited to introduce health care reform in his second term, the national health care market would have more closely resembled Minnesota's market and might have been more conducive to reform.

Despite the disappointment of the failed Health Security Act, Minnesota's effort to increase health care coverage through MNCare has had a lasting impact on the federal debate over health care reform. MNCare, however, is only one of several state programs affecting health care in Minnesota. A variety of other programs also help make health care available to large numbers of residents who might otherwise go without care. These programs blend federal and state dollars, with the federal government generally setting broad parameters within which state policies operate.

Other health care programs

Minnesota's other health care programs meet a variety of health care needs for different segments of the population. A brief tour of other important health care programs in Minnesota would include the following:

Medical Assistance (MA) Medical Assistance is the name of Minnesota's version of Medicaid, a federal program established in 1965 to make health care available to the poor. The federal government establishes broad parameters for eligibility and coverage under the program, and then provides Medicaid funds to the states, who in turn determine the specific population to be served, the specific benefits to be provided, and the level of payments to providers who serve Medicaid clients. States can thus exercise considerable discretion in the allocation of federal Medicaid funds.

Minnesota has historically been on the generous end of the spectrum of state programs operated under the auspices of Medicaid. A wide range of health care services which the federal government designates as "optional" are included in Minnesota's Medical

Assistance program, such as medical transportation services, hospice care, occupational therapy, vision care and eyeglasses, and a variety of mental health services. Minnesota is reimbursed by federal Medicaid dollars for the cost of part of these optional services, and the state picks up the balance. In addition, Minnesota has successfully petitioned the federal government for so-called "waivers," which permit the state to receive partial reimbursement for health care services which are neither mandatory nor optional under the original legislation establishing Medicaid. These "above and beyond" services are targeted primarily to elderly and disabled Minnesotans (Bellis and Chaffee, 1995).

The rules governing eligibility for Medical Assistance are extremely complex and have changed over time. Generally speaking, however, the population of persons served by Medical Assistance is poorer than the population of persons served by MNCare. Most people eligible for welfare (previously known as AFDC, or "Aid to Families with Dependent Children," and now known as TANF, or "Temporary Assistance to Needy Families") or for Supplemental Security Income (a federal program which provides financial assistance to needy elderly and/or disabled persons) are also eligible for Medical Assistance. Some (such as pregnant women and infants up to age one, and some categories of persons with disabilities) are eligible for MA even though their income is higher than that of most welfare clients. However, although the majority of MA *recipients* are also welfare recipients, the bulk of MA *expenditures* are targeted to elderly, disabled, or blind clients who are not on welfare (Bellis and Chaffee, 1995). Long term care for these clients accounts for approximately 40 percent of MA spending. As the population continues to age and as eligibility requirements for Medical Assistance are expanded, it is expected that state spending for Medical Assistance will continue to increase (MDH, 1995).

For the most part, Minnesota's health care providers have cooperated in ensuring access to care for MA clients. This has not been the case in many other states because of the way health care services are paid for under the auspices of the federal Medicaid program.   Providers are reimbursed by their state, using a combination of federal Medicaid and state dollars for the services rendered to Medicaid clients. However, Medicaid reimbursement levels are often lower than the fees normally charged by many providers. Consequently, many clinics and hospitals will not accept patients whose services will be paid for by their state's Medicaid program. But in Minnesota, with the exception of dental clinics (many of which limit the number of MA clients they are willing to accept), health care providers generally have been willing to serve MA clients despite the lower fees they are able to collect for their services (Evans, Rice County Social Services, personal communication, September 30, 1997). Minnesota has thus attempted to make optimum use of federal Medicaid dollars in its implementation and administration of Medical Assistance.

Medicare This is a federally-funded program which makes health insurance available to elderly and disabled persons whose medical expenses might otherwise impoverish them. Established in the mid-1960s, the program is funded by a special payroll tax on employees and their employers. Although it is a federal program, it is important to mention it as part of the overall picture of the health care system in Minnesota, primarily because Medicare covers more Minnesotans (approximately 15 percent of the state's population) than any other publicly-funded health care program (MDH, 1995: 20). Moreover, Minnesota's integrated network of private providers and health insurance carriers is responsible for the actual administration of benefits and payments.

As is also the case with Medical Assistance, providers are reimbursed with federal Medicare dollars for the health care they give to Medicare clients, but the Medicare reimbursement rates are generally lower than the fees the providers normally charge. In the past, this meant that providers were faced with an economic disincentive to accept Medicare patients. However, several provisions in MNCare have reduced these economic disincentives, so there has been a gradual increase in the percentage of "participating providers" (i.e. providers who agree to accept Medicare reimbursement as payment in full for the services rendered), a move which has increased access and choice for many Medicare recipients. In 1995, estimated Medicare participation rates varied from approximately 50 percent of health care providers in a number of Greater Minnesota counties to as many as 90 percent in other counties, and it was expected that, over time, more providers would be added to the list of participants, thereby making services even more available to Medicare clients (MDH, 1995: 86).

General Assistance Medical Care (GAMC) and the Minnesota Comprehensive Health Association (MCHA) These two programs provide additional "safety net" coverage for a small but important population of Minnesotans. GAMC is a completely state-funded program established by the Minnesota legislature in 1975 and administered by the Department of Human Services. The program serves needy people who do not qualify for Medical Assistance, and persons whose high medical expenses severely limit their disposable income. In 1993, approximately 50,000 Minnesotans were served by GAMC each month.

Unlike MNCare, GAMC does not require clients to pay a monthly premium. Most recipients' income levels are not much above the poverty level. GAMC does not cover as extensive an array of health care services as Medical Assistance and Medicare, but it does make basic health care (including hospital care, prescription drugs, eye exams and eyeglasses, selected chiropractic services, and services for the mentally ill) available to a small population who cannot afford even the low premiums charged to MNCare clients. County social services agencies are responsible for determining whether applicants are eligible for GMAC and for helping those who do not qualify for GMAC to apply for other publicly-funded health care programs (Bellis and Chaffee, 1995).

Another population with special health care needs includes persons with chronic ailments, such as heart disease, AIDS, chemical dependency, and leukemia. Most private health insurance programs treat persons with "pre-existing conditions" (that is, health care needs like these which existed before the person applied for insurance) differently from other members. This is because people with pre-existing conditions usually need more care and are therefore among the more expensive members of an insurance company's "risk pool." The company can control health care costs by denying them membership, by limiting their benefit package, or by charging them a significantly higher premium. The Minnesota Comprehensive Health Association (MCHA) was established in 1976 to fill the gap for Minnesotans whose health care needs restrict their access to affordable private insurance. People with pre-existing conditions can purchase health insurance from Blue Cross Blue Shield of Minnesota at standard market rates under the auspices of MCHA. In 1993, MCHA covered approximately 1 percent of the state's population (MDH, 1995: 20). Although this is a relatively small group of beneficiaries, it includes many of the medically neediest people in the state.

Special Supplemental Food Program for Women, Infants, and Children (WIC) The WIC program was established by the federal government in the mid-1960s as part of the Johnson administration's War on Poverty. It is a preventive health care program, intended to meet the nutritional needs of low-income pregnant and nursing women, infants, and children up to the age of five. WIC is administered by the state Department of Health, and services are generally provided through county-level Public Health Nursing agencies.

Most people are familiar with the "food vouchers" WIC participants can exchange at their local grocery stores for nutrition-rich foods such as dairy products, grains, and fruit juices. A less familiar but equally important component of the program is the nutrition education WIC provides. WIC professionals are particularly pro-active in encouraging WIC moms to breastfeed their babies, not only because breastfeeding is by far the healthiest way to feed a baby but also because it is much more economical than formula feeding. In fact, if half the mothers participating in the WIC program were to breastfeed their babies for one month, the federal government would save approximately $2.5 million in the cost of vouchers for infant formula (Fischer, Rice County Public Health Nursing Service, personal communication, January 1997). Because of the health and economic benefits of breastfeeding, and because of the additional nutrition needs of nursing mothers, WIC provides additional vouchers for other nutrition-rich foods to participants who are breastfeeding their babies. Finally, the WIC program helps participants find out about other kinds of services for which they might be eligible. The public health nurses and other professionals who work with WIC clients frequently put their clients in touch with immunization programs, Head Start, Early Childhood Family Education, MNCare, education and training centers, and other health and social services.

WIC resembles Minnesota's Medical Assistance program in that Minnesota has chosen to invest considerable state resources over and above the federal WIC funding. The additional state dollars enable Minnesota's WIC program to serve more clients than it would be able to serve with federal dollars alone; state dollars are also used for continuing education for WIC providers. Minnesota's Department of Health offers a variety of Maternal and Child Health special projects grants, which some local Public Health Nursing Services have used to develop innovative programs or provide extra services for selected WIC clients (Fischer, Rice County Public Health Nursing Service, personal communication, October 1997). WIC typifies Minnesota's general preference for preventive rather than ameliorative public policy, particularly in the health care arena.

Assessing the Impact of Health Care Policy in Minnesota

Lively debate continues on the degree to which Minnesota's mix of private and public health care policies is helping to achieve the goals of quality, cost control, access, and choice. The debate is complicated by a serious lack of broad-based, systematic data; by contradictory research results; by continuous change in both the private health care market and the public regulatory environment; and by the difficulty of determining whether specific outcomes should be attributed to market forces, policy decisions, or some combination of the two.

Nevertheless, there are some trends worth noting. First, MNCare coverage has clearly improved access to health care in the state of Minnesota. One indicator of this improvement is the relatively low proportion of uninsured Minnesotans. Estimates on the number of uninsured vary somewhat, but in a recent speech celebrating the five-year anniversary of MNCare, Governor Carlson (evidently now a convert) noted, "Through MinnesotaCare, we have reduced the number of chronically uninsured children to 7 percent in Minnesota, compared to 14 percent nationally" (Office of the Governor, October 1997). Only five other states have an even lower proportion of uninsured residents. Moreover, while the proportion of uninsured citizens has been rising nationwide, it has remained stable in Minnesota (MDH, 1995: 21-22).

Given this expanded access, what has been the impact of policy change on the cost of health care? The data are quite preliminary, but early indications suggest that Minnesota has stayed within the growth limits on health care expenditures established in the 1992 HealthRight legislation. Moreover, the rate of growth in some categories of medical spending, such as the cost of insurance premiums and the percentage of the state's Gross Domestic Product devoted to health care, has actually slowed (MDH, 1995: 14-19). Perhaps most significantly, programs like MNCare appear to be saving state dollars in other social policy efforts, notably welfare (see below). It will be easier to assess the cost effects of MNCare and other state health programs in the future, because MNCare includes requirements for standardized data collection and analysis.

Perhaps the most important question to ask is, what has been the impact of this mix of programs on the actual health of Minnesota's citizens? That is a surprisingly difficult question to answer. By a variety of measures, Minnesota is a relatively healthy state — by some accounts, the healthiest in the nation. For example, using data from the US Departments of Health, Commerce, Education, and Labor, ReliaStar Financial Corporation has tracked health outcomes in each of the fifty states for the last nine years. The research is based on a wide range of health indicators in several dimensions of population health, such as prevalence of heart disease, occupational fatality rates, rates of selected infectious diseases, rates of cancer cases, and infant mortality rates. ReliaStar's 1997 results ranked Minnesota as the state with the best health outcomes for the fifth time in the eight years it has published its findings (ReliaStar, 1997).

But it is hard to ascertain the degree to which these relatively favorable health outcomes are attributable to the programs and policies described above. The ReliaStar report itself testifies to this: "[M]any factors contribute to Minnesota's No. 1 ranking. The state ranks in the top three for high rate of high school graduation (86.8 percent), high access to primary care (more than 95 percent) and low premature death (4,016 years lost per 100,000 population) . . . In the last year, Minnesota has decreased the prevalence of smoking from 21.6 to 20.5 percent and decreased the rate of motor vehicle deaths from 1.5 to 1.3 deaths per 100,000,000 miles driven" (1997: 2-3). Only some of these causal factors are directly related to public policy in the health care arena.

Second, policy choices do not affect all health care delivery systems in the same way. For example, nearly one-third of all Minnesotans receive their health insurance from "self-funded" plans operated by their employers, rather than from an insurance company under contract with their employer or from a public program such as MNCare or GAMC. Under a "self-funded" plans, an employer collects premiums from its employees and then pays health care providers directly out of company funds for the employees' health care services.   Self-funded plans, unlike the plans provided by insurance companies, are not subject to state regulation (MDH, 1995: 61-63).

There is also a big difference between *having access to health care* and *being healthy*. Not everyone who is eligible for a program actually participates in the program; for example, there may be as many as 96,000 uninsured Minnesotans who are eligible for MNCare but are not enrolled in the program (Office of the Governor, October 1997). And even when people are "covered," they may be unaware that they need care, unsure what services are included in their health care plan, or unwilling to follow the advice of their health care providers.

Finally, some health problems are attributable to environmental factors beyond the reach of either individual choices or public health care programs. And others are simply intractable even with the best possible treatment. Despite these uncertainties, health care policy makers at all levels of government are continuing to work cooperatively with health care providers to improve the accessibility, affordability, and quality of health care in Minnesota.

WELFARE REFORM

A variety of state-level policies and programs, many developed in the context of federal legislation, affect personal and family income in Minnesota. State and local tax codes, minimum wage legislation, workers' compensation, unemployment insurance, food stamps, and housing subsidies are just a few examples. While many of these issues have been on the state's agenda in recent years, few have received as much sustained attention as welfare reform and child support enforcement. Like health care, welfare and child support programs in Minnesota reflect a complicated mix of federal and state initiatives.

Antecedents, Assumptions, and Public Assistance

"Welfare" is a term that encompasses a number of programs for the poor, some of which provide cash grants and others of which provide "in-kind" benefits (such as vouchers which may be exchanged for food, or subsidies to help defray the cost of rent). But when most people speak of "welfare," they are referring to a cash assistance program which, until 1996, was known as AFDC, or "Aid to Families with Dependent Children." AFDC, now replaced by TANF, or "Temporary Assistance to Needy Families," exemplifies what some scholars have called the "residualist" approach to social policy. In the words of Marmor, Mashaw, and Harvey (1991: 25-26):

> Most of those who think of the welfare state as 'residual' believe that its aim should be temporary assistance and its administration highly decentralized. They aspire to a system in which the distribution of 'relief' is closely supervised by officials who are thoroughly familiar with the circumstances of their clients' lives, thereby ensuring that only the 'deserving' poor receive assistance . . . Advocacy of decentralization presumes that individual families will typically assure the welfare of their members. When that fails, institutions close to those families — charitable groups, then local and provincial or state programs — constitute the safety net protecting against destitution.

The AFDC safety net was originally intended primarily for single parents. Although the net was stretched to include selected two-parent families under the federal 1988 Family Support Act, the overwhelming majority of adult welfare clients have always been mothers. However, the *rationale* for this safety net has changed over time, due largely to changes in cultural attitudes toward parenting, work, and the role of the state. The forerunners to AFDC — the Progressive era "Mothers' Pensions" of the early 1900s and the "Aid to Dependent Children" (ADC) programs enacted during the

Depression — were explicitly designed to help widows stay home and care for their children. In the absence of government assistance, it was argued, single mothers would be forced either to institutionalize their children in orphanages, or to join the workforce. Both of these alternatives were considered risky for children and ultimately more expensive than government assistance. State investment in fatherless families which enabled mothers to stay home, according to Frances Perkins, Franklin Roosevelt's Secretary of Labor, was not only "the most satisfactory way from the point of view of the moral, the ethical, and the social principles involved," but also "vastly the most economical method" (Berkowitz, 1991: 96-97). ADC was thus enacted to provide assistance to adults who could not be gainfully employed because of the obligations of childrearing.

The postwar years saw a dramatic change in the cultural assumptions about work and parenting. The main barrier to employment for AFDC recipients, according to the reformers of the mid-1960s and beyond, was no longer considered to be the presence of small children who needed care, but rather a combination of inadequate incentives to work and inadequate preparation for work. A series of reform proposals ensued which retained the "temporary safety net" character of AFDC but on radically different grounds. Assistance was to be provided, not until the children were grown and no longer needed care, but rather until the parent could find a job and become "self-sufficient." Thus, the common goal of most welfare reform proposals since the early 1960s has been to help parents leave welfare by working.

In spite of this near-consensus on the principal objective of welfare reform, it has proved extremely difficult to achieve a major overhaul. The challenge of welfare reform is rooted in a number of factors. First, although "everyone hates welfare," they hate it for different reasons. Critics make very different assumptions about the causes of poverty and the consequences of government help. Welfare has thus been simultaneously criticized for keeping people poor; discouraging work; contributing to the rise in single-parent households; promoting widespread fraud and abuse; encouraging illegal immigration; sapping federal and state budgets; and promoting long-term dependency.

A second major obstacle to welfare reform has been the thoroughly federalist character of AFDC and its corollary programs. They are funded by a combination of federal and state tax dollars and administered by county-level social service agencies which must comply with a Byzantine maze of federal and state regulations. The result is enormous variation in eligibility rules and benefits. In 1990, a family living in Alabama would have received $115 per month in cash assistance; that same family would have received $637 had they lived in California (Beld, 1995). These variations are intended to accommodate state-to-state differences in cost of living, job availability, and related social policies (e.g. child care, health care, and transportation), but they make systematic reform a daunting prospect.

Minnesota's Experiment in Welfare Reform

While the federalist character of welfare policy poses challenges, it also creates opportunities. States can seek permission from the federal government to experiment with new approaches to welfare through small-scale "demonstration projects" in welfare reform. Minnesota has been at the forefront of this effort, launching a major initiative in 1992 known as the Minnesota Family Investment Program, or MFIP. This initiative was developed as a multi-pronged effort to change the structure of requirements and incentives embedded in public assistance programs and to broaden and integrate the kinds of support available to welfare recipients in Minnesota. MFIP has received national attention as one of the most thoughtful and comprehensive state-level experiments in reforming the system of public assistance to the poor.

The process which led to the enactment of MFIP was remarkably similar to the process which led to the enactment of MNCare. MFIP originated in the recommendations of a bipartisan

Commission on Welfare Reform established by the Governor in 1986. The Commission drew heavily on conversations with eight focus groups, three of which were comprised of welfare recipients, and on the advice of several advocacy organizations, in preparing its recommendations to the legislature. After the 1989 legislative session authorizing the broad contours of the experiment, a series of work groups and advisory councils continued to work on the details of the final program, prior to its implementation in 1994. These groups represented a broad cross-section of Minnesotans interested in and directly affected by welfare reform, including current and former welfare recipients, county social workers and case managers, legal aid professionals,   business and industry representatives, advocacy organizations, educators, and local elected officials (Minnesota Department of Human Services [MDHS], 1992).

Like the prewar Mothers' Pensions and Aid to Dependent Children programs, MFIP is predicated on the belief that assistance programs which strengthen family functioning as well as family finances are, in the long run, less expensive for the state and better for families. The statutory language authorizing MFIP is quite clear on this point (Minnesota Statutes 1990, 256.031, Subd.2.):

> The legislature recognizes the need to fundamentally change the way government supports families.   The legislature finds that many features of the current system of public assistance do not help families carry out their two basis functions: the economic support of the family unit and the care and nurturing of children. The legislature recognizes that the Minnesota family investment plan is an investment strategy that will support and strengthen the family's social and financial functions. This investment in families will provide long-term benefits through stronger and more independent families.

The key provisions of the program, which went into effect in 1994 in seven Minnesota counties, included a simplification of the system; a requirement that participants prepare for and enter the workforce; an effort to create support systems for existing families; and providing a means to carefully document outcomes (MDHS, 1992; Johnson, MFIP Director, MDHS, personal communication, October 1997).

Finally, MFIP was designed to ensure that families are always economically better off working, even if they are also receiving some cash assistance. It accomplishes this in a number of ways, including: eliminating the "100-hour" rule (under AFDC, families could not receive assistance if they worked more than 100 hours in a month, no matter what their earnings); disregarding the first 38 percent of a family's earned income in calculating the amount of assistance for which they are eligible; not reducing a family's assistance until after the family's total income (earnings [minus the 38 percent disregard] plus assistance) is 20 percent higher than what their income would be if they relied on assistance alone; continuing to provide assistance until the family's income is approximately 40 percent above the federal poverty level; increasing subsidies for child care (so that parents would not be prevented from working because they can't afford child care); and continuing to provide help with child care expenses for at least a year after a family leaves MFIP.

Minnesota's experiment in welfare reform has been groundbreaking in several respects. First, whereas the primary purpose of welfare reform in other states has usually been to reduce *welfare caseloads*, the primary purpose of MFIP has been to reduce *poverty*, particularly among working families. Second, the reform effort in Minnesota has also been much more comprehensive and far-reaching than that in many other states, some of which have simply tinkered with application forms or eligibility rules. Finally, Minnesota's experiment is thoroughly research-driven. Extensive documentation of long-term changes in the state's labor market and family structures, and a close examination of the true extent and causes of welfare dependency, informed all the major provisions of the program. Furthermore, as a demonstration project, MFIP is itself a data source. The careful experimental design guiding the implementation of the project, and the data collection requirements built in to the program, were intended to allow policy makers to evaluate MFIP's outcomes and compare them with the traditional package of public assistance programs (MDHS, May 1992).

However, as any policy analyst will tell you, one of the major differences between a laboratory experiment and a field experiment is that the real world of politics can disrupt even the best-laid plans. Even though state policy makers had committed themselves to waiting until MFIP's evaluation results were in before deciding whether to move forward with statewide implementation, their hand was forced by the feds (MDHS, May 1992). "Welfare as we know it" ended with the passage of the 1996 Personal Responsibility and Work Opportunity Reconciliation Act (PRWORA). This major federal reform required the states to make some fundamental changes in their assistance programs for the poor, changes which have been at least as hotly debated as the programs they modified.

Enter the Feds

The 1996 legislation transformed welfare from a federally-dominated "entitlement" program (in which the federal government guaranteed assistance to all those who meet the eligibility requirements for as long as they continue to qualify for it) to a state-dominated "block grant" program (in which assistance is available, but not guaranteed, from state programs partially funded with federal dollars and designed to reach federally-specified performance goals). The legislation operates on a system of economic incentives both for state policy makers and for individual welfare clients. States will only receive their full allotment of federal dollars for welfare spending if they meet performance goals within federally-specified timetables. Individuals will only receive their welfare checks if they comply with several specific provisions for work and/or education. This dual system of incentives was developed to move people off the welfare rolls and into the workforce as expeditiously as possible.

Although the Personal Responsibility and Work Opportunity Reconciliation Act was billed as "welfare reform," it actually encompassed a wide range of programs in addition to AFDC (Katz, 1996). For example, many disabled children and elderly persons have long received financial help under the auspices of the federal Supplemental Security Income (SSI) program. The PRWORA reduced the number of children and older adults who qualify for SSI benefits by changing the definition of "disability" and restricting eligibility to citizens. Eligibility for the federal Food Stamp program was also restricted to citizens; work requirements were imposed on selected Food Stamp participants (primarily those without dependents); and benefit levels were cut. The Act also consolidated and block-granted several federal programs providing funds for child care assistance, and required that states spend a specified portion of their child care block grant dollars on subsidies for current or potential welfare recipients, on quality improvement in child care services, and on care for selected age groups. The legislation included cash "bonuses" for the five states with the best record in reducing births to unmarried mothers without increasing abortions. Finally, the welfare reform law made several important changes to strengthen federal child support policies.

The PRWORA ended welfare as we know it primarily by restricting and regulating access to assistance. It abolished the sixty-year-old AFDC program and replaced it with TANF, or "Temporary Assistance to Needy Families." The major provisions affecting welfare recipients include time limits on assistance, requiring additional work for TANF recipients, restrictions on education and training, and restrictions on eligibility for unmarried teens (Katz, 1996).

All states are required to incorporate these rules into their programs for welfare recipients in order to receive their share of federal welfare dollars. The PRWORA legislation also included several optional provisions which states could implement if they wished. In particular, states could decide to deny welfare benefits to all unmarried parents under age 18. They could refuse assistance to children born to parents who were already receiving assistance. And they could establish a "two-tier" benefit schedule, in which newcomers to a state would receive the same level of benefits they would have received in their previous state for the first year of residence in their new state.

State policy makers were also subjected to an array of economic incentives and regulatory mandates under the terms of the federal welfare reform legislation. Although states were authorized to use their federal welfare dollars "in any manner reasonably calculated to accomplish the purposes" of the reforms, the federal government maintains some control through a system of financial penalties for states which do not comply with federal regulations or achieve federally-established goals. In other words, if states don't play, the feds won't pay. The list of goals and standards to which the states must adhere is quite long and complex. Some of the more important aspects of the legislation include a requirement that states meet federally-established goals for "work participation rates"; a requirement that states make periodic reports to the federal Department of Health and Human Services outlining state welfare goals, services, and administrative procedures; and assurances that states comply with federal spending targets (Katz, 1996).

The PRWORA required states to develop their plans for using their block grants by July 1, 1997 in order to receive their share of federal welfare dollars. States thus had less than one year to develop and pass their own welfare reform legislation within the federal parameters described above. What did Minnesota do once the ball was in the states' court?

Minnesota Responds to Federal Welfare Reform

Given the very short time line for state response, Minnesota did the logical thing: it adopted a modified version of the experimental MFIP program. After all, the basic structure of MFIP had already been crafted, and there was enough consensus on its merits for the state legislature and the governor to have agreed in 1992 that it should be piloted on a trial basis. Thus, early in the 1997 legislative session, Governor Carlson proposed MFIP-S ("Minnesota Family Investment Plan — Statewide") and urged the legislature to pass it by the end of March in order to "capture all available federal block grant dollars" (MDHS, January 1997). The Governor's plan blended many of the basic provisions of the MFIP demonstration project with the requirements of the federal welfare reform legislation.

After extensive hearings involving recipients, researchers, advocacy organizations, state agencies, and county human service workers, the legislature passed a modified version of the Governor's plan, and it was signed into law in May 1997. The MFIP-S will be implemented beginning January 1, 1998, affecting more than 51,000 Minnesota families. (Once the MFIP demonstration project is concluded, Minnesota's welfare program will be known simply as "MFIP" rather than MFIP-S.) According to the legislative summary prepared by the Minnesota Department of Human Services (August 1997), the essential provisions of MFIP-S include the following:

- *Simplifying the system.* Like the original MFIP demonstration project, statewide welfare reform combines AFDC, food stamps, Family General Assistance, and several employment and training programs into one umbrella program.

- *Requiring participants to enter the workforce quickly.* Minnesota's statewide reform plan requires work even more quickly than either the MFIP demonstration project or the federal reform provisions. Two-parent families must begin work activities immediately; single parents must work or go to school within six months (unless they have an infant under age one). Parents who do not comply with these requirements will have a portion of their TANF grant withheld.

• *Providing limited education and job search assistance.*
In the words of the MDHS summary, "The emphasis will
be on quick job placement with job supports. Recipients
will be expected to take the most direct path to a job."
Accordingly, Minnesota increased its contribution to
employment and training programs for welfare recipients
by $26 million for 1998 and 1999.

• *Making work pay.* Like the MFIP demonstration
project, MFIP-S attempts to make sure that families are
always better off economically when they work by, in part,
eliminating the old AFDC "100-hour" rule, which
prevented any family with a parent who worked more than
100 hours in a month from receiving assistance. In
addition, MFIP-S permits case managers to disregard the
first $30 and one-third of all subsequent earnings in
calculating the amount of assistance a family could receive
(this represents no change from the old AFDC rules).
Finally, MFIP-S will continue to provide cash assistance
to families until their total income (earnings [minus the
disregard] plus the TANF grant) is approximately 20
percent above the poverty level.

• *Enforcing citizenship and residency requirements.*
Partly in response to restrictions imposed by the federal
Personal Responsibility and Work Opportunity
Reconciliation Act, and partly as a consequence of state-
level decision making, access to welfare in Minnesota is
now much more restricted than under the AFDC
entitlement.

• *Requirements for unmarried teens.* In accordance with
federal regulations, most unmarried minor parents must
live with a parent or in another adult-supervised setting,

and must complete an appropriate educational plan, in order to receive welfare benefits.

• *Diverting welfare applicants into other assistance programs.* State policy makers argued that the "culture shift" emphasizing work and imposing time limits on assistance "will prevent many families from ever applying for welfare" (MDHS, August 1997: 3).

Minnesota's welfare reform provisions were complemented by changes in related programs affecting current and potential welfare recipients. At the governor's request, the 1997 legislative session more than doubled state spending for subsidized child care for low-income families who are not receiving cash assistance, allocating $92.5 million over the next biennium. Child care funding for families on welfare was increased 181 percent to $99.2 million (Children's Defense Fund–Minnesota, June 1997). Child support enforcement was also strengthened. Minnesota was already doing most of what the federal government required of all states under the 1996 welfare reform legislation, such as requiring employers to report new hires to the state so the state can check the employees' child support obligations, and suspending occupational and drivers licenses for adults who owe child support. Additional measures accompanying the state's 1997 welfare reform package included penalties for parents receiving assistance who do not cooperate with the establishment of paternity, and improvements in the state's ability to track child support orders and provide information to custodial parents.

Assessing the Impact of Welfare Reform in Minnesota

It is far too early to predict the impact of this combination of federal and state-level reforms in public assistance programs for the poor, especially since reform will not be officially inaugurated until 1998. However, there are several things policy makers will need to watch as welfare reform unfolds.

First and foremost, can Minnesota's overhauled welfare system really move recipients from welfare to "self-sufficiency"? On the one hand, many advocates of welfare reform pointed to the very low unemployment rate in Minnesota as evidence of the feasibility of placing welfare families in the workforce. They also point to early indicators of success from the MFIP demonstration project. Recent evaluation data cited by Governor Carlson show that, after 18 months on the experimental MFIP program, over half of the long-term recipients were working after 18 months, compared to approximately 12 percent of the recipients in the AFDC control group (Carlson, October 1997).

However, critics argue that these projections are optimistic. For one thing, the experimental MFIP program provides much more access to education and job training services than does Minnesota's statewide welfare reform. For another, *work* and *self-sufficiency* are two very different things. One advocacy coalition, using data from the Research and Statistics Office of the Minnesota Department of Economic Security, calculated that there are more than eight job seekers for every job in Minnesota that pays a "self-sufficiency wage" capable of supporting a single parent family of three (currently about $10/hour). For people with no post-secondary education, there are approximately 14 job seekers for every job requiring only a high school diploma and paying $7.50/hour (less than the self-sufficiency wage) (B. Steuernagel, Jobs Now Coalition, personal communication, December 19, 1996). Given the restrictions on publicly-funded postsecondary education in Minnesota's 1997 reform bill, the declining real value of the minimum wage, and the likelihood of recession in the next several years (just when states are required to increase the proportion of their welfare recipients who are working), policy makers will need to pay close attention to the rate at which welfare recipients move, not just to work, but to work that can support families.

Second, it is unclear whether the changes in other programs affecting low-income Minnesotans will be sufficient to help them avoid welfare. Advocates for child care programs were gratified by the unprecedented increases in funding for child care. However, many are also concerned about whether Minnesota's child care system can accommodate the increased demand. The state doubled its investment in child care development, from $3.56 to $7.7 million over the next biennium (Children's Defense Fund–Minnesota, June 1997), but it remains to be seen whether this will meet the needs of Minnesota's expanded workforce.

Similar questions arise with respect to child support enforcement. Recent research suggests that support enforcement is more likely to benefit families who are *not* on public assistance, than it is to benefit welfare families (Glass, 1990). Ironically, this will probably be even more true under welfare reform. Prior to reform, when the state collected support payments on behalf of a welfare family, the custodial parent was permitted to keep the first $50 of support and the remainder went to the state to compensate the state for its cash grant assistance to the custodial parent. But under welfare reform, this $50 "pass-through" ends. Furthermore, as noted by Laura Kadwell, Director of Minnesota's Office of Child Support Enforcement, "poor women tend to marry poor men."   Thus, although successful child support enforcement allowed over 9,000 families to leave welfare in fiscal 1995 (deFiebre, 1996), many of the support payments owed to welfare recipients would not be sufficient to keep them out of poverty and off of welfare. This will not change under welfare reform.

Transportation policy will be another area to watch. According to the Jobs Now advocacy coalition, there is a 'geographic mismatch' between welfare recipients and job growth, particularly in the central cities and in rural counties. For example, the central Twin Cities are home to nearly 64 percent of the welfare recipients, but only 34 percent of the jobs, in the seven-county metropolitan area (Steuernagel, 1996). Minnesota's welfare reform legislation makes some exceptions in work requirements for families facing serious transportation problems. But it remains to be seen whether there will be sufficient transportation for the state to meet its required "work participation rates."

Many questions remain concerning the impact of welfare reform on newcomers to Minnesota and on non-citizens. Some non-citizens, such as the elderly relatives of Hmong immigrants, face major obstacles to obtaining citizenship. Once the reduced and temporary state assistance substituting for federal food stamps expires, what will happen to non-citizens who have not obtained citizenship in spite of the additional funding for citizenship programs? It will also be interesting to track the feasibility of the 'two-tiered' welfare benefit system, in which newcomers to Minnesota will only receive benefits equal to what they would have received in their previous state. County financial workers will face a major task keeping track of other states' eligibility requirements and benefit levels. This provision has also been challenged in the Minnesota courts in a class action lawsuit, on the grounds that it compromises constitutional guarantees of equal protection (Minnesota Public Radio, October 1997).

Of all the policies and programs described in this chapter, the program with the best track record in helping families avoid welfare appears to be MNCare. Prior to MNCare, health care was available to low-income families primarily through Medical Assistance, which was tied to AFDC. Some families went on AFDC, or chose to remain on AFDC once they entered the system, primarily because that was the only way they could get health insurance for their children. MNCare de-coupled health insurance and welfare. Thus, as of the five-year anniversary of MNCare, it was estimated that 4,600 families were able to stay off welfare because of the availability of health insurance under MNCare (Office of the Governor, October 1, 1997 [website news release]). If "successful" welfare reform means helping families avoid both welfare and poverty, then the state will need to continue, if not expand, its investment in health care, child care, child support enforcement, and transportation.

CONCLUSION

Health care and welfare reform are just two of the many policies affecting the daily lives of Minnesota's residents.   This brief examination has demonstrated that policy choices like these are shaped by a wide variety of factors: the economic environment of public policy; the inclusiveness of the process by which policies are crafted; the values and commitments of policy makers in both the legislative and executive branches; and the precedents established by previous programs. This chapter has also demonstrated that policy choices at the state level and policy choices at the federal level are inextricably linked. Either may inspire, parallel, or constrain the other; but neither can be fully understood in isolation from the other.

REFERENCES

Beld, J. 1995. "Politics Around the Dinner Table: Families and Public Policy." In G. E. Dickinson and M. R. Leming, eds. *Understanding Families: Diversity, Continuity, and Change.* 2nd Edition.Boston, MA: Harcourt Brace. Pp. 495-535.

Belkin, L. 1996. (December 8). "But what about quality?" *New York Times Magazine*: 68-71, 101, 106.

Bellis, M., & Chaffee, K. 1995. *Minnesota Welfare: A Guide to Public Assistance Programs in Minnesota.* St. Paul, MN: Minnesota House of Representatives Research Department.

Berkowitz, E. D. 1991. *America's Welfare State: From Roosevelt to Reagan.* Baltimore, MD: Johns Hopkins Press.

Carlson, A. 1997. (October 22). "Minnesota Welfare Off to a Successful Start." *Northfield News*: 5A.

Children's Defense Fund–Minnesota. 1997 (June). "1997 legislative wrap-up." *You Should Know....* St. Paul, MN: Author.

Chun, R. 1997. *The MinnesotaCare Program.* House Research Information Brief. St. Paul, MN: Minnesota House of Representatives Research Department..

deFiebre, C. 1996. (May 22). "Shrinking rolls, growing debate." *Minneapolis Star Tribune*: A1.

Ellwood, D. T. 1988. *Poor Support: Poverty in the American Family.* New York, NY: Basic Books.

Federal Register. 1997. *The HHS Poverty Guidelines.* [On-Line]. Available: http://asoe.os.dhhs.gov/poverty/97poverty.htm

Glass, B. L. 1990. "Child Support Enforcement as a Means to Reduce Poverty: A Critical Essay." *Family Perspective.* Volume 24: 345-354.

Katz, J. L. 1996. (September 21). "Welfare overhaul law." *Congressional Quarterly*: 2696-2704.

Marmor, T. R., Mashaw, J.L., & Harvey, P. L. 1991. *America's Misunderstood Welfare State: Persistent Myths, Enduring Realities.* New York, NY: Basic Books.

McMenamin, B. 1994. (September). "In bed with the devil." *Forbes.* Volume 154: 200-210.

Minnesota Department of Health [MDH]. 1995. *Minnesota Health Care Market Report. 1995.* St. Paul, MN: Minnesota Department of Health, Health Policy and Systems Compliance Division, Health Economics Program.

Minnesota Department of Human Services [MDHS]. 1997. *Administration's Welfare Reform Plan: Work, Responsibility, and Families.* St. Paul, MN: Author.

Minnesota Family Investment Plan, Minnesota Statutes 256.03. 1990.

Minnesota Public Radio. 1997. (October). Broadcast.

Office of the Governor. October, 1997. *Governor Carlson Celebrates Five Years of MinnesotaCare: Affordable Health Coverage for Working Minnesotans.* Press Release, On-Line. Available: http://www.governor.state.mn.us/news/1997/1001new1.htm.

Patel, K., & Rushefsky, M. E. 1995. *Health Care Politics and Policy in America.* Armonk, NY: M.E. Sharpe.

Reliastar. 1997. *The Reliastar State Health Rankings: An Analysis of the Relative Healthiness of the Population in All 50 States.* Minneapolis, MN: Author.

Sherer, J. L. 1993. "Pioneer's progress: Three states move ahead with their reforms." *Hospitals and Health Networks.* Volume 67: 14-16.

U.S. Department of Commerce–Small Business Administration. 1993. *The Health Security Act of 1993: Health Care That's Always There.* Washington, DC: Author.

Chapter 11

SERVING THE PUBLIC'S INTEREST: ENERGY POLICY IN MINNESOTA[1]

Steven M. Hoffman
University of St. Thomas

INTRODUCTION

The contemporary system of energy production and consumption is the result of a complex web of private decisions influenced to a great extent by public policies. This chapter will discuss the creation of this policy in the state of Minnesota, focusing primarily upon the development of the electric power industry. The chapter begins with a brief description of energy production and consumption in the United States and Minnesota. This is followed by a history of the electric industry and the major policies that have affected its development. The chapter then turns to the evolution of the current regulatory system, arguing that the development of the system can be understood as the product of a continuing tension between basic principles of economics and regulation within a federal system of governance. The chapter concludes with review of a

---

[1] The author wishes to acknowledge the assistance of Mr. Steve Downer, Mr. William Grant, Dr. Burl Harr, Dr. Steven Hatting, Mr. Michael Noble, and Mr. Lee Sundberg. Any errors and omissions are, of course, the sole responsibility of the author.

number of important policy debates that have occurred over the last decade.

ENERGY FACTS

The world's total output of primary energy — petroleum, natural gas, coal, and electric power (hydropower, nuclear, geothermal, solar and wind) — increased from 314 quadrillion[2] Btu in 1986 to 361 quadrillion Btu in 1995. Three countries — the United States, Russia, and China — combined to produce forty percent of the world total. The United States, however, is by far the world's largest supplier of energy, producing over 69 quadrillion Btu of primary energy as compared to Russia's 40 quadrillion Btu and China's 35 quadrillion Btu (EIA, 1997b).

Almost all of this energy is supplied by fossil fuels. In 1995, petroleum (crude oil and natural gas plant liquids) accounted for over 39 percent of world primary energy production, a 12.5 percent increase since 1986, or approximately 7.5 million barrels per day (60.4 to 67.9 million barrels per day.) Coal was the second most heavily used primary fuel source, satisfying approximately 25.3 percent of the world's energy demand. Natural gas was the world's third most important energy source in 1995, accounting for 21.4 percent of total energy production. It also has experienced the most significant level of growth, with production increasing some 23 percent between 1986 and 1995, or from 63 to 78 trillion cubic feet annually (EIA, 1997b).

Electricity production also increased significantly during the same period, with nuclear power accounting for the largest share of the increase. In 1986, the world's nuclear reactors generated 1.5

---

[2] One Btu (British thermal unit) is equal to 252 calories of energy or about the energy produced by one kitchen match. A quadrillion Btu is equal to 10^{15} Btu.

trillion kilowatt-hours (kWh), a figure which rose to 2.2 trillion kWh in 1995, a 45 percent increase. While the percentage increase in electricity generated by nonfossil fuels (geothermal, solar and wind) was significant (225 percent) the amount of production was modest, rising from 34.2 billion kWh to 111.2 billion kWh. This compares with hydroelectric generation, which experienced an increase of 22.8 percent over the same period, rising from 2.0 trillion kWh to 2.5 trillion kWh (EIA, 1997b).

Global consumption patterns are similarly differentiated. The United States consumed some 88 quadrillion Btu of primary energy in 1995, as compared to Russia's 26.75 quadrillion Btu and China's 35.67 quadrillion Btu. Overall, the U.S. consumed over 24 percent of the world's available energy, though it accounts for just over eight percent of the world's population (EIA, 1997b).

Electricity consumption illustrates the extent of global disparities. African countries stand at the bottom of the world's electricity ladder. The average Zairian, for instance, consumes only 122 kWh of electricity per year a rather generous figure compared to the average Ethiopian, who consumes a mere 24 kWhs in the average year. The average Indian consumes a somewhat higher 353 kWhs per year. This compares to the typical individual living in China who has access to approximately 728 kWhs per year, or approximately one-seventh of the 5,233 kWhs per year consumed by the average Russian. Residents of the United Kingdom are slightly better off, consuming some 5,559 kWhs per year, an amount somewhat less than the average German's 6,330 kWhs per year. All of these, however, pale in comparison to the consumption levels of those living in the United States (12,797 kWhs per year), Canada (16,551 kWhs per year) and Norway (24,809 kWhs per year) (EIA, 1997a).

Minnesota's Energy Facts

Minnesota's energy patterns reflect these worldwide trends. Coal and petroleum supplied just over half of the state's total consumption needs in 1995 (28 percent and 27 percent, respectively), followed by natural gas (20 percent).[3]   Most of the state's energy dollars, however, were spent on electricity. As shown in Figure 1, 40 percent of the $7.1 billion dollars that Minnesotans spent on energy was used to purchase electricity as compared to 35 percent for petroleum and 19 percent for natural gas (MDPS, 1996).

Figure 1

1994 Expenditures by Fuel

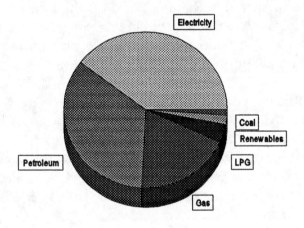

Source: MDPS, 1996. Figure II-6: 12.

---

[3] There are two ways of looking at energy consumption: (a) primary use or fuel directly consumed by the final consumer. In 1995 in Minnesota, petroleum satisfied 42 percent of primary use, followed by natural gas (32 percent) and electricity (17 percent); and (b) end-use consumption, or the indirect consumption of primary fuels through the use of electricity which is primarily generated through the combustion of fossil fuels. In 1995, primary energy production amounted to 1,541.9 trillion Btu while end-use consumption equaled 1,040.9 trillion Btu. The difference is accounted for through losses which occurred during the transmission and distribution of electricity from power stations to the end-users.

While consumption decreased somewhat between 1977 and 1987, since that time virtually every sector of the economy (i.e., transportation, agriculture, industry, commercial and residential) has shown a consistent increase in energy usage (Figure 2). In 1995, the largest single consumer of energy was the transportation sector, which used 40 percent of the state's 1,040 trillion Btus. The industrial and residential sectors consumed 22 and 21 percent respectively of the total, while the commercial sector consumed almost 140 trillion Btu or 13 percent of the total. The agricultural sector required the least amount of energy, using only 4 percent of the total (MDPS, 1997a).

Figure 2

Energy Consumption (trillion kWh)

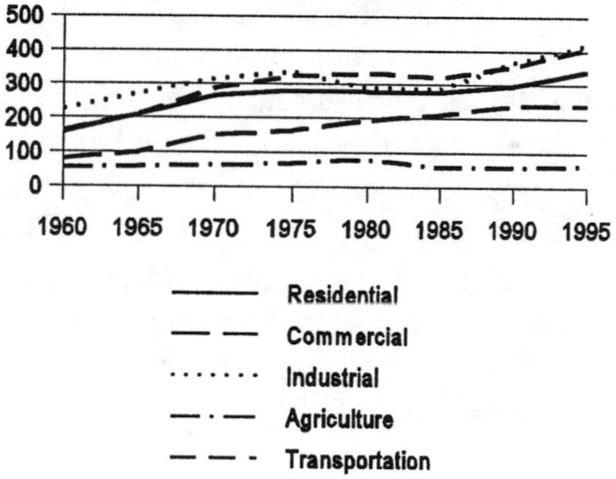

	Residential
— —	Commercial
·······	Industrial
— · —	Agriculture
— — -	Transportation

Source: MDPS, 1997. Table 30: 58.

Per-capita consumption has also been increasing over the last decade. Spurred on by the energy crises of the 1970s, consumers were somewhat successful in decreasing their energy usage. However, since the end of the 1980s, consumption has been moving upward and now exceeds the previous high in 1979. It should be noted, however, that some of these trends are strongly affected by weather patterns, particularly in the case of natural gas used mostly for space-heating. Thus, weather-normalized trends (i.e., adjusting for cold weather) shows that per-capita natural gas consumption has actually decreased since 1973. Electricity and petroleum consumption, on the other hand, has increased steadily over the last several decades, though weather-normalized electricity consumption does appear to have leveled out since 1990 (MDPS, 1997a).

NATIONAL ENERGY POLICY

The present system of energy production and consumption has evolved in response to a number of economic, social, and technological forces. In many instances, individual states such as Minnesota have little ability to influence the nature of these forces. This is particularly true in the case of petroleum. As noted in the Department of Public Service's 1996 Quadrennial Energy Policy and Conservation Report, "crude oil is a commodity whose price is set by the world market," the consumption of which is dictated largely by the sprawling nature of contemporary urban development (1996: 63). On the other hand, the states can and have played an important role in many aspects of the electrical network and its development. A review of Minnesota state energy laws enacted since 1973 attests to this emphasis on electric policy: almost without exception, these laws have dealt with electric issues in one form or another (Minnesota House of Representatives, 1994). For this reason, the remainder of this chapter will focus on the history and regulation of the electric power industry.

Three underlying and oftentimes competing forces explain much of this industry's history: the economics of the industry; the nature of American federalism; and the extent to which electricity can be considered a good "affected" with the public interest. At various points in time, policies have been structured so as to give dominance to one or another of these forces. At the same time, however, consolidation and a subsequent concentration of economic power have been evident throughout the industry's history.

Electrifying America

The origins of the electric power industry are usually traced to September 4, 1882, the day when Thomas Edison flipped the switch at his Pearl Street Station in New York City (Hughes, 1983). While his station served only 59 customers with enough power to light several hundred light bulbs for a few hours per day at a cost of about 24 cents per kWh, the growth possibilities associated with electricity escaped neither Edison nor his competitors. Soon after Edison opened his station, New York and many other cities became dotted with small power stations, each limited to service within a few blocks of the station.

Because cities were the first to experience the benefits, and costs of this emerging industry, municipal authorities were also the first to struggle with defining a regulatory structure adequate to protect the public's interests. Two primary options emerged in this period. First, municipal officials granted "franchises" to private operators such as Edison who, in return for a license to operate in the city, agreed to provide service under a defined set of conditions and terms. Second, and often times simultaneously, cities competed with private operators by building municipally-owned and operated plants for purposes of suppling power for public goods such as street lighting and trollies (EIA, 1996).

By the turn of the century, growing economies of scale hastened growth and consolidation within the industry. One of the most influential of the newly emerging class of energy industrialists was Samuel Insull. Insull's home turf was Chicago, where he arrived in 1892 to take control of Chicago Edison, one of some thirty electric companies operating in the city at the time (Anderson, 1981: 34). Insull initiated a series of mergers and acquisitions that would become the dominant mode of operation in the electric industry for the next thirty years. Aggressively buying out and then retiring the equipment of competitors, Insull soon became the exclusive supplier of electricity for the city of Chicago.

As a result of his experience in acquiring Commonwealth Edison in 1897, and the attendant intrusion of Chicago's machine-style politics, Insull began to urge the elimination of the municipal franchise system in favor of state regulation. In part, this was the result of technological changes and the industry's ability to serve larger geographical areas with ever-larger generating stations. The public had also discovered that it was undesirable to have multiple companies performing the distribution function, i.e., stringing wires from home to home to deliver the power from the generating unit to the consumer. Indeed, in many cities, competition had resulted in a jungle of wires as competing companies literally ran rows of wires in parallel down the same street. Taken together, these characteristics created what economists refer to as a "natural monopoly", that is, an industry where competition is undesirable since fewer firms with larger plants can achieve significant reductions in costs and prices.

The ever more imposing systems invited public scrutiny and increasing demands for public regulation, particularly as private firms came more and more to dominate the industry. The inevitability of public regulation did not escape Insull; the only question was the form of regulation. Insull argued that local regulators were likely to be "rigid, spasmodic, and inept, if not corrupt" (The Twentieth Century Fund, 1948: 42) and that municipal ownership defied the economic logic of the emerging utility industry. Equally distrustful of federal intervention, Insull and his contemporaries at the National Electric Light Association (the leading trade association of the day) turned to the other alternative in the American federal system, the states.

According to Douglas Anderson, "state regulation received the public support of leading men in the electric power industry as early as 1898; after the movement for regulation was successful . . . the electric utilities vigorously defended the jurisdiction of the [state] commissions against encroachment by local and federal authorities" (1981: 33). In essence, says Anderson, the electric utilities saw state regulation as the best means of preserving their autonomy while acknowledging the inevitability of public oversight.

Buttressed by the progressive ideas of the day and the call for "scientific regulation" of the industries such as electric utilities, the first commissions were established in New York State and Wisconsin in 1907. By 1941 forty states and the District of Columbia had established commissions with jurisdiction over the rates and services of private electric utilities (Twentieth Century Fund, 1948: 52, Table II-1) and by the mid-1970s all of the states had established such commissions (Gordon, 1982: 133, Table 4-1).

At the heart of state regulation was the so-called "regulatory compact". Under the terms of the compact, utilities were granted exclusive service territories, in turn, accepting an "obligation to serve" any and all customers within the territory. In order to more efficiently meet this obligation, investor-owned utilities (IOUs) continued their development of "vertically integrated" corporate structures, performing the entire array of generation, transmission, and distribution functions required to bring electrical power from the generating station to the end-user.

Having secured an agreeable regulatory system the utilities were able to continue the historical pattern of consolidation and the concentration of economic and political power. The preferred method of operation was the *holding company*, which according to Black's Law Dictionary is a (1968:865):

[S]uper-corporation which owns or at least controls such a dominant interest in one or more other corporations that it is enabled to dictate their policies through voting power; . . . any company, incorporated or unincorporated, which is in a position to control or materially influence the management of one or more other companies by virtue, in part at least, of its ownership of securities in the other company or companies.

Electric utility holding companies were spectacularly successful enterprises, so much so that in the eight years following World War I, 3,744 public utility companies disappeared through merger or acquisition. During the same time period, slightly more than one percent of the utility corporations in the country came to own 84 percent of all utility assets. Consolidation continued throughout the teens and twenties, such that by 1924, the 16 largest holding companies controlled 75 percent of the industry's generating capacity; the seven largest of the holding companies controlled 40 percent of all generation in the country (Hughes, 1983: 391-2).

To a great extent, the trusts achieved their power with the implicit encouragement of the American people and its government. As President Warren Harding said, "We want a period in America with less government in business . . . and more business in government" (quoted in Price, 1979: 24). Large-scale consolidation of business was encouraged in the early twenties with explicit government endorsement of the "great trade associations and powerful corporations" (Price, 1979: 24). In this respect, the utility holding companies served as a model of corporate efficiency, necessary for the provision of capital and technological expertise in an era when both were in short supply (Hughes, 1983: 393).

By the early 1930s, however, with the onset of the Depression and the collapse of several leading electric holding companies due to widespread financial abuses, the trusts became the target of sweeping federal legislation. The utilities were accused of many abuses, including "control of an entire system by means of a small investment at the top of a pyramid of companies, sale of services to subsidiaries at excessive prices, buying and selling properties within the system at unreasonable prices, intra-system loans at unfair terms, and the wild bidding war to buy operating companies" (Hyman, 1994: 11, quoted in EIA, 1996).

The major piece of legislation enacted in response to these abuses was the Public Utilities Holding Companies Act (PUHCA). Under PUHCA, the Securities and Exchange Commission (SEC) was given the power to break up the trusts by requiring them to divest their holdings until each became a single consolidated system serving a circumscribed geographic area. The law additionally permitted holding companies to engage only in business that was essential and appropriate for the operation of a single integrated utility (EIA, 1996: 25). Title II of PUHCA also empowered the Federal Power Commission to regulate the transmission of electricity across state lines (IEA, 1996: 21).[4]

The 1930s also saw the emergence of a viable system of public power. While municipal systems had survived throughout the period of private power dominance, by 1932 they contributed only 5 percent of total generation (EIA, 1996: 106). In the mid-thirties, however, municipal power was supplemented with two new forms of public power. The first, cooperative electric associations, were created by the Rural Electrification Act of 1936. The Act established the Rural Electrification Administration (REA) with the goal of bringing electrical power to the rural parts of the country not served by private utilities. As a result of the work of the REA, the number of farms with power tripled between 1932 and 1941 (EIA, 1996: 107).

Second, the federal government began to develop its own generating resources, centered mainly around large hydroelectric facilities such as Hoover and Grand Coulee dams. The federal government also established the Tennessee Valley Authority and the Bonneville Power Administration in order to secure the economic development potential of Appalachia and Washington State. The scope of public building was such that between 1933 and 1941, half of all new capacity was provided by federal and other public power installation and by 1941, public power contributed 12 percent of total utility generation with federal power alone contributing almost 7 percent (EIA, 1996: 107).

By the mid-1930s, then, the essential framework for both the provision and the regulation of electricity in the United States was in place. First, the various forms of ownership, i.e., rural electric

---

[4] The FPC was created in 1920 by the Federal Act. The FPC was renamed the Federal Energy Regulatory Commission, or FERC, in 1978 (Garvey, 1993: 62).

cooperatives, municipal systems, federal authorities, and investor-owned utilities (IOUs) were all secured.[5] Second, a regulatory system had been created which respected both the federal character of the U.S. form of government, and the technological and economic imperatives of the industry, as well as its political power. Under this system, the federal government was charged with matters affecting the interstate transmission of electricity while the state commissions had authority over rates and other matters of local interest.

The Minnesota Story

The development of Minnesota's electrical system paralleled that of the national system. The history of the state's two largest IOUs, Northern States Power Company (NSP) and Minnesota Power Company (MP), illustrates the extent to which Minnesota's electric system was a reflection of developments at the national level.

NSP, the state's largest private utility, began operation under the leadership of Henry Marison Byllesby who, in 1881, joined Thomas Edison as a draftsman responsible for drawing up the plans for the inventor's Pearl Street Station.[6] Four years later, one of Edison's chief rivals, George Westinghouse, lured Byllesby away with an offer to become a $10,000 vice-president and general manager of the Westinghouse Electric Company. After six years of working for Westinghouse designing electricity-powered appliances, Byllesby was hired by Charles A. Coffin, president of Thomas-Houston Electric

---

[5] The basic mix of generators remains in place today. Of the 89 percent of total generation that is produced by utilities, 74 percent is produced by IOUs, 9 percent by federal power generators, 6 percent by cooperatives, and 11 percent by other public entities, principally municipal utilities. The remaining 11 of generation is produced by so-called non-utility generators, i.e., cogenerators, independent power producers, and other exempt wholesale generators (EIA, 1996: 17, Figure 7).

[6] This history is drawn from Carol Pine. 1979. *Northern States People: the Past 70 Years.* North Central Publishing.

Company and was sent to St. Paul, Minnesota to run the company's northwest subsidiary. Four years later, Thomas-Houston merged with Edison's General Electric Company.

By 1902, Byllesby was secure enough in his own abilities that he left the now-expanding General Electric Company to form his own engineering and operating firm in Chicago. The firm was run largely by colleagues Byllesby had known from his days at both GE and Westinghouse. For the next decade Byllesby would follow a policy of mergers and acquisitions that ultimately led to one of the nation's largest electric utility holding companies.

The frenetic pace of acquisition led Byllesby to seek out investors and creative financing solutions. For much of this advice and assistance, he turned back to Chicago and Samuel Insull. Following Insull's lead, Byllesby created two companies, Northern States Power Company of Delaware (1909) and Standard Gas and Electric, or SG&E (1910). The former was one of many operating companies that purchased financial, engineering, and management services from SG&E. Byllesby continued his expansive ways throughout the 1910s and 20s, extending his reach beyond the Midwest into California, Kentucky, Colorado and Oklahoma. In addition, Byllesby's SG&E created a lucrative investment securities business. So successful was the holding company that Pennsylvania Governor Gifford Pinchot, a leading reformer of the period, identified Byllesby and SG&E as one of the principle targets in the anti-trust movement, along with others such as Insull's Middle West Utilities Company, J.P. Morgan and his associates who controlled General Electric, and Harry Doherty of Cities Service Company.

As was true of the other holding companies, PUHCA required that SG&E dismantle itself and that the controlling interests in Chicago sell their stock back to the company. NSP was forced to go through a painful period of revaluation, since most of the company's assets were found to be the beneficiary of the creative methods typically practiced by SG&E accountants. The process by which NSP was forced to become a wholly independent utility company was not completed until after World War II.

Minnesota's second largest IOU, Minnesota Power (MP), followed a similar corporate path.[7] MP began as a small company competing for market share in and around Duluth. Employing the same sort of merger and acquisition philosophy as most other electric companies of the day, the company had been transformed by 1923 into the Minnesota Power and Light Company (MP&L) with operations in many parts of northern Minnesota. The company had long been associated with another major electric holding company, Electric Bond and Share (EB&S), which had added one of MP&L's corporate predecessors, Duluth Edison Electric Company, to its holdings in 1906. Eventually, a corporate structure evolved which found MP&L to be an operating company of the American Power and Light Company (established in 1909) which in turn was controlled by ES&B.

The same sort of abuses that led to the downfall of the holding companies ultimately found their way to MP&L. For instance, in hearings before the Federal Trade Commission, the agency found that (Beck, 1985: 284):

> American Power and Light had written up its property by a total of $68.5 million; of that total, MP&L's share came to more than $21.5 million. FTC's investigators charged that MP&L's plant on the Kawishiwi River had been built in 1922 without a permit from the Federal Power Commission. Phoenix Utility Co. sold the hydro development and its flowage rights to American Power and Light in December of that year for $48,000. In November 1923, American Power and Light sold the same

---

[7]   Much of this history is drawn from Bill Beck. 1985. *Northern Lights: An Illustrated History of Minnesota Power.* Eden Prairie, MN: Viking Press, Inc.

property to MP&L for $534,000 as part of the Minnesota's subsidiary consolidation.

Similar sorts of abuses were found in regards to the valuation of stock and other company assets. While company officials argued that such inflated values were perfectly proper and a matter of "business judgement" (Beck, 1985: 285), MP was forced to reinvent itself as a wholly independent company, a process which again was not completed until after World War II.

The development of municipal and cooperative power systems also paralleled national developments. Municipal utilities, for instance, were found as early as the 1890s as towns such as Preston, Litchfield, Granite Falls and many others built power generations to satisfy the demands of both individual residents and public facilities (Centennial reports for the towns of Litchfield, and Granite Falls; *Municipal Plants*, June 1933, Volume 1, Number 1).

Similarly, the state's forty-seven electric cooperatives were established following the Rural Electrification Act. Throughout the 1930s, cooperatives were established, though they often struggled to provide reliable and cost-effective service. Often times, small cooperative merged with other organizations. For instance, in 1937, six cooperatives merged to form the Rural Cooperative Power Association for purposes of building their own generation station and transmission facilities. A similar strategy was followed in other parts of the state (UPA, 1997). Eventually, two types of cooperatives emerged: large generation and transmission cooperatives such as United Power Association and Cooperative Power Association, and distribution-only cooperatives who purchase their energy from a variety of producers for distribution to the end-user.

The structure that evolved during the first half of this century remains in place today. Of the 55,758 Gigawatt hours (GWH) of electrical energy consumed in Minnesota in 1995, 68 percent was provided by IOUs. Cooperative and municipal utilities provided 16 percent and 13 percent of total consumption respectively with the remaining 3 percent being self-generated (MDPS, 1997b). However, both the customer base and the types of sales vary widely among the various types of utilities. IOUs, for instance, serve largely urban areas, while the cooperative and municipal utilities serve mainly rural areas and the small cities of Greater Minnesota. Of the 1.255 million customers served by IOUs, less than one percent are farm customers. In fact, the largest of the state's IOUs, NSP, served no farm customers in 1995. Conversely, nearly one-third of the 563,311 customers served by cooperatives are farm based. By the same token, municipal and cooperative utilities serve mainly residential customers, while the IOUs, and in particular Minnesota Power, devote much more of their load to industrial and commercial customers. Sixty-one percent of the IOUs total consumption is supplied to industrial customers (and 80 percent of MP's load) while municipals sell only 50 percent of their load to industrial customers and cooperatives an even smaller 10 percent (MDPS, 1997b: various tables).

Electric Utility Regulation in Minnesota

Several agencies are presently responsible for the regulation and oversight of electric utilities in the state, including the Public Utilities Commission (PUC), the Department of Public Service (DPS), and the Office of the Attorney General (OAG). The Environmental Quality Board (EQB) also becomes involved in energy issues while assessing the environmental impact of proposed facilities. In the same way, Administrative Law Judges associated with the Office of Administrative Hearings often consider energy-related cases in quasi-judicial hearings.

The fragmented character of regulation is part of the state's historical legacy. Dean Abrahamson's 1974 study of state energy policy, for instance, indicated that the two regulatory authorities with primary responsibility for energy matters were the now-defunct State Energy Agency, which had oversight authority for large energy facilities and the issuance of certificates of need, and the EQB, which was responsible for overseeing the construction of transmission facilities and the issuance of site compatibility permits. In addition, a number of other state agencies, including the Pollution Control Agency, the state Fire Marshall, the Department of Health, the Department of Labor and Industry, and the Highway Department were tangentially involved in energy-related decisions (Abrahamson, 1974: 50-54).

The energy crisis precipitated by the Arab oil embargo of 1973 led the state into taking a more activist role in energy policy, a principle expression of which was the creation of the Minnesota Energy Agency (MEA). Established in 1974, the MEA was charged with managing the state's energy supplies and serving as a center for information, analysis and policy development concerning energy resources, supplies, production, conservation, prices and trends (State of Minnesota, DOA, 1992: 412). Reorganized and merged with other agencies several times since 1974, much of the MEA's work is now performed by the DPS's Energy Regulation and Resource Management division, which serves as a public advocate before the PUC and as the chief source of information about the state's energy system.

The mid-1970s also saw the state become the 48th state to institute rate regulation of electric utilities. The power to exercise this authority was given to the Railroad and Warehouse Commission, which had been established in 1871 for purposes of approving the rates charged by railroads operating in the state (State of Minnesota, DOA, 1992: 532). The Commission was eventually given authority to set rates for trucks and buses, warehouses, grain elevators, weights and measures, telephone and telegraphs and was renamed the Railroad and Warehouse Commission.

Over the years the Commission had been divided into a number of divisions, each dealing with a particular category of rates and/or service. In 1967, the Commission was abolished and replaced by the Department of Public Service (DPS). Over time it was argued that the two electricity-related roles assigned to the DPS, that is, serving as both a public or ratepayer advocate as well as chief regulator of the industry, presented a fundamental conflict. The Commission also expressed a desire for a greater degree of administrative independence. In July of 1980, an administrative separation between the DPS and the PUC, with clearly delineated advisory and advocacy roles, was approved.[8] In 1983 a further reorganization took place, when the responsibility for regulating surface transportation (trucks, buses and warehouses) was transferred to the Minnesota Transportation Regulation Board; the PUC continued to retain authority over electric, gas, and telecommunications utilities (PUC, 1997).

The PUC's present authority is based on state statutes requiring IOUs doing business in the state to provide fair and reasonable rates and adequate service (Chapter 216, Minnesota Statutes). The Commission's authority over municipal utilities applies only to rates or services of customers outside city limits and to cooperatives only when the members of the cooperative elect to become rate-regulated. In addition to its responsibility for rate regulation, the PUC issues certificates of need for so-called 'large energy facilities,' including high-voltage transmission facilities, pipelines for gas and liquid energy products, nuclear processing facilities, and nuclear storage facilities, among others (State of Minnesota, OAH, 1992: 532).

In addition to the PUC and the DPS, the OAG has several divisions which are heavily involved in energy issues. These include the Public Utilities Division, which serves as the chief legal council for the PUC, the Telecommunications and Energy Division and the Residential Utilities Division (RUD), both of which appear before the PUC on behalf of residential and small business customers (State of Minnesota, DOA, 1992: 77-78).

---

[8] The administrative fragmentation that characterizes Minnesota is relatively unique among the states.

RECENT POLICY ISSUES

The final section of this chapter will review a number of the most important issues that have come before Minnesota's policy makers over the last decade.   Each of these cases illustrates both the complexity of the policy process and the many public authorities and private interests that insert themselves into the process. The issues that will be considered include the specification of externalities associated with electricity production; the storage of high-level nuclear waste; and presently unfolding debates over the restructuring of the electric industry.

Externalities and Electricity Production

Economists define 'externalities' as benefits or costs, generated as a by-product of economic activity, that accrue to a party not involved in an economic transaction. *Environmental externalities* are benefits or costs, or changes in economic welfare, that manifest themselves through changes in the physical-biological environment. As a result, the price of a good is misspecified. If it is overspecified, that is, if the price is too high because too many costs are reflected in the price, underproduction occurs. In most instances, however, environmental externalities are generally considered in the negative: as a result of certain kinds of economic activity, damages are inflicted upon the environment which are not reflected in the price of the good produced by that activity.   In this case, there exists an 'under-specification' of price which leads to an excess level of production.

It is important to realize the implications of this perspective: the problem of externalities is not environmental damage per se, but the *inefficient allocation of productive resources*.   In essence, the purpose of quantifying and then internalizing externalities, that is, adjusting the price of the good so that all environmental damages are represented in that price, is not to clean up the environment or even to prevent pollution but to correctly allocate incomes and resources. The concern is not about pollution as such but only about *inefficient pollution*. Thus, even if all externalities are fully incorporated into the price of the good, society might very well choose to continue its polluting ways. The difference is that society will, to the extent that it can put a price on nature, be paying the 'right' price for the privilege of pollution.

The determination of environmental externalities associated with electricity production involved a long and complicated procedural history. The first step occurred in May of 1993 when the state legislature enacted a law which contained a number of provisions related to renewable energy and resource planning, including a requirement that the Commission quantify and establish a range of environmental costs associated with each method of electricity generation. The law further required each utility to "use [these values], in conjunction with other external factors . . . when evaluating resource options in all proceedings before the Commission" (Laws of Minnesota, Chapter 356, Minn. Stat. section 216B.2422 [Supp. 1993]). The legislation, which became effective August 1, 1993, set March 1, 1994 as the deadline to establish interim environmental cost values which were to expire when final values were set.

Given the deadlines specified in the legislation, the PUC decided upon an expedited generic proceeding to determine and establish interim values for a number of air emissions most commonly valued in other jurisdictions engaged in externality quantification, e.g., sulfur dioxide (SO_2), nitrogen oxides (NO_x), lead (Pb), carbon monoxide (CO), particulate matter less than ten microns across (PM_{10}), and carbon dioxide (CO_2). The Commission adopted a range rather than a discreet set of values which, according to the Commission, acknowledged the uncertainty attending externality valuation.

In consideration of the complex nature of the issue, and in order to provide Minnesota-specific data, the Commission ordered a *contested case hearing* for the purposes of setting final values. Accordingly, the case was argued before an ALJ appointed by the Office of Administrative Hearings. The ALJ received and reviewed testimony from numerous parties, including the State of North Dakota, the major IOUs, cooperatives and municipal utilities in the state, large industrial consumers, environmental organizations, low-income advocates, and a number of state agencies, including the AGRUD, the DPS, the Department of Trade and Economic Development, and the Pollution Control Agency.

A number of critical issues were involved in the case, including the selection of the most appropriate method for putting a dollar value on the externalities caused by electricity generation. Two principle methods were considered: cost-of-control and damage cost. Most economists agree that the most methodologically rigorous approach is the latter. According to critics, the 'costs of control', usually measured by the expenditures necessary for end-of-pipe technology, may be too high or too low, depending upon whether regulators over- or under-controlled emissions relative to the optimal (socially-desired) level of pollution. The damage cost method is said to provide a more exact accounting since it associates emissions with specific human impacts such as illness and loss of life and their economic costs. A major part of the proceeding therefore was a very expensive damage-cost study performed by Triangle Research Associates on behalf of NSP.

A second controversial issue involved the question of global climate change. Parties to the case took dramatically different points of view. Coal interests, for instance, argued that climate change was either scientifically unproven or, if it was true, any increase in temperature caused by the buildup of carbon in the atmosphere was likely to prove beneficial to crops and other vegetation. These parties also argued that Minnesota's contribution to global climate was so negligible as to render any efforts at reduction unwarranted and meaningless. Other parties relied primarily upon the work of the U.N.-sponsored Intergovernmental Panel on Climate Change (IPCC) to claim that climate change is occurring and that the effects are likely to be profound and potentially catastrophic. The Judge found that global climate change was, in fact, a real phenomenon with actual, if somewhat difficult to measure, costs. The ALJ also found that since emissions from power plants contribute to the anticipated temperature changes it was appropriate to attach some additional costs to power plants that might be constructed in the future (State of Minnesota, March 22, 1996).

These findings and a recommended set of values were provided to the PUC and on December 16, 1996 the Commission directed that the following values be applied to all future resource planning decisions (PUC, 1996):[9]

Pollutant	Urban	Metro Fringe	Rural	Within 200 miles of MN
SO $/ton	112-189	46-110	10-25	10-25
PM $/ton	4,462-6,432	1,987-2,886	562-855	562-885
CO $/ton	1.06-2.27	0.76-1.34	0.21-0.41	0.21-0.41
NO $/ton	371-978	140-266	18-102	18-102
Pb $/ton	3,131-3,875	1,652-1,955	402-488	402-488
CO $/ton	.30-3.10	.30-3.10	.30-3.10	.30-3.10

Source: PUC. *Order Establishing Environmental Cost Values.* Docket No. E-999/CI-93-583. December 16, 1996.

Nuclear Waste Storage

A second equally complex issue has been the controversy over the storage of high-level nuclear waste produced by NSP's nuclear reactors at Monticello and Prairie Island. Throughout the history of

---

[9] Under Minnesota law, the recommendations of the ALJ are advisory only. The referring body, in this case, the PUC, can accept, reject, or modify the findings as they deem appropriate.

the nuclear project, a variety of technical solutions have been proposed to deal with the waste generated during the various phases of the nuclear fuel cycle. The preferred option for dealing with high-level spent fuel is reprocessing an operation which, in theory, turns the fuel into additional quantities of useful atomic material (Carter, 1987; Cassedy and Grossman, 1990).

While reprocessing remains the ultimate hope of many in the industry, the limited technological and economic success demonstrated to date has forced the industry to pursue an alternative strategy. Rather than presuming that spent fuel can be reused, the industry, in league with the U.S. government, has sought a means to permanently isolate the material from the environment. As stated in the 1982 Nuclear Waste Policy Act, this strategy is predicted on the U.S. Department of Energy's (DOE) ability to identify a passive, non-engineered storage medium, that is a naturally occurring geological formation which would not be subject to invasion or movement. The search for such a deep-site geological storage repository has been on-going for well over a decade. Initially focusing on a number of sites assumed to possess stable geological formations, the effort is now limited to a single site, namely, the old atomic testing grounds of Yucca Mountain, Nevada (Hancock, 1993).

Unfortunately for the industry, the site characterization process has become bogged down in the politics of federalism, the inherent mistrust inspired by the responsible federal agency, the DOE, and the very nature of atomic waste, i.e., its longevity and basic hostility to all forms of life. Initially, the site was to be opened in January 1998. However, because of delays associated with site characterization, principally involving recurring debates over the stability of the region and a newly discovered aquifer laying underneath the proposed chambers, it is now anticipated that the site will not be able to receive waste until well into the first decade of the 21st century, if ever (see Hancock, 1993).

The rapidly declining prospects for Yucca Mountain has left the industry in a difficult situation. Historically, the industry has operated on the presumption that the DOE would, at some point in the future, be in possession of an operating permanent waste storage facility, allowing DOE to fulfill its legal responsibility as owner of the waste. At best, the operators have been assuming that even in the absence of a permanent repository, the DOE would make available interim-period monitored retrievable storage (MRS) facilities. In essence, the plant operators assumed that someone other than themselves would have to deal with the waste problems generated by nuclear plant operations. On the basis of these assumptions, plant operators have been storing the waste in on-site storage pools located in the containment structures housing the reactors.

All of the assumptions regarding permanent and interim storage have been proven incorrect. What has proven to be true is that operators are rapidly running out of temporary pool storage capacity. While reracking, i.e., reconfiguring the waste in the storage pool, offers a near-term solution in some cases, some plants including the Prairie Island facility, were faced with the prospect of shutting down prematurely (that is, before the end of their operational life) because of inadequate storage space. As a result, operators of these plants have been aggressively seeking an interim storage option. The option most favored by the industry is dry cask storage. Under this scenario, the spent fuel would be stored in large, free-standing above ground casks for approximately 25 years or until a permanent facility is readied. Unlike an MRS facility, no attempt is made to isolate the waste geologically. In this respect, dry-cask storage represents an option midway between pool storage and an MRS facility.

The controversy over the so-called Independent Spent Fuel Storage Installation (ISFSI) at Prairie Island, a site adjacent to the Mississippi River, has involved an extremely complex set of legal and regulatory procedures. While the case was formally initiated on April 29, 1991 with a filing brought before the Minnesota Public Utility Commission for a Certificate of Need by NSP, the controversy had, in fact, been underway for several years prior to that time. Several years before the Commission's acceptance of NSP's application for a Certificate, the state's Environmental Quality Board had prepared an

Environmental Impact Statement which had considered the matter in some detail. Begun in December 1989 and released to the public on May 6, 1991, the Final EIS found that the facility would cause no significant harm to the natural and human environment, if certain revisions to the initially proposed siting plans were followed.

While public comments regarding the EIS focused on several important issues, including the likely health effects of the facility, the most significant issue in question was the permanency of the facility. Opponents to the facility argued that given the history of the federal effort in finding a permanent repository, any facility would, de facto, become permanent rather than temporary. The issue of permanency became sufficiently contentious that the PUC ordered a contested case hearing.

The ALJ's finding, issued in April of 1992, offered a serious challenge to NSP's contention that the facility was both limited and temporary. The ALJ first found that the "past two decades have been one missed deadline after another, and the future does not appear to be substantially different" (State of Minnesota, OAH, 1992: 19). Further, the Judge found that this record of failure is likely to inspire a search for an alternative path on the part of the U.S. DOE. According to Judge Klein (State of Minnesota, OAH, 1992: 19):

> There is a substantial risk that the Federal effort at Yucca Mountain will fail, and that Federal policy makers will abandon the search for a single permanent repository, and instead look for new ways to deal with the expanding quantities of waste accumulating around the country. If Prairie Island already has some dry casks in operation, the path of least resistance for the Federal (and state) decision makers will be to just let NSP continue to add more dry casks.

In other words, the facility, once operational, would not only become a permanent repository, but it would also become an importer of spent fuel from facilities around the country.

The finding of permanency was critical since under the Minnesota Radioactive Waste Management Act (RWMA) construction of any permanent nuclear facility required the permission of the legislature (Minn. Stat. Sect. 116C.71, subd. 7, 1990). Thus, if the Judge's finding of permanency was validated by the PUC, then the company would have to seek legislative approval.

On August 10, 1992, the PUC issued its findings pursuant to the application for the ISFSI. It found that the ALJ was mistaken in presuming that facility would, in fact, be permanent, arguing instead that the DOE "has no intention of abandoning its nuclear waste management responsibilities" and the Department "will begin to remove the stored waste within a time frame reasonably close to the one enunciated by that agency" (PUC, 1992: 10). Consequently, the Commission (PUC, 1992:10):

> Emphatically reject(ed) the notion that allowing limited dry cask storage is an irreversible step toward the inevitable creation of a permanent nuclear waste storage facility at Prairie Island . . . The Commission reject(ed) as not credible the assumption that all federal and state officials at every level will fail to carry out their responsibility and will allow Prairie island to become a permanent nuclear waste storage facility by default.

As a result, the Commission concluded that the MN RWMA did not apply and that legislative approval was not required.

The findings of the Commission regarding the permanency issue and the subsequent requirement for legislative approval became the grounds for judicial appeal by a number of groups previously involved at the regulatory level. This appeal was successful and on May 9, 1993 the Minnesota Court of Appeals ruled that "we have concluded that NSP's proposed facility is properly classified as one in which waste is permanently stored" (*Star Tribune*, April 7, 1994). As a result of this finding, the company was forced to seek legislative approval for the ISFSI.

After what has been described as one of the most contentious debates ever seen in the Legislature, approval was granted for the construction of an ISFSI. The initial approval was for nine casks, with additional casks being dependent upon the identification of an alternative site away from the river, a requirement which has subsequently been eliminated. Perhaps the most important outcome of the legislative debate, however, was the requirement that NSP develop significant amounts of wind and biomass energy. According to a report by the Union of Concerned Scientists, Minnesota has some of the finest wind resources available in the nation (Brower, et al., 1993). The Prairie Island legislation provides assurances that these resources will, in fact, be taken advantage of and that Minnesota will become a world-wide leader in alternative energy. In addition to 125 megawatts (MW) of biomass energy by the year 2002, the legislation also requires that 425 MW of wind energy be developed in the state by 2002, with an additional 400 MW required if wind can be proven to be the least-cost resource. [10]

Restructuring the Electric Industry

The debates over externalities, nuclear waste and renewable resources were significant milestones in the recent history of energy policy in the State. However, these debates have taken place within the context of a system that has functioned for the last fifty years and which has provided the state with some of the nation's cheapest electrical energy. The last policy issue to be considered here has the potential to fundamentally reshape the entire electric system in the state.

Beginning with groundbreaking federal legislation enacted in both 1978 (the Public Utilities Regulatory Policy Act, or PURPA) and 1992 (the Energy Policy Act or EPAct), the American electric industry is the latest in a series of key economic sectors to be the

---

[10] The debate continues, of course. NSP continues to seek legislative modifications to the agreement and there is significant debate over the least-cost requirements concerning the next 400 MW.

subject of demands for greater degree of competition. Alternatively referred to as 'retail wheeling', 'restructuring', or 'retail competition', proposals are being made that would move the industry from its historical status as a regulated monopoly to one characterized by a greater degree of competition. In essence, advocates of reform are seeking to transform electricity from a highly regulated good affected with the public interest to one that will be increasingly subject to the rules of the marketplace. In its simplest form, restructuring refers to the vertical 'disintegration' of electric utilities whereby the present system of vertically integrated utilities would be broken up into separate generation, transmission and distribution companies. While the so-called TRANCOs and DISCOs would likely remain regulated monopolies, generation companies would compete for customers.

The potential consequences of this transformation are enormous. Advocates of restructuring, for instance, argue that the process will result in significantly lower electricity prices that will multiply into billions of dollars of new economic growth (Maloney and McCormick, 1997). Critics of restructuring, on the other hand, claim that the most likely result of retail competition will be a highly segmented market structure, where lower prices for one market segment, such as large industrial consumers, will mean higher prices for other segments, mainly residential and small commercial consumers. As evidence, critics point to the recently deregulated telecommunications industry, where such trends are already clearly visible (National Consumer Law Center, 1997). In particular, critics worry that low-income households and neighborhoods, as well as rural customers, will experience degraded service and higher costs while specialized and generally lower-cost services will be made available to the wealthiest segments of society.

Similar debates are taking place regarding the environmental consequences of restructuring. For instance, proponents suggest that renewable energy will experience a renaissance similar to the days of the energy crises of the 1970s if people are given the option of choosing their electricity supplier. 'Customer choice,' says the market advocate, means that people will finally be able to act upon long-expressed preferences for purchasing green energy. Critics envision a very different outcome. In their scenario, restructuring is a death knell for renewable energy as wind and other forms of capital-intensive green energy are forced to compete with coal plants that have long been fully amortized and are operating at low capacity factors. The result of this unfair competition will not only be the demise of the renewable industry but increased levels of emissions as utilities attempt to price-compete by ramping up output from dirtier, but cheaper, coal plants.

In addition to distributional and environmental impacts, there are a host of technical questions that are being considered as the restructuring debate unfolds (Hoffman and Matisone, 1997; Hunt and Shuttleworth, 1996). For instance, many critics question whether service standards will be maintained under a highly competitive system, arguing that reliability will be severely degraded as companies try to cut costs by reducing labor and other supporting infrastructure. On the other hand, proponents argue that customer choice will mean that companies will be forced to maintain reliability under the threat of losing market share to more reliable providers. By the same token, there are strong indications that demand-side management programs, i.e., energy efficiency and weatherization programs designed to curtail energy consumption, will be eliminated as firms try to eliminate all but the most essential of items. This is particularly likely to happen as firms turn away from a conservation ethic to one based on maximizing the sale of electricity as a way of maximizing profits. Critics are also concerned about maintaining consumer protection laws and regulations. Again, many commentators have argued that electricity deregulation will be accompanied by widespread fraud and abuse as well as annoying and intrusive marketing campaigns.

Finally, there is the enormously contentious issue of 'stranded costs' that is, costs associated with generating plants that are no longer cost competitive due to significant debt burdens or high operating costs. While most analysts do not perceive this to be a problem in Minnesota, in other parts of the country, particularly in those states with a significant number of nuclear plants, stranded costs dominate the policy discussions. Indeed, many analysts argue that the principle impetus for restructuring comes from industries in high-cost states seeking a way to purchase power from low-cost states such as Minnesota.

The restructuring issue involves the usual panoply of federal and state actors. For instance, in 1996, the Federal Energy Regulatory Commission (FERC) issued Orders 888 and 889 (FERC Docket No. RM95-8-000 and RM94-7-001; Docket No. RM95-9-000, respectively). These orders established the rules for so-called "open access transmission" that will allow newly-competitive generators access to privately-owned transmission systems. At the same time, high-cost states such as California and Rhode Island have adopted comprehensive plans calling for the rapid deregulation of the electric industry in their respective states while low-cost states, including Minnesota, have adopted a much more patient attitude towards restructuring.

CONCLUSION

The restructuring debate is yet another illustration of the dynamic character of American energy policy. As has been the case throughout the century, the debate concerns fundamental principles inherent in the American policy making system. In some respects the debate is reminiscent of the holding company period, particularly since the threat of deregulation has prompted a wave of mergers among utilities. The irony of this situation, that is, the inconsistency between calls for greater and greater competition in theory and fewer and fewer firms in practice, has not escaped notice. The trend toward larger and fewer firms is also inconsistent with the new economics that supposedly now characterizes the electricity industry. Unlike earlier in this century when assumptions of economies of scale and natural monopoly provided the analytical framework for policy makers, today's economics are said to favor smaller generating stations and hence more active competition among a greater number of firms. Thus, while the historic trend of industrial consolidation continues, the traditional rationalization for consolidation seems to be evaporating (EIA, 1996: 88).

Mergers are also creating entirely new types of firms. ENRON, a large power marketer, has recently announced a merger with Portland Gas and Electric, a traditional vertically integrated utility. Other deals are being made that will merge companies operating in different states and/or regions of the nation. Some commentators are also calling for the repeal of PUHCA. Using language typical of the proponents of repeal, Senator D'Amato of New York State has argued that recent developments "have called into question the relevance of the model of regulation established in the Act" (Preamble, Senate Bill 621, introduced on April 22, 1997).

All of this poses significant challenges to the existing regulatory system. It was argued above that state regulation was a satisfactory solution to an industry, and to a nation, tired of municipal regulation and distrustful of federal intervention. Today, the expanding geographic bounds of the industry calls into question the appropriateness and perhaps even the possibility of state-based regulation. Should restructuring move forward on a national scale, it is clear that some sort of regional regulation will be necessary (Andrews, 1995). Yet, there are few working examples of effective regional regulation in American history. The recent experience with efforts to implement a multi-state compact for the siting of low-level nuclear waste facilities is certainly not encouraging. Perhaps this is the central challenge for policy makers: to craft a regulatory system that recognizes the new economics of electricity while continuing to respect the fundamental features of American federalism.

REFERENCES

Anderson, Douglas D. 1981. *Regulatory Politics and Electric Utilities: A Case Study in Political Economy*. Boston, MA: Auburn House Publishing Company.

Andrews, Clinton J. 1995. *Regulating Regional Power Systems*. Westport, CT: Quorum Books.

Beck, Bill. 1985. *Northern Lights: An Illustrated History of Minnesota Power*. Eden Prairie, MN: Viking Press.

Blacks Law Dictionary. 1968. Revised, 4th Edition. St. Paul, MN: West Publishing Company.

Brower, Michael C., Michael Tennis, Eric Denzler, and Mark Kaplan. 1993. *Powering the Midwest: Renewable Electricity for the Economy and the Environment*. Cambridge, MA: Union of Concerned Scientists.

Carter, Luther. 1987. *Nuclear Imperatives and Public Trust: Dealing with Radioactive* Waste. Washington, DC: Resources for the Future.

Cassedy, Edward S. and Peter Z. Grossman. 1990. *Introduction to Energy: Resources, Technology and Society*. New York, NY: Cambridge University Press.

Energy Information Administration (EIA). 1997a. *Country Analysis Briefs (various tables)*. Washington, DC: Energy Information Administration.

_____. 1997b. *International Energy Annual: 1995*. Washington, DC: Energy Information Administration.

_____. December, 1996. *The Changing Structure of the Electric Power Industry: An Update*. Washington, DC: EIA, Office of Coal, Nuclear, Electric and Alternative Fuels, U.S. Department of Energy.

Garvey, Gerald. 1993. *Facing the Bureaucracy: Living and Dying in a Public Agency*. San Francisco, CA: Jossey-Bass Publishers.

Gordon, Richard L. 1982. *Reforming the Regulation of Electric Utilities*. Lexington, MA: Lexington Books, DC Heath and Company.

Hancock, Don. 1993. "FOR SALE: Nuclear Waste Sites — Anyone Buying?" *The Workbook.* Albuquerque, NM: The Southwest Research and Information Center.

Hoffman, Steven M. and Sandra Matisone. 1997. *A Citizens Jury on Minnesota's Electricity Future.* Minneapolis, MN: The Jefferson Center for New Democratic Processes.

Hughes, Thomas P. 1983. *Networks of Power: Electrification in Western Society, 1880-1930.* Baltimore, MD: The Johns Hopkins University Press.

Hunt, Sally and Graham Shuttleworth. 1996. *Competition and Choice in Electricity.* Chichester, UK: John Wiley and Sons.

International Energy Agency. 1997. *Energy Statistics of OECD Countries.* Paris, France: IEA.

International Energy Agency. 1997. *Energy Statistics and Balances of Non-OECD Counties.* Paris, France: IEA.

Maloney, Michael T. and Robert E. McCormick. 1997. *Customer Choice, Consumer Value: An Analysis of Retail Competition in America's Electric Industry.* Washington, DC: Citizens for a Sound Economy Foundation.

Minnesota Department of Public Service (MDPS). 1997a. *Minnesota Energy Data Book: Energy Trends From 1965 Through 1995.* St. Paul, MN: Minnesota Department of Public Service.

_____. 1997b. *The 1995 Minnesota Utility Data Book: A Reference Guide to Minnesota Electric and Natural-Gas Utilities Through 1995.* St. Paul, MN: Minnesota Department of Public Service.

_____. December 1996. *1996 Energy Policy and Conservation Report.* St. Paul, MN: Minnesota House of Representatives.

Minnesota House of Representative. 1994. *State Energy Laws: 1973-1994.* St. Paul, MN: Minnesota House of Representatives, Research Department.

National Consumer Law Center. 1997. Congressional Testimony.

Price, Carol. 1979. *NSP: Northern States People for the Past 70 Years.* North Central Publishing.

Public Utilities Commission (PUC). 1997. *PUC Employees Manual.* St. Paul, MN: Public Utilities Commission.

_____. December 16, 1996. *Final Order,* St. Paul, MN: Minnesota Public Utilities Commission.

_____. August 10, 1992. *Order Granting Limited Certificate of Need.* Docket No. E-002/CN-91-19. St. Paul, MN: Minnesota Public Utilities Commission.

Research Department. July, 1994. *A Guide to Major State Energy Laws 1973-1994.* St. Paul, MN: Minnesota House of Representatives.

State of Minnesota. Department of Administration (DOA). 1992. *Minnesota Guidebook to State Agency Services 1992-1995.* St. Paul, MN; State of Minnesota, Department of Administration.

State of Minnesota. Office of Administrative Hearings (OAH). For the Public Utilities Commission. March 22, 1996. *In the Matter of the Quantification of Environmental Costs Pursuant to the Laws of Minnesota: Findings of Fact, Conclusions and Recommendation.* St. Paul, MN: Office of Administrative Hearings.

_____. April 10, 1992. *In the Matter of the Application of Northern States Power Company for a Certificate of Need for the Construction of an Independent Spent Fuel Storage Facility: Findings of Fact, Conclusions and Recommendation.* St. Paul, MN: State of Minnesota.

Twentieth Century Fund. 1948. *Electric Power and Government Policy: A Survey of the Relations Between the Government and the Electric Power* Industry. New York, NY: The Twentieth Century Fund.

United Power Association. 1997. Web site: www.upaweb.com/frames/story.

Chapter 12

MINNESOTA'S ANSWER TO ESCALATING MEDICAID COSTS: THE MINNESOTA PREPAID MEDICAL ASSISTANCE PROJECT

Patricia J. Bodelson
Associate Professor

Steven C. Wagner
Assistant Professor

Department of Political Science
St. Cloud State University

INTRODUCTION

Health care is a contentious issue. Debate tends to come down to the issue of whether therapeutic interventions are a privilege or a right. Shifts in the discussion throughout the century reflect changing perspectives on the issue. Presently, the focus is on cost containment. Since the late 1970s, policies have focused on controlling publicly reimbursed health services. Nationally, Medicaid changes have been in the purview of states by nature of the program's design. Unlike the centralized bureaucracy of Medicare, Medicaid is enmeshed in several layers of government. Rapidly escalating expenditures that grew nearly five-times from 1970 to 1980 provided impetus for the federal government to seek alternative state models for delivery of Medicaid services (Holahan and Cohen, 1986). One innovative attempt to ensure quality while containing costs was recently implemented in Minnesota. On July 1, 1985, Minnesota was granted a waiver from federal Medicaid regulations to implement a proposed cost containment plan. The infrastructure of the plan mirrored managed care.

Managed care was first introduced by the Committee on the Cost of Medical Care (CCMC) in the 1930s. Managed care is presently referred to as Health Maintenance Organizations (HMOs). The model did not receive support until the Nixon administration because of the unanticipated rise of health care costs of Medicare and Medicaid. The rationale for the model is its ability to address preventative health care with cost containment. The philosophical shift in the health care debate from enhanced accessibility to cost containment in the 1970s gave further impetus for legislation that promoted managed care. Throughout the 1970s, debate centered on several policies designed to reign in skyrocketing health expenditures. One of these efforts was the adoption of the HMO Act of 1973. Since then, the HMO model of health care delivery has become an archetype for the formulation of several innovative programs, one of which is the subject of this chapter: the Minnesota Prepaid Medical Assistance Program (PMAP). This chapter traces the development of United States health care and the emergence of managed care, examines Minnesota's innovative implementation of managed care, and analyzes some of the impacts of the program.

THE DEVELOPMENT OF HEALTH POLICY IN THE UNITED STATES

The focus of health policy in the United States shifted during the 20th Century. The change in direction was in response to the social, economic, and political influences of the time. According to Paul Starr, this evolutionary pattern can be divided into three eras: progressive, expansionary, and containment (Starr, 1982b).

The Progressive Stage

During the progressive stage (1900-1920), proposed policies emphasized income maintenance for ill or disabled employees. The problem the reformers of the progressive stage addressed was that of stabilization of income during illness. Prior to the 20th century, workers were insured through sickness funds sponsored by mutual societies, unions, and employers to provide cash benefits in case of illness to compensate for lost wages. Such programs dwindled by the turn of the century and after the passage of worker's compensation interest in health insurance developed (Anderson, 1985). As the Progressive era ended in the 1920s, there was no national policy that would respond to the crisis of wage loss due to illness. What is noteworthy about the Progressive era is that, although unsuccessful, citizens' groups and professional associations emerged who thought the government should become involved in the issue.

The Expansionary Stage

This shifted as the country moved into the expansionary stage (1920-mid 1970) which focused on providing access to health care regardless of financial status or geographic location. Policies developed and implemented in the expansionary stage are partially responsible for the fiscal crisis facing the Congress today. There was very little activity on health care issues in the 1920s and early 1930s. Yet, the issue of health insurance did not totally dissipate (Anderson, 1985). The concept of health insurance received attention during the New Deal and following World War II. The problem was that "the costs of services were rising to the point that not only wage earners, but also people of 'moderate means', were finding them hard to meet. And as a result of this economic barrier, society was failing to meet individual's health care needs" (Starr, 1982a: 82). The cost of both physician's fees and hospitalization increased, but primarily the latter.

The increase in physician's role came from improved quality of services due to scientific advances and increased monopoly power due to licensing restrictions. The latter gave physicians higher returns on their investment in education than was perhaps justifiable (Friedman, 1945). The rise in hospital costs was related to the transformation of hospital care: as hospitals became centers for surgery and acute care their construction and operating costs soared. Moreover, as the care became more common and derived more income from services, their charges increased (Goldwater, 1905).

In 1926, a group of health care professional gathered in Washington D.C. to discuss the social and economic aspects of health care. The Committee on the Cost of Medical Care was created during the Washington meeting (Anderson, 1985). The CCMC identified several areas for intensive analysis. The studies done by the CCMC found that "the need for medical care as defined by professional standards was higher than the rate of utilization even among the highest income group" (Falk, Rorem, and Ring, 1932: 5). The CCMC also called for changes in the delivery system focusing on the prepaid capitation group practice model for health care versus the already prevalent fee-for-service model. The CCMC's stance requiring increased expenditures to meet the health needs of the nation marked a shift in health policy from a means of distributing wage losses and medical cost through insurance into expansionary financing to facilitate access (Starr, 1982a).

During the expansionary period, many proposals were offered to solve the problem of restricted access to medical care. Presidents Roosevelt and Truman recommended national health care programs. Neither could rally enough support to insure the enactment of any national health policy. Other proposals include the introduction of Senate bill 1920 by Wagner of New York, the Caper bill in 1941, the Eliot bill in 1942, and the Wagner-Dingell bill in 1945 (Starr, 1982a). The major issue that led to the demise of these proposals was ideological. Endorsement of the programs was not forthcoming because it was considered inappropriate for the government to use payroll deduction and/or taxation to finance health services for everyone (Anderson, 1985).

There was not enough support to enact a national health care plan until the Johnson landslide election in 1964. When the 89th Congress convened in 1965, a national health care plan was a priority for both congress and the administration. The plan covered only the elderly (Medicare) and indigent (Medicaid).

Medicare is a centralized national program associated with Social Security. It mirrors the distributive policy attributes of the Social Security system. *Medicaid*, on the other hand, is administered by states according to a mix of federal and state guidelines and regulations. The federal government encourages state participation and compliance in several ways. For example the federal government provides matching grants to states to encourage them to expand their Medicaid programs. Presently, the federal Medicaid matching ratio varies from a minimum of 50 percent to a maximum of 83 percent. Furthermore, states have the option of administering the program or devolving it to their counties (Patel and Rushefsky, 1995). The Health Care Financing Administration (HCFA) is the federal agency charged with oversight of the Medicaid system. It is from this agency that Minnesota received its waiver for the demonstration project.

Medicaid targets children and mothers who are eligible to receive Aid to Families with Dependent Children (AFDC), the elderly poor over the age of sixty-five, and disabled or blind persons who qualify for Supplemental Security Income (SSI). The federal guidelines set the income limits for the SSI program. Therefore, state Medicaid programs must include the categorically needy persons (Brown, 1984). States may elect to provide coverage to those not required to be covered by federal regulation. States are eligible to receive matching funds for coverage of optional groups. These include medically needy families with dependent children whose incomes are above the state Medicaid means test limit and elderly who do not qualify for cash assistance but have large medical and skilled nursing facility bills (Grannenmann and Pauley, 1983).

The Medicaid enabling legislation requires states to cover certain services, including hospital and physician services, family planning, care in nursing homes, diagnostic services, and screening. Optional benefits include prescription drugs, dental care, and care in intermediate-care facilities.

States may demarcate services per beneficiary or use health care models other than fee-for-service. Originally, under Medicaid, states had to pay hospitals and physicians according to the "reasonable cost" principle, determined by the health care provider. The reasonable cost principle meant that service providers could set costs and government would reimburse. Presently, states now reimburse physicians the same rate as Medicare mandates or on a fee schedule. All providers must accept Medicaid's reimbursement as payment in full. Because of low physician pay rates in many states, a significant number of physicians refuse to treat Medicaid clientele (Ginsburg, 1988).

Initially, Medicaid was perceived as a limited entitlement program. Over time, however, Medicaid has broadened to include payment for the health care of low-income, pregnant women and long-term institutional care for the elderly, disabled, and mentally retarded (Schneider, 1988).

The Cost Containment Stage

The enactment of Medicaid and Medicare was the culmination of the expansionary era and played a role in the shift to the present stage of health care. This present stage, referred to as the cost containment era, emphasizes control of rapidly escalating health care costs (Starr, 1982a).

As noted above, the Medicaid program experienced dramatic increases in outlays as it evolved. Medicaid also experienced a steady growth in the number of recipients. Those receiving Medicaid benefits nationwide increased from 17.6 million in 1972 to 21.6 million in 1980. By 1990, the number had grown to 25.3 million people (Ginsburg, 1988). Total Medicaid expenditures increased from $5.3 billion in 1970 to $24.8 billion in 1980 (Holahan and Cohen, 1986). The fee-for-service delivery model for Medicaid inflated rising health costs in part because there was no coordination of care. For example, Medicaid recipients were able to self-refer, thereby seeing a neurologist instead of a primary care physician for a headache. Moreover, Medicaid recipients could use hospital emergency rooms as their source of primary medical care which is far more costly than ambulatory care facility.

By the mid 70s, proposed health policies began to reflect the need to control the ever-rising costs of health care. In part, the change was due to the shift in power within the health care delivery system. Hospital administrators began to emerge as institutional leaders in health care. Along with increasing power within the care institutions, administrators also became more influential in the formulation of health policies and regulations. The emergence of this new interest affected a shift in the focus of health policy from one that addressed the amount of care provided to one that emphasized the economic efficiency of health care (Alford, 1975).

For a variety of reasons, the complexity of the Medicaid program led to calls for reform. First, because health services are reimbursed by a third party there is no incentive to limit services. Furthermore, those that provide services have limited incentives to curb services and costs. Second, Medicaid is administered through several layers of government: national, state, county and special districts. This makes effective program coordination nearly impossible. Finally, Medicaid recipients are relatively uninformed health care consumers. Therefore, their ability to evaluate the amount and type of services is minimal. The combination of these factors create a convoluted matrix of health care delivery models.

Cost containment proposals reflect two strategies for controlling costs: regulation and increasing competition in the health market (McClure, 1981 and Berki, 1983). The advocates of health regulations argue that market short-comings inhibit the health care industry from controlling costs (Ellwood, 1975). A physician who is provider of services and consultant to patients in a fee for service model is not motivated to limit therapeutic interventions and subsequent health care expenditures. The third party reimbursement model renders this an especially acute problem because the patients are not responsible for medical costs. Instead, insurance companies or the government reimburses physicians and hospitals for services. Thus, regulation seemed justified to ensure quality and monitor hospitals and physicians regarding type and price of care (Marmor, 1983).

The market strategy of cost containment relies on the assumption that access to health care had improved to such an extent that competition among providers, which in a free market would normally contain costs, is lost (Enthoven, 1982). Advocates of a market strategy argue that incentives could increase competition among health care providers. Dr. Paul Ellwood, a key health care advisor in the Nixon Administration, combined the two strategies and reintroduced the CCMC's concept of prepaid group health plans (or HMOs) to the policy debate (Brown, 1981).

DEVELOPMENT OF MANAGED CARE

As long ago as the 1920s, the CCMC advocated the HMO model of delivery. It was not until the passage of the HMO Act of 1973 that HMOs received support despite ongoing physician's resistance to the concept of managed care.

Managed care refers to an integrated health care delivery model (Starr, 1982b). Members prepay a capitated rate for an entire range of services, from acute care to emergency response to annual physical examinations (Starr, 1982b). A primary care physician coordinates all health care. Hospital costs, office visits and preventive medicine are all included and subscribers are not charged for the specific services that they use if approved by the primary care physician (Hillman, 1987).

The prepaid captitation model has piqued public and private interest. The incentives inherent in the HMOs for physicians and members are more compatible with cost containment in health care than the more traditional fee-for-service model. Increased services results in diminished provider revenue unlike the fee-for-service model. It appears the intent of HMOs is to cut health care costs under the guise of efficiency.

Research substantiates that medical care provided through HMOs is generally less costly than fee-for-service care. This may be due to the fact that HMOs tend to deliver a different mix of services and provide care for a different demographic cohort. Most HMOs are not required to provide services to Medicare recipients, the most avarice consumers of health care. While HMO enrollees visit health providers somewhat more often than patients who pay for each visit, they have a lower hospitalization rate than other insured populations (Sorkin, 1986). Cost savings may also may be related to the demographics of those enrolled in the plan as compared other health care recipients (Fetter, Thompson and Kimberly, 1985).

Despite the introduction of prospective capitation health plans in the 1920s, the model as an alternative to traditional fee-for-service was not well received by health care professionals. Starr reports that many viewed the concept as utopian and perhaps even subversive (1982b). The model integrates health care providers and insurers into a corporate model. The medical profession perceived the introduction of corporate dominated competition in health care delivery as a threat to their sovereignty and autonomy in clinical practice. In the 1970s, the rapid escalation of health care costs and a shift in power in the delivery system led many to assess a prepayment option as a relatively conservative form of health care management (Brown, 1983).

The emergence of the HMO as a viable competitive medical care delivery model received a significant boost beginning in 1971, when Nixon used discretionary funds for federal assistance to plan and establish HMOs (Rosoff, 1975). Nixon's early efforts culminated in 1973 when Congress passed the Health Maintenance Act. The legislation allocated $375 million to be used to finance initial start-up cost of HMOs. The legislation also required employers with 25 or more employees to offer an HMO option in addition to traditional health care services. It was thought that this would give an HMO the essential assistance to become established and rapidly become competitive (Brown, 1983).

Nearly immediately it became apparent that high costs created by outliers may constrain the ability of organizations to start an HMO. Therefore, legislation contained provisions that protected HMOs from catastrophic losses. Moreover, statutes required that all federally supported HMOs provide comprehensive care, maintain open enrollments, limit copayments, and price services on a community rate (Patel and Rushefsky, 1995). These restrictions prohibited many HMOs from obtaining federal start-up funds. Subsequently, in 1976 and 1978, amendments to the HMO Act reduced the comprehensive care requirement and limited enrollment. These two actions, coupled with allowing Medicare and Medicaid recipients to seek care at HMOs, helped to insure initial success. It is noteworthy, however, that the HMO Act, as amended, did not require HMOs to accept high risk and potentially costly clientele into their practices.

STATES AND MEDICAID

An interesting feature of Medicaid policy is the integral role played by state and local governments. Although the national government took an increasingly significant policy formulation role in the 1960s, financing and management of subsidized health care remain divided and shared among nearly all levels of government (Patel and Rushefsky, 1995). As previously stated, Medicaid is funded by national and state governments but administered by state and local governments. Subnational management, according to national parameters represents an excellent example of intergovernmental policy management.

The importance of state and local government involvement in health care delivery is partially historical. The provision of financial assistance for maternal child health care, as well as services for the mentally ill and disabled, are traditionally state and local functions (Marmor, 1973). States have traditionally licensed health care professionals, regulated insurance, and more recently, have acted to contain hospital and physician costs through rate setting, price fixing, and even rationing (Leichter, 1992).

The ability of state and local governments to respond to the emerging health care needs in their territories diminished shortly after they obtained authority to respond. Citizen initiatives to reduce taxes, a recession in the early 1980s, and Reagan-sponsored reductions in Medicaid spending all hindered states from continuing to increase health care access (Thompson, 1986). Nevertheless, states were given authority to suggest and seek changes and innovations in Medicaid administration (Leichter, 1992).

Presently, the level of state and local government spending in health care is significant. In 1993, total state and local government spending was $107.3 billion compared to $280.6 billion expended by the national government (Levit, 1994). Of the $107.3 billion expended by state and local governments, approximately 39 percent or $42 billion were for Medicaid reimbursement (Levit, 1994). State and local expenditures for health care in general and Medicaid in particular are accounting for an increasingly large share of state and local resources. A significant portion of these funds are allocated for long term care for senior citizens who have exhausted their Medicare entitlement. In Minnesota this group comprises one-quarter of the Medical Assistance (MA) population, but accounts for three-quarters of all expenditures. Because of this statistic, this cohort was included in a state-initiated innovative cost containment program: the Minnesota Prepaid Medical Assistance Program (PMAP).

THE MINNESOTA PREPAID MEDICAL ASSISTANCE PROGRAM

The Health Care Financing Administration (HCFA), a bureau of the Department of Human Services responsible for fiscal policy, allows states to develop cost containment alternatives for payment and delivery of Medicaid services through waivers of service options. In the early 1980s, the HCFA provided development or planning grants through waiver number 1115, permitting states to seek support for the preparation of cost containment strategies. In 1982, the state of Minnesota proposed the Minnesota Prepaid Assistance Program. (Minnesota Department of Human Services, 1995a). In Minnesota, Medicaid is managed and partially funded at the county level.

The actual design of the PMAP resulted from the efforts of an advisory or planning committee consisting of Minnesota Department of Human Services staff (DHS), county officials, consumers, health care providers, and HMO representatives. The State sought three county sites for the initial phase of the program: one each representing rural, suburban, and urban centers (Minnesota Department of Human Resources, 1995a).

Itasca County, approximately two hundred miles north of the Minneapolis/St. Paul metropolitan area, volunteered as the rural county. Dakota County, part of the Minneapolis-St. Paul Metropolitan Statistical Area, located in the southeastern part of the urban area, was willing to participate as the suburban county. Hennepin County, where Minneapolis is located, participated as the urban county despite the lack of unanimous support from the County Board.

Concomitantly, the PMAP received support from the State legislature with passage of Minnesota State Statute 256B.69 in 1983. The statute allocated funds for county expenses connected with or resulting from participation in the project. Previously, each county in Minnesota assumed responsibility for 50 percent of the administrative costs of its Medicaid program. Federal outlays accounted for the remaining 50 percent. In addition, the state offered to reimburse each county 50 percent of its normal costs for Medicaid services. The financial incentive propelled the planning committee to finish the program guidelines or protocols. In early 1985, the program protocols were submitted to the HCFA (Minnesota Department of Human Services, 1995a).

The final plan resulted in a prepaid, capitated managed care program for Medicaid eligible individuals. The selection of this model was based on the previously stated premise that it removes incentives for uncoordinated and excessive provision and consumption of services. Most AFDC, needy children, pregnant women, and elderly Medicaid recipients are included as participants. The participants choose a collaborating health plan, such as Blue Cross and Blue Shield, and receive services through the provider. Each month, the State pays a capitation rate to the health plan on behalf of each participant (Minnesota Department of Human Services, 1995a).

The health plan delivers all Medicaid covered services. The capitation rate is calculated on an actuarial analysis of the State's historical cost experience with groups of recipients and other cost and use factors. Capitation payments for skilled nursing facilities and Intermediate Care Facilities for Mentally Retarded (ICF/MR) residents cover all services except the residential per diem. Initially, the State reimbursed individual plans for their Medical Education (ME) and Disproportionate Population Adjustment (DPA) costs. This was an attempt to insulate the plans from the negative fiscal impacts caused by their service to lower income and generally more severely ill clientele. Beginning in 1992, the State built these costs into the capitation rates, based on utilization rates of teaching and DPA hospitals. The State also offers hospitals inpatient stop-loss protection, which prohibits providers from terminating coverage to high risk or expensive patients. Coverage is set at 80 percent of costs above a $15,000 threshold. Participating health plans may opt to have the State supply the reinsurance or privately purchase it. If they choose the latter, the capitation rate reflects the value of the coverage (Minnesota Department of Human Services, 1995a).

Of the three demonstration sites, Itasca County implemented the PMAP on July 1, 1985. The remaining two counties implemented the PMAP in December 1985. In Hennepin County, 35 percent of those eligible were enrolled in the PMAP, with the remainder enrolled in a fee-for-service plan to provide a control group for comparison purposes. The demonstration was to run through December 31, 1988 (Minnesota Department of Human Services, 1995a).

During the first two years of the PMAP, the State contracted with eight prepaid health plans. Health plans had the option of enrolling only one high risk and potentially expensive Medicaid population. However, the State stipulated that any health plan contracting to enroll AFDC eligible individuals, including the MA population categorically related to AFDC, MA needy children, and pregnant women program recipients, was also required to cover one of the higher risk populations: either aged or blind and disabled. Five health plans served Dakota County, while seven served Hennepin County (Minnesota Department of Human Services, 1995a). In January 1988, the PMAP underwent two major changes. Blue Cross and Blue Shield withdrew from the program and the blind and disabled populations were disenrolled. The remaining plans served all covered populations: AFDC, aged, and needy children. With the withdrawal of Blue Cross and Blue Shield, there remained four plans serving Dakota County and six serving Hennepin County for year three of the PMAP (Department of Human Resources, 1995a). A separate plan, administered by Itasca County, served that county's eligible population.

Although it was initially thought that three and one-half year's experience would provide sufficient time to collect data for evaluation, it became clear that this was insufficient. In 1987, problems obtaining service data and delays in enrollment compelled the State to request a two year extension through 1990. The HCFA lacked legislative authority to grant the request. The HCFA, however, suggested that the State pursue permission to continue the demonstration project through another waiver: 1915b (Minnesota Department of Human Resources, 1995a).

The State pursued both waivers. Minnesota considered it crucial to obtain an extension of the original 1115 waiver, which allowed the state to require health plan enrollees remain with a provider for a 12 month period. The 1915b waiver did not allow a similar lock-in device. The State requested plan providers submit a letter of intent to participate under either 1115 or 1915b waivers. One of the providers, Physicians Health Plan (PHP), indicated it could not continue participation without the 1115 waiver. Another provider, Preferred One, indicated that it significantly favored operating under the 1115 waiver. The State and the HCFA sought a temporary extension of 1115 through legislative action. The HCFA was eventually successful in obtaining authority to extend 1115 waivers through 1990 (Minnesota Department of Human Resources, 1995a).

Considering initial cost evaluation of the demonstration counties, the State legislature authorized the use of the prepayment plans in other counties. In the fall of 1989, Hennepin County decided to expand enrollees from 35 percent of eligible recipients to 100 percent. In the fall of 1990, the State received U.S. legislative authority to expand the PMAP to other viable counties through 1996. In early 1995, the State obtained approval to operate PMAPs until June 30, 1998. From early 1993 to late 1995, an additional nine counties, all in the greater Minneapolis/St. Paul metropolitan area, developed

PMAPs. The remaining 71 counties suggested that it would take about one year for their counties to reach full implementation (Minnesota Department of Human Resources, 1995b).

The PMAP also reduced or contained Medicaid expenditures. The Department of Human Services estimated a saving of over $5 million in 1987, $6.5 million in 1988, and $1.5 million for 1989 (1995a). The estimated saving in 1987 and 1988 may be inflated due to lower capitation rates used during these years. The capitation rates in 1987 and 1988 were based on historical per capita cost experience for 1986 Medicaid fees-for-service. The rates were also discounted up to 17 percent for AFDC eligible enrollees (Minnesota Department of Human Services, 1995a).

The DHS (1995a) suggests the more moderate saving for 1989 was primarily due to an increased capitation rate paid for aged enrollees. Minnesota laws dealing with care equity and financial liquidation make Medicaid more attractive to the state's elders than is the case in most other states. In 1989, the capitation rate for the aged population was based on 1987 historical fee-for-service expenditures and adjusted for inflation. The capitation rate was 124 percent of 1987 estimated fee-for-service costs. However, the 1989 Medicare Catastrophic Coverage Act reduced costs for fee-for-service Medicaid recipients for that year (Minnesota Department of Human Services, 1995b).

The importance of capitation rates for cost comparison with fee-for-services was obvious. If the rates were based on old or incorrect data, they may be too high or too low. The DHS determined rates annually, taking into account costs for the previous year, differences between metro and non-metro areas, and the age of each enrollee (1995a). The rates did not vary by provider. In Hennepin County the rates were higher than in other metro counties due to a higher rate of hospitalization, which was related to the County's demographics. This adjustment took into account the use of teaching hospitals that qualified for ME and DPA payments. The capitation rate for the

AFDC eligible enrollees averaged 10 percent less than fee-for-service costs. The capitation rate for the elderly averaged 5 percent less than estimated fee-for-service costs (Minnesota Department of Human Services, 1995a).

The DHS estimated that the PMAP resulted in a cost saving of $2.5 million in 1990 and $4.3 million in 1991 (1995b). The estimated cost savings in 1992, compared to fee-for-services trend, was $3.0 million. In 1993, DHS estimated the PMAP cost $18.9 million more than estimated fee-for-services expenditures. The DHS reports the PMAP costs were higher than estimated fee-for-service costs due to several factors (1995a).

One factor responsible for the increase was that in the beginning of 1990, the State assumed the risk for catastrophic cases and reimbursed providers on an individual basis. This continued until 1993, when stop-loss differential spending was incorporated into the capitation rates. This diminished the variability of expenditures among the population and equalized the costs for treatment of catastrophic illnesses. In 1992, the State reimbursed $898,014 to individual providers for stop-loss expenditures. In 1993, State spending for stop-loss differentials accounted for $6,073,288 of total capitation payments made to providers. Another factor related to the increase was the 1993 metro capitation rate, established at the beginning of 1993, was higher than estimated end of year fee-for-service expenditures. Moreover, services available to PMAP enrollees, such as interpreter services, plan education, services to pregnant individuals experiencing substance abuse and outreach were not available to Medicaid fee-for-service beneficiaries (Minnesota Department of Human Services, 1995b).

The total capitation payments made during the seven years of initial demonstration and enlargement of the experiment was $452.7 million. The DHS estimated the Minnesota Prepaid Medical Assistance Program resulted in a net saving of $3.3 million (1995a). The estimated savings were based on comparison of actual capitation expenditures versus estimated fee-for-service payments (Department of Human Services, 1995a). Most recent fiscal data indicate PMAP had a net savings of over 18 million dollars or five to ten percent of total MA budget. The DHS projects an increased net savings directly proportional to the longevity of the program (Chase, 1997).

CONCLUSION

The savings obtained by Minnesota's innovative medical assistance health care delivery model contributes to the state's fiscal solvency. This experiment and its successful outcome were made possible through cooperation among several layers of government. The national government waived medical assistance reimbursement regulations permitting the state to develop the model. Subsequently, counties began to implement the plan. Cooperation of this nature provided the opportunity for a state to find a creative and innovative solution to a contentious issue, namely, cost control and quality assurance for government reimbursed health care. This is an excellent example of successful policy implementation in a cooperative federal environment.

REFERENCES

Alford, Robert A. 1975. *Health Care Politics: Ideological and Interest Group Barriers to Reform*. Chicago, IL: University of Chicago Press.

Anderson, Odin. 1985. *Health Services in the United States: A Growth Since 1875.* Ann Arbor Michigan, MI: Health Administration Press.

Berki, S.E. 1983. (July). "Health Care Policy: Lessons from the Past and Issues of the Future." *Annals of the American Academy of Political and Social Science*. Number 468: 231-246.

Brown, Lawrence D. 1981. (Spring). "Competition and Health Cost Containment: Cautions and Conjectures." *Milbank Memorial Fund Quarterly/Health and Society*. Volume 59, Number 2: 145-189.

_____. 1983. *Politics and Health Care Organization: HMOs as Federal Policy*. Washington, DC: Brookings Institution.

_____. 1984. *Health Policy in the Reagan Administration: A Critical Appraisal*. Washington, DC: Brookings Institution.

Brown, Richard E. 1984. "Medicare and Medicaid: Band-Aids for the Old and Poor." In Victor Sidel and Ruth Sidel, eds. *Reforming Medicine: Lessons of the Last Quarter Century*. New York, NY: Pantheon. Pp. 50-76.

Chase, James. Director Managed Health Care Programs Division, Minnesota Department of Human Services. October 3, 1997. Personal Interview.

Ellwood, Paul M. 1975. "Alternative Regulation: Improving the Market." In *Institute of Medicine, Controls on Health Care*. Washington, DC: National Academy of Sciences. Pp. 49-72.

Enthoven, Alain C. 1982. "Competition in the Marketplace: Health Care in the 1980s." In James R. Gay and Barbara J. Sax, eds. *Competition in the Marketplace: Health in the 1980s*. New York, NY: Spectrum Publications. Pp. 11-19.

Falk, Rorem, and Ring. 1932. *The Cost of Medical Care. CCMC Medical Care for the American People*. Chicago, IL: University Press.

Fetter, Robert, John D. Thompson and John R. Kimberly. 1985. *Cases in Health Policy and Management*. Homewood, Illinois, IL: Richard D. Irwin, Inc.

Friedman, M. Kuznets. 1945. *Income From Independent Professional Practice*. New York, NY: National Bureau of Economic Records.

Ginsburg, Paul B. 1988. "Public Insurance Programs: Medicare and Medicaid." In H.E. Freech III, ed. *Health Care in America: The Political Economy of Hospitals and Health Insurance*. San Francisco, CA: Pacific Research Institute for Public Policy. Pp. 179-215.

Goldwater, S.S. November 9, 1905. "The Cost of Modern Hospitals." *National Hospital Record.* Pp. 39-48.

Grannenmann, Thomas W. and Pauley, Mark V. 1983. *Controlling Medicaid Costs: Federalism Competition, and Choice*. Washington, DC: American Enterprise Institute for Public Policy Research.

Hillman, Alan L. 1987. (December 31). "Financial Incentives for Physicians in HMOs: Is There a Conflict of Interest?" *New England Journal of Medicine*. Number 27: 1734-1748.

Holahan, John. F. and Joel W. Cohen. 1986. *Medicaid: The Trade-Off Bewteen Cost Containment and Access to Care*. Washington, DC: Urban Institute Press.

Leichter, Howard M. 1992. "The States and Health Care Policy: Taking the Lead." In Howard M. Leichter, ed. *Health Policy Reform in America: Innovations from the States*. New York, NY: M.E. Sharp. Pp. 3-23

Levit, Katharine R. 1994. (Fall). "National Health Expenditures." 1993. *Health Care Financing Review*. Volume 16, Number 1: 280.

Marmor, Theodore, Donald A. Wittman, and Thomas C. Heagy. 1983. "The Politics of Medical Inflation." In Theordore R. Marmor, ed. *Political Analysis and American Medical Care*, Cambridge, Cambridge, England: Cambridge University Press. Pp. 33-50.

Marmor, Theodore. 1973. *The Politics of Medicare*. Chicago, IL: Aldine Press.

McClure, Walter. 1981. (Spring). "Structural and Incentive Problems in Economic Regulation of Medical Care." *Milbank Memorial Quarterly/Health and Society*. Volume 59, Number 2: 107-144.

Minnesota Department of Human Resources. 1995a. *Prepaid Medical Assistance Cost*. Study and Addendum. St. Paul, MN: State of Minnesota.

_____. 1995b. *Prepaid Medical Assistance Cost and Study Addendum*. St. Paul, MN: State of Minnesota.

Patel, Kant and Mark E. Rushefsky. 1995. *Health Care Politics and Policy in America*. New York, NY: M.E. Sharpe.

Rosoff, Arnold J. 1975. (Fall). "Phase Two of the Federal HMO Development Program: New Directions After a Shaky Start." *American Journal of Law and Medicine*. Volume 1, Number 2: 209-243.

Schneider, Saundra K. 1988. (July/August). "Intergovernmental Influences on Medicaid Program Expenditures." *Public Administration Review*. Volume 48, Number 4: 756-763.

Sorkin, Alan L. 1986. *Health Care and the Changing Economic Environment*. Lexington, MA: D.C. Heath.

Starr, Paul. 1982a. (January). "Public Health Then and Now." *American Journal of Public Health*. Volume 72, Number 1: 78-88.

_____. 1982b. *The Social Transformation of American Medicine*. New York, NY: Basic Books.

Thompson, Frank J. 1986. "New Federalism and Health Care Policy: States and the Old Questions." *Journal of Health Politics, Policy, and Law*. Volume 11, No.4 (Tenth Anniversary issue): 647-669.

Chapter 13

AGING POLICY IN MINNESOTA

Carolyn M. Shrewsbury
Mankato State University

INTRODUCTION

At the beginning of this century, a special focus on policy needs and concerns of older persons would have had a very small audience. Few lived to old age; families cared for most of the elders needing assistance. Poorhouses, usually run by municipalities, served to warehouse the rest. By the end of the century, though, issues surrounding old age have entered center stage. Old age policy issues illustrate all the complexity of policy making. These issues have a major impact on young as well as old. Our ability to resolve them satisfactorily will have a major impact on American politics far into the 21st Century (Torres-Gil, 1992; MacManus, 1996).

While the national big budget issues of Social Security and Medicare received most of the media attention, the American states were engaged in less visible but equally important activities surrounding old age. The quality of life for all Minnesotans will continue to be affected by decisions made and not made in areas as diverse as long-term care, work force policies, health care, housing, transportation, and criminal justice, all areas which have significant dimensions important for aging policy. Old age policy is no longer a concern just for the old.

For the most part, Minnesota has not been a leader among states on aging policy issues. Given the state's general prominence as a policy leader, and particularly the state's prominence as a leader in health care issues, one might expect Minnesota to be on the forefront (Litman and Robins, 1997; Fox and Inglehart, 1994). The state's image of being progressive, pragmatic, and innovative would not be supported if one looked only at aging policy (Gieske, 1984). The primary purpose of this paper is to explore some of the reasons for this anomalous performance.

Fischer and Forester note that (1993: 1-2):

[P]olicy-making is a constant discursive struggle over the criteria of social classification, the boundaries of problem categories, the conceptual framing of problems, and the definition of ideas that guide the ways people create the shared meanings which motivate them to act.

Ideas about age and policy matter. What people think about age and politics matters. It may be Lester Thurow asking: "Will democratic governments be able to cut benefits when the elderly are approaching a voting majority?" (1996: 47). He goes on to say that "In the years ahead, class warfare is apt to be defined as the young against the old rather than the poor against the rich" (Thurow, 1996: 47). Or, from a different, albeit also gloomy perspective, Laura Katz Olson suggests that "the American political economy is inherently incapable of providing for the real needs of the elderly, especially those who are frail" (1994: 1). These and other perspectives are a part of the current policy debate in Minnesota.

The importance of aging issues becomes apparent as one looks at the changing demographics of the state. The proportion of the aged population has been increasing and that increase will escalate as the baby boomers reach old age. Some believe a crisis will be upon us unless we begin to make changes now. Thus, our discussion begins with the demographics of old age in Minnesota.

Policy leadership requires an institutional setting conducive to translating ideas into workable programs. The second section of the paper develops this structural setting. Finally, to illustrate the course of aging policy development in Minnesota, the third section will look at one fairly narrow and specific policy issue, prescription medications, and one much broader policy issue, long term care. Together, these will illustrate why Minnesota has not emerged as a policy leader on aging issues.

DEMOGRAPHICS

"Apocalyptic demography" refers to the comments by pundits who proclaim that the increasing proportion of the population who are aged are undermining American prosperity. The pejorative "greedy geezers" is used to paint an image of wealthy seniors enjoying a luxurious retirement at the expense of adequate schools for children. An army of older voters are seen as ready to march against any politician who dares even to suggest cutting benefits to seniors. Increasing numbers of frail elders are seen as likely to topple the health care system with end-of-life medical needs.

Apocalyptic demographers do have one point. The baby-boom generation has had a profound effect on our society as the sheer size of this cohort has moved through the life cycle. What that impact will be when all the baby-boomers have turned gray is yet to be decided. That the impact will be great has escalated the rhetoric surrounding age and public policy.

Minnesota's elderly population has continued to grow, with the growth rates highest at the more advanced ages. In the 1990 census, 16 percent of the population, or 718,154 people, were 60 or older.

Between 1980 and 1990, the numbers of those 85 and older grew by 30 percent, those 90 and older by 45 percent. The projections for the year 2020 show continued growth (see Table 1). The increases in the old-old are especially significant since they are much more likely to be poor (16 percent of the men 85 and older live in poverty compared to only 6 percent of men between 60 and 74; the comparable numbers for women are 26 percent versus 20 percent) and are more likely to be institutionalized (8 percent of those over 65, but 33 percent of those over 85, and 48 percent for women over 90) (McMurry, 1995).

TABLE 1		
Older Minnesotans as a Percent of Total Population		
Year	*1990 (actual)*	*2020 (projected)*
60-64	3.9%	7.2%
65-85	10.9	25.1
85+	1.6	2.3
total 60+	16.4	25.1

Source: Minnesota State Demographer's Office.

Insofar as the very old are particularly likely to be frail and to have mobility or self-care limitations, the comparative weight of that group is of concern to policy makers. Using 1990 census sample data, the National Aging Information Center ranked Minnesota 34 among states in terms of the proportion of its population over 60, but 13th for the proportion 85 and older (1996). If you couple this with the growth in Minnesota spending on Medical Assistance (114 percent between 1980 and 1990) as reported in *Trends in State and Local Government Spending* (1996), and note that 32 percent of that is for nursing home care, mostly for the aged, then the potential escalation in spending with increased numbers of the old-old becomes apparent.

Although suburban areas are now beginning to see the growth in the numbers of those over 65 that had earlier occurred in central cities and small towns, communities differ significantly in the proportions of the population that are older. For example, in the South Central region of the state, Eagle Lake, a growing suburb of the regional center, Mankato, had a low 4.9 percent of its population 65 and older while the proportion in Winthrop, a small rural town was over six times as great at 32 percent.

A 1996 survey published by the Minnesota Board on Aging based on telephone interviews of 805 non-institutionalized residents of Minnesota age 60 or older provides more detailed information regarding the diversity among seniors. Besides the differences in poverty rates noted above, women's greater longevity results in men being much more likely to be married (almost 2 to 1, or 66 percent of the men compared to 34 percent of the women at age 75 and over). Women are then much more likely to be living alone than are men (38 percent to 16 percent for those 60 and older). About 69 percent have a child living within 30 minutes and most have personal or telephone contact with their children regularly. However, about 4 percent could be considered socially isolated having little contact with anyone.

While the majority of older persons have retired, a significant number remain active in the work force (29 percent of the men and 20 percent of the women in the 65-74 age category; 7 percent of the men and 2 percent of the women over 75). Much larger numbers engage in productive activities by providing voluntary services to individuals (51 percent) or to organizations (61 percent). Many provide services (baby-sitting for grandchildren, caregiving for relatives) to their families (59 percent).

Many elderly continue to engage in vigorous physical activity (56 percent including many of those 75 and older). On the other hand, about 3 percent of the non-institutionalized adults in the sample, because of a health or physical problem, had difficulty doing personal care for themselves.   Another 6 percent had difficulty with activities like preparing meals, shopping for groceries, or light housework. By age 75, 16 percent have some difficulty performing at least one functional activity.

The growing numbers of older people and the needs associated with old age have been a concern to state policy makers for some years.   Concerns about the burden on the state treasury because of the high cost of nursing homes led the state to make significant attempts to control those costs in the early 1980s.   And in 1989, the lead article in the Economic Report to the Governor tried to generate concern about the implications for the labor force of an aging work force.   At the same time, the figures noted above point to the diversity among older residents of the state.   While age is not meaningless, it is also not one of those characteristics with which people strongly identify, nor one which gives people a lot in common.

Part of the problem Minnesota has had in becoming a leader in aging policy has been in finding a sufficiently clear focus for diverse policy issues.   As the population in Minnesota has aged, other significant demographic trends have attracted attention.   For example, the continuing growth of the major metropolitan area of Minneapolis-St. Paul and, until recently, the decline of greater Minnesota, occupied more attention than age changes (*Regional Diversity*, 1991).   In addition the meaning of other aging related characteristics of the population has not yet become a part of public discourse.   For example, the informal caregiving activities that families are giving elders is still relatively invisible in public discussions, albeit very much a part of private conversation.   States that are innovators in this policy area have had leaders and institutional bases for translating demographics and other issues into public policy concerns.   The next section will show how hard that has been in Minnesota.

A STRUCTURAL MAP OF AGING POLICY

Minnesota, as other states, is engaged in identifying ways to cope with the increasing numbers of seniors and to develop a coherent policy that reflects the diversity of that population. Situating aging policy in the political arena illustrates the difficulty the state is having in developing an aging policy that matches its overall progressive and innovative image. Political leaders, state agencies, and interest groups (and in some cases political parties) all have an impact on the visibility and development of policy issues (Nice, 1994). In the area of aging, none of these have provided the leadership that would make Minnesota a model for other states.

Historical patterns

In one review of Minnesota aging policy, Lammers and Klingman saw the state as strong on health, welfare and tax relief, but as a late adopter of regulatory provisions and only an average ranking on social services (1984). With the exception of Orville Freeman and Wendell Anderson, governors have rarely played any leadership role on aging issues. Legislative leaders in the 1970s, in particular, then-Speaker of the House Martin Sabo and Senate majority leader Nicholas Coleman, played key roles. Since then, while individual legislators have been important on one or another bill, the top leadership has not been prominent in aging issues. Nothing in more recent history would change the general perspective of Lammers and Klingman.

Likewise, while individuals in state agencies have played important roles on specific issues, department heads in Minnesota are rarely policy leaders and with one exception, Mike Hatch as Commissioner of the Department of Commerce on long-term care insurance, that is also true for aging policy. The Board on Aging, led from 1966 to 1994 by a single individual, focused on management more than advocacy.

Aging policy issues have a further disadvantage in state agencies because these issues cross so many substantive policy domains. While the Departments of Human Services and Health are most central to aging policy, Veteran's Affairs, Transportation, Economic Security, Labor and Industry, and Commerce, among others, also have important roles. While there have been a variety of structural attempts to integrate policy concerns, none have endured over time. Even within departments such as Human Services, organizational structures dealing with aging come and go with only the Board on Aging, itself mandated by Federal law, being a constant.

Governmental perspectives

Although there is no real history of major state political leadership on aging issues as a whole, and there has not been a policy area in aging where Minnesota's historical leadership would focus attention to the state, grassroots efforts can be the source of important policy innovations. Aging policy has a particular advantage here. One of the more interesting accomplishments of the Older American Act (OAA) has been to establish an "aging network" around the country. Besides requiring an agency on aging in each state, the Board on Aging in Minnesota, the OAA mandated that Area Agencies on Aging (AAAs) be created within each state. Of the 14 AAAs in Minnesota, nine are housed in Regional Development Commissions, three are free-standing nonprofit entities, one is a joint powers arrangement among nine counties and one is an Indian tribal organization.

These agencies serve as focal points on aging in their geographical region and are advised by a citizen advisory council. Besides advocating for the elderly, offering technical assistance to aging programs, planning on behalf of older persons, the AAAs administer a grant program for their region that supports ongoing state-wide efforts like a nutrition program serving meals in centers and in-home settings and grants to develop and/or support programs to benefit the elderly in their region. Although the amount of funds involved have been relatively small, these funds have been used to help increase the services available to seniors. Chore services, telephone reassurance, hospice, forms assistance, senior center renovations, adult day services, retirement counseling, and transportation programs are just a few of the many kinds of activities developed around the state through the efforts of the AAAs and the OAA funds they have granted.

The structural location of AAAs has been a strength and a weakness. In general, while they have been important in terms of enhancing the infrastructure of home care and community services (through their planning and grantmaking activities), they have played only minor roles in the overall aging policy of the state. As Falcone, Ensley, and Moore indicated in their 1992 study of Oregon and North Carolina, statewide, informed and sustained advocacy is required for significant policy leadership. Minnesota's Board on Aging and AAAs have instead intentionally focused their efforts on developing the infrastructure and enhancing the diversity of services for the aged. "We really believed the seed money concept would work, we guarded maintenance of effort very carefully, and, we were faithful to the notion that the Aging Network was to develop the capacity of other organizations - rather than ours - to serve older persons" (Minnesota State Unit on Aging, 1996: 13).

Counties, and in some service areas municipalities, also have a role in aging policy development. Counties have differed considerably in terms of the interest in and focus on the needs of their older residents. Since only about ten percent of their social services spending goes to the elderly, one might expect that aging services would be less visible than those for other needy individuals and families. Although there are a small handful of counties that might be viewed as policy innovators, and although in some counties there are staff who are particularly innovative in developing local programs, overall county activity in aging services has not translated into leadership in aging policy as a whole.

Interest groups

Minnesota's strong political parties have tended to moderate the impact of interest groups in the state. Nevertheless, interest groups do play an active role in the policy process. Although the popular image may be that aging interest groups led by the gigantic American Association for Retired People (AARP) always get their way, in Minnesota aging interest groups have never had an easy time of it. Neither have they been led by the AARP which only began to decentralize and play a role at the state-level after the debacle of Catastrophic Health Insurance at the national level. AARP's membership of over a half million Minnesotans overstates its strength in the state as most members have very minimal, if any, ties to local chapters.

On the other hand, the Senior Federation, with only about a tenth the membership of AARP, is a state focused organization and most of its members have stronger ties to local chapters. The Senior Federation has had a strong political focus and active lobbying effort since its founding in 1976 during a nursing home controversy in the state.

Some interest groups representing senior citizens are smaller, more specialized organizations, like the Older Women's League (OWL). Others, for example, the Minnesota AFL-CIO, identify aging concerns as only a small part of their overall policy agenda. For several years, many of these groups have been sharing information and cooperating on their legislative agendas in a group convened by the Board on Aging. The Senior Organizations Network (SON) present a united legislative front when possible.[1] Many of these groups also

---

[1] Members of the SON include the Minnesota Senior Federation, AARP, Gray Panthers, Minnesota Board on Aging, Retired Educators Association of Minnesota, Older Women's League of Minnesota, Minnesota Alliance for Health Care Consumers, Minnesota AFL-CIO, Minnesota Education Association – Retired, and the Minnesota Council on Black Aging.

support Senior Citizen days at the Capital and other efforts to engage their members more actively in the legislative process.

There are also a number of groups representing professionals, service agencies, proprietary organizations and others that align themselves for or against specific issues that affect some segment of the aging population. The Minnesota State Medical Association is such a group that Grau listed among the top lobby spenders in the 1979-85 period (1993). One group that actively opposed the senior's lobby on Living Will legislation, the Minnesota Citizens Concerned for Life (MCCL), was listed as one of the most effective groups at election time as well as in direct lobbying.

If there is a perception of Seniors as powerful political players easily getting their way, the history of the Adult Health Care Decisions Act, more generally known as the Living Will, shows the more typical course of long hard battles and many compromises even for issues on which senior organizations are relatively united. Living Will legislation had been introduced seriously since 1985. In 1987 a major push was made to pass this legislation with the primary opponent being the Minnesota Citizens Concerned for Life. After failure in 1987, a broad-based coalition of senior citizens, physicians, nurses, hospitals, nursing home residents and lawyers was formed. That coalition was broadened during the 1989 session to include organized labor and other groups. Over a million Minnesotans were represented by the coalition. Citizens throughout the state wrote letters to their legislators and to local newspapers, talked to their legislators, and sought editorial support. Strong legislative leadership supported by broad public support finally lead to passage of the bill in 1989.

Searching for a Focus

Since 1961, White House Conferences on Aging have been held roughly once a decade. In the early years these Conferences were focal points to bring together a coherent picture of the needs of older

Americans and to suggest bold policy initiatives to address them. Like much of the rest of American politics at the national level, the White House Conferences have become the victims of partisan wrangling with substantive discussions giving way to symbolic manipulation. At the state level, in recent years these events have been a vehicle to provide more citizen involvement in the pressing aging issues of the day and to form networks of active seniors and to raise the visibility and discussion of aging issues. The last Conference began at local levels where each Area Agency on Aging brought together seniors, their families, professionals in the field, and academics to develop recommendations for their region. These recommendations were then consolidated, discussed and prioritized at a state conference in late 1994. These then were sent on to the national conference.

A look at the process, the state conference, and the recommendations demonstrates the current central problem of aging policy in Minnesota. There is no core. Nor is there a clear leadership helping center the discussion of issues. In other words, there is little that holds the diversity of the aging interest structure together.

One can look back and see the embryos of many attempts to build such a core. The 1989 Wilder Foundation study resulting in a report entitled *Older Minnesotans What Do They Need? How Do They Contribute?* and the Board on Aging's *1995 Survey of Older Minnesotans* have been used more to see how older people are faring than to buttress a focused policy discussion. Project 2030 (referring to the date by which all baby-boomers will have turned 65), an initiative of the Department of Human Services could provide such a core. A similar effort by the Administration on Aging, "Redefining Retirement," involves the AAAs in Minnesota and provides a supporting opportunity for a clear policy focus. These, along with existing programs discussed below, provide the professional and staff support to policy development, so critical but often overlooked (Sabatier and Jenkins-Smith, 1993). But a political champion(s) will be needed for these to become more than just another study, another initiative, or another round of incremental change.

ISSUES

Almost any issue has a special aging dimension. In this section we will focus on only two issues to illustrate more about the aging policy process in Minnesota. Most attention will be given to long-term care which in many respects is the defining issue for aging policy. It intimately involves all ages. A 1997 national study, *Family Caregiving in the U.S.*, noted that one in four families are actively involved in caring for aging kin and that it is a costly undertaking. Expenditures by the state of Minnesota in FY1995 just for nursing home expenses alone were $819 million. Other states are taking many different and innovative directions as they develop long-term care policy, with Oregon the most widely admired (see, e.g. Justice, 1988). Minnesota has some innovative programs in long term care, but still has no real long term care policy. Prescription medications presents us with a case with a much narrower focus, but further illustrates how difficult it is in Minnesota to be innovative in aging policy.

Long-term care

According to a 1996 national survey, 87 percent of the respondents felt that providing long-term care is a big problem in this country. At the same time, only 30 percent passed a quiz on the basic facts about long-term care. Even fewer were preparing for possible long-term care needs (Miller, 1997). Both the awareness of the issue and the confusion about its dimensions and what to do about it are in part a consequence of the aging of the population and a shift in long term care policy from an emphasis upon institutionalization to community-based care.

Minnesota, too, is trying to make this transition from nursing home to community based care. However, Minnesota has been more dependent upon nursing homes than most states and that greater dependence makes the transition particularly difficult. Depending on the precise measure used, Minnesota's rate of nursing home beds per 1000 age 65+ ranged from 82-94 while the national average was 52-65 (*Responsibly slowing...* ,1994*)*. The high cost of nursing home care poses a burden for everyone. Even a short time in a nursing home can impoverish middle class residents. Consequently, public dollars pay for over 65 percent of all nursing home costs (*Trends in State...*, *1996*). Indeed, the bulk of state long-term care dollars goes to nursing home care. This leaves very few state dollars available for community care.

Many in Minnesota would agree upon appropriate goals such as the 20-year mission proposed in 1991 in A *Strategy for Long Term Care*: "[T]o create a new community based care paradigm for long term care in Minnesota to 1) maximize independence of the frail older adult population and 2) maximize cost-effective use of financial and human resources" (1991: 4). How to accomplish that mission is more problematic.

The state first had to control costs and decrease the reliance upon nursing homes. It then had to make a community-based care policy that would control costs and meet the needs of the frail elderly. This section will focus on the central problem of Minnesota aging policy and its failure to develop a coherent, cohesive, and focused policy. In this brief review, we will focus on three policy directions in which one might classify state community-care programs. Each direction has both philosophical and practical incompatibility with the other. The state is still searching for a focus for its long-term care policy.

Cutting costs for nursing homes

Community-based care is both more desired by frail older persons and is, at least in many cases, more cost effective than nursing home care. However, given the many demands upon state budgets, resources for community-based care depended upon slowing the growth in nursing home costs. One way to slow cost increases and to decrease the reliance upon nursing homes was to keep existing facilities from expanding and new facilities from being built. A moratorium on building new beds was promulgated in 1983.

Since then, the role of the nursing home has changed. Where once the place one went to die, nursing homes for many residents are now a transition stage from acute care to home care following a significant illness or accident. This new role, coupled with the growing population of the older population, meant an increased demand for nursing home care. If supply could not be increased because of the moratorium, then demand would have to be cut. Because the state controlled nursing home rates, demand could not be cut sufficiently by increasing rates. One state response was a pre-admission screening process which at first tried to divert potential nursing home residents to home based care and then was used to deny nursing home admission to the least disabled applicants. As more assisted living and other in-home services become widespread, one might expect that nursing home admission standards would increase even further and that the role of nursing homes would continue to evolve.

The state has also sought other ways to control costs. Minnesota adjusted reimbursement formulas, put caps on reimbursement increases, even used a purchase of services approach instead of a cost-based reimbursement system. It is difficult to identify whether any of these approaches have had an appreciable impact in that Minnesota, according to a study by the Legislative Auditor's Office, has a higher reimbursement rate than neighboring states (1997).

At the same time the state was trying to cut its expenditures, nursing homes, mostly for-profit institutions, were trying to sustain profitability. Diversification was one answer. The other would be to increase revenues. If the state were to hold the line on payments for poor or medically poor residents, perhaps private pay patients could be asked to pay more. While that has been the practice in every other state except North Dakota, Minnesota has prided itself on its common rate structure, regardless of the source of the money. But the linking of private and public pay rates has been under attack by the nursing home industry and by those who seek an unregulated marketplace. In 1995, ten years after the Supreme Court let stand an Appeals Court decision upholding Minnesota's rate equalization law (one of the long-term care policies of the state that might be viewed as innovative, progressive and pragmatic), the legislature began to backtrack by allowing some experimentation with differential rates at some facilities.

Community-based care: the role of the state

Decreasing institutionalization has both financial and personal benefits, if there are adequate alternatives available. The development of those alternatives is complicated by the historical reliance on nursing homes (and the poorhouse before it), by the financial restrictions in current federal law governing Medicare and Medicaid, by the lack of an infrastructure of alternative services, by the attitudes of elders and their families, by the centrality of the health care system in long term care (as practice and as idea), and by a plethora of unresolved policy issues. While all states face these problems, they have been particularly troublesome for Minnesota.

These policy issues are complex and here we can only indicate some of their dimensions. Still unsettled and most central is what is the role of the state. Three dimensions of the role of the state have characterized Minnesota's attempt to develop a coherent long-term care policy. The first has to do with how the state assists frail elders and their caregivers. The second has to do with the role of managed care. The third has to do with public-private partnerships.

Elder and caregiver support In Minnesota, as elsewhere, the vast majority of care given to frail elders is provided by the informal sector, that is, family, friends, and neighbors. Even if the state wanted to shift more of that responsibility to the formal sector it could not afford to do so. The question then becomes whether the state has any role in supporting and/or facilitating the work of the informal sector, especially as the demands on it increase. For example, Shenk argued in her study on rural women that many such women would far prefer to receive help from family and neighbors, but that such help would be best as part of a reciprocal exchange (1987). If the person were eligible for funding under the Alternative Care Grant program, for instance, might it be as appropriate to provide the client with dollars she could spend as she wanted rather than with services provided by the formal care sector. The answers to such questions rest not just on the pros and cons of this particular case, but upon deeply held perceptions about the role of government, about accountability, about oversight, about process, and about outcomes. Minnesota did provide some opportunities for elders to receive funds rather than services and Consumer Support Grants passed in 1997 should expand that.

Another approach placing maximum autonomy in the hands of the consumer was Minnesota's 1995 Elderly Housing with Services Act. The Act covered apartments, board and lodging establishments, and corporate foster homes serving seniors. Rather than regulation by the state, the key quality assurance mechanism was a contract made between the resident and the establishment. The contract covers what services are provided, the fees for those services, and how to amend the contract. Individuals don't stand totally alone because the ombudsman's scope has been expanded from advocating for nursing home residents to long-term care in general.

Managed care moves policy in a very different direction. Health care reform, an area in which Minnesota has been very innovative, has essentially centralized a good deal of the power and authority involved in health care decisions. Managed long-term care would involve case managers, as gate-keepers and/or as service coordinators for frail elderly. Rather than vesting authority in the consumer as above, managed care vests it in professionals and bureaucracies, either public or private. Minnesota is involved in several managed care initiatives including the first state-sponsored program in the country for those eligible for Medicare and Medicaid, the Long Term Care Options Project partially financed by a grant from the Robert Wood Johnson Foundation.

The analogy with health care issues does raise other questions. Minnesota's leadership in health care makes the commingling of medical and social issues in long term care seem natural. The Long Term Care Options Project integrates long term and acute health care under the management of a health plan or integrated service network. In many ways this is simply an extension of the way much of long term care has been delivered. The nursing home is dependent upon physician orders. Services for the poor have been paid for primarily through Medicaid, a medical program. The disabilities movement has been able to separate the need for various kinds of assistance to maintain one's independence from one's medical needs. The elderly have not yet successfully uncoupled the two. While Minnesota has not committed to the medical model as the primary direction for community-based long term care, it has invested significant resources in that model.

Public-private partnerships are another twist on the role of the state. SAIL (Seniors Agenda for Independent Living) grew out of recommendations made by the Board on Aging and the Minnesota Interagency Board for Quality Assurance in their 1990 report *Seniors Agenda for Independent Living*. SAIL began with six projects, each involving several counties. SAIL's basic mission to move long-term care in Minnesota from its institutional center to a community based center provides opportunities for many different kinds of activities. The SAIL legislation mandated a public awareness campaign to help change public attitudes about long-term care and to inform the public and professionals about alternatives in long-term care. Chore Corps was a project that was rather ingeniously, as the saying goes, designed to kill several birds with one stone. Chore Corps refers to community vendors who have received a seal of approval. These vendors provide a variety of fee-for-service assistance. Seniors benefit by being able to have some confidence in the quality of the services they are buying while the vendors benefit by getting increased sales. The public role is a small subsidy that pays for the administration of the program.

The intention of the advertising for the program was not only to highlight the availability of Chore Corps, but also to buttress the idea that buying aging services is simply an extension of normal life activities. It fit with the paradigm change in long-term care that the SAIL media consultant identified as one from "people accept care so they can survive" to "independent people buy services so they can enjoy life." (SAIL, 1993: iv). Also noted in the report was the need to instill "a new cultural attitude whereby Minnesota seniors will want and be willing to pay privately for early assistance to help them be as independent as possible for as long as possible, and can accomplish this through changes in cultural attitudes and public policy" (SAIL, 1993: 4-5).

Long term care is such an intimate policy area affecting the details of everyday life for the frail elder that the preference structures of those persons could be seen as something one needs to change or take into account. There is considerable diversity in those preference structures (Shrewsbury and Janovy, 1995). As long as people are purchasing what they want/need, the marketplace provides opportunity for diversity, at least in Metropolitan areas where the population base is sufficiently large to provide niches for diverse services. For those who need some assistance in securing services, honoring diversity runs into the management emphasis in modern state government. As Justice noted (1988: 1):

> The organizational challenge to state governments is to integrate the resource allocation and policy development activities of the various state offices responsible for some aspect of long-term care so that a coordinated system of care can be developed, rather than one reflecting a diffuse constellation of individual programs.

The emphasis upon public/private partnerships may turn out to be long-term care policy for the middle class, while managed care may be the state policy for the poor and medically poor.

Issues of long term care raise a number of policy issues for the state. The most central issue is what should be the role of the state. To date, Minnesota has no overall coordinated policy. There have been numerous demonstration projects, some of which find broader application, but rarely did they get broader recognition nor did they lead to broader policy visibility. Besides the general commitment to community based services rather than institutionally based ones, the direction of the evolution of state policy is still emerging. We discussed three policy directions, none necessarily compatible with the other, and none clearly dominating the state policy scene at this writing. There have been numerous attempts to chart a state course. For the latest, Project 2030, to be determinative in state policy, more statewide, visible policy leadership and champions may need to emerge. But if not, as the other attempts before it, Project 2030 will nudge the state in incremental ways. A project here or there may get noticed beyond the state. But without clearer vision and direction, aging policy in Minnesota will continue to belie the tradition of the state.

Seniors and prescription medications

Long-term care covers many issues and developing a coherent policy in this area is admittedly a complex task. Developing a policy for helping impoverished seniors acquire prescription medications is a much narrower, focused, and conceptually easier policy area for which one could develop a program. The story of seniors and prescription medications, however, also demonstrates the weaknesses of policy entrepreneurship in Minnesota for aging issues.

Many people think of Medicare as a full coverage health program. However, Medicare does not cover prescription drugs, significant cost items for many older adults. The Catastrophic Health

Care bill passed by Congress in July, 1988 would have corrected this by, after a $700 deductible, paying 80 percent of the costs of FDA approved medications using generics when appropriate. However, Congress repealed that legislation the next year, leaving those seniors (about half the over 65 population) without either supplemental insurance policies or Medicaid eligibility continuing to pay all prescription drug costs out of pocket. The Clinton health care proposals in 1994 included prescription drug coverage but failed to pass. Several states developed state subsidized programs to ameliorate a situation where many seniors had difficulty in affording expensive, but medically necessary, medications.

The high cost of prescription medications has long concerned seniors. Those who can afford to do so purchase a policy supplemental to Medicare to cover those costs. Many cannot afford supplemental policies or policies that cover prescriptions. If they are lucky, their medication costs are low. If they are unlucky, their prescription costs can be very burdensome. As shown in Table 2, a

TABLE 2			
Percentage of Minnesota Seniors Without Prescription Drug Coverage with Annual Expenditures in Excess of $1000 by Income Range			
	Income Range		
Seniors w/o prescription drug coverage	*Up to 100% poverty*	*100%-150% poverty*	*150%-300% poverty*
% with annual prescription expenditures > $1000	21.1%	19.3%	5.6%
% with annual prescription expenditures > $500	35.8	36.2	33.5
Source: *Senior Spotlight*. Spring, 1997. "Many low-income seniors have high drug expenses."			

survey commissioned by the Pharmaceutical Manufacturers of America and reported in the *Senior Spotlight* in the Spring of 1997 showed a large number of low income seniors with significant prescription drug costs.

Prescription medications have higher costs in the United States than in other countries and the costs of those medications has increased at a rate exceeding that of inflation. Seniors have been vocal in their concerns over those costs and in Minnesota the Senior Federation for many years made prescription drug coverage a mainstay of their legislative activities.

The state, however, has been very hesitant to move in this area. That hesitancy can be seen in a Feasibility Study for a state-funded prescription drug assistance program published in 1991 pursuant to a legislative mandate passed in 1990 and in subsequent publications from the Departments of Human Services and of Health. The state operated a number of medical facilities in state institutions and had long been involved in purchasing prescription medications. Indeed the Department of Administration won awards for its cooperative purchasing arrangements in which it acted on behalf of other states and the city of Chicago. The state had also been involved in prescription medications through its Medical Assistance program (Medicaid) where it used several standard cost control devices, including formularies, prior authorization, and manufacturer rebates. The state also was involved through the state health plan for its employees

Thus, while it might seem an easy step for the state to develop a plan to assist low-income seniors with prescription drugs, that has not proved to be the case. The Board on Aging advocated for such legislation for several years. The first legislation, passed in 1995, established the Senior Drug Discount Program as part of Minnesota Care, the ground breaking Minnesota health program. The drug discount program was to provide a prescription drug discount to seniors with incomes between 100 and 200 percent of federal poverty guidelines. The program was never implemented.

The Department of Health's 1996 report on the program to the legislature tactfully noted that "the legislation as passed may have been structured too tightly to allow the necessary innovation in program design to effectively implement the program" (1). There was little support in the bureaucracy for the program. As structured it was a voluntary program requiring pharmacists, manufacturers and seniors to come to the table to negotiate a program. The state was not putting dollars into the program. In effect, all participants opposed the program as passed. Whatever hope seniors had from the passage of the program was misplaced. The question was whether the bureaucracy had faith that any program could be structured. Without the support of the state departments, it was very unlikely that any program would be successful.

The legislature responded in 1996 with legislation requiring the Departments of Health, Human Services, and Administration to hammer out a plan. Several bills were introduced in the 1997 legislative session. Finally passed and approved by the Governor as a part of the Minnesota Care bill was a very limited and narrow program providing prescription drug coverage for low-income seniors not eligible for Medical Assistance (Medicaid) who pay a $120 annual premium and a $25 monthly deductible credited toward a $300 annual deductible (S.F.1208). The law is to take effect on January 1, 1999.

The story of prescription drug programs for seniors demonstrates some of the weaknesses of aging policy in the state. A deficiency in a national program, Medicare, leaves many low income seniors unable to afford the medications they need for maintenance of health and even life. While the Board on Aging and the most legislatively active seniors group, the Senior Federation, long pushed for some type of prescription drug program, there was little legislative agreement over details and little support in the state departments about whether any program was appropriate. When a bill was finally passed, it was not implemented. Some changes were made and a weakened proposal passed.

CONCLUSION

Talk to any politician and the importance of old age to policy concerns in the state is recognized. Beyond that there is little consensus. And although the title of this chapter is aging policy in Minnesota, one might even question whether there is such a thing. We made brief mention of Living Will legislation. But although older persons may have special interests in living wills and durable powers of attorney, these are instruments that are also of importance to people of all ages. We discussed long term care policy and that is often what many think of as aging policy. Even here, although we did not consider other dimensions, long-term care has also traditionally been of importance to those with mental illnesses and to those with developmental disabilities. Policy concerns here have many points of common interest as well as some important differences. We also discussed prescription drug assistance and that too is not just an issue for older persons, although the health plan for older persons, unlike most health plans for those under 65, peculiarly does not cover prescriptions.

Old age may be a status that most people desire to attain, but that does not make it a characteristic with which people strongly identify. And among the old, there is great diversity. While the "greedy geezer" described by some does exist, there are far more elderly just over the poverty line, struggling to maintain lives of quiet dignity. While some are locked in the dependence of Alzheimer's, others are actively involved in their communities, are reaching out to nurture and mentor not only their own grandchildren and great grandchildren but other young people in their communities. And while some may look with nostalgia about "the good old days," others are happily surfing the internet looking for new frontiers of knowledge and interest. It is no wonder that the interest group structure representing the old is so relatively weak. Beyond the universal entitlement programs like Medicare and Social Security (neither of which apply exclusively to the old), there is little that would automatically draw the attention of this group.

But old age, if for no other reason than the sheer weight of the baby-boom generation, is thrusting its need for a policy focus upon us. In these circumstances, the need for policy champions is particularly great, if the policy area is to attain visibility and to attain the level of discussion necessary to develop some consensus. Barring a policy champion, a clear structural center with enough clout to bring people together, if not to lead on its own, facilitates innovation. Occasionally a program can provide such leadership. Demographic forces have a way of asserting themselves whether we are ready for them or not. The baby boomers move into old age is about as inevitable as things get in a chaotic universe. If Minnesotans want to maintain their image as a progressive, innovative, and pragmatic state, there is much work to be done in aging policy.

REFERENCES

Falcone, D., et al. 1992. "Political Culture, Political Leadership, Sustained Advocacy, and Aging Policy Reform: the Oregon and North Carolina Experiences." In H.M. Leichter, ed. *Health Policy Reform Innovations from the States*. Armonk, NY: M.E. Sharpe. Pp. 73-101.

Family Care-giving in the U.S. Final Report Findings from a National Survey. 1997. Washington DC: American Association of Retired People.

Final Report of the Minnesota Board on Aging in Minnesota. Age in Place Project. On-site Coordinators to Arrange Support Services for Senior Housing Tenants. 1993. St. Paul, MN: Minnesota Board on Aging.

Fischer, F. and J. Forester. 1993. "Editors Introduction." In F. Fischer and J. Forester, eds. *The Aurgumentative Turn in Policy Analysis and Planning*. Durham and London, England: Duke University Press.

Fox, D. M. and J.K. Inglehart, eds. 1994. *Five States that Could Not Wait Lessons for Health Reform from Florida, Hawaii, Minnesota, Oregon and Vermont*. Cambridge, MA: Blackwell Publishers.

Gieske, M.L. 1984. "Minnesota in Midpassage: A Century of Transition in Political Culture." In M.L. Gieske, ed. *Perspectives on Minnesota Government and Politics*. 2nd Edition. Minneapolis, MN: Burgess Publishing Company. Pp.104-114.

Grau, C. H. 1993. "Minnesota: Labor and Business in an Issue-Oriented State." In R.J. Hrebenar and C.S. Thomas, eds. *Interest Group Politics in the Midwestern States*. Ames, IA: Iowa State University Press. Pp. 145-164.

Justice, D. 1988. *State Long Term Care Reform: Development of Community Care Systems in Six States*. Washington, DC: Health Policy Studies, Center for Policy Research, National Governors Association.

Lammers, W.W. and D. Klingman. 1984. *State Policies and the Aging.* Lexington, MA: Lexington Books.

Litman, T.J. and L. S. Robins. 1997. *Health Politics and Policy.* Third Edition. Albany, NY: Delmar Publishers.

MacManus, S.A. 1996. *Young v. Old Generational Combat in the 21st Century.* Boulder, CO: Westview Press.

McMurry, M. 1995. *Minnesota's Elderly Population: A 1990 Census Profile Working Paper #4-95.* St. Paul, MN: Minnesota Planning Office of the State Demographer.

Miller, B. 1997. *Worries About Long-Term Care.* American Demographics.

Minnesota State Unit on Aging (Board on Aging) and Minnesota Area Agencies on Aging. 1996. *Managed Care and the Aging Network: Current Status and Future Directions in Minnesota.* St. Paul, MN: Minnesota Board on Aging.

National Aging Information Center. 1996. *Older Persons with Mobility and Self-care Limitations: 1990.* Washington DC: Administration on Aging, U.S. Department of Health and Human Services.

Nice, D. C. 1994. *Policy Innovation in State Government.* Ames, IA: Iowa State University Press.

Nursing Home Rates in the Upper Midwest. 1997. St. Paul, MN: Program Evaluation Division, Office of the Legislative Auditor, State of Minnesota.

Olson, L. K., ed. 1994. *The Graying of the World: Who Will Care for the Frail Elderly.* New York, NY: Haworth Press.

Prescription Drug Study: A Report to the Minnesota Legislature on the Prescription Drug Market. 1994. St. Paul, MN: Health Economics Program, Division of Health Care Delivery Systems, Minnesota Department of Health.

Recommendations for Implementing the Elderly Housing with Services Registration Program. 1996. St Paul, MN: Division of Facility and Provider Compliance, Minnesota Department of Health.

Regional Diversity: Reexamining the Urban-Rural Dichotomy. 1991. St. Paul, MN: Minnesota State Planning Agency.

Responsibly Slowing the Growth of Minnesota's Long Term Care Spending: Recommendations for Reducing the Rate of Expenditure Growth and Ensuring the Quality of Care. 1994. St. Paul, MN: Minnesota Long Term Care Commission.

Sabatier, P.A. and H. C. Jenkins-Smith, eds. 1993. *Policy Change and Learning: An Advocacy Coalition Approach.* Boulder, CO: Westview Press.

SAIL (Seniors Agenda for Independent Living). 1993. *Report to the Minnesota Legislature.* St. Paul, MN: Minnesota Department of Human Services.

Senior Drug Discount Program: A Progress Report to the Legislature. 1996. St. Paul, MN: Minnesota Department of Health, Health Economics Program.

Senior Spotlight. 1997. *Many low-income seniors have high drug expenses.* Volume 26, Number 1: 7.

Shenk, D. 1987. *Someone to Lend a Helping Hand: The Lives of Rural Older Women in Central Minnesota.* St. Cloud, MN: Central Minnesota Council on Aging.

Shrewsbury, C. and D. Janovy. 1995. *Long-term Care Service Preferences of Rural Seniors in South Central Minnesota. A Report Prepared for Long Term Care Services* Minnesota Department of Human Services. Mankato, MN: Center on Aging, Mankato State University.

State Planning Agency. 1987. *Long-term Care for the Elderly. Trend Reports.* St. Paul, MN: Author.

A Strategy for Long Term Care in the State of Minnesota, Developed in Response to the SAIL 1990 Report. 1991. St. Paul, MN: Minnesota Departments of Human Services, of Health, of Finance and the Minnesota Board on Aging.

Thurow, Lester. 1996. (May 19). "The Birth of a Revolutionary Class." *New York Times Magazine*: 46-7.

Torres-Gil, F.M. 1992. *The New Aging Politics and Change in America.* New York, NY: Auburn House.

Trends in State and Local Government Spending. 1996. St. Paul, MN: Program Evaluation Division, Office of the Legislative Auditor State of Minnesota.

Chapter 14

STRUCTURING METROPOLITAN GOVERNMENT

John J. Harrigan
Hamline University

INTRODUCTION

If imitation is truly the sincerest form of flattery, residents of the Minneapolis-St. Paul metropolitan area have reason to wonder about the praise that has been given to their system of metropolitan governance over the years. Widely praised but never copied could easily be the logo put above the door of the Twin Cities Metropolitan Council. Indeed, for the past fifteen years, the Metropolitan Council has probably received more praise from outside the Twin Cities than from within it.

However prominent the Metropolitan Council might look from afar and however successful it was in the past, there is a great uneasiness in the Twin Cities today about whether the Metropolitan Council can provide direction on three overriding challenges — the need to position the region to compete effectively in the changing global economy, the need to alleviate the growing central-city suburban disparities that are seen to threaten the region's quality of life, and the need to gain better control over suburban sprawl .

This chapter will address these concerns by (1) sketching out the challenge of global competition, (2) outlining the patterns of central city-suburban disparities, (3) relating this to the Twin Cities governance model, (4) explaining a growing disenchantment with the governing model in the 1980s, and (5) describing significant changes that were made in the model in the 1990s .

POSITIONING FOR GLOBAL COMPETITION

A useful guidepost for assessing an area's comparative advantage is John Mollenkopf's identification of three different adaptations to the nation's transformation from an industrial to a post-industrial economy (1983: 31-36) . Some old industrial cities like Detroit failed to make the transformation and have gone into severe economic decline. Newer cities, such as San Diego or Phoenix, had the good fortune to hit their growth phase precisely when the post-industrial economy went into high gear, and thus they virtually grew up as service and/or administrative sites for high-technology industries. Still others, such as Boston or San Francisco, transformed themselves from dependence on industry into significant service centers for finance, medical care, and corporate services.

The Twin Cities area is a moderately successful example of the third type of adaptation. During the early twentieth century its economy was heavily based on manufacturing, railroading, grain milling, and the stockyards. All of these sectors declined over the past four decades, but the region itself prospered. There is currently great concern over the ability of the metropolitan area and the broader economic region to continue adapting successfully to the changing global economy.

Positive Signs for Global Positioning

The Twin Cities possess several economic advantages. Minnesota has enjoyed above average job growth in the North Central region (Statistical Abstract, 1993-94: 418) and below average unemployment rates (New York Times, 1994). The state was ranked by the Corporation for Enterprise Development as one of only eight states best poised for future economic growth (Star Tribune, 1994c: C-2). The state has also been a dynamic leader in medical services innovation. Among the medical technology firms located in the Twin Cities, for example, are the nation's premier manufacturers of artificial heart valves and heart pace makers. The region houses two leading research medical complexes at the University of Minnesota Hospitals and the nearby Mayo Clinic. Minnesota's overall economic output is fairly consistent with its size. Ranking 20th in population, the state ranks 19th in gross state product and 17th in median household income (Statistical Abstract, 1993 and 1994: xii, xix, 444.)

Also, despite an outmigration of retirees, the Twin Cities experience a net in-migration of people . Most of these come from the five state region of Minnesota and its immediate neighbors (Star Tribune, 1993b: 12A). The vast majority of counties in the five state region lost population in the 1980s, and a goodly portion of the rural emigres from these counties wound up in the Twin Cities suburbs (Star Tribune, 1991a: 5B).

Finally, the Twin Cities metropolitan area dominates this broader region economically and culturally. It is the regional mecca for financial services, advanced medical services, long range air travel, upscale shopping, and entertainment. Major league sports is the most visible symbol of this dominance. There is no other major league sports team within a radius of more than 300 miles. Because of its geographical location, Minneapolis-St. Paul is not overshadowed by giant neighbors the way that Milwaukee is overshadowed by Chicago. Furthermore, there are hopes that the 1993 NAFTA agreements will dramatically stimulate North-South trade routes as distinct from the historic traditional patterns of East-West trade routes. If this happens it could give an important economic boost to mid-continent metropolises such as Minneapolis-St. Paul.

Much of this positive picture is summarized in Table 1. Among the 25 largest MSAs, both the central cities and the suburbs of the Twin Cities compare favorably in terms of education, income, poverty rates, and violent crime rates.

TABLE 1		
How the Twin Cities Ranks Among the 25 Largest Metropolitan Areas		
Characteristic	*Central Cities*	*MSA*
Poverty rate (1989)	17 (18.5%)	24 (8%)
Population	14 (640,000)	16 (2,464,000)
Population growth 1980-90	12 (-.2%)	12 (15%)
Central city share of the MSA population	12	
Percent of population racial minority	24 (20%)	25 (8%)
% of H.S. dropouts among adults	21 (11%)	24 (7%)
% of adults with 4 years of college	7 (29%)	6 (27%)
Median family income	9 ($33,364)	5 ($43,252)
Violent crime rate	18 (1,344)	23 (478)
Married couples as % of all households	17 (36%)	3 (55%)
Source: Twin Cities Metropolitan Council, 1994a: 17.20.		

Ominous Signs for Global Positioning

In contrast to these positive signs of regional dynamism, there are also some ominous signs. The geographic position that enables the Twin Cities to dominate a large region also isolates manufacturing businesses from large consumer markets. In comparison to other states, Minnesota is only average in its share of U. S. exports (Statistical Abstract, 1993 and 1994: xxii). Minnesota lags most other states in the formation of new corporations. Most of the state's large manufacturers have programs of plant expansion in other states, while many of their in-state facilities are aging and need replacement (Citizens League, 1994). Business leaders complain that they are discouraged from expanding in-state because of Minnesota's high-tax, high-spend environment and its rigorous regulatory atmosphere. It is difficult to weigh the merits of these complaints, but 'business climate' has been an issue for several years.

Although the region is a leader in medical technology companies, it has lost ground in other high technology sectors, especially computer hardware. Two regional computer firms (Control Data and Cray Research) were decimated by the shift away from mainframe and super computers.

GROWING CENTRAL CITY-SUBURBAN DISPARITIES

Some urbanists argue that the overall economic health of a metropolitan area is directly tied to the health of its central city. Dynamic central cities produce dynamic metropolises. Decaying central cities produce decaying metropolises (Rusk, 1993; Ledebur and Barnes, 1992; Savitch, 1993). As Table 1 suggested, Minneapolis and St. Paul have not decayed nearly as much as many other central cities, but there is nevertheless reason for concern. The trend for the past twenty years has been toward growing disparities between the two central cities and the surrounding suburbs. It is not as though the region did not try to revitalize the central cities. The two central business districts have been rebuilt over the past two decades, and enormous public funds have been poured into festival market sites, gentrified historic neighborhoods, downtown redevelopments, and industrial parks in the two cities. Despite these efforts, disparities have grown, especially along three critical measures.

A Sharply Increasing Minority Population

Compared to metropolitan areas of similar or larger size, the Twin Cities do not have a large minority population. Nevertheless, the minority population has sharply increased over the past twenty years to nearly a quarter of a million people. The minorities come from four population categories and no one category dominates. This gives the Twin Cities a much more diverse minority population than is the case in most metropolitan areas. The most profound change came in the Asian population, which by 1990 had become the second largest minority group. This growth was largely due to the influx of thousands of Hmong refugees from Laos and immigrants from Korea, China, and Vietnam.

As Table 2 shows, the suburbs are picking up a larger share of the minority population as time goes on and the concentration of blacks and Hispanics decreased in the 1980s. In 1990, 15.5 percent of blacks lived in census tracts that were a majority black, down from 25.7 percent in 1980 (Star Tribune, 1991b: 3Be). Nevertheless, most minorities still live in the central cities. During these same years, the number of whites in the central cities declined by almost 200,000. Minorities now comprise about twenty percent of the two central cities, and they comprise a majority of students in the public school systems.

Spreading Poverty

Poverty has gotten worse in the central cities. In 1970, the two central cities had only 19 census tracts with more than 25 percent of persons living below the poverty line. This expanded to 34 census tracts in 1980 and 51 in 1990. The only census tracts to drop out of this grouping (3 in St. Paul and 2 in Minneapolis) were those in the gentrifying areas in or near the central business districts (Twin Cities Metropolitan Council, 1994a: 10-5). Until 1970 poverty in the Twin

TABLE 2				
Population Growth by Race				
	1970	*1980*	*1990*	*1970-90 Change*	*1980-90 Change*
Central Cities					
White	703,000	566,900	512,800	190,200	54,900
Minority	41,380	74,286	127,818	86,438	53,532
Suburbs					
White	1,091,612	1,314,317	1,573,859	483,247	257,542
Minority	19,896	42,973	83,965	64,069	40,992
Region					
White	1,874,612	1,881,225	2,086,659	212,047	205,434
Minority	61,276	117,259	211,783	150,507	94,524
Black	32,140	49,270	89,459	57,319	40,189
Asian	4,953	29,970	64,583	59,630	34,613
Hispanic	11,700	21,866	36,716	25,016	14,850
Indian	9,958	15,666	23,340	13,382	7,674
% minority in central city	67.5	63.3	60.4		

Source: Twin Cities Metropolitan Council. 1992: 6-8.

Cities was concentrated in four or five main pockets. Today, census tracts with 25 percent poverty rates extend in an unbroken belt from the East Side of St. Paul roughly parallel to Interstate 94 through the center of Minneapolis to the western boundary of that city. As poverty spreads geographically, it puts pressure on nearby working class neighborhoods and even some of the inner ring suburbs (Star Tribune, 1992: 5). Not surprisingly, the high concentration of poverty in the central cities is accompanied by a higher concentration of social problems than in the surrounding suburbs. The central cities contain over 80 percent of the region's homeless population (Twin Cities Metropolitan Council, 1994a: 5-4). They have the highest rates of births to single women, the highest percent of low-weight births, the highest percent of mothers with no prenatal care, and the highest rates of crime and violent crime (Twin Cities Metropolitan Council, 1994a: 9, 12, 11, 31-36). Furthermore on most of these statistics, the current rates are higher than those of ten years or twenty years ago.

Negligible Job Growth in the Central Cities

While the last twenty years have brought a big influx of immigrants, a tripling of the minority population, and a significant increase in people below the poverty line, there has been negligible job growth in the central cities. This is shown in Table 3. Hundreds of millions of dollars were spent on Minneapolis and St. Paul redevelopment projects in the 1980s, but only 5,447 net new jobs were added in the central cities. The inner suburbs added only 52,933. The bulk of job growth took place in the outlying developing area where there was a 75 percent increase in jobs.

Topping off the cities' meager job growth has been a loss of manufacturing jobs. From 1988-92, the State Department of Jobs and Training counted a loss of 11,208 manufacturing jobs in the central cities and a loss of another 10,470 manufacturing jobs in the suburban balance of Hennepin (Minneapolis) and Ramsey (St. Paul) counties (St. Paul Pioneer Press, 1994a: 8D). This is a critical loss because of the key role that manufacturing jobs historically played in making the city a place of upward mobility for millions of European immigrants and American born lower-class people. The loss of unskilled production jobs is especially hard on those immigrants and minorities with educational and training deficits.

TABLE 3			
Twin Cities Area Job Growth: 1980-1990			
	Number of Jobs		
	1980	1990	Change
Central Cities	445,371	450,818	5,447
Inner Suburbs	326, 760	379,693	52,933
Fully Developed Area Total	772,131	830,511	58,380
Developing Areas	214,237	374,273	160,036
Rural Area	53,643	88,337	34,694
Regional Total	1,040,011	1,293,121	253,110
Source: Twin Cities Metropolitan Council. 1994b: 9-16.			

This migration outward of jobs would not be so devastating if the core area residents could commute easily to the developing areas where the jobs are growing. But many core area residents have no car. Surveys of core neighborhoods indicate that 48 percent of black, 56 percent of Native American, and 36 percent of Asian households lack an automobile (Twin Cities Metropolitan Council, 1992: 21). Public transit does not make up for the dearth of cars, because bus service is minimal beyond the major shopping malls.

THE GREAT HOPES FOR METROPOLITAN GOVERNANCE

What makes the growing regional disparities especially discouraging for concerned Twin Citians is that they took steps a quarter century ago to forestall urban decline.   In 1967, the Legislature created a governing structure for the seven central counties and gave it responsibility for grappling with land use, housing, transit, sewage, and other metropolitan issues. At the top of the regional governing structure was the Metropolitan Council which, for the next decade, did an outstanding job of tackling those issues. The question today is whether this metropolitan governing structure can provide direction on the threefold issues of regional disparities, suburban sprawl, and positioning the region for global competition.

An Innovative Governing Model

The governing model in the Twin Cities had two fundamental principles. First, it was a bifurcated model that separated metropolitan policy making from program implementation. The center piece of the model is the Twin Cities Metropolitan Council, which was responsible for setting policies on transit, water quality, housing, land use, and other issues of metropolitan significance.   Those policies were implemented, however, not by the Metropolitan Council but by other governing bodies.   This bifurcation of policy making from implementation was established with the Council's first major success, its solution to a metropolitan sewerage crisis. Many growing suburbs had neither a central sewer system nor a central water supply. The State Department of Health reported that nearly half the homes it tested in these suburbs were using drinking water polluted by backyard septic tanks (Harrigan and Johnson, 1978: 27). The Federal Housing Administration threatened to stop insuring home mortgages if the homes were not tied into a sewage treatment system. When the Legislature created the Council in 1967, it specifically instructed the Council to find a solution to this problem. The Council recommended the creation of the Metropolitan Waste Control Commission to run a metropolitan-wide system of treatment plants and trunk sewer lines. Policy control over where these sewer lines would be built was vested in the Metropolitan Council and that gave Council leaders great optimism that they could shape future growth of the metropolitan area. They would simply restrict sewer capacity in places where they wanted to inhibit growth.

The second significant feature was a Legislature-guided process of incremental fine tuning. Each legislative session saw the Metropolitan Council ask the Legislature for authority and funding to deal with a major issue. In 1969 the Legislature dealt with the transit issue by putting the Metropolitan Transit Commission under the policy guidance of the Metropolitan Council. Further increments took place in the 1973-74 session when the regional governing model was restructured, the Metropolitan Council was given greater control over the Waste Control Commission, the Transit Commission, the Airports Commission, and other regional commissions. A Housing and Redevelopment Authority was created, and this gave the Metropolitan Council the ability to build moderate income housing in the smaller suburbs which lacked the resources to do so on their own.

Thus, within a decade of its creation, the Metropolitan Council sat atop a complicated system of metropolitan governance. It appointed the members of most metropolitan commissions, had approval power over their capital budgets, and through the Metropolitan Development Guide laid out the policies that these commissions were supposed to implement. Because of its legislatively guided incremental innovation, this governing model avoided the paralyzing conflicts over metropolitan consolidation referenda that failed three-fourths of the time (Marando, 1979). It also avoided the paralyzing weaknesses of the Council of Government (COG) model (Mogulof, 1971). Unlike a COG, the Metropolitan Council had financial independence through its own tax base and its ability to win federal grants. Also unlike a COG, the local governments were not represented in the Metropolitan Council. The 16 Metropolitan Council districts lapped over municipal boundaries and each was roughly coterminous with 2 state Senate districts.

In sum, by 1977 the Twin Cities had created a bifurcated metropolitan governing apparatus characterized by (1) separation of policy making (by the Metropolitan Council) from program administration (the other governments) and (2) a Legislatively guided process of incremental innovation. This bifurcated system was very complicated in that different service areas had different

implementation structures. Sewerage services were most susceptible
to policy direction by the Metropolitan Council because of its control
over the Waste Control Commission. Airport services, on the other
hand, were least susceptible to policy direction by the Metropolitan
Council, since the Metropolitan Airports Commission enjoyed much
more autonomy than did the Waste Control Commission.

A Decade of Unprecedented Accomplishments

Not only was this model a structural innovation, it also produced
a string of impressive accomplishments in its first decade.   It
developed a solution for the sewage crisis and a systematic regional
approach for solid waste disposal. It forced the affluent suburb of
Golden Valley to develop a plan for low- and moderate-income
housing. It vetoed plans of the Airports Commission for a second
international airport, and it also vetoed plans of the Metropolitan
Transit Commission to build a rapid rail transit system. These vetoes
over these two huge metropolitan authorities constituted a significant
political achievement.

Perhaps its most renowned achievement came in 1971. The
Legislature passed the Council's proposed Fiscal Disparities Act which
provided that the entire metropolitan area, including the central cities,
share in the tax base created by new commercial real estate.

Another far reaching achievement was the creation of a seven
county system of regional parks. The Council achieved bonding
authority to purchase land for parks and open spaces. True to its
principal of separating policy from administration, the Metropolitan
Council issued the bonds but turned the money over to the counties
which actually acquired the land and built the parks. The result today
is an extensive system of regional parks in places that would most
likely have become shopping centers or residential neighborhoods.

Even more far reaching was a systematic approach to land
planning set up in 1975-76. In 1976, the Council passed the
Development Framework Plan which divided the region into five

development areas — the Central Cities, the Fully Developed Area, the Developing Area, the Rural Area, and the Free Standing Growth Centers. Around the developing area was drawn a Metropolitan Urban Services (MUSA) line that roughly paralleled the Interstate highways that encircle the Twin Cities. By channeling future growth to the developing area and the freestanding growth centers, the Council hoped to contain suburban sprawl and save local taxpayers from spending $2 billion for public infrastructure over the next two decades.

In 1976 the Legislature put teeth in this plan by passing the Metropolitan Land Planning Act. This Act required all of the region's municipalities and townships to submit a comprehensive plan to the Council for approval. If a local plan was inconsistent with the growth projected for its municipality by the Development Framework, the Council had authority to hold up the plan's approval, and this gave the Council considerable power to pressure the local government into bringing its plan into conformity with the Development Framework. The net result was an elaborate, multi-year process of negotiating back and forth between the Council and local municipalities as they went about the task of implementing the Development Framework. Finally, adding even further strength to the Council's control over land use, the Council in 1976 was given power to review proposed projects of 'metropolitan significance' to ensure that those projects were consistent with the Development Framework and other policies of the Metropolitan Development Guide.

Again, consistent with the role bifurcation model, the Council did not implement any of the local development plans. It established the overall metropolitan land planning policy, and put limits on the growth that would be permitted to each municipality. Just how and where that growth would occur was left to each municipality to decide for itself using zoning codes, building permits, variances, subdivision requirements, and all the other tools of land management. But they had to use these tools within the confines of overall metropolitan land planning policy. With a few exceptions such as Hawaii, Vermont, and the Coastal Zone Commissions in California, this was the most systematic attempt to control metropolitan sprawl that the nation had yet seen (Haskell, 1973; Mogulof, 1975).

In sum, by the tenth anniversary of the Metropolitan Council in 1977, the bifurcated governance model had gained considerable legitimacy, had evolved an innovative governing structure that fit the desires of regional elites, and had scored an impressive array of accomplishments in carrying out its mission. There were great hopes that this system of metropolitan governance would lead the Twin Cities into a bright future and serve as model that would be copied by other regions around the country.

THE GREAT HOPES GONE SOUR

By 1990 those great hopes had gone sour. The Metropolitan Council faced persistent criticism throughout the 1980s from the Legislature (Legislative Commission on Metropolitan Governance, 1983), the Legislative Auditor (1985), the Citizens League (1984), and an editorial writer for the Minneapolis Star Tribune with a long history of supporting the Council (Whiting, 1984). Despite its vaunted powers of metropolitan significance, the Council played only a bit role in some of the most significant land use decisions over the past twenty years, ranging from the building of a domed stadium which turned out to be a success, to a race track which ended up in bankruptcy (Klobuchar, 1982). In between were a World Trade Center for St. Paul, a velodrome for the northern suburbs, the nation's largest shopping mall for the southern suburbs, a state of the art basketball arena for downtown Minneapolis, numerous industrial parks and numerous festival markets, some of which are in severe financial trouble.

There is no way to know how a strong, resourceful Metropolitan Council would have ruled on any of these developments, because the Council did not try to impose its will on any of them. The more important the project was to big development interests, the less that the Council seemed to affect the decisions.

The result is that the siting of most of these projects resulted from the traditional politics of land use rather than from a guided land use policy directed by the Development. The racetrack is a good example. In the 1980s, Minnesota voters approved a Constitutional amendment removing any constitutional impediments to parimutuel betting. From that point on it was evident that a race track would be built someplace in the metropolitan region. The key contestants for the site were Blaine in the northern suburbs, Woodbury in the eastern suburbs, and Shakopee in the southwestern suburbs. These municipalities competed with proposals for tax increment financing, industrial development revenue bonds, and other enticements. There is no evidence that the Metropolitan Council used its powers of metropolitan significance to shape the siting decision in accord with its own metropolitan land use plans. Shakopee finally won the prize, which turned out to be a bit tarnished when the novelty of horse racing eventually wore off and attendance declined. The race track went bankrupt in 1993.

Perhaps the single largest land use decision with the most far reaching implications on the metropolitan area was the decision to build the Mall of America on the site of the former baseball-football stadium in the southern suburb of Bloomington. This site had been vacant since the domed stadium opened in downtown Minneapolis. The site was located along the largest strip of commercial real estate in the Twin Cities, and Bloomington was eager to develop the empty space. When constructed, the Mall of America became the largest shopping mall in the nation.

Although the Metropolitan Council appears to have had no influence on the decision to build the Mall of America, it did influence the Mall in ways that reduced congestion, increased the amount of retail space, and prevented the construction of a proposed convention center next to the site (Israel, 1994). The jury is still out on this development's ultimate impact on the Twin Cities, but to date the Mall of America appears to be financially sound. So it is conceivable that in the long run the region is better off that the Council was bypassed in the Mall of America decision.

In addition to being bypassed on significant land use decisions, there were other signs that the Metropolitan Council was losing its dynamism by the late 1980s. Despite their important decision-making potential, Council members are almost invisible to the general public. The Council found itself in a decade-long irresolvable controversy with the Transit Commission over the management of the bus system, planning for transit policy, and light rail transit. It also came under criticism for permitting expansions in the MUSA line (Alnes, 1992). Although the Metropolitan Urban Services Area expanded by only 2 percent since 1986 (Reddick, 1994) the Minneapolis Star Tribune accused the Council of becoming an "easy mark for leapfrog developers and tax-base hungry fringe suburbs" (Star Tribune, 1994b: 14A).

A new governor in 1991 threatened to eliminate the Council if it failed to bring about service efficiencies through the consolidation of local government services. Budget problems forced a twenty percent reduction in planning staff in 1993. It was clear that another major crisis was brewing for the Metropolitan Council.

REGIME CHANGE AND THE METROPOLITAN CRISIS

No government exists in a vacuum. Urban scholars often use term 'regime' for the vague system of leadership ties between public and private sector elites (Stone, 1987). In the late 1960s when the metropolitan governing model was created, a dynamic metropolitan regime existed that provided powerful support for the Metropolitan Council's approach to metropolitan issues. One of the most serious metropolitan problems today is that regime changes over the past quarter century have dissipated important sources of support for the Metropolitan Council. And much of the explanation for the collapse of the bifurcated governing model in the 1990s can be traced to these regime changes. The most important of these involve the Legislature, the business community, the political parties, and the failure to create a position of metropolitan leadership.

The Legislature

The Legislature historically played a key role by enacting Metropolitan Council initiatives into law. In the early days, when the Council marched from one stunning success to another, Council successes reflected positively on legislators who had in turn supported Council initiatives. Today, however, it has been a long time since the Council has scored a stunning, highly visible success. The Legislature has very little institutional memory of the Council as a dynamic positive force in the Twin Cities. Few legislators are left who can build political support for themselves by pointing to their work on Metropolitan Council initiatives as positive achievements. Of the 201 representatives and senators in the 1993-94 session, only 2 held office at the creation of the Council, and only 24 held office during the Council's first decade of success (Legislative Manual, 1993). Only twelve of these old-timers are from the seven county region where the Council operates, and of that dozen none is a prominent advocate of the Metropolitan Council or the regional governing structure. The Council sorely needs some victories to end its orphan status and to get some legislators to share in the credit for those victories.

The Business Community

Even more ominous than the changes brought by legislative turnover are the changes in leadership of the Twin Cities business community (Israel, 1993: 10). Some of the most important forces for metropolitan reform in the 1960s came from prominent business figures — members of the Pillsbury family and the Dayton family, for example. This generation of business leaders has passed, and the most prominent of the old families no longer control the corporations that bear their names. The change is most symbolic in the case of Dayton-Hudson. As a locally based retailer in the 1960s, Dayton's had a vested, financial interest in the well-being of the Twin Cities, and Donald Dayton was an original appointee to the Council. This financial vested interest in the area is much less the case for Dayton-Hudson now that it has become a national retailing chain. Dayton-Hudson is still a generous contributor to local causes but rising stars in the corporate hierarchy are no longer tied to this particular metropolitan region (Oslund, 1994). It is no accident that the top officials of major corporations take less interest in metropolitan issues and organizations such as the Citizens League (Byrum, 1994). The new leaders of these corporations have less need to show a local commitment to the Twin Cities than did their predecessors a generation earlier.

The Political Parties

Compounding these leadership problems has been a decline in the ability of the political parties to play a stabilizing role in Twin Cities politics. Increasingly in the late 1980s and 1990s, the party activists who control party endorsements and party platforms have come from the ideological extremes. This is especially pronounced in the Independent Republican Party where Pro-Life forces dominated the state conventions in 1990 and 1994 and endorsed gubernatorial candidates who were extremely divisive. It is hard to reconcile today's limited issue Republican leadership with the broad-based Republican leaders who created the Metropolitan Council in 1967. To a lesser degree, the mirror image of the Republican activist appears in the Democratic Farmer Labor Party, where the most dominant activists are Pro-Choice, Gay Rights, feminist advocates, and people who actively seek to shut down the state's nuclear power plants.

It is possible that the ideologues who dominate the two parties may well have the answers to today's global problems, but they exhibit little interest in the metropolitan governing model. For this reason, the parties are in a poorer position today to provide the stabilizing political role that they performed in the 1960s when the Metropolitan Council was created.

No Position of Areawide Leadership

Finally, the metropolitan governing model deteriorated because there is no highly visible political figure whose own political base depends on coping with the metropolitan issues of central city-suburban disparities, suburban sprawl, and positioning the region to compete in the global economy. In many instances, political leaders would be harmed by trying to develop such a political base.

This is certainly true of the governor. As the political parties increasingly marginalize themselves by falling under the sway of ideologically extreme factions, the governor increasingly gets elected through a personalized campaign aiming more at constituencies that cross over party labels than it does at party loyalties. In this type of electoral campaign, metropolitan issues are either non-existent or they emerge in codewords dealing with crime, jobs, and poor educational achievement. Although reducing metropolitan disparities and positioning the metropolis for the global economy come pretty close to what Paul Peterson called "unitary interests" that would benefit everybody in the region, it is hard to imagine anybody capable of winning the governorship campaigning on these issues (1981).

The most visible metropolitan positions are the mayors of Minneapolis and St. Paul. For the past twenty years, those offices have been held most of the time by liberal individuals who want to address the issues of urban decline. Nevertheless, their cities compete bitterly for the same limited amount of development dollars and their political representation in the Legislature declined as they fell behind in population growth. For these and other reasons, neither mayor has become a major force on the urban issues addressed here.

Finally, the Metropolitan Council has failed to turn itself into a position of metropolitan leadership. The Metropolitan Council staff has done a first rate job of producing planning documents and analyses of the region's demographic and economic trends. But, once the Council's first decade of achievement was over, the Metropolitan Council chairperson and members failed to use their positions to dominate metropolitan issues. The problem is that Council members have no political base of their own. They are alternately ignored by the governor and dominated by the governor (Israel, 1993). With the legislative turnover described earlier, they have lost their base of support in the State Legislature. There is a serious fear that the

Council has become little more than another state agency competing for the favor of the governor (Israel, 1994).

TINKERING WITH THE SYSTEM IN THE 1990S

To recapitulate, the dawn of the 1990s saw several adverse developments that hindered the ability of the metropolitan governing system to cope with the issues of the day. The nature of the most pressing issues had changed from physical development issues in the 1960s to the much more intractable issues of social deterioration in the 1990s. Economic and demographic change worsened the central city-suburban disparities. Changes in the metropolitan leadership regime diluted the base of support for the Metropolitan Council and its priorities. The Council's authority to cope with urban issues was not expanded. It suffered a decline in federal grants-in-aid monies during the Carter and Reagan administrations, and the State Legislature did not make up those shortfalls by increasing its own grants or increasing the Council's taxing powers.

Most important, the Council had failed to develop an independent political base. As an appointive rather than an elective body, it lacks the political clout to confront the governor, key legislators, and sometimes even local officials. While the Metropolitan Council was losing political power, the counties were gaining influence. As their budgets grew and as the county governments modernized themselves, they became formidable forces for defending their turf against metropolitan level policy making. In 1993, the counties proposed legislation that would have reduced the Council's influence even further (Star Tribune, 1994a: 18A).

In the 1993-94 sessions of the Legislature, two developments brought these issues to a head. The first was transportation and the second was a package of bills authored by a persistent Minneapolis legislator who wanted to address the growing central city-suburban disparities.

Transportation and Metropolitan Reform

Transportation had been a sticky issue for many years. Although the Metropolitan Council had effectively vetoed the Transit Commission's (MTC) plans for a rapid rail line in 1974, rail advocates came back in the 1980s with proposals for a light rail transit (LRT) system. With the MTC's planning role reduced and the Metropolitan Council opposed to rail based transit, LRT advocates complained that overall transportation policy was being neglected. The Legislature responded in 1989 by creating a Regional Transit Board (RTB) that was placed under the Metropolitan Council and over the MTC. However, this structural change did not resolve the transit conflicts. It replaced a two level system with three levels in which the MTC was primarily an operating agency nominally responsive to both the RTB which advocated rail transit and the Metropolitan Council which historically opposed rail transit and had at best become a skeptical and cautious supporter of it.

Muddying the issue further, Hennepin County and Ramsey County approved plans for an LRT system and asked the Legislature in 1993-94 to fund a plan that would essentially follow the same rapid rail paths that the Metropolitan Council had vetoed in 1974. The counties funded a `grass roots' group called Minnesotans for Light Rail Transit to build public support for LRT and lobby the Legislature (Dornfield, 1994: 6A). While these transit conflicts were going on in the background, a highly visible transit issue undermined both the RTB and the MTC. The MTC and later the RTB had operated Metro Mobility which provided on-demand transportation service for disabled people. In 1993 the RTB awarded the Metro Mobility contract to a new service provider which promptly ran into snags with its dispatching system. Service deteriorated and, as complaints mounted, the governor responded by calling out the National Guard to drive the Metro Mobility vans until a solution could be found. Metro Mobility riders sued over their poor service and eventually received a $1.3 million settlement from the RTB (Pioneer Press, 1994b: 1A).

As if this were not enough to undermine the transit system, the MTC board fired the MTC's chief administrator whom the governor viewed as having done an excellent job of rebuilding bus ridership. The governor responded by trying to force the MTC to hire back the administrator it had just fired.

These events turned out to be the coup de grace for the bifurcated model of metropolitan transit. On paper the MTC board was ultimately accountable to the governor, since the MTC board was appointed by the RTB which was in turn appointed by the Metropolitan Council which was in turn appointed by the governor. From one perspective, the governor's attempt to reinstate the fired transit chief was an unwarranted intrusion into the operational affairs of a metropolitan agency. From the opposite perspective, the MTC was an agency out of control, impervious to democratic oversight. There was no way to look at the transit crisis of 1993-94 without concluding that the traditional bifurcated model of governance was in a shambles.

Thus, the Metro Mobility crisis and conflicts over LRT set the stage for metropolitan reform in 1993-94. Issues were raised that were not resolvable within the bifurcated model.

A Metropolitan Legislative Package

The second thing that provoked a metropolitan restructuring in 1993-94 was a package of legislative bills named after its author, Minneapolis State Representative Myron Orfield. Orfield addressed the growing central city-suburban disparities with a package of bills that would provide for: an elected Metropolitan Council; mandating the Council to prescribe low- and moderate-income housing goals for each suburb; giving the Council authority to enforce its low- and moderate-income housing goals by denying sewers and highway extensions to suburbs out of compliance; and a housing reinvestment fund. For each new home valued above $150,000, a percent of the excess tax base valuation would go into a housing reinvestment fund that would be used to increase the supply of low- and moderate-income housing.

Orfield calculated that three-fourths of the suburbs would benefit from the reinvestment fund, and only one-fourth of the suburbs would pay more into the fund than they got out of it. That one-fourth, however, were the most affluent suburbs in the region, and they bitterly opposed the proposals. Orfield spent the better part of two years testifying at hearings and traveling throughout the region to address any group that was willing discuss his proposals and to look at his many charts on growing central city-suburban disparities.

Incremental Tinkering in 1994

All of these proposals were put before the 1993-94 sessions of the Legislature. Orfield's housing bills passed the DFL controlled legislature in 1993 but were vetoed by the Republican governor. The Legislature put off a decision on funding for the LRT proposals. And in 1994 the bill for an elected Metropolitan Council failed by a single vote in the House and just five votes in the Senate.

The most significant action that did take place was a major change in the bifurcation governing model which had been in place since 1967. The Legislature abolished both the RTB and the MTC and turned all transit operations and planning over to the Metropolitan Council. Likewise, the Legislature abolished the Metropolitan Waste Control Commission and gave its operations to the Council as well. Since the Council would now be a major operating agency, the Legislature created the position of Regional Administrator who was expected to serve as a city manager for Metropolitan Governance. Finally, to tighten accountability over metropolitan governance, the governor was given authority to dismiss as well as appoint members of the Metropolitan Council.

CONCLUSION

The 1994 changes in the metropolitan governing model were significant. They discarded the bifurcation model for transit and waste control operations by, for the first time, making the Metropolitan Council responsible for both policy planning and operations. It is not likely that the other metropolitan commissions (Sports Facilities and Airports) will also lose their operating responsibilities, unless a crisis emerges similar to the one that brought the governor directly into the dispute over transit.

The restructuring of 1994 also suggest that a new metropolitan leadership regime might be emerging. Both the Orfield package and strengthening the Metropolitan Council received solid support from the daily newspapers and the Association of Metropolitan Municipalities. Even suburban Republican legislators admitted the need to deal with the regional disparities and proposed a milder version of Orfield's package that was dubbed "Orfield Light" by the press. Only the counties and a small number of affluent suburbs stayed consistently in opposition. If this new metropolitan leadership regime stays in place as the metropolitan issues return in future years, it will greatly enhance the prospects for action.

Nevertheless, the issues that provoked so much activity in 1993-94 have not been resolved. Despite the fact that transit operations have now been centralized in an agency that has historically been cool to rail forms of transit, the proposal to build an LRT system still has many vocal and influential advocates. And the guerrilla warfare over LRT will probably continue.

The Orfield package to alleviate housing disparities between the central cities and the suburbs will also remain on the agenda. Many elites in the region seem to believe not only that the disparities are growing but that they pose a threat to the overall quality of life and the region's economic stature.

However, the Legislature failed to take the single biggest step it could have taken to resolve these issues — namely providing for an elected Metropolitan Council in order to create a position of metropolitan leadership with its own political base. Instead, the 1994 Legislature increased the dependence of Council members on the governor. This means that the Council's ability to address the growing central city-suburban disparities will depend primarily on the good will of the next governor. If the governor favors taking the political risks to address those issues and is willing to back up the Council's efforts along those lines, then it is conceivable that considerable progress could be made. In the long run, however, tying the Council so closely to the governor makes action on metropolitan issues dependent on the whim of the governor who has little to gain politically from involving himself or herself in the divisive issues of regional disparities and growth control. There is a great danger that the Council will simply become another State agency. Like other state agency heads, the pressure on the Metropolitan Council members will be to avoid doing things that might cause problems for the governor. But action on regional disparities and suburban sprawl inherently causes problems for the governor.

In the last analysis, the key issue is still a political one. Alleviating regional disparities, containing sprawl, and positioning the region for global competition cannot be achieved by a bureaucratic agency. It can only be done by a position of leadership that has its own political base of support. Rather than creating such a base of support by providing for an elected Metropolitan Council, Minnesota in 1994 decided instead to make the Metropolitan Council's political strength dependent on the governor. This might work. But it probably won't.

Savitch, *Regional Politics,* #45, pp. 206-228, © 1996 by Sage Publications. Reprinted by Permission of Sage Publications, Inc.

REFERENCES

Alnes, Steven. 1992. (December 15). "Met Council Faces Push for New Roles Amid Calls for More Power in Old Ones." *Minnesota Journal*. Volume 9, Number 12: 1, 4.

Byrum, Oliver. 1994. Statements at a seminar on metropolitan organization. Hamline University, Master of Arts in Public Administration seminar. St. Paul, Minnesota. April 1994.

Citizens League. 1984. *The Metro Council: Narrowing the Agenda and Raising the Stakes*. Minneapolis, MN: Author.

_____. 1994. *Call for Membership Applications to Global Positioning Task Force*. St. Paul, MN: Author.

Dornfield, Steven. 1994. (July 18). "A Lot of Public Bucks Go Into Backing 'Grass-Roots' Citizens Group for LRT." *St. Paul Pioneer Press*: 6A.

Harrigan, John J. and Johnson, William C. 1978. *Governing the Twin Cities Region: The Metropolitan Council in Comparative Perspective*. Minneapolis, MN: The University of Minnesota Press.

Haskell, Elizabeth and Price, Victoria S. 1973. *State Environmental Management*. New York, NY: Praeger.

Israel, Roger. 1993. "Twin Cities Intergovernmental Relations: The Changing Landscape." Unpublished paper.

_____. August, 1994. Comments to the author.

Klobuchar, Amy. 1982. *Uncovering the Dome*. Prospect Heights, IL: Waveland Press, Inc.

Ledebur, L. C., and Barnes, W. R. 1992. *Metropolitan Disparities and Economic Growth*. Washington, DC: National League of Cities.

Legislative Manual of Minnesota. 1993.

Legislative Commission on Metropolitan Governance. 1983. *Report of the Legislative Commission on Metropolitan Governance*. St. Paul: Author.

Legislative Auditor of Minnesota. 1985. *Metropolitan Council*. St. Paul, MN: Author.

Marando, Vincent L. 1979. (December). "City-County Consolidation: Reform, Regionalism, Referenda, and Requiem." *Western Political Science Quarterly.* Volume 32, Number 4: 409-422.

Minneapolis Star Tribune. 1991a. (March 9): 5B; 1991b. (October 4): 3Be; 1992. (October 13): 5; 1993b. (April 25): 12A; 1994a. (January 6): 18A; 1994b. (March 5): 14A; 1994c. (June 30): C-2.

Mogulof, Melvin B. 1971. *Governing Metropolitan Areas.* Washington, DC: Urban Institute.

_____. 1975. *Saving the Coast: California's Experiment in Inter-Government Land Use Regulation.* Lexington, MA: Lexington Books.

Mollenkopf, John H. 1983. *The Contested City.* Princeton, NJ: Princeton University Press.

Oslund, John J. 1994. *Fewer Firms Set Fixed Goals for Corporate Giving.* Minneapolis Star Tribune. April 4: 1D.

Peterson, Paul. 1981. *City Limits.* Chicago, IL: University of Chicago Press.

Rusk, D. 1993. *Cities Without Suburbs.* Washington, DC: The Woodrow Wilson Center Press.

Savitch, H. V., Collins, D., Sanders, D., and Markham, J. P. 1993. "Ties That Bind: Central Cities, Suburbs, and the New Metropolitan Region." *Economic Development Quarterly.* Volume 7, Number 4: 341-57.

St. Paul Pioneer Press. 1994a. (February 4): 8D; 1994b. (March 8): 1.

Statistical Abstract of the United States: 1993 and 1994. Washington, DC: United States Government Printing Office.

Stone, Clarence N. 1987. "Summing Up: Urban Regimes, Development Policy, and Political Arrangements." In Clarence N. Stone and Heywood Sanders, eds. *The Politics of Urban Development.* Lawrence, KS: University of Kansas Press. Pp. 269-290.

The New York Times. 1994. (June 30): C-2.

Twin Cities Metropolitan Council. 1992. *Trouble at the Core: The Twin Cities Under Stress.* St. Paul, MN: Author.

_____. 1994a. *Keeping the Twin Cities Vital. Appendix 5: Social Indicators*. St. Paul, MN: Author.

_____. 1994b. *Keeping the Twin Cities Vital. Appendix 9: Job Location*. St. Paul, MN: Author.

Whiting, Charles C. 1984. "Twin Cities Metro Council: Heading for a Fall?" *Planning*. Volume 50, Number 3: 4.